Castle Builders

Castle Builders

Approaches to Castle Design and Construction in the Middle Ages

Malcolm Hislop

First published in Great Britain in 2016 by
Pen & Sword Archaeology
an imprint of
Pen & Sword Books Ltd
47 Church Street
Barnsley
South Yorkshire
S70 2AS

Copyright © Malcolm Hislop 2016

ISBN 978 1 78159 335 6

The right of Malcolm Hislop to be identified as the Author of this Work has been asserted by him in accordance with the Copyright, Designs and Patents Act 1988.

A CIP catalogue record for this book is available from the British Library

All rights reserved. No part of this book may be reproduced or transmitted in any form or by any means, electronic or mechanical including photocopying, recording or by any information storage and retrieval system, without permission from the Publisher in writing.

Typeset in Ehrhardt by
Mac Style Ltd, Bridlington, East Yorkshire
Printed and bound by Replika Press Pvt. Ltd.

Pen & Sword Books Ltd incorporates the imprints of Pen & Sword Archaeology, Atlas, Aviation, Battleground, Discovery, Family History, History, Maritime, Military, Naval, Politics, Railways, Select, Transport, True Crime, and Fiction, Frontline Books, Leo Cooper, Praetorian Press, Seaforth Publishing and Wharncliffe.

For a complete list of Pen & Sword titles please contact
PEN & SWORD BOOKS LIMITED
47 Church Street, Barnsley, South Yorkshire, S70 2AS, England
E-mail: enquiries@pen-and-sword.co.uk
Website: www.pen-and-sword.co.uk

Contents

Preface — vii
Acknowledgements — viii

Chapter 1   Introduction — 1
Chapter 2   Earthworks — 10
Chapter 3   Building In Timber — 29
Chapter 4   Building In Stone — 54
Chapter 5   Great Tower Builders Part 1: *c.* 900–1190 — 87
Chapter 6   Great Tower Builders Part 2: *c.* 1100–1500 — 110
Chapter 7   Military Engineering Part 1 — 137
Chapter 8   Military Engineering Part 2 — 165
Chapter 9   Domestic Engineering — 186
Chapter 10 The Castle Builder's Aesthetic — 210

Afterword — 237
Glossary — 238
Referenced Works — 240
Notes — 247
Index — 258

'For Anne, with love'

Preface

The book covers the medieval period from *c.* 1000 to *c.* 1450. The study area is primarily Britain, and, to a lesser extent, northern France, although there are occasional mentions of other continental sites. It is not intended to be a straightforward architectural history of the castle within the dates described, but it does contain elements of architectural history and one intention, where possible, has been to provide a chronological narrative of certain elements of the castle so that the book can be used as a more general work on its evolution than might be implied from the title.

Building measurements are generally given in metres with imperial equivalents; longer distances are given in miles. British sites are located with respect to their pre 1974 county boundaries. No particular significance should be attached to the use of the terms *keep*, *great tower* and *donjon*; they are used here as similes of one another in order to enrich the text, except in the index where *great tower* is used exclusively to refer to all three.

Acknowledgements

A number of individuals and institutions facilitated the task of preparing this work and bringing it to publication. Philip Davies' Gatehouse website (www.gatehouse-gazetteer.info), John Kenyon's *Castles, Town Defences and Artillery Fortifications in the United Kingdom and Ireland: a bibliography 1945–2006*, and the *Castle Studies Group Journal* and *Bulletin* have all been invaluable sources of information. In addition, John Kenyon was kind enough to comment on a draft of the text and to make suggestions in respect of illustrations and sources. I am indebted too to Bob Meeson, Cadw and English Heritage for permission to publish a number of the illustrations; these are acknowledged in the individual captions.

Chapter 1

Introduction

From a retrospective and art historical viewpoint, the term 'castle builder' may sometimes seem synonymous with 'master mason'. That might be a broadly accurate supposition for the later medieval period, when castle building usually (though not always) meant building in stone. By that time, it was the master mason that normally had overall charge of a substantial castle-building project, while other building crafts played a subordinate role. However, it was not always so, and it is part of the purpose of this book to highlight the roles played by other major contributors to the development of castles, notably the carpenters and earthmovers, who at different times played a more significant part than the mason.

Although we know a good deal about the instigators of castle construction and their motives, we know less about the designers and craftsmen involved; for the most part they remain as anonymous as the builders of most parish churches. What we may be able to do, however, is to trace the influence of certain individuals in the architecture. Without documentary evidence this can be a precarious task, subject to many pitfalls, but the general principle that individual masters had identifiable repertoires of craft traits holds true.

Few building craftsmen worked exclusively on castles, but one specialist that was particularly associated with castles was the engineer. In a medieval context, the term 'engineer' is not one that can be readily defined in all cases. The responsibilities of Ailnoth the engineer (*fl.* 1157–1190), the keeper of Westminster Palace during the reign of Henry II, were primarily architectural, and his recorded building activities are mostly domestic in nature. On the other hand, it is clear that many engineers, including Ailnoth's contemporary Urricus (*fl.* 1184–1216), were essentially makers of siege engines.

There are, then, two strands to the title, but there are a number of well-documented instances to show that some engineers, including another of Ailnoth's later contemporaries, Elias of Oxford (*fl.* 1186–1203), were adept in the execution of both functions. Indeed, Ailnoth's own appointment in 1175–1176 to dismantle Framlingham and Walton castles (Suffolk) provides a hint of a background in military engineering. It is reasonable to suppose that the makers of siege engines, who were skilled in the destruction and circumvention of fortifications, might also turn their minds to improving the design of defensive works, on the grounds that expertise in field ordnance involves an understanding of defensive installations and *vice versa*. Further, once the principle of the engineer as a castle builder had been established, it was perhaps only a short step from the design of a castle's defences to the design of its domestic buildings.

While it might be expected that makers of timber-framed siege engines would have been carpenters, by Ailnoth's time the term 'engineer' in an architectural sense transcended individual crafts, being applied to both carpenters and masons. Ailnoth's contemporary, Maurice (*fl.* 1174–1187), Henry II's master builder at the castles of Newcastle-upon-Tyne and Dover, who we only know as a castle builder, was described as a mason at Newcastle and an engineer at Dover. Ailnoth himself was not identified with any particular craft, but the range of his structural responsibilities included lead roofing, stonework, timberwork and glazing.[1] The King's servant, Elias of Oxford (*fl.* 1186–1203), was variously styled carpenter, mason and engineer.[2] In the last quarter of the thirteenth century and the first quarter of the fourteenth century, Richard the engineer, of Chester, one of Edward I's key men in his north Wales castle-building programme, was responsible for works in both wood and stone, including bridges, castles and siege engines, although, like Ailnoth, his own craft status is unknown.[3]

The ambiguous roles of such men are a reminder of how wide a range of skills a medieval master builder might be expected to encompass. One is reminded of the description of William of Sens, the architect of the eastern arm of Canterbury Cathedral from 1174, as 'a craftsman most skilful in both wood and stone'.[4] Familiarity with more than one branch of building craftsmanship was a powerful asset when masterminding a major architectural project, and particularly so where castle building was concerned. The array of expertise encompassed by castle builders at different times included earthwork construction, carpentry, masoncraft and water engineering, as well as all the minor building crafts. While the master builder might be able to call on the services of all kinds of building craftsmen, it was he who had to devise a scheme's overall strategy and the manner in which the various aspects of the design fitted together.

An interesting document with respect to this topic is the indenture of 1380 between John of Gaunt, Duke of Lancaster, and the carpenter, William Wintringham, in which the latter agreed to undertake a major building operation within the duke's castle of Hertford.[5] These buildings were essentially of timber, but Wintringham was to be responsible for all elements of the construction work including foundations, chimneys, tiling and leadwork. The foundations and chimneys would have been in stone, and indeed Wintringham was given permission to obtain stone from the quarries of Hertford. No doubt the construction of the fireplaces and chimneys would have been sub-contracted to a mason, but they were Wintringham's responsibility and subject to his dictate and approval. This rather unusual delineation of a carpenter's responsibility for all aspects of the building work is owed to the fact that, in this case, Wintringham was acting as a building contractor rather than a direct employee, but it can only reflect the broad reality that in castles that were substantially of timber the carpenter would have been pre-eminent.

Where stone was the dominant building material, the timber adjuncts could not be designed in isolation, because the stonework had to be fashioned to accommodate them. Offsets, corbelling, sockets and chases were all incorporated in the masonry at one time or another in order to lodge flooring, roofing, hoarding and other timber trappings. Similarly, gateways had to be planned to hold portcullises, gates and drawbridges, all of which were aspects that had to be considered at the design stage. Timber was also used in significant quantities for scaffolding and centring. Erection of the former would have been within the remit of the masons; the latter may have been constructed by the carpenters, but its form would have been dictated by that of the vault and approved by the master builder.

It is reasonable to suppose, then, that the medieval master builder would have had an interest in and knowledge of all aspects of building construction, and may, indeed, have been proficient in more than one of them. The wide-ranging subjects of the early thirteenth-century sketchbook of Villard de Honnecourt, for many years regarded as the work of a master mason, are reflective of the types of themes that might fall within his sphere of concern: building plans and elevations, timber roof structures, practical geometry, mechanical devices including lifting machines and siege engines, figure studies, and decorative detail. The effective master builder needed more than proficiency in a particular craft; he had to be able to see the wider picture and maintain a grasp on all aspects of building construction including the sourcing of materials, recruitment of personnel and logistics.

Regarding the castle builder in particular, defensive considerations encompassed the choice of a tactically advantageous site and the design of the defences to counter whatever siege tactics were current. Fire, escalade, mining and assault by siege engines, including bombardment, were all employed at one time or another. The design of mechanical devices, like the drawbridge and the portcullis, can be recognized as falling within the sphere of a maker of siege engines: they were all machines, the conception of which required the same kind of aptitude. These mechanisms, along with the lifting machines required to manoeuvre heavy building materials into place, were part and parcel of the castle builder's remit.

On the other hand, attention had to be paid to the domestic practicalities, including heating and sanitation arrangements and facilities for the preparation and cooking of food. The resolution of these issues became more challenging as the medieval period progressed, and the demand for high quality accommodation became more exacting. In the later Middle Ages, a castle architect's ability to deal with complex spatial planning took precedence over defensive considerations. Thus, Richard Lord Scrope's Castle Bolton (*c.* 1377–1395), in the Yorkshire Dales, is primarily a high-rise courtyard house with defensive trimmings, the whole thrust of the design being focused on the planning of the residential accommodation. In castles like this it was skill in domestic rather than military engineering that was required.

There was also an artistic dimension to the castle builder's work, both in general effect and in architectural detail. In the medieval period, a powerful aesthetic sensibility often went hand in hand with mechanical ability, and the medieval builder would have seen nothing incongruous in the mixture of artistic and technological interests that Villard de Honnecourt's sketchbook implies; the art of the period was, after all, rooted in technical craftsmanship: in early castles, in which the defences were often blatantly functional, the focus of aesthetic attentions was the great tower, a prestige building that was to a great extent separate from the wider castle. Subsequently, it was rivalled, and in some cases surpassed, as an architectural centrepiece by the gatehouse. In the later Middle Ages aesthetics might be the overriding factor in determining the form of the entire castle.

The Responsibility for Design

The responsibility for design was shared between the patron and/or his servants and the master builder. The patron dictated his requirements and the castle engineer used his technical expertise to accommodate them into his plan. We seldom have any direct references to this relationship and only occasionally do we catch glimpses of the dynamics involved, but design was a two-way process in which the patron issued instructions, the master builder made proposals for the manner in which they might be fulfilled, and the patron either gave his approval or demanded modifications. The patron, then, played an essential role in influencing the design of a castle by expressing his initial vision, preferences and models.

Sometimes the patron took a very personal interest in the enterprise, as did Richard the Lionheart at Château Gaillard (Eure); but then Richard's noted expertise in war set him in good stead to play an influential role in devising the form that the castle ultimately took. Edward II seems to have been particularly involved in the design of the new keep raised at the royal castle of Knaresborough (Yorkshire) between 1307 and 1312. Edward's order to demolish the old keep and to build another 'as we have more fully indicated' intimates that he had given fairly explicit instructions regarding the new work. The theory is corroborated by subsequent events when the master of works, Hugh of Tichemers, who was a London-based mason,[6] left the site on four occasions to find the King, wherever he might be at the time, 'in order to find out his express wishes and intentions concerning the works'.[7]

In other cases, possibly the more mundane projects or certain aspects of them, the responsibility for approving the scope and design might be delegated to a third party, as when Henry III asked his brother, Richard, Duke of Cornwall, to advise on fortifications at the royal castles of Dover (1243) and Oxford (1255).[8] A project that may have been more appealing to Henry, with its promising of an exciting architectural centrepiece in the form of the new keep, was the reconstruction of the old motte and bailey castle at York. In this instance it was the king's mason, Henry de Reyns, the man who was shortly to be entrusted with the rebuilding of Westminster Abbey, and his colleague, the royal carpenter, Simon of Northampton, who, in 1244, were sent to view the castle in order to organize the work. Part of their brief was to consult other experts in the field: such a consultative process being fairly common in the field of medieval architecture. Some 200 years later, in 1442, when the royal mason, Robert Westerley, was charged with building a new tower at Tutbury (Staffordshire), a castle of the duchy of Lancaster, it was masons from the fellow duchy castle of Pontefract (Yorkshire), William Hamell and John Swillyngton, who came over to give their advice.

Episodes such as these illustrate the collaborative nature of medieval building design. Exactly what was expected or gained from such meetings is uncertain, and probably varied. However, local knowledge about the qualities of the subsoil, the sources of materials, the recruitment of suitable personnel and other practicalities would have been useful to an outsider, but views on the feasibility of the plan and its structural implications would also have been valuable, particularly if the consultants had been involved in similar projects.

Henry de Reyns and Robert Westerley are unlikely to have spent much time at their respective provincial sites. Both had more important responsibilities elsewhere: at Westminster Abbey and Eton College (Buckinghamshire) respectively. In both these cases there must have been a deputy to whom the day-to-day running of the site was delegated. During Hugh de Tichemers' absences from Knaresborough, Hugh of Boudon, the master mason of York Minster, took on his responsibilities on site, but where a master had simultaneous charge of more than one building project, so that his visits were of necessity infrequent, there had to be a resident mason. Such was the situation at Kirby Muxloe (Leicestershire) where the master mason, John Cowper, also had charge of Tattershall church (Lincolnshire), a distance of some 100 miles away. In the first building season (May to October 1481) he was at Kirby on four occasions on each of which he stayed for three or four weeks, which, in total, amounted to about half the time that building work was being carried on. His deputy, or warden, initially a man called Robert Steynforth, was present the whole time, and therefore had charge of the work while Cowper was away.[9]

This kind of arrangement was probably common enough in the later medieval period, but Kirby Muxloe is an exception in the extent and clarity of the documentation. In some other cases we can only make the inference, as in the case of the Durham-based mason, John Lewyn, who, in 1378, entered into major castle building contracts at Castle Bolton (Yorkshire), Carlisle (Cumberland) and Roxburgh (Roxburghshire). The distances between these sites are: Bolton–Carlisle, 60 miles; Carlisle–Roxburgh, 50 miles; Roxburgh–Bolton, 95 miles. They probably imply a two-day journey by horse in the case of the first two, and a three-day journey in the case of the third (though a stop-over in Durham would have been likely in the latter instance). It's clear that Lewyn couldn't have stayed at any of these sites for long periods and that he must have had a site manager at each.

In Lewyn's case, although he was the contractor, it is also highly probable that he was the designer as well.[10] This wasn't always the case; there is, for example, good reason to suppose that Lewyn's contemporary, the royal mason, Henry Yevele, was the designer of John Lord Cobham's castle of Cooling (Kent), which was raised under a licence to crenellate of 1381.[11] At Cooling, at least three, and possibly four, main building contractors were involved in the construction work.[12] On behalf of one of these contractors, Thomas Wrek, Yevele acknowledged receipt of payments from Lord Cobham for building work at Cooling. In the case of two others, William Sharndale and Thomas Crump, Yevele certified their work on the castle on behalf of Lord Cobham. His close involvement with the project, and the use of several contractors, suggests that he was the architect behind the design.

A great deal of contract work was going on in individual castle-building projects from the thirteenth century onwards, much of it low level, though sometimes, as at Cooling, on a substantial scale.[13] Occasionally, even where he was employed directly, the master builder himself undertook specific elements of his own project on a contract basis. One example is James of St Georges who, in addition to having overall charge of Edward I's castle-building programme in north Wales, also entered into an agreement at Conwy (Caernarvonshire) to erect the masonry works of the principal domestic buildings at a fixed rate.[14] Similarly, John Box, the principal mason for Queenborough Castle (Kent) over the period 1361–1371, who took a salary of 12d. per day for the direction of building operations, was also party, with others, to building the outer curtain by contract. It isn't always easy, then, to determine a particular craftsman's role from an isolated reference, and we cannot always be sure that the name we have is that of the architect.

Dissemination of Style

The building trades, masoncraft in particular, were peripatetic professions, a condition that provided a natural opportunity for the dissemination of ideas. In the field of castle building, the royal works with their central organisation, large budget and national distribution of sites, played a major role in influencing castle design. It is a fact that from the thirteenth century at the latest royal craftsmen were often being sent from the south-east into the provinces. We have already noted that Henry de Reyns and Simon of Northampton were sent to York, Hugh de Tichemers to Knaresborough, and Robert Westerley to Tutbury. There are also other instances where the influence of the royal masons is evident on stylistic grounds.

A phenomenon that seems as though it ought to have been significant in the diffusion of architectural ideas is the large-scale national conscription of construction workers that occurred under Edward I in the late thirteenth century, and under his grandson, Edward III, in the late fourteenth century.[15] The first mobilisation concerned the castle building programme in north Wales[16] and the second the reconstruction of the royal apartments at Windsor Castle (Berkshire).[17] These large concentrations of building craftsmen from all over the kingdom in particular localities would seem to provide the ideal conditions for the dissemination of concepts, techniques and architectural style.

In practice, the effect is difficult to evaluate with much degree of certainty, and the concept of a royal 'school' of castle building should not be overstated. It would be erroneous to think of a body dominated by a south-eastern clique, because many of the royal craftsmen themselves had their origins in the provinces, as indicated by the large numbers of toponymical surnames that occur amongst them: Elias of Oxford, Simon of Northampton, John of Gloucester, Robert of Beverley (Yorkshire), Walter of Hereford (Gloucestershire),[18] John Sponlee (Gloucestershire), William Wintringham (Yorkshire), William Wynford (Somerset), Henry Yevele (Derbyshire),[19] Thomas Mapilton (Derbyshire), Robert Westerley (Gloucestershire), William Colchester (Essex), Michael of Canterbury (Kent). It is likely that these men took their own ideas, experiences and working practices with them and helped to mould the character of the royal works.

It is also a fact that a number of provincial master builders, who stayed close to their roots were commissioned to carry out work on the royal castles within their own regions. The north of England in particular appears to have retained a good deal of independence based on the palatinate of Durham and the patronage of its bishop. Bishop Hugh du Puiset's master mason, Richard Wolveston, who undertook the rebuilding of the great tower of Norham (Northumberland) sometime between 1157 and 1174 and who may have been behind Du Puiset's building work at Durham Castle, including the North Hall, is probably to be identified with Richard the engineer, who, in 1171, was working on the royal keep of Bowes (Yorkshire).[20] There is also some reason to believe that his contemporary, the royal mason, Maurice, the builder of Newcastle keep, was a northerner as well (see pp. 107–109 and 139–143). In the late fourteenth century, the Durham mason, John Lewyn, dominated castle building in the northern region. Lewyn's successor at Durham, Thomas Hyndeley, carried out work for the crown at Scarborough Castle (Yorkshire).

Moreover, in some notable examples it was the nobility rather than the king that led the way in innovation. William Marshal's castles of Pembroke (Pembrokeshire) and Chepstow (Monmouthshire) owe little or nothing to the royal works, and in at least one instance directly influenced royal practice (see pp. 167–169). The twin-towered gatehouse at Chepstow, now believed to date from *c.* 1190, is the earliest of its kind in England and Wales, only to be emulated by the royal works some 15 years later at Dover. Furthermore, two of the defining concepts of the Edwardian castles of north Wales, one of the high points of royal castle building – concentricity and the great residential gatehouse – appear to be borrowed from the works of the earls of Gloucester at their castles of Tonbridge (Kent) and Caerphilly

(Glamorganshire).[21] In the fourteenth century, the north developed its own distinctive style that, under John Lewyn, imposed itself on the royal castles of the region.

The royal works, then, were an important element in the development of the castle, but the story isn't a simple one in which an official style was diffused from a central body, but rather a collection of episodes and individuals. Instead of encountering a large degree of conformity, one is surprised at the high level of originality in each royal castle, even in those that are close in date to one another. Although there are discernible trends, as might be expected, there isn't a great deal of replication. The great castle builders were men at the top of their profession, confident in their own abilities, susceptible to ideas, but nevertheless strong personalities with their own views on design and construction. It might be anticipated that these views would develop over the course of a career as new experiences and challenges arose and enriched a master builder's creative capacity.

Theoretically, it should be possible to trace the course of architectural progress and attribute particular buildings to individual architects through comparative analysis. In practice, the process is fraught with difficulty: comparatively few craftsmen's names have survived, well documented castles are rare, and too many of the links in the chain have been broken because of demolition and alteration. Further difficulties are the versatility of the craftsmen themselves and the disparate natures of the buildings on which they might be engaged. Nevertheless, despite these obstacles, the attempt is worth making, and there is still a good deal of potential for making further inroads into the subject. Castles, in contrast to great churches, tend to have few distinctive decorative details that might provide clues towards establishing authorship. Planning concepts and structural characteristics are often more fruitful lines of enquiry, particularly in the case of master builders with wide-ranging responsibilities, who might delegate aspects of the design to subordinates or colleagues.

One aspect that is seldom given the importance to which it is entitled in tracing architectural relationships is the straightforward matter of size. Planning analogies might suggest a common source, but correspondence in the dimensions tends to confirm them. There are a number of such correlations in castles, which seem to suggest that the architect of one building had a detailed knowledge of another. Regarding the royal works, cases like these might be explained by the existence of a centrally-held repository of building craftsmen's drawings such as survive for a number of continental cathedrals.[22] However, given that no archive of this nature appears to subsist, despite the fact that many royal records from the period have been preserved, it is difficult to be sure. An alternative supposition is that individual master builders had personal knowledge of potential models, either because they had been involved in their construction or because they had studied them for the express purpose of broadening their repertoire and recording the information in their own sketch books for future use.

Process

The process of medieval architectural design is relatively well known. Geometry was the corner stone, and, for the master builder, a facility with practical geometry was a *sine qua non*, the forms of mouldings, window tracery and often entire buildings being based on geometrical constructions. The defensive role of the castle meant that the character of the terrain and other practical considerations were often the determining factors in planning

8   Castle Builders

the outline, rather than abstract concepts, but it is nevertheless true that geometry had its place in castle design, and was sometimes the overriding factor in formulating the plans of individual buildings within the castle curtilage, and, occasionally, of whole castles.

Usually, the figure that underpinned the plan was the square or the circle, other constructions being derived from them, notably the hexagon from the former, and the octagon from the latter. It was also from the square that two of the most popular proportional systems of measurement were derived; a third proportional system was based on the equilateral triangle. In such schemes the measurements of the plan, and other aspects of the building, were all consequent upon a single module. The equilateral triangle was also one of the geometrical figures on which the sectional profiles of buildings were often based; another was the square.[23] The process of geometrical design was not a complicated one and relied on mastering traditional practices rather than academic theory. Such geometrical tricks of the trade were within the range of all competent master masons, rather than being hallmarks of certain individuals, though particular combinations or preferences might contribute to an assessment of whether two buildings are the work of the same master.

To take one simple example of a geometrical plan and the manner in which it might be transferred to the site we might look at the great tower of Houdan (Yvelines) in northern France (Fig 1.1). A reconstruction of the steps taken by the architect to draw up the plan might be as follows:

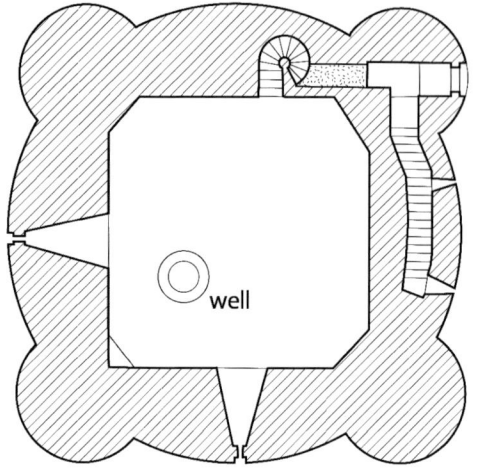

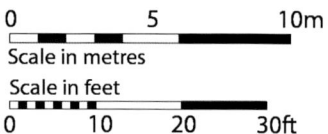

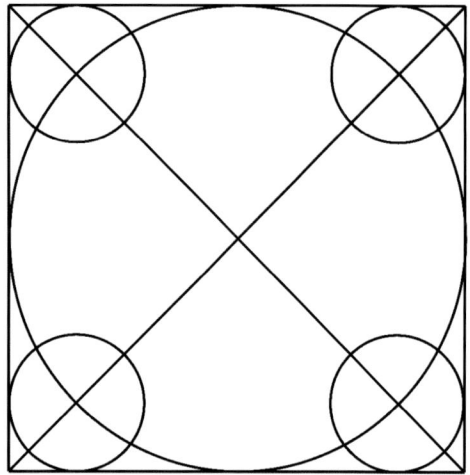

Fig. 1.1. Houdan (Yvelines) a) Basement plan of the donjon (second quarter of the twelfth century), after Viollet le Duc 1875, b) Geometrical basis of the plan.

1. Draw a square and its diagonals.
2. From the intersection of the diagonals inscribe a circle using the side of the square as its diameter.

3. From the intersection of the circumference of the circle and the diagonals of the square inscribe four circles within the corners of the square to represent the projecting turrets.
4. Create a smaller square within the first to represent the interior walls.

In replicating this layout on the building site, the greater square would have been set out first with ropes and wooden pegs, the regularity of the right-angled corners relying on the use of the 3:4:5 triangle technique;[24] then the diagonals, would have been strung out; a post would have been hammered into the ground at the intersection of the diagonals and used as the fulcrum from which the circular line of the exterior wall was inscribed in the earth using a rope and marker. Then, the turrets would have been set out in the same way as the main circle. After marking out the inner square, work on the foundation trenches could have begun almost immediately.

In the case of Houdan, the method seems to have been fairly straightforward, but in some other cases it is quite clear that the progression from drawing board to completion was more complicated, and that some aspects of design were finalized only during the construction phase. A comparison of building contracts and the finished products, for instance, often highlights anomalies, which point to changes of tack while work was in progress.[25] In some cases then, the initial plan was only a starting point and the ultimate design was, in part, a product of the construction process. Such changes of plan were commonplace in medieval buildings, and hint either in alterations to the patron's specification, or at unanticipated difficulties that were encountered as building work progressed.

Building on a virgin site was one thing, but a large amount of castle building was 'brownfield development': either additions to, or reconstruction of existing castles, or adaptations of even older fortifications, including prehistoric and Roman forts and Anglo-Saxon *burhs*. In these circumstances the design was to some extent dependent on the restrictions imposed upon it by the confines of the site. This might be considered as obstructive to a successful outcome, but the best master builders were able to rise to the challenge and produce stimulating designs that might not otherwise have seen the light of day.[26]

Conclusion

To pull all these various strands together, the castle builders of the Middle Ages were rooted in the practical world of craftsmanship, masters of their trades, sometimes with a grasp of more than one trade. While a few names are known, which may be linked to particular developments, all too many have been lost, to the detriment of the overall narrative. Of the many surviving monuments, some can be tied to known individuals, but, at the other end of the scale, there is a glaring absence of evidence regarding date, patron and master craftsman. What these structures nevertheless suggest is that their perpetrators were essentially pragmatists, but that they were also capable of reconciling the practical with the idealistic to produce stunning works of art. It is the details of the monuments: their structural characters, planning concepts and decorative schemes that provide us with the means of furthering our understanding of the castle builder's art, of filling in the details of the evolutionary process, and of constructing a fuller appreciation of the part played by the extraordinary individuals who oversaw the castle-building phenomenon.

Chapter 2

Earthworks

Rarely given the consideration to which he is due, yet fundamental to the initial construction of most castles (particularly during the early period, when the majority of superstructures were of timber), the earthwork builder must have been pre-eminent amongst the castle engineers of the tenth and eleventh centuries. On virgin sites it was very often the earthwork builder who had to assess the topography and understand the implications of the local geology. He was consequently a powerful influence on the ultimate form of the castle.

Motte Construction

Perhaps the most conspicuous and considered of castle earthworks is the motte, a natural or artificial mound, or indeed a combination of the two, serving as an observation post and a defence work. Usually surrounded by its own ditch, and thereby isolated from the rest of the castle, it was crowned by a palisade, and sometimes surmounted by a tower and/or other buildings. As a matter of sound structural principle mottes were usually built in the form of truncated cones with a broad base tapering to a smaller summit. Although dimensions and proportions varied enormously, this was the basic model to which motte builders generally adhered.

Thus, the motte of Baile Hill on the right (south-west) bank of the River Ouse, York, has a diameter of approximately 55 m (180 ft) at the base and 21 m (70 ft) at the top, and rises to a height of some 12 m (39 ft) above current ground level[1] and a conjectured 18 m (59 ft) from the base of the ditch.[2] The angle of inclination is approximately 40 degrees.[3] Another Yorkshire castle, at Sandal, near Wakefield, has diameters of 40 m (130 ft) and 15 m (48 ft) and reaches a height of 10.25 m (33 ft) above the bailey or 17 m (56 ft) from the base of the ditch.[4] The sides have inclines of 40 to 45 degrees.

At Tutbury (Staffordshire), the present dimensions are approximately 80–83 m (262–272 ft) at the base, 25 m (82 ft) at the top, and 12 m high above the inner bailey, but 24 m (79 ft) high above the base of the outer ditch.[5] The sides slope at angles of about 40 degrees towards the bailey, but 50 degrees towards the exterior, where the natural hillside forms the lower part of the mound. The diameters of the base and summit of Stafford motte have been estimated at 80 m (262 ft) and 40 m (131 ft) respectively, and at least 16.5 m (54 ft) above the present level of the ditch base;[6] this would give an angle of inclination of around 40 degrees.

To take two instances in the south of England, the maximum diameters of the motte of Bramber (Sussex) are *c.* 60 m (200 ft) and *c.* 25 m (82 ft). The mound rises to a height of *c.* 8m (29ft) the sides sloping at an angle of between 25 and 30 degrees. Dwarfing all these examples, the motte of Thetford (Suffolk) is 90 m (295 ft) at the base, 26 m (85 ft) at the summit and 25 m (82 ft) high, giving an average angle of about 38 degrees.

Owing to the difficulties of calculating the degree of attrition to which they have been subjected, these figures can only be approximations of the dimensions to which the monuments were originally built; they are therefore limited in what they can tell us about building practices. Although there are some points of correlation the figures do not support a theory of a universally accepted formula of proportion, and it seems more probable that the motte builders of the eleventh century had an empirical approach to their work that took account of individual circumstances, which would have included the peculiarities of the site and the nature of the materials they had to work with. On the other hand, an angle of around 40 degrees would seem to represent the optimum incline – some mottes were intended to be mounted by steps, in which case, too steep a profile would have been impractical.[7]

The dimensions above also give a broad picture of the scale of the earthworks in general and the magnitude of the building operation. A few attempts have been made to calculate how long it took to build a motte. At Bramber, the volume of the eleventh-century motte has been estimated at more than 13,0000m³ (474,572 cubic feet), and the amount of labour required to build it has been calculated as 228,269 man hours; assuming a workforce of 100 working a ten-hour day it has been suggested that it would have taken at least nine months to build.[8] The respective estimates for the smaller motte at Castle Neroche (Somerset) are a volume greater than 89,000m³ (315,2752 cubic feet), 165,360 man hours, and a construction period of at least four to six months.[9] There are, of course, many imponderables in such calculations, but they illustrate the point that mottes were major undertakings that would have required the procurement of a substantial work force for a prolonged period.

Where the mound was raised from a comparatively level surface, the base may well have been set out as a regular circle, as seems to have been the case at Bramber.[10] By using a length of cord attached to a central peg as the radius, the circumference could be rapidly delineated with further pegs. Once the edge of the motte had been defined it is generally assumed that the material from the excavation of the surrounding ditch was then used to construct the mound so that the two features were fashioned in tandem. This might suggest that the dimensions of one were determined by the those of the other, but a (necessarily tentative) calculation of the respective volumes of earth involved in the excavation of the ditch and the construction of the motte at Bramber have suggested that the ditch could only have supplied approximately 70 percent of the material in the motte, so that the remainder must have been transported from a greater distance.[11]

One frequently mentioned piece of pictorial evidence for the method by which mottes were built is the section of the Bayeux Tapestry that shows the motte of Hastings (Sussex) under construction. The mound is depicted with an obvious horizontal stratigraphy implying that it was constructed in a series of carefully prepared layers. Although selective excavation of the motte in the 1960s found no evidence to support the accuracy of this representation,[12] observations elsewhere tend to suggest that such layering was indeed employed by some motte builders, which leads to the conclusion that the stitchers of the Tapestry were representing a known eleventh-century technique.

Some evidence of this structural method has been obtained from the two mottes raised by William the Conqueror in the 1060s at York on opposite banks of the River Ouse. North-east of the river, observations made in 1903 during excavations for the underpinning of the thirteenth-century keep (Clifford's Tower) recorded a series of horizontal layers of different types of earth.[13] In 1968, archaeological excavation at the foot of the motte of Baile Hill, on the south-west side of the river, suggested that the lower part of the motte, at least, comprised a series of horizontal layers of different coloured soils.[14] A variant of this general construction principle of layering, modified to take account of the materials that were available locally, is the motte of Carisbrooke (Isle of Wight), an earthwork dating from *c.* 1100. A section excavated through the Carisbrooke motte in 1892 revealed a basal layer of stone, mainly flints, surmounted by alternate layers of loose and rammed chalk.[15]

A different type of construction technique has been recorded during excavations at two eleventh-century motte sites in Staffordshire. At Stafford, the motte raised by Robert de Stafford soon after 1071 was built with carefully arranged deposits of clay, sand and gravel, probably taken from the excavation of the surrounding ditch.[16] Work began by depositing the construction material in a ring or doughnut shape. Then, when the ring had reached a certain height, the central hollow was in-filled with further deposits of the same material. Finally, the top of the motte was capped with clay. A similar method seems to have been used at William Fitz Ansculf's castle of Dudley, some 21 miles to the south of Stafford. Here too, the initial stage in the construction of the motte of *c.* 1070 was to erect a clay ringwork. Next, the interior was in-filled with limestone rubble, and then the rubble was capped with clay.[17] The solidity of the clay rings meant that they acted as revetments by which the looser material might be contained and the stability of the mottes upheld. At Stafford and Dudley, the relatively small scale of the motte excavations, which were confined to the tops of the mounds, leave as yet unanswered questions about the substructures.

A related technique has also been discerned at York Castle, where the original eleventh-century motte was heightened sometime after the late twelfth-century destruction of the timber great tower that stood on its summit, most probably in preparation for the construction of the current keep in the 1240s. The method used in raising the height of the motte was to build an outer ring of firm clay, and to then level up the interior by piling in looser material.[18] At York, the ringwork formation is, seemingly, a feature of the later, uppermost, part of the motte, but there is no indication that it was also used in the earlier motte. This does not seem to be a typological sequence, because both the ringwork technique and the horizontal layering technique were being used in the eleventh century; it might, however, reflect the adoption of a construction principle that had its origins in a different region.

The clay ring formations described here were constructed in much the same manner as a contemporary enclosure castle, or ringwork, and it is evident that this type of motte construction method did in fact derive from the ringwork. Supportive evidence comes from the excavation of the motte of More Castle (Shropshire), where a comparable construction sequence has been recovered.[19] At More, however, the phasing represents the conversion of one type of structure (a ringwork) into another (a motte) rather than the planned stages of a single construction project. The More ringwork probably dates from the late eleventh century, with the conversion to a motte taking place in the early twelfth century. A similar structural sequence has been demonstrated for the motte of Aldingham on Morecombe Bay (Lancashire).[20]

This principle was also applied in the construction of the twelfth-century motte of South Mimms (Hertfordshire) where construction began with the raising of a 6 m (20 ft) wide clay bank around the intended perimeter of the mound. That this material was considered to have particular structural properties conducive to the project is evident from it having been imported to the site.[21] This clay bank, however, was only 1 m (3.25 ft) high, and seems to have served as the base for a timber revetment that contained the motte material. Roughly contemporary with the construction of the clay bank was the erection of a timber tower within it. Then, the space between the bank and the tower was filled in with dumps of chalk rubble, which probably came from the excavation of the motte ditch. After that, with the builders able to take advantage of the in-fill as a working platform, the timber revetment was constructed on top of the bank and the raising of the motte continued.

The motte of South Mimms was approximately 24 m (80 ft) in diameter at the base, and it is estimated that it was over 3 m (10 ft) high.[22] At Goltho (Lincolnshire) the motte, which was dated to c. 1080–1150, had a similar-sized base and, prior to excavation, rose approximately 3.3 m (11 ft) above the bailey, although it was probably higher originally.[23] This motte also seems to have been revetted, foundation trenches 0.82–1.8 m (2.5–6 ft) deep having been dug around the proposed outline of the mound, except at those points where it was to be abutted, and therefore buttressed, by the bailey bank. There does not seem to be much doubt that these slots were intended to accommodate upright timbers, although large numbers of pebbles found in the trenches were interpreted as facing material, perhaps used in conjunction with turf. It is not clear whether all these materials were contemporary or whether they represented different phases.

Unlike its counterpart at South Mimms, the Goltho motte was constructed of clay, and was therefore an inherently more stable structure, so that the revetment seems to have been less of a structural necessity and may have had as much to do with supporting a palisade than containing the motte. If the motte had the profile of a truncated cone, as Davison has suggested for South Mimms,[24] then it would have placed minimal thrust on the timberwork, so that stability would have been more easily maintained, and the preservation of the timber would have been enhanced through minimal contact with the damp earth. It has been argued that the South Mimms revetment and its continuation as a palisade rose to a total height of c. 4.5 m (15 ft);[25] timbers of such length would have been readily available in the twelfth century. The height of the motte of Goltho is less certain, though Beresford argued for a maximum of c. 6 m (20 ft) based on the limiting factor of available timber length.[26] There is every possibility that it was closer to the 3.3 m (11 ft) that it stood at latterly.

Excavated evidence suggests that a similar arrangement may have been intended at Aldingham. Here, the twelfth-century motte had a base diameter of around 33 m (108 ft) and rose to a height of c. 2.5 m (8 ft).[27] Subsequently, it was partially raised to a height of c. 4 m (13 ft) before being abandoned, and, as part of this heightening exercise, a 1.8 m (6 ft) deep foundation slot with flat bottom and near vertical sides was dug at the base of the mound, evidently for a substantial timber revetment. In this particular instance it has been suggested that the diameter of the summit would have equalled that of the base so that the motte would have been in the form of a drum.[28] Structures such as these with sheer revetments would have had a military advantage over a mound with sloping sides by being more difficult to mount, and, secondly, by providing the defenders at parapet level with a direct drop to the base of the defences.

Something of the appearance of such structures may perhaps be conveyed by similar encasings of mottes in stone, of which the most obvious survivors are Berkeley (Gloucestershire) and Farnham (Surrey), both twelfth-century constructions and therefore broadly contemporary with the timber counterparts discussed. The shell wall at Farnham is an addition to an existing motte, which probably dates from the second quarter of the twelfth century, having been raised for Henry of Blois, bishop of Winchester as a revetment to a great tower.[29] Here, possibly in the later twelfth century, a step was cut into the lower part of the motte to accommodate the inner face of the surrounding wall, and then, once the wall had been built, the void between it and the sloping sides of the motte were in-filled to the level of the motte summit, so creating a spacious enclosure. The process must have been somewhat similar at Berkeley, where an existing, perhaps eleventh-century motte, was encased in stone in the 1150s.

The motte of Farnham was approximately 47 m (155 ft) in diameter at the base narrowing to 26 m (85 ft) at the summit, and rose to a height of 10.7m (35 ft) above the original ground level. The dimensions are less certain at Berkeley but the enclosure at summit level is now about 34m (110 ft) across at its greatest extent and the top of the motte is around 7 m (22 ft) above courtyard level. It is, of course, possible that the height of motte has been reduced and the material used to in-fill the void between the mound and the surrounding wall. Farnham and Berkeley were larger structures than the timber-clad mottes and their substantial stone ring walls, which were heavily reinforced at the base, would have had no problem in containing the thrust produced by the infill material that was deposited on the sides of the motte in order to produce a level surface.

One wonders whether a timber revetment would have coped so well if the motte had been given a drum-like profile like its modified counterparts at Farnham and Berkeley, because the in-fill material would have exerted considerable outward pressure on upper parts of the timbers. Perhaps in a structure like the South Mimms motte, which was relatively small, and where the tower occupied a large part of the interior, and acted as a second revetment for the in-fill material, such an arrangement was a feasible means of retaining the motte make up. However, in larger and more solid structures it is questionable as to whether a timber revetment of the kind implied by the excavation of South Mimms would have been adequate. In which case, it may be that the void between the motte top and the wall was simply covered over with timber decking.

It is not possible to be certain whether stone encapsulations of mottes were simply stone replacements of existing timber structures, or whether they were novel solutions (adapting timber models) to accommodating an outmoded earthwork when remodelling a castle in stone. Such examples are rare and the cost must have been prohibitive when weighed against the limited increase in accommodation that the schemes provided. The question of what to do with the motte when reconstructing a castle along less militarily functional lines was to confront castle builders time and again in the later medieval period.

Bank and Ditch Construction

While mottes were popular entities, more universal and fundamental forms of earthwork defence were those that formed the main enceinte. This often consisted of a bank, or rampart, capped by a wooden palisade, with a ditch in front and a low counterscarp bank on the outer side of the ditch. These earthworks were designed to break up the impetus of an attack and to prevent the besiegers from coming too close to the palisade.

At Goltho, the late eleventh-century moat was about 11 m (37 ft) wide and 3.6–4.5 m (12–15 ft) deep. The ditch was flat-bottomed, the outer side sloping at an angle of *c.* 60 degrees and the inner side at *c.* 45 degrees.[30] The Norman ditch of Canterbury Castle, which was flat bottomed like that of Goltho, measured somewhere between 10 m (33 ft) and 11.5 m (38 ft) wide and some 3.2 m (10.5 ft) deep. The incline of the inner side had a relatively gentle slope that increased from 10 to 40 degrees between bottom and top; the outer side was slightly less regular, the slope averaging about 35 degrees.[31]

Such flat-bottomed ditches were common in the medieval period, although other profiles also existed. At South Mimms, the ditch around the motte was V-shaped, the slope of the outer side being steeper than the inner side at 70 degrees and 40 degrees respectively. It seems to have been a more serious work of defence. The two sections recovered through archaeological excavation showed a variation in their respective dimensions of *c.* 10 m (33 ft) wide by 4.5 m (15 ft) deep and 8 m (26 ft) wide by 3.5 m (11.5 ft) deep.[32] A not dissimilar profile has been recorded for the twelfth-century motte ditch at Newnham (Kent) where the outer and inner sides have angles of approximately 70 and 45 degrees respectively. The dimensions are *c.* 8 m (26 ft) wide by 4 m (13 ft) deep.[33] A third V-shaped ditch, around the bailey of Sandal, dwarfs these motte ditches at 21.8 m (72 ft) wide and 7 m (23 ft) deep, but the profile is much gentler having angles of 35 and 30 degrees respectively.[34]

For the castle builder the main function of the ditch was to provide the material for its accompanying bank(s), the two operations being carried out in tandem. The evidence from some sites is that bank building was an operation undertaken with methodical care. At Hen Domen (Montgomeryshire), one of the first tasks of the eleventh-century builders of the bailey bank was to construct a low bank of boulder clay capped by turf along the line of the proposed rampart. It was approximately 0.75 m (2.5 ft) high and 1.5 m (5 ft) wide, and its structural purpose seems to have been to level up the natural slope and to act as a base for a line of posts, the archaeological indication of which was a series of clay pads.[35] A second line of pads towards the bailey, some of which were clearly paired with those of the front line, implies a framed structure that acted as a skeleton for the earthen bank that was built around it.

So far, Hen Domen has proved to be the exception rather than the rule, but other castle banks have occasionally produced evidence for the use of timber in their construction to assist stability. One example is a probable timber revetment to the rear of the bailey bank of South Mimms, which would have been erected along the proposed inner line of the bank either before or shortly after the excavation of the ditch had begun.[36] Layers of soil and chalk from the ditch were piled up against the revetment, the foot of which, towards the bailey, had a clay bank built against it in order to counteract the thrust from the earth.

In contrast, however, many excavated earthworks have produced no signs of associated timberwork. One of these is the early twelfth-century bailey bank of Sandal, archaeological sectioning of which revealed evidence for the initial construction of a low marking-out bank of turf on the edge of the ditch, the upcast from the ditch being piled up behind it.[37]

At Stafford, partial sectioning of the eleventh-century inner bailey bank also produced indications that the initial stage in its construction was the erection of a low marker bank (Fig 2.1). Otherwise, the section revealed a sequence of marl dumps, mostly comprising redeposited natural clay.[38] Tip lines indicating the sequence of dumping were all from the exterior to the interior, indicating that the material was probably hoisted into position directly from the surrounding ditch as it was being excavated. The ditch is now 10 m (33 ft) below the level of the bailey on this side, so we can conclude that there was either some form of mechanical hoist to haul the earth up from below, or that it was thrown up in stages, perhaps onto a series of temporary platforms. The workers finished off by capping the bank with a narrow layer of marl.

The builders of the early thirteenth-century bank at Odiham (Hampshire) began by depositing a low dump of grey clay mixed with flint on the edge of the moat; it was *c.* 4 m (13 ft) wide and no more than 0.5 m (1.5 ft) high. Then, a 1 m (3.25 ft) high deposit of yellow clay with flint was heaped over and behind it, thereby extending the width to the bank to at least 10 m (33 ft).[39]

A more extensively excavated bank is that of the outer earthwork of Portchester (Hampshire), which comprises an inner bank and outer ditch sequence, probably of the fourteenth century.[40] Here, evidence was recorded for an initial dump of turf and topsoil positioned approximately 5 m from the edge of the ditch, which formed an approximate

Fig. 2.1. Stafford The inner bailey bank (left) with counterscarp bank to the right (last third of the eleventh century).

centre line for the main bank.[41] This initial deposit, then, may have been a marker bank, designed to give guidance to the diggers, and as such, it is indicative of a systematic approach to the construction work. Some calculation of volume was presumably made and the line of turf and topsoil marker bank positioned accordingly. Subsoil was piled on top, and, finally, chalk rubble from the bottom of the ditch, which was spread over the top and sides.

These purely earthen structures, composed as they were of loose material, must have been revetted in some way in order to prevent slumping. Archaeological indications of such practice seldom survive, although we do know that at Caernarfon (Caernarvonshire) the earthworks of the town defences, which were being built in tandem with the castle, were revetted with turf.[42] Turfing was probably the principal method of revetment for most castle earthworks, for reasons of economy and speed.

Double Bank and Ditch Systems
In some instances, the defences of the enceinte were more extensive. At Hen Domen, for instance, there was a double line of defences comprising (from inside to outside) bank, ditch, bank, ditch and counterscarp bank.[43] It is probable that a similar eleventh-century sequence existed at Tutbury Castle (Staffordshire).[44] The fact that this rare earthwork arrangement existed at these two particular castles is of interest because, *c.* 1071, Hugh d'Avranches, the first lord of Tutbury, was transferred to the Welsh marches as Earl of Chester. His fellow marcher lord to the south was Robert of Montgomery, Earl of Shrewsbury, who was the builder of Hen Domen between *c.* 1071 and 1086. The two men would inevitably have co-operated, and it is perhaps conceivable that the design of Hen Domen's defences was, in some measure, derived from Tutbury.

There are, however, other examples of double enceintes dating from soon after the Conquest. One is at Berkhamsted (Hertfordshire), built by Robert, count of Mortain, while another is at Castle Neroche, which is also thought to have been built by Robert of Mortain.[45] Interestingly, at Helmsley (Yorkshire), which was yet another of Robert of Mortain's properties, there are also two ditches separated by a bank, although these latter are usually attributed to an earlier period. In these three instances it would be strikingly coincidental if the planning of these rare double enceintes was unconnected, and it is more likely that the correspondence is a result of the common ownership.

Miners and Quarrymen
Where the ditch was dug through rock, miners and/or quarrymen might be employed. These two occupations had a considerable degree of overlap in that some quarrying was done underground, and some mining was open cast, and would have involved stone extraction. At Corfe castle, in 1207, eleven miners were engaged in creating the great ditch that lies to the south of the inner ward.[46] This ditch was dug right across the castle from east to west before turning abruptly south-west across the face of the south-west gatehouse, and then down the slope of the hill outside the curtain wall. Its inner face forms a continuation of the steep natural slope of the elevated inner ward, and the outer face is nearly vertical. Further ditch digging was carried out in 1214 when fifteen miners and quarrymen were recruited to carry out the work.[47]

It was miners from the Forest of Dean that were involved in excavating the foundations of Henry III's new castle at the hill top site of Montgomery, which was begun in 1222. Their equipment included the standard quarrying tools of picks, mallets, levers, and wedges.[48] Presumably these men were miners of iron ore, iron extraction being an industry for which the Forest of Dean was noted, the practitioners of which were being recruited in the thirteenth century to undertake siege-related mining operations.[49]

Substantial rock-cut ditches are features of several thirteenth-century castles, King John being a particularly enthusiastic ditch digger, not only at Corfe, but also at Chinon, Knaresborough, Nottingham and elsewhere. In the West Midlands a small group of non-royal castles with rock-cut ditches demonstrates a wider trend. The earliest in the series is the late twelfth-century castle raised by Bertram de Verdon (d. 1192) at Alton (Staffordshire), which is sited on the edge of a precipitous cliff overlooking the Churnet Valley. Here, the enclosure is isolated from the land to the south by a 7.6 m (25 ft) deep ditch cut through solid rock. Verdon was the guardian of the young earl of Chester, Ranulf de Blundeville, whose hilltop castle of Beeston (Cheshire), raised *c.* 1220, incorporates a very similar feature around the inner ward (Fig 2.2). Two further castles with rock cut ditches, were built at Heighley (Staffordshire) and Red Castle (Shropshire, licensed 1237). Both were raised for Henry de Audley, who was an adherent of the Earl of Chester and a kinsman of the Verdons.[50] It is possible, then, that this particular facet of this group of castles had a common origin. At all four of these Midland castles it is evident that most of the work must have been undertaken by experienced quarriers, that the material from the ditch was used

Fig. 2.2. Beeston (Cheshire) The inner ward enceinte perched on the edge of the rock-cut ditch from the north (*c.* 1220).

in the construction of the castle, and that it was probably the source of the wall facings. In addition to being accustomed to extracting stone, quarriers were also experienced in its grading and working, qualities that could be efficiently employed in such circumstances.

Tunnelling

A less obvious aspect of castle earthworks is the underground passage or tunnel. Tunnelling was, of course, extensively employed in siege warfare, both by the besiegers, who used it to undermine fortifications, and by the besieged, who excavated counter-mines with which to intercept those of the enemy.

An interesting application of the skill in respect of castle planning is to be seen at the twelfth-century castle of La Roche-Guyon (Val d'Oise). Sited on the right bank of the River Seine, the castle comprises two components situated respectively at the top and bottom of the one of the chalk cliffs that overlook this part of the river. The upper castle, apparently of purely military character, was sited close to the cliff edge, and was linked to the lower castle next to the river by a tunnel cut through the chalk. The yielding nature of the stone would have facilitated the project, but the work would have required the input of experienced miners.

In England, the sandstone on which Nottingham castle is built is another medium that proved easy to work, and, as a consequence, was eminently suitable for tunnelling. The most famous of the Nottingham caves with medieval associations is probably Mortimer's Hole, which extends a distance of 105 m (344 ft) from the inner bailey on the top of Castle Rock, the natural sandstone motte, to Brewhouse Yard at its foot. Possibly, this is the postern built in 1194 to give access to the motte,[51] the immediate proximity of the River Leem at the foot of the rock probably being the reason for this particular position.

One of the most extensive tunnelling projects to be carried out in a castle was at Dover, constructed in the 1220s, and now much altered, so that its original form is uncertain. This thirteenth-century network of passages was associated with the remodelling of the defences at the north-west apex of the castle, following the revelation of their inadequacies during the siege of 1216. The scheme included the blocking of the main outer gateway built by King John, and the construction of a sequence of outworks along the line of approach. The tunnels provided a concealed route between the outer ward of the castle and the outworks, from which route the outworks could be manned with impunity, and sallies made against a besieging army. The excavation and concealment of the Dover tunnels would have come under the remit of the master fossator, who name is given as Master Ralph of Popeshal, a man of Kent who took his name from the manor of Popeshall in Coldred parish, some 7 miles north-west of Dover.

Tunnels are not uncommonly found in association with castle wells. In the castle of Chinon a tunnel leads from the Tour du Coudray to the well shaft of the inner ward (Fort du Coudray) at a depth of 18 m (59 ft) from courtyard level. Some 79.2 m (260 ft) below the courtyard of the inner ward of Beeston, an abortive tunnel (possibly intended as a sally port) was excavated from the shaft of the well for a distance of nearly $c.$ 12 m (40 ft) through the bedrock before being abandoned.[52]

Water Engineering: Wet Ditches and Other Water Features

Dry ditches were the norm, but wet ditches were favoured wherever the topography made them possible. Some ditches were partially/seasonally wet owing to the natural water-retaining qualities of the underlying geology. Two examples are the early ditches at Canterbury and Goltho, which are cut through brick earth and boulder clay respectively (both relatively impervious materials). In other instances, the moat, or wet ditch, was a deliberate creation effected by harnessing a natural water supply and then maintaining consistent water levels. This latter process was a task for a specialist who understood water management technology. Such expertise was in evidence in England, soon after the Conquest, at Robert of Mortain's castle of Berkhamsted (Hertfordshire), which was one of the earliest examples of an English wet-moated castle. Built to control the valley of the River Bulbourne and the Roman road of Akeman Street, it is a castle of motte and bailey type, and is unusual in its double-ditch system. Both ditches were wet, being fed from the north by a stream that was diverted through them before draining into the River Bulbourne to the south. The relative complexity of the scheme implies that an expert had been at work, and in this respect, the entry for Berkhamsted in the Domesday Book is of great interest in that it lists the presence of a *fossarius* or dyker, who was retained to construct and/or maintain the ditch system.[53]

Interestingly, a wet ditch scheme may also have existed at Helmsley, which was also held by Robert of Mortain, which as we have seen, is another property with a double-ditch system. The south-east end of the castle was adjacent to the River Rye, and the north-west end close to one of its tributaries. It is at this north-east end that there appears to be a feeder channel into the outer ditch.[54]

A wet ditch scheme of comparable intricacy to that of Berkhamsted was created for at Bourne Castle (Lincolnshire). The chosen site was adjacent to St Peter's Pool, a natural artesian well that forms the source of the River Bourne Eau. Here, the master dyker incorporated the river into the castle defences, in addition to excavating a number of other channels to define the castle enclosures. The result was an inner bailey with a motte at its southern extremity, and a concentric outer bailey around the north, east and west sides, all three components being surrounded by water-filled channels.

Control of the water supply to a moat was usually achieved by damming a natural watercourse to create a head of water that would mitigate seasonal inconsistencies in the flow and help to maintain the moat water level. Where circumstances allowed, the damming of a watercourse was undertaken to make a more extensive feature than a moat. At York, the River Foss, which flowed past the royal castle of 1068 on the way to its confluence with the Ouse was blocked close to the main gatehouse, the dam serving as a causeway over which the castle was approached. Not only were the ditches of the castle filled with water, but an artificial lake, known as the King's Pool, was formed which protected the castle on its east side and also acted as a royal fishery.[55]

A similar notion was adopted by the engineer behind the water defences of Kenilworth Castle (Warwickshire), built by Geoffrey de Clinton in the 1120s (Fig 2.3). The chosen site was a modest sandstone eminence overlooking the confluence of the Finham and Inchford brooks to the southeast. These two watercourses provided the inspiration and means for an ambitious scheme of water defences. On the south side of the castle a causeway was constructed across the stream to the east of the confluence in order to flood the valleys

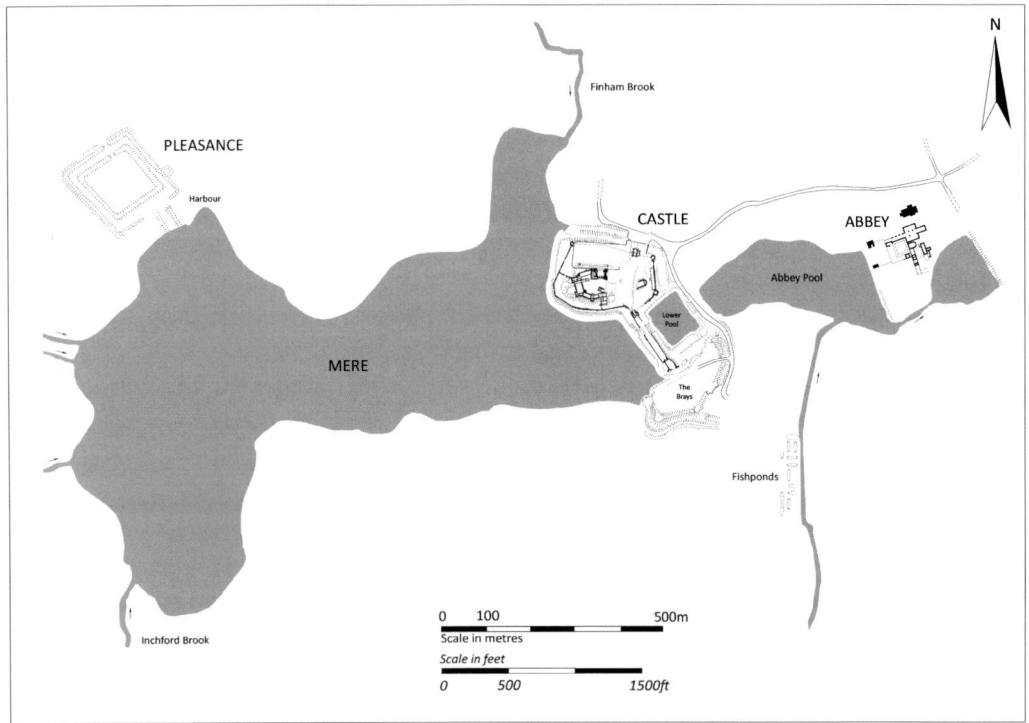

Fig. 2.3. Kenilworth (Warwickshire) The castle showing the extent of the Mere and associated water features; after Thompson 1977a.

to the south and west of the castle. The encirclement of the castle by water was achieved by cutting a moat around the north and east sides. Kenilworth was appropriated by the crown in 1174, and substantial works were carried out by King John in the early thirteenth century, a programme that included the heightening of the dam in order to raise the level and extent of the water. The result was an artificial lake (the Mere) that extended for a distance of nearly a mile.

Kenilworth was to gain fame (or notoriety) in the great siege of 1266; it was here that some of Simon de Montfort's supporters gathered after the Battle of Evesham and continued to defy the royal forces. The effectiveness of the water defences thus exemplified may well have provided the inspiration for at least one major thirteenth-century scheme. This is the one associated with Gilbert de Clare's castle of Caerphilly (1268–1271), begun only two years after the siege, in which Gilbert de Clare had taken part. Situated within the Rhymney Valley (Gwent), it was built on an eastward-extending raised gravel spur of glacial origin flanked by two watercourses, both tributaries of the Rhymney, the Nant y Gledyr to the south and the Nant yr Aber to the north (Fig 2.4). It was a site, therefore, that had natural advantages as a defensive position. Gilbert de Clare's master dyker fashioned three islands by cutting ditches across this spur in order to accommodate the central core of the castle and two outworks. The Nant y Gledyr was dammed to the south of the eastern island to create a large lake to the south of the spur; the dam was later extended to the north to block the Nant yr Aber and create a lake on this side of the spur as well.

22 Castle Builders

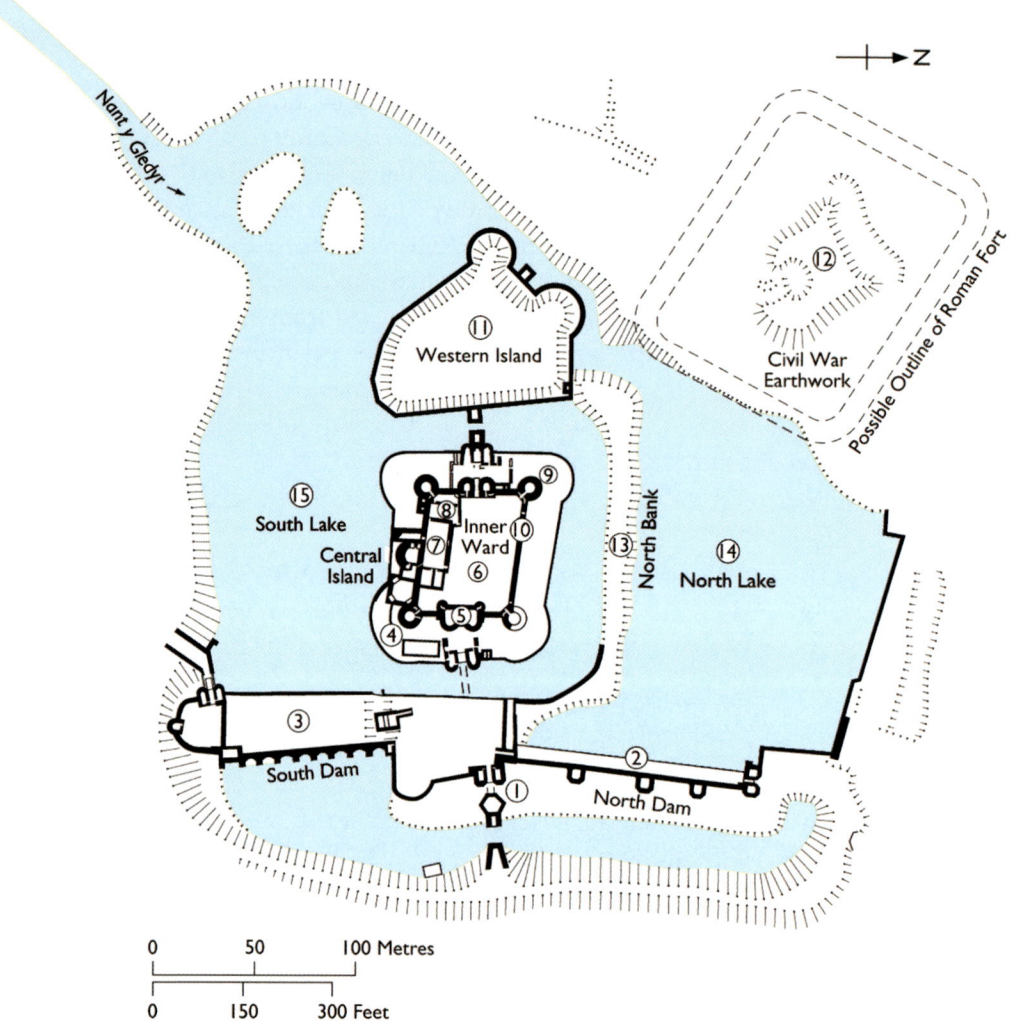

Fig. 2.4. Caerphilly (Glamorganshire) Site plan showing the extent of the water defences (last quarter of the thirteenth century). © Crown copyright (2015) Cadw.

Leeds (Kent) is another castle that stands within a great lake, which in this case was formed by the construction of a dam across the course of the River Len that flows past the castle. Edward I, who had also been present at the siege of Kenilworth, acquired the manor in 1278 and remodelled the castle, so it is possible that this too was in part inspired by Kenilworth. Prior to his acquisition of Leeds, Edward had already demonstrated an interest in water engineering at the Tower of London and elsewhere. The first attempt to create a water-filled moat around the Tower, which was made $c.$ 1190, using the Thames as the water source, was not a success, because the ditch failed to retain water.[56] It is possible that inadequate thought was given to the ebb and flow of the river so that there was a consequent inconsistency in the water supply.[57] Some fifty years later, $c.$ 1240, when the ditch was extended in association with Henry III's expansion of the castle to the north and west, it was a Flemish master ditcher, John le Fossour, who was called in to supervise the works. Flemish ditchers appear to have had a good reputation, no doubt owed to the development of their expertise on the dyke systems of the Low Countries.

Confirmation of such regional expertise is suggested by Edward I's employment of another Fleming: Master Walter of Flanders to mastermind the remodelling of the moat as part of his expansion of the Tower from 1275. This project involved the creation of a narrow outer ward immediately outside the existing outer curtain, on all four sides, and was achieved through an impressive programme of land reclamation from the existing ditch and the river frontage, accompanied by the creation of a more substantial moat extending to approximately 35 m (115 ft) in width. The moat was fed from one of the tributaries of the Thames,[58] which was, perhaps, a more reliable source for maintaining the water level than the tidal waters of the Thames alone. Master Walter was employed at the beginning of the project, when the details of the scheme were worked out, and towards the end when he supervised the directing of the water supply into the moat.

Water played a substantial role in Edward's northern Welsh castles during the last quarter of the thirteenth century. Several were situated so that they could be supplied by sea. Beaumaris (Anglesey), Caernarfon and Harlech (Merionethshire) were sited on the coast, while Conwy (Caernarvonshire) and Flint (Flintshire) lay on the estuaries of the rivers Conwy and Dee respectively. At Rhuddlan (Flintshire), which is situated on the right bank of the River Clwyd approximately 2½ miles from the coast, a major ditching exercise was carried out between 1277 and 1280 in association with the construction of the castle, involving the diversion and canalization of the River Clwyd in order to ensure sufficient draught for shipping of the requisite tonnage. It has been estimated that the project would have employed an average of seventy-seven *fossatores* working six days a week for three years.[59] The principal figure amongst the *fossatores* at Rhuddlan appears to have been Master William of Boston from the Lincolnshire fens, another area from which some of the leading dykers of the Middle Ages were drawn.

Edward I's works in Scotland
A master dyker who played a prominent role in the castle building programme that accompanied the Edward I's invasion of Scotland was, perhaps, another native of Flanders, a man called Adam the Fleming who, nevertheless, hailed from Bury St Edmunds in Suffolk, not too far from the fens. Where possible, Edward's castle builders took advantage of and enhanced natural water defences. Master Adam is first mentioned in 1300 when he contracted to complete the wet moat system around Dumfries (Dumfries and Galloway) peel and castle, and also to enlarge the existing moats so that they would contain water 20 ft wide and 10 ft deep.[60] The destruction of Dumfries Castle and the landscaping of the site as a public park prohibits any interpretation of this system, but as the castle stood beside the River Nith it was probably from this source that the moats were intended to be fed.

Although the details of the ditch system at Dumfries are obscure, a rather better preserved arrangement survives at Lochmaben Castle (Dumfriesshire), which lies approximately 8 miles to the north-east of Dumfries, and whose earthworks were probably underway at around the same time. It is quite likely that Master Adam was also involved here. Lochmaben Castle is built on a promontory that juts out into Castle Loch; a main ditch extended along a slightly irregular path across the neck of the promontory, isolating it from the mainland by linking the two sides of the loch. It also defined the south side of the outer ward, the east and west sides being marked by northward extending offshoots from the main ditch. A further east–west aligned ditch, which separated the outer ward from the inner ward, also extended right across the promontory to join the waters of the loch and act as a canal to allow boats into the castle.[61]

Subsequently, in 1302, Master Adam had charge of the earthworks at Linlithgow Castle (Linlithgowshire). Like Lochmaben, Linlithgow was a promontory site, lying on the south side of Linlithgow Loch. The main ditch on the landward side was intended to cut off the promontory, and was made deep enough to allow it to be filled by the waters of the loch. In addition, a ditch was to be dug around the promontory to protect against a waterborne attack. Linlithgow provides an interesting insight into the organization of the dykers, showing that they were divided into work gangs of 20 or 30 strong each with its own leader (*vintenarius*).[62] We can probably assume that these gangs were assigned to different sections along the planned route of the ditches.

Later medieval water schemes
Water schemes associated with castles proliferated in the fourteenth and fifteenth centuries. At Dunstanburgh (Northumberland) the coastal headland location of the castle that Thomas earl of Lancaster began to build from 1313 was turned to advantage by utilizing the low-lying land to the west for the creation of a chain of large freshwater lakes, or meres, and other water features that extended around the landward side of the castle site for a distance of some 800 m, effectively converting the headland into an island.[63] The meres were fed by a spring brought to the site from a distance of 600 m by the construction of an artificial, stone-lined channel. Preparatory earthworks for the scheme included the raising of two small dams, the excavation of a deep, 100.6 m (330 ft) long by 24.4 m wide (80 ft), ditch or moat linking two of the mere sites, and the making of overflow channels to conduct excess water from one feature to another or towards the sea.[64]

A late fourteenth-century scheme at Ravensworth (Yorkshire) also made full use of the natural terrain to form what may have been an extensive lake around the castle.[65] The castle itself is sited on a steeply scarped platform within a valley bottom surrounded by a marshy depression except for a narrow neck of land to the north-west that links it to higher ground. The natural elevation of the castle platform above a topographically wetland terrain, was a promising basis for a master dyker seeking to encompass the castle within a large expanse of water. A 20 m (65 ft) wide ditch was excavated through the north-west causeway to link the marshy ground on either side, and a bank was raised along the west and south-west sides of the marshy area to dam the area on this side. Otherwise, the containment of the water seems to have relied on the natural topography.

A near contemporary system in the south of England was at Bodiam (Sussex) where Sir Edward Dallingridge built a new castle under a licence of 1385, but also created a wet landscape that included not only a wide moat, but also a series of fishponds and a extensive mill pool. The castle sits on a low spur overlooking the River Rother to the south, with gently rising land to the north. Major factors at this site that allowed the creation of such a landscape were the existence of numerous springs that might be harnessed to feed the water features, and a level building platform in the form of the spur that was elevated above the river and which thereby provided a means of draining the excess water.

Another extensive system of water features had been created somewhat earlier in association with Mettingham Castle (Suffolk), which was built for John de Norwich under a licence to crenellate of 1344.[66] The moats enclosed two sub-rectangular courtyards, north and south, and, in the north-east corner of the southern one, a small further enclosure. A plan of the castle published in 1896 shows an additional moated enclosure, of even greater extent, attached to the east side of this main complex, and there is a hint that another such feature may have existed towards the west.[67]

Although the full extent of the wet features at Mettingham is currently uncertain, some 80 years later Sir John Fastolf repeated the moated double courtyard arrangement that formed the basis of its plan at the brick castle he built some 18 miles north-west of Mettingham at West Caister (Norfolk) between 1432 and *c.* 1446. Preparations for the construction of Caister Castle probably included the excavation of a canal known as the Barge Ditch, which formerly connected the moat system to the navigable River Bure, via a stretch of water known as the Pickerill Fleet, a total distance of approximately 2.5 miles. It would have provided a convenient and cost effective means of transporting the building materials, including those that came from overseas. The account for the first year of activity (1432–1433), which refers to the taking down of existing buildings and to the repair of the hedges and ditches of the manor,[68] suggests that the castle was built on the site of an existing moated manor house. In the two subsequent years (1433–1434 and 1434–1435) there is reference to the making of new ditches,[69] implying that the character of the earlier moat system was extended to form the double courtyard plan.

Roughly contemporary with Fastolf's work at Caister is Ralph Lord Cromwell's rebuilding of Tattershall Castle (Lincolnshire), a project that was carried out between 1434 and 1446, and which, like Caister, was a transformation of an existing manorial site. Prior to the fifteenth-century rebuilding, Tattershall was a thirteenth-century enclosure castle with round or D-shaped wall towers. It must have been somewhat similar to Bolingbroke Castle (Lincolnshire), which lies approximately 10 miles to the east, and was built on roughly the same scale, perhaps in imitation of it. The earlier castle at Tattershall was surrounded by a wet moat, which was retained in Cromwell's redevelopment of the site.

Cromwell's master ditcher at Tattershall was Matthew Dyker, who was paid at piecework rates. His work began in March 1434 when he and his team undertook the scouring and emptying of the waters of the existing castle ditches. This was necessary preparatory work for the construction operations that were about to ensue, in particular, the revetment of the moat in brick. In the same year Matthew and his fellow dykers remade or excavated a number of watercourses around Tattershall amounting to 739 rods or 3,717 m (12, 194 ft).[70]

It is uncertain how much of this work was directly concerned with the castle but in low-lying areas like Lincolnshire sound drainage schemes were, of course, essential to prevent flooding.[71] As far as the castle was concerned, however, these works resulted in a principal moat around the inner ward, which was, in turn, surrounded by an outer moat. A feeder stream extended from the River Bain approximately 190 m (625 ft) to the east, and a channel led from the outer to the inner moat.

At this distance, the workings of few medieval moat schemes are completely understood. However, some of the best evidence for the construction of a castle moat pertains to William Lord Hastings's never to be completed quadrangular castle of Kirby Muxloe, the accounts for which survive, and which show that the moat and its related features were constructed between October 1480 and September 1481 (Fig 2.5).[72] Restored to its former dimensions in the early twentieth century, the moat ranges in width from 13.7 m (45 ft) to 21.3 m (70 ft) and was fed from a stream that flows past the south-east side of the castle, a feeder channel branching off to the moat and returning to it downstream.

In the accounts, if the nomenclature is consistent, the main stream, now known as Kirby Brook, is described as 'le Broke' and the feeder and outlet channel is known as 'Lytyl Broke'. The mouth of the feeder channel is some 35 m (115 ft) to the north-east of the castle. The supply of water was maintained by the construction of a stone dam across Kirby Brook, the waters of which were channelled through a hollowed oak log at the foot of the dam, which could be plugged in order to build up a head of water from which the channel could be fed.[73] Where the channel joins the north-east corner of the moat another dam was built. The water was conveyed via a vertical brick shaft to a sluice at the foot of the dam and thence into the moat. The device for closing the sluice was a leather covered timber plug, which fitted into the shaft. There was another dam at the outlet from the

Fig. 2.5. Kirby Muxloe (Leicestershire). The moat of Lord Hastings' unfinished castle from the south (1480–1483).

moat, which has not survived, and so the details of the original arrangement are unknown. Beyond it, the channel fed a stew pond, and thence carried on to rejoin Kirby Brook.

The principal dyker was a Welshman called John Powell or Ap Howell; the fact that several of his men also had Welsh names, suggests, perhaps, that he had recourse to a regular team of workers. The first reference to work on the moat and its attendant features dates from the first week of the project (beginning 30 October) when Powell and his men spent four days on 'le Broke' and on 'cleaning Lytyll Broke for a water-course and at directing the moat as far as the said water-course'. From then until the week beginning 22 January 1481 Powell and a team of three were generally working on the moat. At that point they broke off to spend two weeks on a pool. The week beginning 5 February was spent on the moat, the following week on 'le Brooke, to make the water-course', and the week after that on 'le lytull broke'.

From the week beginning 26 February until the week beginning 11 June, Powell and his men worked solidly on the moat. During those fifteen weeks the team, including Powell, varied in number from four to twelve and put in an average of 46.5 man days per week, the greatest effort being concentrated on the five weeks from 30 April onwards when an average of 61.1 man days was worked each week. After this, the operation was reduced, and, during the week beginning 11 June, Powell and his gang spent only a few days in the moat, and for the next three weeks are recorded as being on non-specific tasks, or on digging the foundations of the castle. During the week beginning 9 July the dykers' time was divided between working on wall foundations in 'le Courte' and the moat. No further work on the moat was recorded until the week beginning 30 July when Powell and eight others expended 50 man days on squaring the sides of the moat, a project that extended into the following week, and which was, perhaps, in preparation for the revetment of the inner face of the moat in brick.

In fact, this latter task had probably begun a few weeks earlier, the bricklayers having started work during the week beginning 7 May. For the first two weeks they were paid a day rate, and the week after that they do not appear in the records, but during the week beginning 28 May the bricklaying was being done at piecework rates, which implies that the layers had an unrestricted site on which to work. The appearance of the bricklayers coincides roughly with the increased urgency with which the work on the moat was carried forward and it is highly probable that the revetment would have been the first of the brick walling to be erected. It is perhaps significant that during the same week that the master bricklayer, John Horne, and his team began laying in earnest, John Powell and four of his men spent a night in the moat keeping watch for water, presumably to prevent the new brickwork from being spoiled.

The week beginning the 20 August 1481 Powell's team spent four days on 'le Brooke kestyng', or the final consolidation of the watercourse. What appears to be the ultimate phase of work on the moat was not recorded in the accounts until the week beginning 28 October 1482, when Powell received £24 for 'kestyng le moote'. Apparently it had been finished by contract and represented three months work. The hiatus between the tailing off of the work in the summer of 1481 and its resumption over a year later was perhaps in part owed to the necessity of waiting for the mortar of the revetment to cure before the water could be released into the moat.

Conclusion

The Kirby Muxloe accounts give a rare insight into the work pattern of a master dyker and his crew, and their interaction with other members of the workforce. Apart from defining the parameters of the castle platform and designing the moat system, the dykers worked closely with the masons and bricklayers in undertaking the ground works for foundations and revetment walls. This is one illustration of the integral role played by the groundworkers in the castle-building process and their essential contribution to the creation of the infrastructure.

The involvement of such men was even more critical in situations that demanded the rapid establishment of defended bases in hostile territory. In these circumstances the earthmovers formed the advance guard, playing a fundamental part in setting up the initial circuit of ditch and bank, earthworks which could be quickly converted into a defensible complex by the addition of a timber superstructure, and then modified in safety at a more leisurely pace later on.

Digging and banking might be thought of as unskilled work, but digging effectively in specific terrains, and to a tight schedule, needs experience of a particular kind. We have seen something of the specialisms – dyking, mining and quarrying - that were to be found amongst the workers taking part in earthmoving programmes. Furthermore, the creation of banks and mottes wasn't simply a matter of piling up heaps of earth and hoping for the best; there were recognised techniques that contributed towards stability, including the use of revetments, timber lacing, layering and compaction, all of which required a depth of experience and a grasp of structural principles. Though seldom celebrated for their often prodigious feats of workmanship, the diggers and earthwork builders of the Middle Ages, played a vital role by moulding the landscape itself, and thereby creating the underlying character upon which the castle's ultimate form was to be based.

Chapter 3

Building In Timber

The earth movers may have been responsible for laying out the fundamental framework of the castle, but, because the buildings and defensive superstructures of most early castles were primarily of timber, it was the workers in wood that made it habitable and defendable. Consequently, it is probable that the majority of military engineers of the eleventh and twelfth centuries had a facility with timber, a circumstance that reinforces the notion that in this early phase the makers of siege engines and the designers of castle defences might often have been interchangeable. When stone replaced timber as the main building material for defences, this dynamic altered, although it has been demonstrated that as an instrument of war and conquest the timber castle held its own into the fourteenth century.[1]

In addition to the application of timber to military installations, much castle-related carpentry was of a domestic nature, quite independent of any defensive scheme, and did not require its practitioners to have skills additional to those that might be needed on an undefended site. As the use of wood as a defensive medium receded, so then did a greater proportion of domestic buildings come to be built in stone, although most ancillary and some main buildings continued to be made in timber. Even where a castle was primarily of stone it incorporated large areas of timberwork, including floors, roofs, internal partitions, gates and doors.

A difficulty in assessing carpentry techniques in the early years of castle buildings is that few upstanding timber buildings of any kind survive from before the thirteenth century. Our primary source for timber construction practices, then, for the first 150 years of castle building in England, is archaeological excavation, and the evidence is mostly in the form of negative features, including postholes and foundation trenches, although surviving timberwork has sometimes been recovered in waterlogged conditions. Supplementary information can be gleaned about timber structures from accommodations in the walls of stone buildings for roofs and floors. From the late twelfth century we are on firmer ground, because even though the amount of medieval woodwork to have survived in castles is small, we have the means of drawing analogies with existing buildings of other types.

Early Timber Structures

Palisades

Although few vestiges of carpentry have survived from the eleventh and twelfth centuries, archaeology has revealed evidence of earthfast-post construction, sometimes combined with timber-framing techniques. An early example of the latter is suggested by Meeson's incisive interpretation of the excavated evidence for the eleventh-century bailey defences of Tamworth Castle (Staffordshire).[2] Here, at the north-east angle of the bailey, a row of postholes was recorded along the edge of the bailey, as well as a double row of postholes at a lower level extending along a horizontal ledge at the edge of the outer ditch. Alignments of postholes from all three rows were identified at regular intervals, suggesting to the excavator that the three sets of timbers were linked structurally and that they represented a single timber-framed structure. This interpretation was supported by the manner in which the scarp from the bailey edge to the ditch had been shaped – the upper part at an angle of 45 degrees, which, it was reasoned, was designed to accommodate the angle of the timber members that linked the post alignments, and then an almost vertical drop to the outer ledge.

The shapes of the postholes suggested that the main timbers were squared - a sign of proper carpentry. In the conjectural reconstruction drawing of the Tamworth defences, the angled timbers that linked the post alignments are depicted as passing braces lap-jointed or halved into the posts (Fig 3.1). The earliest known examples of passing braces to survive in England date from the later twelfth century, and they are a frequent feature of aisled construction, extending across the aisle in order to bind it to the timbers of the main vessel, so presenting a solution to the problem of transverse stability which might otherwise arise in a structure of this type. The nature of the framework at Tamworth lends itself to this type of stiffening, and it is quite possible that passing braces were in use in the eleventh century, and that the designer of the defences applied a familiar technique to an unusual construction.

To form a continuous framework, or timber skeleton, along the length of the earthwork defences, these transverse trusses would have been linked by horizontal timbers. Further archaeological indications suggested that on the lines of the outer and middle sets of posts, there was a double row of timbers, apparently linking the main posts and providing a continuous outer barrier and an inner revetment to the lower part of the scarp. The whole construction formed a substantial line of timber defences incorporating an alure, or wall walk, the back of which was supported on the inner row of main posts. The builders, then, designed the timber superstructure to fit the profile of the scarp, and prefabricated the main frame. Once the scarp had been cut to shape, the principal postholes were excavated, the main posts put in place and the skeleton assembled. Subsequently, the revetment was erected and the platform for the alure laid down. Finally, the outer row of verticals was fixed in position.

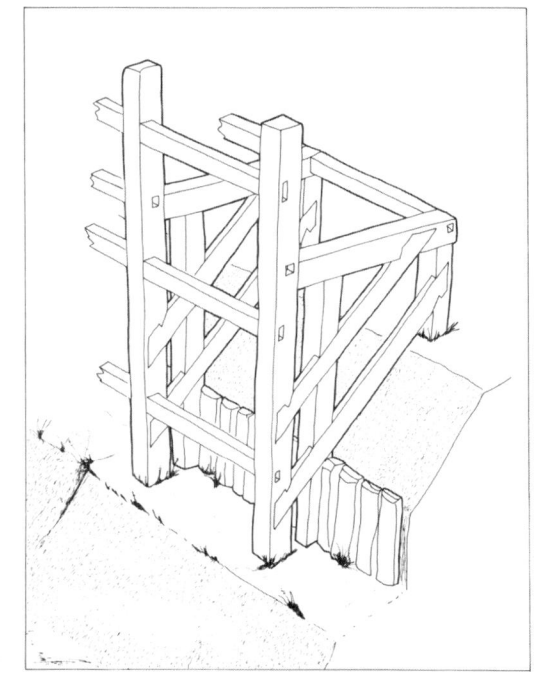

Fig. 3.1. Tamworth (Staffordshire) Reconstruction of the possible form of the timber-framed structure based on the archaeological evidence (third quarter of the eleventh century). Reproduced by kind permission of Bob Meeson.

The excavation of the motte of Abinger (Surrey) also revealed evidence, in the form of postholes, for a defensive timber wall with elements of framed construction around the perimeter of the summit, albeit of a slightly less regular nature.[3] Two concentric lines of postholes were uncovered, the closely-spaced outer line being interpreted by the excavator as a palisade and the more widely spaced inner line as supports for an alure. The inference is that in order to achieve structural stability, the two elements must have formed elements of a single, framed, structure.

The use of postholes at Tamworth and Abinger contrasts with the evidence for the near contemporary (c. 1080) timber defence work around the bailey of the marcher castle of Hen Domen (Montgomeryshire). Instead of being placed within postholes, the main supports for the timber superstructure along the line of the bailey perimeter were set on clay pads.[4] These were arranged in two parallel rows and, as at Tamworth, the inner posts appear to have been paired with the outer ones. The whole arrangement suggests an integrated framed structure, which, once in position, was self supporting without having to resort to postholes to ensure stability. In contrast to Tamworth, the ground surface along the front line of the defences was raised by the construction of a low earthen bank in order to provide a flat construction site. An additional factor at Hen Domen, though, is that the framework appears to have been intended as a skeleton around which an earth bank was raised.

Towers

Probably contemporary with these framed defences is the earliest building on the motte of Hen Domen. It was approximately 5.5 m (18 ft) square, and was supported by earth-fast posts which were placed in position simultaneously with the raising of the motte, rather than inserted into postholes after the motte had been built.[5] The posts were squared, several being about 0.3 m (1 ft) square, and were buried up to 1.1 m (3 ft 6 in) deep. Lengths of foundation trench indicated that there were walls between the main posts, containing either sill-beams or intermediate posts.

In the centre of the motte of Abinger, a collection of postholes has been interpreted as the remains of a tower, dating from the mid twelfth-century.[6] The building was approximately 3.6 m (12 ft) square, and the main supports consisted of four earth-fast corner posts that were embedded to a depth of c. 1.2 m (4 ft) below the surface of the motte.[7] The profiles of two of these postholes suggested that the inner faces of the main verticals were grooved, a detail that probably implies planked sides in which the planks were tenoned into the grooves.

The excavated remains of both Abinger and Hen Domen are indicative of straight-sided buildings, probably low towers, a number of which are illustrated in the Bayeux Tapestry.[8] Excavation indicated a different form of tower on the motte of South Mimms,[9] where the building was erected on 0.9 m (3 ft) wide strips of flint foundations, each containing a 0.22 m (8.5 in) slot, possibly to accommodate a timber sill-beam on which the frame of the tower was erected. These foundations, however, fell short of the corners, which suggests, perhaps, that the main corner posts themselves stood on the ground surface or on padstones, which in turn would imply that the horizontals were jointed into the corner posts.[10] Once the tower had been built, an earthen mound, or motte, was raised round it to an estimated height of 3 m (10 ft) in order to act as a revetment, and perhaps as a form of anchorage. The tower contained a basement within the motte, so the sides of the building must have been covered with a substantial cladding in order to contain the surrounding earth. Planks would be the obvious choice. The South Mimms tower was a much bigger structure than the buildings at either Hen Domen or Abinger, with estimated internal dimensions of 9.6 m (31.5 ft) x 8.4 m (27.5 ft), and it may be for this reason that it was constructed in a different manner. Unlike the other two straight-sided towers, the sides of the South Mimms tower appear to have been tapered at an angle of about 80 degrees.

The below-ground evidence recovered from the excavations at these three sites is not extensive enough to tell us much about the superstructures. Surviving medieval timber bell towers have sometimes been considered as useful analogues in supplementing the unsatisfactory nature of the evidence for timber castle towers.[11] The drawbacks are that the bell towers tend to be later in date than the castle towers, and, therefore, perhaps more advanced technologically. In addition, they are mostly no more than 5 m square, and so, may not necessarily be suitable analogues for larger structures like South Mimms. These caveats should be borne in mind when drawing conclusions.

The earliest of these timber bell towers, and therefore the closest in date to Abinger and South Mimms, is probably that of the church of St Leonard at Yarpole (Herefordshire), for which dendrochronology has indicated a timber felling date of 1195.[12] The timber-framed bell tower measures a little more than 5 m (16.5 ft) across at the base and the lower, twelfth-century portion, rises to a height of slightly over 9 m (30 ft). The mainstays of this structure are four corner posts set on padstones; they have curving profiles and the tower tapers inwards as it rises, as at South Mimms. On each side there are three horizontal beams or rails joining the posts to each other, and, in a measure to ensure the rigidity of the structure, two tripartite sets of passing braces, which cross each other to form a lattice pattern, and which are secured to the posts by barefaced lap dovetails.

A handful of slightly later towers at Pembridge (Herefordshire, 1207–1216);[13] Mamble, (Herefordshire, 1214–1255);[14] and Brookland (Kent, 1262–1274),[15] also have tapering sides and latticed passing braces, but are all set on sill-beams. This latter detail might perhaps suggest that the use of padstones at Yarpole was a transitional stage in the development of this type of carpentered building from a partially-framed technology based on earth-fast posts to a fully-framed tradition incorporating sill-beams, and that South Mimms represents another such transitional structure. South Mimms has been given the broad date range of $c.$ 1140–$c.$ 1200,[16] so there is a possibility that it is closer in date to Yarpole than it is to Abinger, and that it reflects more recent developments in technology.

Twenty-five miles to the north-west of Yarpole, at Hen Domen, the successor buildings of the tower that had capped the motte in the eleventh-century were replaced in the final phase (mid to late thirteenth century) by what was interpreted as a freestanding rectangular building.[17] No structural details can be inferred, other than those of a fully-framed timber building with sill-beams. In the excavation report this is illustrated as a tower with inclined sides, modelled on contemporary bell towers.[18] There is, of course, no way of being certain of the precise form of this building, but the evidence is sympathetic to a hypothesis of a transition from early towers, supported by earth-fast posts, to surface-mounted towers in which the main verticals were carried on a sill-beam, and that this transfer from one form of construction to another occurred towards the end of the twelfth century.

Domestic buildings
Several castle excavations have produced evidence of early medieval timber domestic structures, though they seldom survive above ground level. The width of a building, or, strictly speaking, the width of the space within it was restricted by the length of timbers available for the roof. This was seldom more than *c*. 11 m (36 ft), and buildings of greater width could only be achieved by introducing one or more structural divisions.[19] For this reason, early castle halls of over a certain width were generally of aisled construction, because the addition of aisles allowed a wider building than might have been possible had it been roofed in a single span, the aisles being roofed separately from the central vessel.

Both single- and twin-aisled halls are known. The two arcades of a twelfth-century twin-aisled hall excavated at Sandal Castle each comprised four earth-fast posts set within individual postholes.[20] This central framework of posts supported the main part of the roof and would have been the first element of the building to be erected, all other parts being subordinate to it. The arcades supported arcade plates, horizontal timbers that carried the feet of the rafters. Once the roof was in position the outer walls were raised and then the aisles, the roofs of which leaned against the central framework.

At Goltho, a single-aisled hall, which was excavated in the bailey, probably dated from the construction of the castle in the late eleventh-century.[21] The main roof was carried on the north wall and the arcade, the former being represented by a 0.3 m (1 ft) deep foundation slot, and the latter by a row of 0.6 m (2 ft) diameter postholes up to 0.6 m (2 ft) deep. These elements were the most substantial of the foundations, because they had to carry the greatest load: the main roof. The north wall trench probably contained closely-set posts, or possibly a sill-beam into which the feet of the uprights were jointed.

Wall trenches have also been excavated at Hen Domen, notably for a large conspicuous eleventh-century building (LIa), approximately 15 m (49 ft) x 9.5 m (31 ft) built next to the motte ditch and in direct line of the bridge to the motte.[22] It had the most robustly built foundations of all the Hen Domen structures and is likely to have served as the main residence. The trench, which reached a width of 1 m (3.25 ft), was probably intended to house timber sill-beams like the 0.3 m (1 ft) square beam that formed part of the bridge support, and which was discovered *in situ* within a trench in the motte ditch. Despite being a much wider building than the Goltho hall, no evidence for internal supports was recorded in LIa, so the interior must have been spanned by beams approaching 9.5 m (31 ft) in length to support the first-floor (the size of the foundations suggesting that it was a two-storey structure) and roof. The impression, then, is of a fully framed, strongly constructed, building of much higher quality than the hall at Goltho.

Of particular interest in the catalogue of excavated timber buildings is the thirteenth-century kitchen at Weoley Castle (Birmingham). Owing to the fact that the waterlogged conditions of the site had preserved the lower parts of the walls, it provided an opportunity to study construction techniques in more detail than is usual in excavated structures.[23] This oak-built kitchen, which measured approximately 12.5 m (41 ft) by 7 m (23 ft), was dated by the excavator to *c*. 1200–1260, a time-span that comprised seven structural periods. There were large earth-fast posts at the corners, sunk to a depth of 2 ft 6 in below the floor level, and three others on the line of the long north wall, two of which flanked the entrance. These posts, which provided the building's main structural supports, were linked at ground level by a series of abutting sill-beams that carried the walling material. Vertical posts were morticed into the sills at irregular intervals; both the top of the sill and the sides of the posts were grooved to accommodate horizontal planks or weatherboarding; subsequently, vertical planks were also used.

It can therefore be observed in the foregoing discourse on defensive and domestic structures that fully-framed buildings were in widespread use in English castles during the eleventh century, albeit in different guises. One version, familiar to the builders of Tamworth and Goltho, incorporated the ancient earth-fast post tradition. In a second system, evident at Hen Domen, and reflected, perhaps, in the twelfth-century towers of South Mimms and Yarpole, the main posts stood on the ground surface or on clay or stone pads. A third technique, which also manifested itself at Hen Domen and Goltho, was the use of a sill-beam, into which the uprights were jointed. In addition to the variety of framing techniques there are also signs of different forms of infill between the main supports. Plank walling has been discerned at Abinger and Weoley, and clay cladding at Hen Domen. Manifestations of all these principles have been recorded in later medieval timber buildings, sometimes as distinct elements of a regional building tradition. There is, as yet, insufficient evidence from which to evaluate the extent to which these techniques distinguished particular geographical areas, but given the existence of regional practices of masoncraft there is a strong probability that in some measure they did indeed bear witness to localised patterns of workmanship.

Timber Elements in Stone Buildings

When timber was replaced with stone as the main building material for defences, carpentry was reduced to a more subordinate role. However, timber remained a substantial and necessary element of the structure and often required high levels of ingenuity and skill on the parts of its practitioners. Wilcox has shown that from the eleventh century onwards the practice of reinforcing masonry buildings with timbers was an established part of the English castle builder's repertoire.[24] The interlacing of the stonework with timbers both as part of the foundations and higher up the walls was probably to maintain stability during the time it took for the mortar to cure. Here is another example of castle builders being comfortable with the use of more than one structural medium (see above, pp. 1–2).[25]

Floors in rectangular buildings

Rectangular buildings were floored with heavy timber joists, the ends of which were either embedded within joist sockets or supported on an offset, in which the wall of the floor above was set back to form a ledge. In either case the masonry was tailored in anticipation of the carpentry arrangements, and it is clear that the design of the two aspects was carried out in concert. A general point to be made, based on facility of construction, is that where beams and joists occupied wall sockets, the most effective technique would have been to place the timbers in position on the tops of the partly completed walls first, and, subsequently, to form the sockets by building the walls up around them. The first floor then provided a working platform for the next stage of construction.

As we have seen (above, this chapter) building widths were to some extent determined by the lengths of available timbers. For this reason the larger great towers were divided by at least one crosswall and the resultant cells were floored and roofed independently. One of the earliest great towers to be divided in this way may have been that of Beaugency (Loiret) in France, *c.* 1013–1039, which has an external width of 17.6 m (58 ft), although here the division, which was in the form of an arcade, was initially in timber. Not dissimilar in principle, perhaps, is a structural arrangement that was adopted some thirty years later, in England, by the builder of the great tower of Chepstow in south Wales, a building that probably dates from the 1060s. Here, the pattern of the first-floor timbers is denoted by square sockets within the masonry, closely-spaced along the side walls, and a single socket, placed centrally in each of the two end walls. This arrangement implies a central spine-beam carried on posts, which in turn carried the joists. The spine-beam sockets are at a lower level than those of the joists, which suggests that the latter rested on top of the former. The tower has an internal width of only 8.9 m (29 ft) but the non-correspondence of the joist sockets on the two sides of the building implies that it was spanned with two sets of joists, and that the spine-beam was introduced to bridge the gap.[26] However, the structural character of the first floor itself necessitated an unusual degree of strength from the timber sub-structure because it had to carry a 0.75 m (2.5 ft) thick floor, which comprised thick boards, then a layer of sand, and, finally, stone paving slabs.[27] This, then, may have been the main impetus behind the nature of the timberwork.

An analogous arrangement of first-floor timbers was used in the near contemporary Scolland's Hall at Richmond Castle (Yorkshire), where there is similar pattern of beam

Fig. 3.2. Richmond (Yorkshire) Scolland's Hall from the east, showing the sockets for the first-floor main beam (in the centre of the end wall) and joists (in the two side walls) (third quarter of the eleventh century).

sockets (Fig 3.2). At 7.9 m (26 ft) Scolland's Hall is slightly narrower than the Chepstow keep and the design of the first floor was probably determined by the availability of suitable timber. Richmond itself was rather unusual for a castle of its date in that it had a superstructure of stone rather than timber, and it may well be that there was a general shortage of timber of the right quality in the area. The central beam was supported at intervals along its length by posts standing on padstones, and the 23 m (75 ft) length of the building indicates that it must have comprised at least two, but probably more, timbers jointed end to end.

The obvious construction sequence in this instance is that the posts were propped in position and the beams lowered on top of them; it is likely that the tops of the posts were tenoned and that the soffits, or undersides, of the beams incorporated corresponding mortices. It is also probable that the different lengths of beam were linked by scarf-joints. Usually, however, flooring in large rectangular buildings was more straightforward. In Canterbury keep, of *c.* 1100, which was divided by two internal walls, the floors of the cells were carried on heavy joists set at centres of approximately 0.9 m (3 ft), the ends housed within rectangular sockets in the long side walls, approximately 0.5 m (1 ft 8 ins) square,[28] suggesting that they were designed for 1.5 ft square beams. The spine-beam sockets at Chepstow were of a similar size, while those of the joists were 0.4 m (1 ft 4 ins), implying slightly smaller timbers.

Fig. 3.3. Stokesay (Shropshire) Bracing system for the main beams over the ground floor of the solar block (last quarter of the thirteenth century).

By the later thirteenth century, if not before, the ends of floor beams were being given extra support by an arrangement of wall posts and braces. In the Eagle Tower at Caernarfon, of *c.* 1283, the posts were carried on corbels. At Stokesay the posts of the North Tower undercroft extended from stone floor pads (Fig 3.3). Here, and in the solar, the post and brace rise to a pad, a horizontal timber set immediately beneath the beam; in the solar the pad is jointed into the soffit of the beam by a slip tenon.

Twelfth-century keep roofs in south-east England
If we attempt to reconstruct the form of early castle roofs, the evidence tends to be less telling than it is for flooring, and, often, all we have to guide us are the roofline profiles preserved in the gable ends of the buildings, should these happen to survive. For the early twelfth century the best evidence comes from great towers, and in England the earliest

indications of a keep roof, dating from c. 1100, are at the White Tower (Tower of London) where the profiles of the original roofs are known through a soot imprint and scars in the masonry. There was one each side of the cross-wall, both falling within a pitch range of 40–45 degrees,[29] and rising to a height of about 6 m (20 ft). The wider of the White Tower's two roofs extended across a span of c. 12 m (39 ft), a distance equalled by the widest of the three divisions at the contemporary keep of Colchester (Essex).

These are exceptional spans in the context of great towers and are best compared with the central vessels of contemporary great churches. Unfortunately, no great church roofs of such early date survive for comparison, the closest we have being the reconstructed form of the early Norman roof over the nave of Ely Cathedral of c. 1120. The Ely nave has a slightly narrower span of a little over 10 m (33 ft), although the truss itself, which extended to the outer faces of the sides walls, was actually 14 m (46 ft) long and 6.4 m (21 ft) high.[30] The Ely truss, which had a pitch of 45 degrees, incorporated a tie beam, two collars, king strut, raking struts and two pairs of queen struts secured by lap joints. Although this particular design cannot be extrapolated to the roofs of the two keeps, the latter would have been constructed at a similar stage of technological development, and are likely to have incorporated some, if not all, of these elements.

Nevertheless, these eleventh- and twelfth-century great tower roofs did differ from those of contemporary great churches, in that, rather than surmounting the outer walls, they were sunk within them, a factor that affected their designs. A case in point is the roofing arrangement for Rochester Castle keep (Kent) of c. 1136,[31] where there is slightly more evidence for the character of the carpentry than at the White Tower. Rochester also had two roofs, which were of comparable pitch to those of the White Tower, but here, the side walls of the two compartments also incorporate angled sockets to accommodate the feet of the rafters, an arrangement that implies common rafter roofs without tie beams. There would also have been some form of transverse bracing, probably collars, as in the near contemporary roof of the church of St Mary at Kempley, Gloucestershire, of c. 1128–1132, which has two.[32]

A south-western school of carpentry
There was probably a good deal of variety in the solutions that early medieval carpenters devised for the roofing of great towers. An unusual one is to be found in the keep of Corfe Castle of c. 1105, which is also divided by a crosswall, a normal expedient for roofing a building with such internal measurements (here, 16 m (53 ft) by 14 m (46 ft). In this case, however, instead of placing the wall down the length of the building and covering the entire keep in a longitudinal double-pile arrangement, the division is across the width, and only the greater space to the south was covered by a twin-span roof (the scars for which are visible in the south wall), but without the structural benefit of a crosswall. There must have been a central main beam extending across the 9.5 m (31 ft) between the north and south walls, a length that was very close to the limit for a beam in Norman England.

It may be argued that this aspect of the Corfe roof's design, in which the central valley of the double-pile roof was carried on a beam rather than a wall, is related to the roof in the first phase of Portchester keep (Hampshire), which also dates from the first quarter of the twelfth century. The keep was heightened in the later twelfth century, but the profile of the early roofs that covered the two halves of the two-storey building survive on the end walls of the second-floor rooms.[33] These are highly unusual in having V-shaped profiles, but in common with the double-pile roof at Corfe, the main distinguishing characteristic would have been a central spine beam, or plate, supported by the two end walls, to which the feet of the rafters were fixed; the heads of the rafters were probably fixed to a pair of wall plates. In effect, each cell was covered with a pair of lean-to roofs. The two cells of the Portchester keep are 14 m (46 ft) in length, probably too great a distance to be traversed by a single beam, so clearly some kind of support would have been required from below, and it is probable that it was carried on the first-floor ceiling joists, which were, in turn, supported on offsets along the side walls. This meant that the roof was not open to the room below but had a garret immediately beneath it.

The idiosyncratic nature of this roof might be considered an unsuccessful experiment if it were not for the fact that something very much like it was applied in at least one other great tower. This is the keep of Bridgnorth Castle (Shropshire), which, like Corfe, was probably built in the early years of the twelfth century (Fig 3.4). The single-cell great tower of Bridgnorth had an internal width comparable to those of the two cells of the Portchester keep, but an internal length only a little longer at 6.5 m (21 ft). The surviving north wall retains the roof coping, which shows an identical pattern to that of Portchester. There is a beam socket immediately below the roof valley, and the extended gap in the stonework beneath may indicate the position of a former corbel. A row of joist sockets along the surviving side

Fig. 3.4. Bridgnorth (Shropshire) The early twelfth century great tower has an unusual inverted roof profile. The technique was also used in the early keep of Portchester and may be a product of a regional school of carpentry.

wall suggests that, as at Portchester, the room was ceiled and there was a garret beneath the roof. Quite what advantage these two roofs were considered to have is difficult to imagine,[34] but their unusual nature marks them out as a hallmark of a specific craftsman or a regional style of carpentry. If Corfe is included, we have a small group of buildings dating from the first quarter of the twelfth century centred on the south-west. Evidence that the practices of this school extended well beyond the lives of the early twelfth-century craftsmen who created the style is to be found at Corfe in the west bailey north tower of *c.* 1201–1204. This open-backed tower was semi-circular externally but pentagonal internally. The two wall faces that form the prow retain a V-shaped roof profile, and the tower must have been roofed in the same manner as Bridgnorth and Portchester.

Flooring and roofing round and polygonal towers
Flooring great towers of circular or polygonal plan required different configurations of timberwork. In the larger towers, a radial pattern of beams was often adopted. At first- and second-floor levels the cylindrical keep of Conisbrough (Yorkshire) has offsets rather than beam sockets, so the arrangement of the floor timbers is conjectural, but radially-arranged beams certainly seem to have been used for the floor at parapet level, which was carried on twenty stone corbels extending all around the 8.23 m (27 ft) diameter interior of the tower. Although further details are impossible to confirm it seems most likely that the inner ends of the beams were jointed into a frame of circular pattern at the centre of the floor. A similar system seems to have been used in the donjon of Château Gaillard *c.* 1196–1198.

Two tiers of closely-spaced square beam sockets in the surviving walls of Odiham keep, raised sometime between 1207 and 1216,[35] suggest that the first and second floors were constructed on a radial pattern. In view of the internal span of over 12 m (40 ft) there must have been a central support, probably in the form of a column, which meant that the beams would have to have been no more than 6 m (20 ft) in length. This has been confirmed by excavation of the castle, which discovered the foundation for such a column in the form of a circular arrangement of compacted flint right in the centre of the keep.[36] Although the form of the floor at Odiham cannot be reconstructed other than in a general fashion, it is reasonable to consider that it may have borne some resemblance to the arrangement of the near contemporary floor supporting the hoard over the great tower of Laval (Mayenne), where eight of the floor beams are jointed into the central octagonal post, and the others into an inner ring beam fixed between the eight.

Further evidence for floors of a radial nature comes from a number of other buildings that are only slightly later in date than Odiham. In the donjon of Coucy-le-Château (Aisne) *c.* 1225, directly above the crown of the two lower vaults, the outer ends of the 0.3 m (1 ft) square floor beams were arranged in radial fashion and jointed into a double ring beam embedded within the wall.[37]

The details of the arrangement at Coucy cannot be reconstructed in their entirety, but we know more about a similar contemporary structure in the Wakefield Tower at the Tower of London. Like Coucy, the Wakefield Tower is a cylindrical building with a polygonal interior, the first floor being constructed in concert with an intra mural ring beam into which the floor beams were dovetailed. Although this floor is no longer extant, G. T. Clark recorded it prior to its destruction (Fig 3.5),[38] and archaeological investigation of the tower during

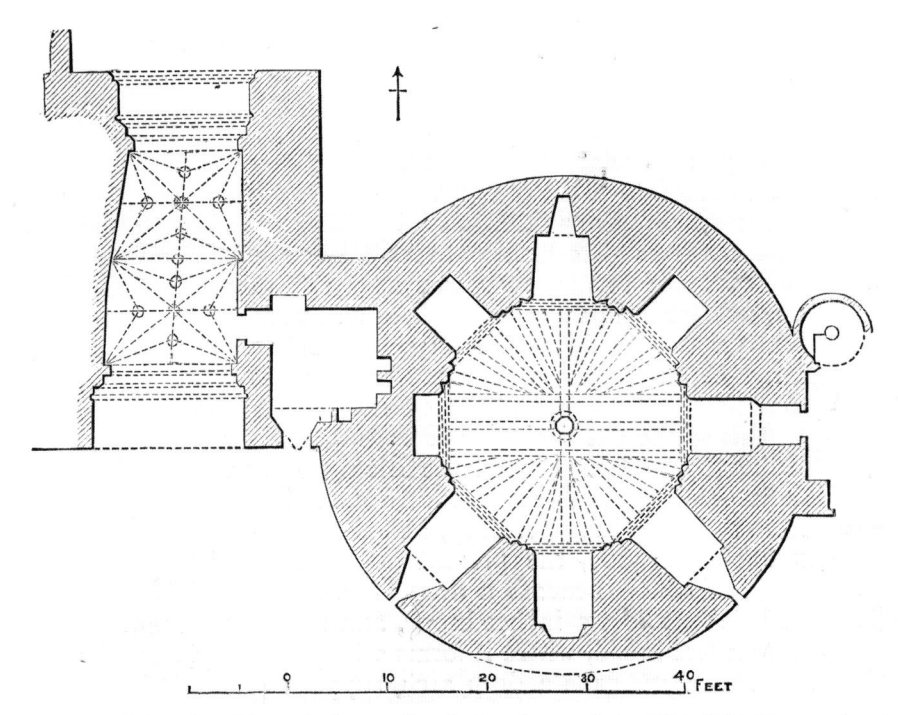

Fig. 3.5. Tower of London Plan of the medieval first-floor of the Wakefield Tower showing the configuration of timbers in the former floor frame (*c.* 1221); from Clark 1885.

restoration work in the twentieth century has added to our knowledge of its structural character.[39] This floor frame, which dated from *c.* 1220, was constructed of 0.28 m (11 in) square timbers. Two of these extended north–south and east–west across the building at right angles to one another, being supported at the centre by a timber post. The east–west timber was flanked by two parallel beams, and a radial pattern of subsidiary beams extended from the intra-mural ring beam to be tenoned into the north–south and the two outer east–west timbers.

Slightly later is the cylindrical great tower of Bothwell Castle (Lanarkshire), which was built in the 1240s. The tower had an octagonal interior, and an elaborate system of internal timberwork. The floors were carried on sixteen beams extending from the angles and the centre of each side, those of the upper floor being supported by posts set within vertical chases immediately below the beam sockets. It is probable that the posts also supported braces that rose to the beam soffits. The system is quite an extravagant one and was dictated by the great size of the keep, which, with a diameter of nearly 20 m (65 ft), was one of the largest cylindrical towers ever to be built in the British Isles. There is some reason to suppose that the design of the building was based on that of Coucy, which also had a radial pattern of flooring.

These radial flooring arrangements were carpentry constructions of the highest quality. Something of the kind also existed in the keep of Pembroke, another building at the higher end of the social scale, but in many round towers quite different, often less sophisticated systems were employed in which various configurations of beams and joists extended across the space in single spans.[40]

Fig. 3.6. Angers (Maine-et-Loire) The flooring arrangement of the Windmill Tower in which the joists rested on top of a pair of main beams, which were themselves strengthened by corbels and braces (second quarter of the thirteenth century).

Fig. 3.7. Rhuddlan (Flintshire) The hexagonal interior of one of the corner towers, showing the alternating orientations of the beam sockets (fourth quarter of the thirteenth century).

Amongst the better quality beam and joist arrangements is a floor of *c.* 1230 in the northernmost wall tower of Angers Castle (Maine-et-Loire). Here, the ends of the beams were set within wall sockets, further support being provided by a pair of stone corbels. A second pair of corbels at a lower level supported braces that extended to the soffit of the beam (Fig 3.6). The inner ends of the joists were carried on the beam, and the outer ends supported by continuous stone corbelling. A somewhat similar method was used in the polygonal towers of Caernarfon Castle from 1283 onwards, although here the upper corbels were dispensed with probably because the ends of the beams were supported by posts carried on the lower corbels.

Apart from their principal function, floor beams also played a role in enhancing the stability of a stone structure. In the cylindrical towers of Rhuddlan Castle (*c.* 1277), which have hexagonal interiors, the angles of the beam sockets indicate that each floor was carried on a single series of parallel beams of uniform scantling extending from two adjacent sides of the interior to their opposite counterparts (Fig 3.7). The beams tied the walls together, but the building was given greater strength through alternating the orientation of the beams between floors. There is little doubt that this was deliberate rather than fortuitous.

Just as the flooring of circular and polygonal towers require different approaches to those for rectangular structures, so too did their roofing. It may have been partly to obviate such technical challenges that the early twelfth-century cylindrical donjon of Houdan was built with a rectangular interior that presented no new challenges for the carpenter, in that it would have allowed the donjon to be floored and roofed in the same manner as a rectangular building. There is also an example in England of an early cylindrical keep, in which the accompanying development of new carpentry techniques has been mitigated. This is the great tower of New Buckenham (Norfolk), which is thought to date from *c.* 1140, and which is unusual on two counts. Firstly, with a diameter of 18.30 m (60 ft), it is one of the largest towers of its kind to be built in England. Secondly, it has a crosswall, a feature that is generally associated with rectangular keeps of the eleventh and twelfth centuries, and which is not encountered in any other cylindrical great tower. The most likely explanation for the cross wall is that it was intended to support the floors and roof, because the diameter of the tower meant that some form of intermediary structure would certainly have been required. It is most likely that the roof was conical, the crosswall serving as a base for the main truss that would have acted as an anchor for other roof members.

While we can only surmise about the form of the New Buckenham roof, there is rather more evidence for that of Orford Castle keep (Suffolk) of *c.* 1165–1167, which is one of the earliest of the polygonal- or circular-plan English great towers after New Buckenham. The conjectural reconstruction of its roof, which covers a circular interior, is based on a series of thirteen stone corbels that extend from the wall at a height of 2.4 m (8 ft) above the floor (Fig 3.8). Slanting chases in the wall immediately above the corbels appear to be housings for steeply pitched rafters, which, if continued to an apex would imply a spire roof with a pitch of about 65 degrees rising to approximately 10 m (33 ft) above the level of the corbels, but mostly hidden within the tower.[41]

The spire roof was a natural enough response to a tower of circular or polygonal plan, though the instinct to conceal it within the building echoed the practice of sunken roofs that was followed for rectangular towers. As a result, the design of the Orford roof is, like that of Rochester, an adaptation of a more conventional structure, in this case a church spire. Few twelfth-century

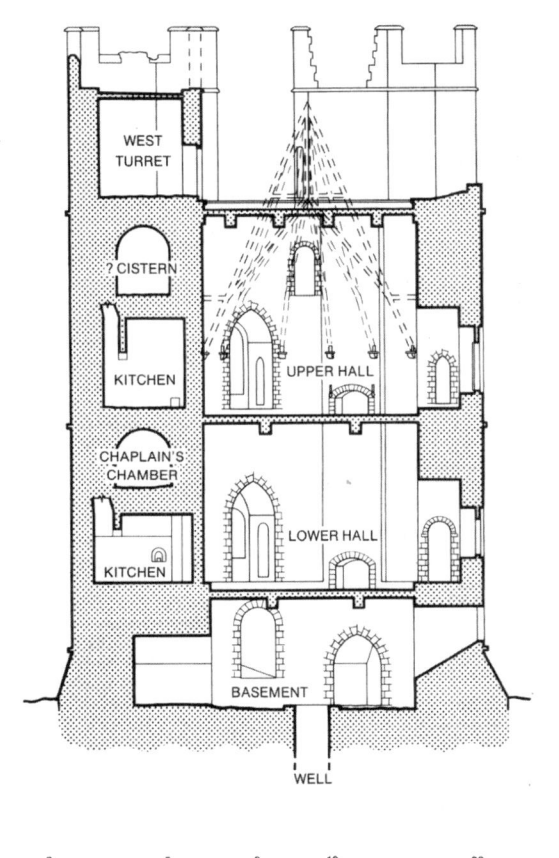

Fig. 3.8. Orford (Suffolk) Section through the keep with conjectured form of the roof. © Historic England.

church spires are known to survive, an exception being the one over the south-east stair turret of Canterbury Cathedral, which has been dated to between 1097 and 1122.[42] Unlike Orford, this structure is supported on a horizontal frame and lies entirely above the stonework, but the main rafters, which rise to the apex, are also at a pitch of about 65 degrees. At an intermediate level the rafters are stiffened by interrupted collars, which are jointed into a central post or mast.

Interestingly, the Orford roof probably bore some resemblance to elements of the existing roof over its near contemporary, the Tour de César in Provins (Seine-et-Marne), built by the count of Champagne between 1152 and 1181. The present roof of this polygonal tower is a product of the sixteenth century, but it is possible that some elements date from the medieval period and that the form was to some degree dictated by its medieval predecessor. The space between the roof and the vault of the upper room is currently occupied by a seventeenth-century bell cage, and the outer part of the roof, which extends from the tops of the medieval battlements to the apex, are clearly part of the sixteenth-century rebuilding. However, if we strip these elements away we are left with the inner part of the roof structure, which is of greater interest. This comprises eight rafters pitched at an angle of approximately 75 degrees, the feet of which are set within chases in the stonework at the angles of the octagonal tower just above the vault. They rise to support a horizontal frame of similar design to the base on which the Canterbury stair turret spire is built (Fig 3.9). This supports a central mast that rises to the apex. The general principle is not unlike that which must have governed the roof of Orford, although at Provins the timber structure now rises some way above the tower.

Fig. 3.9. Provins (Seine-et-Marne) Sectioned model of the Tour de César showing the eastern half of the building (third quarter of the twelfth century).

The largest of these polygonal towers, with an internal span of approximately 13.70 m (45 ft), is Odiham. We have already established that the floors would have been supported by a central column (see p. 39), so it is more than probable that this column would also have played a principal role in supporting the roof. Unfortunately, the loss of the upper part of the building means that there are no surviving masonry details that might provide clues as to its nature. The closest analogues are probably the roofs over polygonal chapter houses in which the underlying vault is supported on a central column. Buildings of this type in which the medieval roof survives include those of Salisbury (*c.* 1250–1260) and Wells (*c.* 1293–1306) cathedrals. The Salisbury roof is nearly flat and has eight principal rafters meeting immediately above the central post, which is itself carried on the central vaulting column. The outer ends of the rafters are supported by posts situated at the angles of the octagonal building and rising from stone corbels level with the top of the vaulting column. The design of the Wells roof, which is a very similar construction, was probably derived from that of Salisbury.

These roofs are somewhat later in date than Odiham, but there is no doubt that the chapter house of Salisbury was strongly influenced by that of Westminster Abbey (*c.* 1246–1259), in which case so may the character of its roof have been derived from the same source, though, sadly, the Westminster roof no longer exists. Westminster Abbey provides a link with the royal school of carpentry and so with Odiham. The master builder in charge of the Westminster chapter house was Henry de Reyns, who, in 1244 had been sent, with the royal carpenter, Simon of Northampton, to York to oversee the reconstruction of the castle. The remit of the royal craftsmen must have included Clifford's Tower, the motte-sited keep that formed part of the new works, and which was built between 1245 and *c.* 1270. It is a quatrefoil building, and although it too is now roofless, a seventeenth-century drawing of the tower, made when it was still covered, suggests that the roof was of low pitch.[43]

This makes a contrast with the roof over the donjon of Étampes (Essonne,) of *c.* 1160, which was probably the model for Clifford's Tower (see pp. 126–128). Étampes is depicted in *Les Très Riches Heures du Duc du Berry* (August), and the illustration appears to show a high pitched roof with rounded hipped ends apparently covering the main body of the tower and two of the four lobes, while the other two lobes seem to be have been covered separately with conical roofs. Such manuscript illustrations suggest that high conical roofs were once common in the towers of French castles. Conversely, there isn't much evidence, pictorial, archaeological, or otherwise, to suggest that this was also the case in England, and it seems more likely that most tower roofs were of low pitch.

This certainly seems to have been the case in the great tower of Stokesay, which dates from *c.* 1300. The medieval roof is no longer extant, but the corbels on which it was carried survive on the interior of the wallhead. These corbels indicate a rather unusual configuration of beams, a concomitant of the highly original plan of the tower, which comprised an irregular polygon with two external lobes and an internal triangular projection on the south-west side. The corbels suggest that there was a main beam extending from the apex of this projection, into which subsidiary beams were jointed. The pattern of corbels is, however, irregular.

Perhaps the nearest we have to a surviving roof over a polygonal tower in Great Britain is that over the decagonal Eagle Tower in Caernarfon Castle, which dates from the early twentieth century but which was based on the original early fourteenth-century structure. As at Stokesay, the main component of this roof is a massive tie beam, which in this case forms the base of a dwarf king-post roof truss. On each side of the room a stone corbel projects from the wall directly below the beam, approximately 1.8 m (6 ft) above floor level. Each corbel carries a post from which an arch brace extends to a stub tie immediately under the beam. The rafters are set at right angles to the roof truss, and extend from the wall plate to the principals to create a nearly flat roof. This bracing system at each end of the tie beam is in most respects similar to the structural arrangement for the first-floors of Stokesay Castle (see p. 36).

Great hall roofs

Although the medieval roof of Stokesay keep has been lost, the more important one over the great hall has survived. This roof, which has been dated to 1284–1285,[44] and which spans a width of 9.5 m (31 ft), is of cruck construction, a technique that had a largely western distribution in the medieval period, and which is found in domestic structures ranging from peasant to manorial status. The Stokesay example, therefore, is towards the higher end of the social scale. At Stokesay, the feet of the crucks extend the greater part of the way down the walls to rest on the lateral corbels. Contrasting with the cruck frames, cross-frames of aisled form are set against the two end walls, the main posts standing on paired corbels (Fig 3.10). The aisled trusses are a reminder that the thirteenth century was a period in which carpenters were developing roof forms that would span the great hall in one, thereby obviating the use of aisle posts. Stokesay seems to be unique in its use of cruck construction to achieve this aim, and the width spanned is exceptional for this form of structure; it is probable that the enterprise represents a strictly local solution to the problem, rather than a widely adopted technique.

The incorporation of stone corbelling in the side and end walls, in order to carry the roof, is paralleled in the late thirteenth-century great hall of Ludlow Castle (Shropshire),

Fig. 3.10. Stokesay (Shropshire) The great hall from the north west with an end truss of aisled construction and main trusses of cruck construction. The feet of the crucks have been truncated and the stone corbels on which they rest extended upward to compensate; originally the crucks would have extended most of the way down the walls (*c*. 1280).

some 6½ miles to the south-east of Stokesay and, at 9 m (30 ft), of comparable width. Projecting from each of the side walls, a little above the level of the window rear arches, is a line of closely-set corbels (Fig 3.11). Beneath them, a little below the level from which the window arches spring, there are four pairs of three-tier corbels, with a vertical chase in the wall above each corbel, in each case rising between two of the upper tier corbels but no further. In the centre of the eastern end wall there is another three-tier corbel, but this is at the height of the upper corbels.

The upper corbels have been interpreted as supports for timber wall plates into which the feet of the roof rafters would have been jointed, and the lower three-tier corbels as supports for bracing for the main roof trusses; it has been further suggested that the roof incorporated crown posts.[45] This is an entirely plausible interpretation of the surviving structural evidence, and probably the best way in which the configuration of corbelling can be understood. We also know that, like cruck technology, crown post construction was in use in Shropshire by the end of the thirteenth century.[46] Crown posts generally occupied a central position between a tie beam and a higher level collar. The posts carried a collar purlin, or crown plate, which in turn supported the collars. If the three-tier corbel in the eastern end wall carried a crown post, then those on the lateral walls must have carried supports for a series of tie beams at the level of the upper tier of corbels. The chases indicate the positions of the supporting posts from which arch braces would have extended to the soffits of the beams.

Fig. 3.11. Ludlow (Shropshire) The late thirteenth-century great hall showing two tiers of corbels; the lower ones carried the bracing for the main roof trusses, and the upper ones wall plates into which the feet of the rafters would have been jointed (last quarter of the thirteenth century).

It is possible that these two examples, in which the principal supports are set a considerable way down the walls, are to be viewed as measures to relieve the wall head of lateral thrust from the roof. Certainly, these roof-related masonry details are evidence of co-ordinated planning in which the design of the timber roof was integrated with that of the stone building. Not only was the stonework designed to accommodate the roof, but the form of the roof itself was a corollary of its association with a stone, rather than timber, substructure.

Another west midlands great hall roof in which the main trusses were raised on corbels survives at Maxstoke Castle (Warwickshire). Here, the hall built in the 1340s, which is 9.5 m (31 ft) wide, is spanned by two base cruck trusses, which, in turn, carry an upper roof of crown post construction.[47] Base crucks, which are related to cruck construction and which may be derivatives of it, are normally associated with high class buildings though perhaps not of the highest class. The technique has a national (English) distribution and had been in use in England since the first half of the thirteenth century. Even more pertinently, the earliest known base cruck truss in a domestic building is in Alcester (Warwickshire), approximately 25 miles to the south-west of Maxstoke, which was probably constructed in 1264.[48]

The raising on corbels of the Maxstoke base crucks and the Stokesay crucks, sets them apart from other examples in the region, because the feet of both types normally extend to floor level and form part of the wall frame of a timber house. In adapting them to stone buildings, it was possible to introduce the modification and thereby make savings in materials and labour.

Ten miles to the south of Maxstoke, is another castle hall in which the stonework of the walls was prepared to accommodate elements of the roof. This is at Kenilworth as rebuilt by John of Gaunt from 1373. The

Fig. 3.12. Kenilworth (Warwickshire) Chase for securing one of the roof trusses in the great hall (third quarter of the fourteenth century).

designer of the roof was probably the carpenter, William Wintringham, who, by 1373, was in Gaunt's employ, and, in 1375, was described by Gaunt as 'master and surveyor of all our works in England'.[49] The great hall of Kenilworth is a particularly interesting building from the perspective of medieval roof development, because at 14 m (46 ft) it is one of the widest castle halls to be roofed in a single span rather than in two or more as in an aisled hall. The side walls of the hall incorporate 1.2 m (4 ft) long vertical chases between the upper sections of the main windows (Fig 3.12). Unfortunately, the evidence is too vestigial for there to be much certainty regarding the form of the roof, but what we can say is that it was a steeply pitched roof rising high above the walls.

The two main possibilities for roofing a wide span at this date were, on the one hand, the hammer beam roof, and, on the other, the arch-braced collar roof, both of which had been in use since the thirteenth century. Although the evidence of the stonework could be construed to accommodate either type, it has been considered most recently that an arch-braced collar roof might have been more likely on the grounds that William Wintringham had erected such a structure over the great hall of Windsor in the 1360s in association with the King's principal carpenter, William Herland.[50] This, however, is simply an opinion, and cannot be corroborated. The great hall of Windsor was narrower than Kenilworth's great hall, and the design of the roof, as depicted by Hollar, would not correlate with the structural evidence at Kenilworth, which leads to the conclusion that the two roofs may have been quite different.[51]

Low-pitch roofs
The roof of Stokesay's great hall has a pitch of 50–55 degrees, a not uncommon angle of inclination in thirteenth-century castle great halls. In the future, however, it was the roof of very low pitch that was to become a favourite of castle builders, and by the late fourteenth century it had become the norm in the increasingly integrated castle. The process was already underway by the 1280s when an almost exact contemporary of Stokesay, the integrated manor house of Robert Burnell, bishop of Bath and Wells, at Acton Burnell (Shropshire), was given a double-pile roof with a pitch of approximately 10 degrees. The only surviving evidence are fragments of the profile formed by the grooves for the flashing, and a series of corbels along the surviving side wall, apparently to accommodate tie beams. A stone arcade divided the manor house longitudinally at first-floor level, and served to carry the inner ends of the beams.[52]

In Herefordshire, the former roof over the early fourteenth-century great hall of Goodrich Castle had a similar pitch to that of Acton Burnell, but a more complex configuration of timbers. Two-tiered corbels at the top of the side walls suggest a series of tie beams, while a corresponding line of corbels at a lower level with angled chases in the wall above them seems to be indicative of angled braces extending to the soffits of the beams. It is also evident that there was a spine-beam extending the full length of the building that was carried on

Fig. 3.13. Carlisle (Cumberland) Roof over the hall of the outer gatehouse made by the carpenter William Wright of Lancaster (*c.* 1381).

the tie beams. The central longitudinal beam suggests a form of roof related to crown post construction.

In the north of England, the great hall of Durham Castle was extended and reroofed by Bishop Hatfield in 1350. It retains the low pitched roof of that date, which was erected by the Yorkshire carpenter John of Alverton.[53] Timber posts on stone corbels rise to cambered tie beams carrying a ridge piece and two pairs of purlins. Very plain roofs like this were not uncommon in later fourteenth-century northern castle halls. That over the Barons' Hall at Raby Castle (Durham) survived until the mid nineteenth century when it was replaced by the current structure, but the Reverend J. F. Hodgson recalled it as 'very similar in effect to that above the nave of Staindrop church; nearly flat, and resting on fine cambered beams'.[54]

At Castle Bolton of 1378–1395, the flashing scars at the ends of the accommodation ranges show nearly flat profiles. Slightly more substantial evidence for the nature of the Bolton roofs is to be found in the sockets and associated corbels in the north wall of the south-east tower, which suggest that the roof over the east range was carried on two pairs of purlins and a ridge plate. Given that there were intermediate walls that could have supported these longitudinal members this may have been the extent of the structural timberwork. Contemporary with the Bolton roofs are those over the outer gatehouse of Carlisle, which were made by the carpenter William Wright, of Lancaster.[55] They have tie beam trusses with dwarf king posts supporting a ridge piece and a single pair of purlins (Fig 3.13). Tree-ring analysis of the solar roof has given a felling date of 1380.[56]

Some 30 years later, in Lancaster itself, the carpenter of the low roofs over the outer gatehouse of the royal castle dispensed with the king post so that the ridge piece was

Fig. 3.14. Lancaster (Lancashire) Roof over the gatehouse (first quarter of the fifteenth century).

supported directly by the tie beam. Here, the greater scantling of the timber may have prompted the use of corbelled posts and arch braces to strengthen the ends of the tie beams (Fig 3.14), a structural expedient that was repeated in the contemporary re-flooring of the keep.

In summary, roofs of low pitch were economical in the use of timber, they simplified building operations, and they complemented the compact aesthetic of many later medieval castles. In addition, they largely eliminated lateral thrust to the wall heads, and obviated the need to introduce mitigating structural schemes like those at Ludlow and Stokesay. In the dynamic between craftsmen in stone and timber they gave greater control to the former and further confined the creative contribution of the latter to decorative embellishment, in those instances in which it was required.

Timber vaults and ceilings
Many roofs were open to view, either (in the case of a great hall) for the practical reason of accommodating a louvre to service an open hearth, or as ostentatious architectural features. Others, however, may have been ceiled. It is unlikely, for instance, that the spire roof of Orford keep was open. Rising to some 42 ft above floor level, it would have contributed to the making of an uncomfortable chamber, and it is probable that a decorative timber ceiling, or perhaps a timber vault, would have been applied to the roof timbers. For example, by extending arch braces from each of the rafters to a central crown and laterally to form wall arcading, a low ribbed vault could have been created.[57]

Although timber vaulting is attested in a number of great churches in England,[58] the extent to which it was used in castles is less well known. The one example that we know to have existed in England was over the chapel of St Edward, of the 1240s, at Windsor Castle, which was modelled on the timber vaulting of Lichfield Cathedral.[59] More tangible evidence for a timber vault exists in the keep of Bothwell Castle, Scotland, of the 1240s, where blind arcading around the walls of the first floor, and chases in the masonry suggest that the room was designed to be covered with a timber vault.[60] The stonework around the upper face of the ribs is grooved to take wooden boards and above each of the responds is a corbel with a dished upper surface and a v-shaped chasing in the stonework above it. The second-floor beam sockets are immediately above the apex of the wall ribs and may have functioned as part of the underlying vault structure. These sockets are at the angles, but also in the centre of each wall face, suggesting a radiating arrangement of beams meeting in the centre of the keep.

Bothwell is a rare instance of a stone castle building retaining evidence for timber vaulting, and, like stone vaulting, it does not seem to have been a very common expedient. However, one other British example might be deduced from structural evidence in the South Tower of Tutbury Castle, which dates from the 1440s. Here, the ground storeys of the main block and annexe were designed for high barrel-vaults. Indeed, the lower courses of both vaults were actually built, before the scheme was discontinued and timber first floors installed instead above the level of the planned vault. The vault in the larger of the two ground-floor rooms, which was provided with faux ribs, seems to have been intended as a highly decorative feature, and it seems probable that this would have been completed in timber rather than left in a half-finished state. Whether this was intended from the outset, or whether it was a

Hoardings

Pictorial evidence suggests that both perimeter walls and towers of timber might be capped with hoardings,[61] the oversailing galleries from which the defence of the castle was largely conducted. Although they have generally perished along with their timber substructures, the feature survived the transition to stone, and timber hoardings continued to form part of the castle builder's repertoire into the late medieval period. Even in these instances, however, few of the structures themselves survive, so our knowledge is to a large extent based on contemporary pictorial representations and a limited amount of archaeological evidence. What the illustrations tell us is that hoardings were roofed, admitting light via lucarnes or dormers, and that the wooden screen wall was pierced with arrow loops. While this gives an idea of the outward appearance, it tells us little or nothing about the structural techniques involved. What knowledge we have is usually based on archaeological evidence, which often consists of no more than a row of square sockets piercing the wall close to the base of the parapet. Nevertheless, such traces clarify the main construction principle in that they must have provided the means by which the main supporting beams might be cantilevered out from the wall face.

The positioning of the main beams, by threading them through the sockets, was an operation that could be carried out safely from inside the wall. Subsequently, to facilitate the raising of the superstructure, a safe working environment was provided by fixing a plank floor over the beams. Using a crane, which was set on the top of the wall, the tenoned main posts that formed the skeleton of the screen wall would be dropped into mortices in the ends of the beams and fixed in place with pegs or wedges. A more rigid structure would be achieved if the posts also supported a plate extending around the whole structure; tie beams and principal rafters would have corresponded with the posts. In order to create a screen wall around the perimeter, the spaces between the main posts were probably infilled with plank walling, a stout building technique of ancient origin in which the planks were slotted into grooves in the sides of the main posts.

Some hoards were temporary buildings to be erected when a castle was put on a war footing. This might seem a cumbersome process to be carried out in an emergency, but in practice, prior warning of a siege was likely, and the construction work was probably a more straightforward procedure than might be imagined, especially if the pre-fabricated timbers were waiting in storage for such an eventuality. Some hoards, however, were certainly intended to be permanent, as evidenced by a surviving example dating from *c.* 1220 that encircles the top of the cylindrical donjon of the Château de Laval (Fig 3.15). Here, the hoard is integral with the roof of the donjon, which covers the oversailing hoard as well as the tower. The ends of the main beams are jointed to the central post, and instead of the principal timbers being supported in slots in the elevation, they surmount the wall head, being carried on a trio of wall plates. Other surviving hoards are integral parts of the roof structure, and therefore of a permanent nature.

Roughly contemporary with the donjon of Laval is that of Coucy, where the masonry provision for hoarding included a series of stone corbels around the tower's perimeter.

Fig. 3.16. Stokesay (Shropshire) Oversailing timber upper storey around the north tower (*c.* 1290).

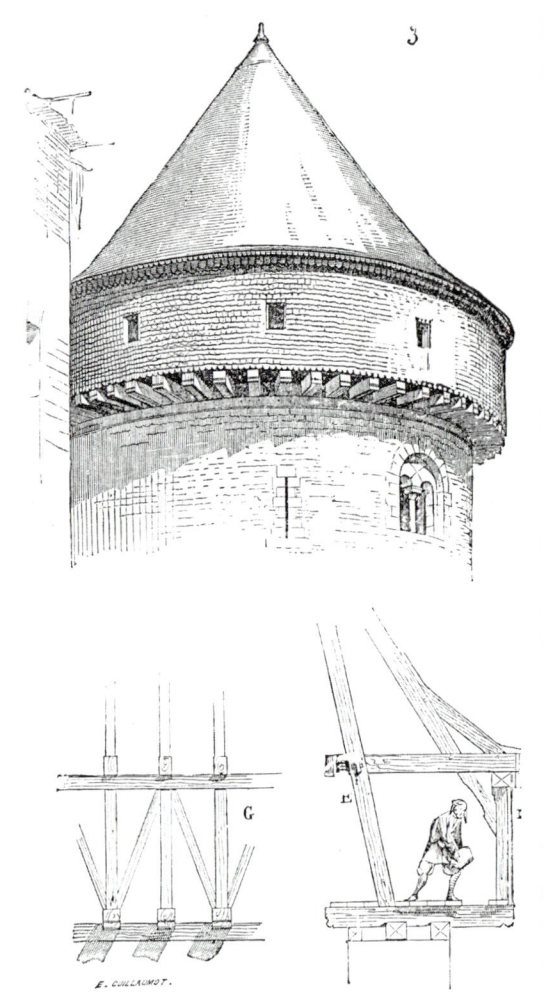

Fig. 3.15. Laval (Mayenne) The hoarding of the donjon (*c.* 1220); from Viollet-le-Duc 1875.

This is one of the first examples of its kind and provides a link between hoardings and the corbelled machicolations that tended to supplant them in the later Middle Ages. However, although stone machicolations were in use from the twelfth century they were unusual before the fourteenth century; furthermore, it was normal for provision to be made for timber hoardings until the end of the thirteenth century and beyond. In the course of Edward I's Welsh castle building programme of the late thirteenth century corbelled machicolations appear at only two sites - Conwy and Beaumaris - where they are confined to the gateways, and as late as *c.* 1370, by which time corbelled machicolations were becoming popular, the earl of Douglas's great tower at Threave (Kirkcudbrightshire) was built with a line of beam slots in order to accommodate a timber hoarding.

It may have been something in the nature of a hoard that the carpenter Henry of Ryhull made in 1301 to surmount the great tower of Flint. A major component of this great work of timber was 'a circular gallery of noble and beautiful appearance'.[62] Given that there was an evident intention to enhance the architectural quality of the tower with this gallery, there is a strong probability that it oversailed the walls of the tower in the manner of a hoard and thereby provided the plain cylindrical substructure with a more diverting termination and focus. The one surviving analogy for such a structure in Britain is the jettied timber upper storey of the north tower of Stokesay, which dates from around 1290 (Fig 3.16). This is a different kind of building but there is no doubt that the projection of the timberwork over the walls adds another dimension to the stone base and enriches the architectural character of this part of the castle.

Conclusion

Initially responsible for much of a castle's superstructure, the master carpenter was both military engineer and domestic builder, and he continued to practise the two aspects of the craft well into the fourteenth century. The carpenter, more than any other craftsman, was experienced in both sides of siege warfare, on the one hand as a maker of siege engines and on the other as a builder of fortifications. Increasingly, however, from the later twelfth century onwards, it was the master mason who came to dominate the building site and the carpenters' work was gradually subordinated to that of the masons. There is no doubt that a single master builder familiar with both crafts, directed the two sets of workers, though, as implied in the introductory chapter, we may do well to reserve judgement as to whether, at the stage of transition from mainly timber to mainly stone castles, those master builders were either carpenters or masons by training.

Chapter 4

Building In Stone

Despite the predominance of the carpenter in the early history of castle construction in northern Europe, stonemasons played an important, albeit more restricted, role from the earliest times, most notably as great tower builders. It was the great tower that gave the master builder with a background in masoncraft his opportunity to excel as an architect. As prestige buildings, desired as much for the esteem they garnered as the security they offered, great towers must have bestowed upon their creators a great deal of professional stature. How far this extended to other aspects of castle building is uncertain, but there was sometimes a more comprehensive role for the mason than that of great tower builder, particularly in those regions in which there was a shortage of suitable timber. Of the castles dating from the early years of the Norman settlement in England a handful may have been built of stone from the outset, or very soon after their initial construction. Exeter (Devon), Ludlow, Richmond and Rochester are all castles with eleventh-century curtain walls. To a great extent these were renditions in stone of timber models, but from the second half of the twelfth century onwards the construction of the defences principally in stone was becoming the norm. From this point onwards most master castle builders were probably masons by training and the other building crafts were secondary to them.

Foundations

Building in stone began with the excavation of the foundation trenches, directed by the master mason via the master dyker. In the case of great towers, these trenches could be very deep. Archaeological investigations on the south side of Colchester keep have revealed something of the nature of the eleventh-century foundations.[1] The bottom of the footings were discovered to be c. 3.65 m (12 ft) below the base of the splayed plinth, a measurement approximately half that of the 7.4 m (24 ft) foundation thickness. The lowest course of construction material comprised a concrete mix of stone and mortar, which had been poured into a 0.75 m (2.5 ft) deep slot at the bottom of the foundation trench. Above this layer were twenty courses of masonry, the quality of workmanship improving in stages as the wall rose higher. The interfaces between these changes in the character of the stonework appeared to correspond with the staged infilling of the foundation trench. At Rochester the wall of the Roman settlement was used as the foundation of the entire south wall of the keep. The foot of the Norman foundations has not been located but excavations inside the keep in 1905 showed that the walls extended at least 4.3 m (14 ft) below ground-floor level,[2] a measurement that equates to one eighth of the height of the tower.[3]

These were exceptional foundations for exceptional buildings; lesser structures were raised on far less extravagant footings. At Warkworth, the foundations for the curtain wall of c. 1200 were cut only 0.15 m (6 in) into the natural clay subsoil. They consisted of two courses of long roughly dressed stones bonded with mortar and shale; above them was a

0.15 m (6 in) layer of soil and then a single course of mortared rubble. These foundations had a total depth of approximately 0.5 m (1.25ft),[4] on the interior, and although it is possible that they were more substantial on the outer side, this cannot as yet be confirmed.

Plinths

Above the foundations of the great tower, wall towers and curtain, there was often a tapering plinth extending from the outer edge of the foundations to the exterior face of the walls. It had a practical function in that it prevented the accumulation of rainwater at the foot of the walls, a structural role in buttressing the base of the building, and an aesthetic purpose in giving a tall building a more elegant profile. As tapered plinths apply mainly to towers and curtains, they probably also had a defensive role. The plinths of two of the earliest great towers in England: the White Tower and Colchester keep were both plain splayed constructions. That of the White Tower, where it has been exposed on the west side, rises to 2.86 m (9ft) in height. In contrast, the Colchester plinth was 4.2 m (13 ft 9 ins) high, but the difference is owed to the nature of the sites, and both plinths were designed to rise to the level of the ground storey.[5] The keep of Rochester also has an external splayed plinth, and although its base is not exposed on the exterior its position may be reflected by an internal offset discovered in 1905 about 1.8 m (6 ft) below ground-floor level on both sides of the keep. If so, it would suggest a plinth of approximately 3.5 m (11.5 ft) in height.

An alternative to the splayed plinth was devised, *c.* 1090, by the architect of Canterbury keep who built a stepped structure with the evident intention of creating a form with greater decorative scope, and indeed, in the Canterbury plinth plain chamfered courses are mixed with mouldings of more pronounced ornamental qualities. The impressive 4 m (13 ft) height of the Canterbury plinth may have been inspired by that of Colchester, and while it wasn't quite as tall, the builder made up for the shortfall by giving the feature a greater projection from the face of the tower of 1.8 m (6 ft) as opposed to Colchester's 1.3 m (4 ft 3 in). Although the architect of Canterbury emulated the prominence of the Colchester plinth he developed this model purely for its decorative possibilities. This is implied by the mouldings, but also, whereas the plinth at Colchester was a practical response to an unusual site, the Canterbury plinth rises high above ground-floor level and so diverges from the structural honesty displayed at Colchester and London, in that the top of the plinth bears no relation to the internal floor levels.

Stepped plinths did not gain much traction in the south of England,[6] but in the north the builder of the great tower of Bamburgh (Northumberland) of *c.*1120 designed another stepped and moulded plinth, which has an average height of 1.68 m (5.5 ft) and a projection of about 1.2 m (4 ft). Although it is a more discrete feature than its counterpart at Canterbury, it too rises above ground-floor level. The mouldings of these two plinths are exceptional, however, and it was the plain chamfered version of the stepped plinth that was to gain a degree of popularity in the north of England. This type is found in the late twelfth-century keeps of Newcastle, Bowes, Middleham (Yorkshire), the early thirteenth-century keep of Pontefract, one of the thirteenth-century wall towers at Prudhoe (Northumberland), and the early fourteenth-century gatehouse of Dunstanburgh.

Notwithstanding this northern fashion, it was the splayed, or battered, plinth that proved most popular. Following the White Tower and Colchester, it was used in the construction of the twelfth-century keeps of Rochester (*c.* 1130), Castle Rising (Norfolk, *c.* 1140), Hedingham (Essex, *c.* 1140), Orford (*c.* 1165), Conisbrough (*c.* 1180) and Pembroke (*c.* 1200), and remained a popular feature throughout the Middle Ages. Visually, it comes into its own with the cylindrical keeps of the late twelfth and thirteenth centuries, being used to great effect at Conisbrough, for instance, where a prominent batter rises to first-floor level, and contains the vaulted basement entirely. This represented a return to the plinth as an external indicator of the floor levels within the keep; at Conisbrough, the top of the plinth indicated the entrance level, for example. This aspect was a feature that was to be incorporated into the designs of a number of other great towers including those of the Louvre (*c.* 1190), Château Gaillard (*c.* 1195), Pembroke (*c.* 1200) and Longtown (Herefordshire *c.* 1220).

In a number of thirteenth-century buildings in England and Wales with battered plinths of this type, entrance-floor level was demarcated more emphatically by employing a bold half roll-moulded string course. Examples include the Welsh keeps of Skenfrith (Monmouthshire, *c.*1220) (Fig 4.1), Tretower (Breconshire, *c.* 1235), Dinefwr (Carmarthenshire) and Bronllys (Breconshire). Although the distribution is predominantly among Welsh castles, proof that it was not solely a regional characteristic is demonstrated by its use on the thirteenth-century twin gatehouse towers of Alton.

Fig. 4.1. Skenfrith (Monmouthshire) Battered plinth of the great tower with bold roll moulding at first-floor level (first third of the thirteenth century).

Another distinctive feature related to plinth construction with a predominantly (though not exclusively) Welsh distribution, is the spurred tower, which came into vogue during the late thirteenth century. Spurred towers were in existence from the late twelfth century in Angevin France, and occurred at a slightly later date at Dover under King John. In these examples, a rounded tower was built on a rectangular base, the visual transition from one shape to the other being achieved by inclined planes splaying outwards and upwards from the angles of the base. While the Welsh spurred towers result from a similar juxtaposition of a rectangular base and round (or polygonal) tower, they are quite different in character, and constitute a distinct type.

In the Welsh examples, inclined planes extend from each of the three exposed sides of the base, so that two planes meet at each corner to form an arris. This produces two corner features (or spurs) in the form of demi-pyramids. The technique as employed in Wales, then, is a complete reversal of the earlier French form, and has more in common with the relationship between the early thirteenth-century glacis around the south and west sides of the inner ward at Krak des Chevaliers and the towers that it protects. In Wales and the Marches spurred towers are generally indicative of a late thirteenth-century date, are occasionally also found in the fourteenth century, and appear to be almost exclusively confined to non-royal castles.

At Caerphilly, which was built by Gilbert de Clare, earl of Gloucester, one of the earliest datable examples of the group is to be found in the south gatehouse of *c.* 1270 (Fig 4.2). At a slightly later date (*c.* 1277–1290) the polygonal towers of the main outer gatehouse and the north dam platform of Caerphilly were similarly treated. Spur buttresses also occur in association with rounded towers at the castles of Coch (Glamorganshire, gatehouse after *c.* 1277), Powis (inner gatehouse *c.* 1270s–1280s), Goodrich (1270s–1290s), Chepstow (Marten's tower, *c.* 1283–1293), Carew (1280–1310), Llawhaden (gatehouse, fourteenth century), and in association with polygonal towers at Carreg Cennen (Carmarthenshire, inner gatehouse and north-east tower, after *c.* 1277), and Kidwelly (Carmarthenshire, chapel tower *c.* 1280s–1290s).

While the principle of construction is the same, there are variations in execution. Whether these differences are the result of typological development or simply variances in interpretation is unclear. What we can say is that in respect of the south gatehouse of Caerphilly, probably the earliest in the sequence, the spurs rise only half way up the ground storey, a characteristic shared by Powys and Carreg Cennen. On the main outer gateway and the north dam towers at Caerphilly, the spurs rise a little higher, to just above the basement windows; this trait also occurs in the south-west tower of Goodrich, the castle tower of Castle Coch and Marten's Tower, Chepstow. Examples of more exaggerated height are to be seen in the south-east tower of Goodrich, Carew and Kidwelly.

Paradoxically, in view of the predominantly Welsh distribution of this feature, its genesis is probably to be found in south-east England, the main conduit being Tonbridge, where the twin drum towers of the gatehouse built *c.* 1250–1265 are set on semi-polygonal bases. The fact that the Tonbridge gatehouse was raised by Richard de Clare, earl of Gloucester, whose son, Gilbert, was to build Caerphilly appears to confirm that this was the source of the Welsh spurs. We also know that the mason employed by Roger Bigod, earl of Norfolk, to oversee his building works at Chepstow, including Marten's Tower, was a Master Ralph, who is described elsewhere as 'Ralph Gogun' and as 'of London',[7]

Fig. 4.2. Caerphilly (Glamorgan) Detail of the south gatehouse from the west (*c.* 1270).

although it is arguable as to whether, in this instance, the spurs are a south-eastern or Welsh contribution to the design. The presence of spurs at the bases of the gatehouse towers of Bigod's Bungay Castle (Suffolk), which dates from 1294, after Master Ralph had died, suggests a two-way process in the dissemination of style.

Although the greatest concentration of spurred towers belongs to the later thirteenth century there are a number of later examples, at Newport (Monmouthshire, 1327–1386) and Caldicot (Monmouthshire, 1385–1389) in Wales, but also at the Middle Gate (early fourteenth century) and Inner Gate (1340–1345) of Alnwick Castle (Northumberland), and at Beaufort-en-Vallée (Maine-et-Loire, later 15th century).

Walling

Types of stonework

Many of the masonry practices of early stone castle builders had their origins in antiquity, deriving ultimately from those of the Romans. Amongst these proto-Romanesque techniques is a distinctive form of rubble coursing derived from the Roman *opus spicatum*, although it tends to be of less formal character in the medieval period and is more popularly known as herringbone masonry in England. In this technique courses of flat stones are laid at an angle of approximately 45 degrees, stability being ensured by alternating the direction of pitch from course to course to give a zig-zag pattern. It was used at Doué la Fontaine (Maine-et-Loire) in the earliest (*c.* 900) of all surviving donjons (Fig 4.3), is prominent in the early eleventh-century donjon of Ivry-la-Bataille in Normandy (Eure), and appears in several early Norman castles in England (eg Colchester, Exeter, Peveril (Derbyshire), Rochester and Corfe).

Fig. 4.3. Doué-la-Fontaine (Maine-et-Loire) Herringbone masonry (last quarter of the ninth century).

Fig. 4.4. Langeais (Indre-et-Loire) *Petit appareil* in the donjon (*c.* 1000).

A type of masonry sometimes found in association with early *opus spicatum* is *petit appareil*, a type of wall facing in which small squared stones were laid in regular courses to provide a façade of uniform pattern, giving a more accomplished finish than ordinary rubble walling. In castle construction, the technique usually predates the twelfth century. It was the principal type of masonry used in the donjon of Langeais (Indre-et-Loire) *c.* 1000, where the facing stones are mostly in the range of 75–150 mm (3–6 in) (Fig 4.4), and also appeared in the eleventh-century donjon of Avranches (Manche).[8]

Most of the early towers incorporate an element of better quality freestone masonry for quoins, buttresses and other dressings. At Langeais this was confined to the buttresses, whereas at Ivry-la-Bataille freestone was used not only for the buttresses, but also the opening surrounds. The increasing use of large dressed freestone blocks culminated in the donjon of Loches (Indre-et-Loire), a building dating from between *c.* 1015 and *c.* 1030, which was faced entirely in this manner with courses in the range of 200–300 m (8–12 in) high and mortar joints typically 30–40 mm thick. It is unlikely to be coincidental that this was one of the first tower keeps, rising through five storeys to a height of 36 m (118 ft), because ashlar provided a stable material that facilitated high-rise construction. Loches, however, was an exception, and it was not until the late twelfth century that full facing in ashlar became commonplace for keeps and other buildings.

In England all the early great towers were rubble built with only the quoins and dressings being executed in freestone. Norwich (*c.* 1090–1120) was the first in which entire storeys were faced with freestone, which, in this case, was mainly Caen stone for the two upper floors. However, others soon followed at Kenilworth (*c.* 1120s), Bamburgh (*c.* 1120–1135), Carlisle (*c.* 1120–1140), Norham (*c.* 1121), Scarborough (1158–1169), Richmond (1156–1171) and

Conisbrough (*c.* 1164–1190). Because the cutting of the blocks to shape required a more highly skilled workforce and the practice itself was slow, preparation was expensive. There were also transport costs to consider if suitable stone could not be obtained locally. However, the construction process itself was simpler, more precise, more consistent and resulted in stronger walls.

Scaffolding

Putlog holes are the square apertures through which the horizontal scaffolding poles were threaded, and which provide the main source of evidence for the character of the scaffolding. Patterns vary; those at Doué-la-Fontaine of *c.* 900 form a gridiron pattern indicating 'lifts' (the frequency with which the scaffolding was raised) of approximately 1.15 m (3 ft 9 ins), a dimension that is also to be found in the donjon of Loches (*c.* 1015–1035). In the tower of Langeais (*c.* 1000) the putlog holes denote lifts of between 1.00 m (3 ft 3 ins) and 1.20 m (4 ft), and at Ivry-la-Bataille the lifts were between 1.20 m (4 ft) and 1.25 m (4 ft 2 ins). These figures range from waist to chest height and indicate the limit at which the masons laying the stones could work comfortably.

Simple gridiron patterns are usual, but the widespread adoption of the round tower in France during the late twelfth and early thirteenth centuries was accompanied by the development of scaffolding that encircled the towers in a spiralling pattern, suggesting that it was intended to support a continuous ramp. It was widely used by the builders of the *Tours Philippienne*, the series of cylindrical great towers built by Philip Augustus between *c.* 1190 and *c.* 1220 (Fig 4.5), was adopted by the architect of Enguerrand III's donjon of Coucy *c.* 1225,[9] and is found a little later in the century in the works of the counts of Savoy, in what is now Switzerland. The technique had a fleeting appearance in north Wales at Conwy and Harlech, whence it was imported by Savoyard masons employed by Edward I for the castles associated with the conquest of Gwynnedd, but it was not a technique that had much currency in Britain.

Fig. 4.5. Villeneuve-sur-Yonne (Yonne) One of several *tours philippiennes* in which the builders employed scaffolding in a spiral pattern around the tower, the evidence for which are the two lines of putlog holes ascending from left to right in an anti-clockwise direction (1205–1212).

Angle stitching

Where two lengths of rubble walling met at an oblique angle the junction represented a structural and military weak spot. During the thirteenth-century military engineers would

Fig. 4.6. Framlingham (Suffolk) Stitching at the junction of two sections of curtain wall (last decade of the twelfth century).

Fig. 4.7. Dover (Kent) Stitching at an angle of the inner curtain wall at Dover (*c*. 1168–1189).

largely eliminate such deficiencies in the defences by placing a tower at the strategic point, but in the late twelfth century a common practice was to stitch the two walls together with splayed freestone quoins. In joining adjacent sections of the polygonal keep at Orford (1165–1173), Henry II's masons used quoins of unequal projection to left and right adjacent to a second, single-faced, ashlar on the short side. A similar technique was used in the rebuilding of Framlingham, of *c.* 1190 for the earl of Norfolk (Fig 4.6). Framlingham has other details in common with Orford and it may represent a regional or possibly a personal trait (see pp. 143–144). A different method was certainly employed in the inner curtain wall of Dover of the 1180s, also built for Henry II, in this case by the master builder, Maurice. In this instance single double-faced quoins alternate with twin quoins jointed on the angles (Fig 4.7).

A third technique, which proved more popular and longer lasting was employed in the curtain of the near contemporary Conisbrough where the stitching comprises roughly dressed single-faced quoins extending alternately to the left or right (Fig 4.9). A related example is to be found at White Castle (Monmouthshire), in a slight change of direction in the south-east curtain to the inner ward, which was reconstructed for Henry III, probably no earlier than the 1250s. A slightly later and more unusual case of this particular manner of stitching together adjacent sections of rubble walling is to be seen at the Tower of London in the western inner curtain built under the direction of the King's master mason Robert of Beverley in the 1270s and 1280s, where straight stretches of curtain and the rounded faces of the Beauchamp Tower are so treated. Why this expedient should have been thought necessary is uncertain. The same kind of stitching was used at the angles of the polygonal towers added to the shell keep of Lewes castle in the thirteenth century and in the construction of the barbican *c.* 1330.

Arches, lintels and joggling
Most arches were semi-circular before the last decade of the twelfth century, after which the form was to a large extent displaced by other types, although it remained in use for some way into the thirteenth century, and is occasionally encountered in some later medieval castles. In the keep of Skenfrith, which is usually dated to *c.* 1220, the doorway and windows were all semi-circular.[10]

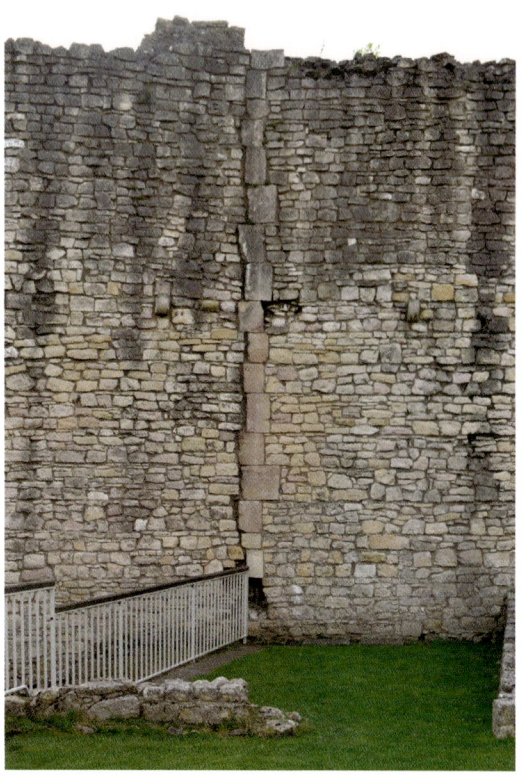

Fig. 4.8. Conisbrough (Yorkshire) Stitching between two sections of curtain wall (last decade of the twelfth century).

The earliest pointed arches in an English castle are probably those in the royal keep of Orford *c.* 1165, where they were used for doorways and window embrasures, although the windows themselves have semi-circular arched openings. These innovatory pointed arches were slow to catch on amongst English castle builders. The royal keeps at Newcastle (1168–1178) and Dover (1181–1187), for example, are entirely Romanesque in detail. However, pointed arches are a prominent feature of the Avranches Tower on the outer curtain of Dover, which is usually dated to the 1180s.[11] By the time John came to build the Gloriette in Corfe Castle in 1201–1204, two-centred pointed arches were an established part of the English castle builder's repertoire and were to remain a staple for the next 350 years. In the Orford examples, the wedge-shaped voussoirs rise from a horizontal base to a mitred apex; an alternative to the mitred apex was the incorporation of a keystone. Sometimes voussoirs of extended length were used, and occasionally, especially in the case of narrow openings, the arch was formed of no more than two stones springing from a flat base and mitred at the apex.

The thirteenth century also witnessed the widespread adoption of segmental and segmental-pointed arches by castle builders. The rounded segmental arch wasn't unknown in the twelfth century, but was usually set beneath a larger semi-circular arch to support a tympanum, as, for instance, in the gateway to the forebuilding of the Newcastle keep, but it was only in the thirteenth century that it was much used independently. The related

Fig. 4.9. Stokesay (Shropshire) Detail of the entrance to the great tower showing slippage between the springer and voussoir, and a crack in the springer (last decade of the thirteenth century).

segmental-pointed arch was in use by *c.* 1190 at the Tower of London in the entrance to the Bell Tower, and slightly later at Corfe in the towers of the west bailey *c.* 1202. Both types were in use at Beeston *c.* 1220 and they were to become a common feature in castles thereafter.

Where an opening was bridged by a pointed arch with straight rather than curved sides, an alternative had to be found for conventional wedge-shaped voussoirs. At Goodrich, where straight-sided pointed arches are a particular feature of the late thirteenth-century masonry, the voussoirs are cut square, except at the base and apex, where the joints are mitred. In the great tower of Stokesay of *c.* 1291, where a similar method was employed in concert with segmental-pointed arches with nearly flat arcs, there have been a number of structural failures in which the voussoirs adjacent to the springers have slipped, and in so doing have put pressure on the springers and caused them to crack (Fig 4.9).

An older form of construction was used in the straight-sided arch at the entrance to the keep of Orford Castle (Suffolk, 1165–1173) (Fig 4.10). Here the arch was joggled, a technique probably derived from Islamic architecture,[12] and which was in use in England from the eleventh century.[13] At Orford the voussoirs are in the form of notched rectangles so that they could be interlocked. Exactly the same form was used for the straight-sided rear arch of the gateway of nearby Framlingham Castle of the 1190s. The keystone arrangement at Orford is complex; the feet of the two ultimate voussoirs are mitred together at the apex of the arch, and the upper faces are notched to accommodate a stone shaped like an inverted trapezium, and, on top of it, forming the apex of the entire construction a stone with a pitched head. The structural concept behind this beautiful piece of workmanship is that

64 Castle Builders

Fig. 4.10. Orford (Suffolk) Joggled gate arch to the great tower (third quarter of the twelfth century).

Fig. 4.11. Conisbrough (Yorkshire) Joggled lintel over the main entrance to the keep with split tympanum and relieving arch (last quarter of the twelfth century).

downward pressure on the arch compresses the voussoirs against one another to create a tighter joint.

In the north of England around this time the builder of the keep of Conisbrough Castle *c.* 1180 used joggling as an alternative to monolithic lintels for the entrance and the first- and second-floor fireplaces (Fig 4.11). The voussoirs are comparable in form to those of Orford and Framlingham, but because the construction is horizontal rather than arched, the sides of the voussoirs are splayed at an angle of approximately 75 degrees in order to keep the notches level. These Conisbrough lintels have proper keystones in the form of T-shaped wedges, a shape that replicates that of the two upper stones at Orford.[14]

A century later, the builder of St Thomas's Tower (1275–1278), the water gate of the Tower of London, applied joggled jointing to the segmental arch supporting the rear (north) wall of the tower. The arch extends across a span of 18.6 m (61 ft), and represents a remarkable piece of engineering. The voussoirs follow a similar general pattern to those described above and are held in place with a T-shaped keystone. This arch would have been the responsibility of Robert of Beverley, principal mason at the Tower in the 1270s.

The examples already given are all variants of a familiar formula. A more unusual and elaborate form of joggling was used in the fireplace lintel of the mid to late fourteenth-century solar tower of Edlingham Castle (Northumberland) (Fig 4.12). Here, there was no keystone and the sides of the voussoirs were scalloped, a form that calls for consummate skill and meticulous workmanship. A less unusual and more economical method of joggling a fireplace lintel in the fourteenth century was to support a single stone block of two shoulders (Fig 4.13).

An application of joggling that was used at Caernarfon from 1283 is to be found in concert with some of the fireplaces, including the Eagle Tower and the Well Tower, the latter probably carried out under master Walter of Hereford. In both instances the lintel is made up of three stones including a large keystone, T-shaped in the former, simply wedge-shaped in the latter. These lintels are in each case surmounted by two further such constructions of progressively reduced proportions (Fig 4.14).

A related concept was adopted for the mid fifteenth-century North and South towers of Tutbury Castle (Staffordshire). Here wedge-shaped stones were incorporated into the wall coursing (Fig 4.15). Their function must have been similar to that of the keystones, that is, to make those parts of the wall self supporting. The fact that this expedient was used solely above openings (fireplaces and doorways)

Fig. 4.12. Edlingham (Northumberland) Fireplace in the upper chamber of the solar tower, with an elaborately joggled lintel (second half of the fourteenth-century), from Turner and Parker 1853.

Fig. 4.13. Castle Bolton (Yorkshire) Fireplace in the south-west tower with joggled lintel on corbelled haunches (last quarter of the fourteenth century).

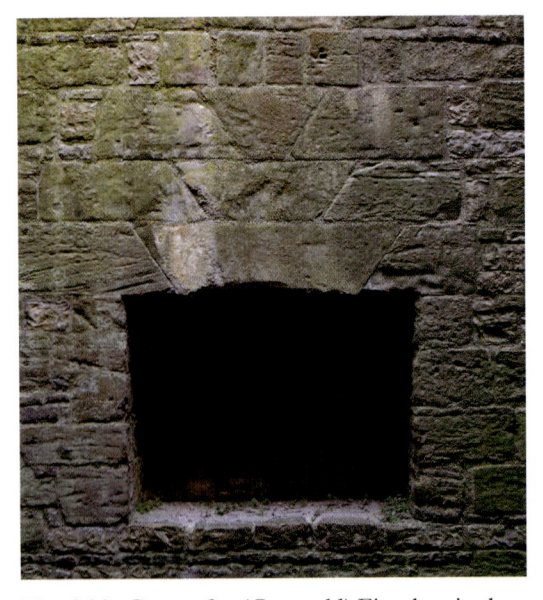

Fig. 4.14. Caernarfon (Gwynedd) Fireplace in the Well Tower with three tiers of joggling (last quarter of the thirteenth century).

suggests that it was intended to relieve pressure on the lintels. It served, then, as an alternative to the relieving arch that was simpler to execute in ashlar-faced buildings like the Tutbury towers.[15] The South Tower, which is the earlier of the two, was the work of the royal mason, Robert Westerley, and the names of the four masons who built the South Tower are also known,[16] but as to whether it was Westerley himself who was responsible for this feature, or the other masons, is not something we can be certain about.

That it was deemed prudent to adopt such measures presupposes that lintels were prone to failure. This may have been one reason for the adoption of openings in which corbels projected boldly beneath the lintel in order to give it support. The most

Fig. 4.15. Tutbury (Staffordshire) Successive wedge-shaped stones above a doorway in the North Tower designed to relieve pressure on the lintel (*c.* 1441–1450).

well known manifestation of this form is the so-called Carnarvon (or Caernarfon) arch (so named because of its widespread use in that particular castle in the late thirteenth century). In this instance the corbels have concave soffits. Early examples of the form were made for the third floor of Carrickfergus keep (Co. Antrim, 1178–1195), where they were used in the construction of large two-light windows surmounted by relieving arches.[17] The relieving arches were a sensible precaution, because the introduction of corbels does not seem to have cured the tendency of lintels to fail.

An instance in which a countermeasure for failing lintels was imposed during the course of construction was at Castle Bolton, which was raised between *c.* 1378 and *c.* 1395. Here, the appearance of cracks in some of the earlier lintels prompted the introduction of relieving arches over subsequent openings.[18] The relieving arch had in fact been in use castles since the tenth century as a means of diverting vertical thrust from the lintel as an integral part of an opening. In the donjon of Langeais, the lintels of at least three square-headed windows of *c.* 1000, were set beneath semi-circular arches (Fig 4.16), which act as relieving arches. This form seems to derive from the semi-circular arched opening and there seems to be no technical purpose behind the adoption of the lintel, because the arch itself extends right through the wall as the window embrasure vault, whereas the lintel is confined to the exterior face where its purpose must have been to support a tympanum. Windows based on the same principle existed in the near-contemporary donjon of Loches (*c.* 1013–1035). A similar technique was employed in the late eleventh-century chamber block at Lillebonne (Seine-Maritime) in Normandy but here, the opening was divided into a twin-light window. This latter form

68 Castle Builders

appears again in the late twelfth-century keep of Conisbrough Castle (Fig 4.17), and a semi-circular relieving arch was used in conjunction with the joggled lintel of the keep entrance (Fig 4.11). The flat lintel with relieving arch enclosing a tympanum was still being employed in the thirteenth century for doorways and rear arches by the builders of Angers Castle, *c.* 1230. At Coucy, (*c.* 1225) the technique was turned to decorative advantage in the entrance to the donjon where the tympanum was decorated with a sculptured relief.

Vaulting

Chapels

Although significant areas of stone vaulting are rare in early castles, there are numerous examples of vaulting on a minor scale from the eleventh century onwards. One of these

Fig. 4.16. Langeais (Indre-et-Loire) Lintelled window with relieving arch in the great tower (*c.* 1000).

Fig. 4.17. Conisbrough (Yorkshire) Window in the keep with broad mullion, common lintel, split tympanum and relieving arch. Note that the lintel has failed and has had to be repaired (last quarter of the twelfth century).

areas was the chapel, where vaulting was favoured either for its acoustic effects or for the purpose of enhancing the aesthetic character of the space and emphasising its ecclesiastical function.

One of the earliest surviving castle chapels in England is the chapel of St Nicholas at Richmond Castle, which is housed in one of the wall towers. The Robin Hood Tower has two barrel-vaulted storeys, of which the lower contained the chapel. The simple semi-circular section vault is carried on a shelf made by the projecting stones of the blind arcades above the benches that line the side walls. A later and larger eleventh-century castle chapel in the north of England is that of the episcopal castle of Durham, which probably dates from the time of Bishop William of St Calais (1080–1096).[19] Understandably, the Durham chapel is a considerably more elaborate building, being divided by six columns into twelve bays, all of which are covered by groined vaults.

Looking towards the south-east, the most ambitious eleventh-century castle chapel in England is the chapel of St John in the White Tower, at the Tower of London, the design for which may date from the 1070s, although the building itself was not completed until *c.* 1100. Groined vaults were also used here, for the aisles and ambulatory, although the nave and gallery are barrel-vaulted, and the apsidal sanctuary is covered with a hemispherical dome. The keep of Colchester, which is a contemporary of the White Tower, also contained a chapel with an apsidal sanctuary, the shape of which is replicated in the two storeys that lie directly beneath it. Excavation within the barrel-vaulted sub-crypt showed that in preparing for the construction of the semi-hemispherical vault over the apse, the builders raised the centring on a series of posts. The main post was centred just above the baseline of the semicircular plan, and a number of lesser posts radiated around the circumference.[20]

Stairs and wall passages
These instances of vaulting were exceptional in the eleventh century, and it was not until the twelfth century that vaulting became a more general staple of castle construction. Mostly this was barrel-vaulting, a cheap and speedy form of construction used on purely structural grounds to cover spiral staircases, mural passages and chambers, window embrasures and other recesses. Early barrel-vaults were made largely of rubble, construction being facilitated by an initial application of mortar onto the centring, into which were set the narrow stones that formed the arch. Where the outer mortar bedding survives (as in the White Tower and Rochester keep) it sometimes retains the impressions of wooden planks, thereby providing us with an insight into the character of the formwork.

In Rochester keep (*c.* 1127) the barrel-vaults of the wall passages are slightly recessed from the faces of the side walls on which they are built, resulting in a narrow ledge on each side. These ledges were probably used to support the semi-circular centring on which the vaults were raised, and may have been sufficient to obviate the need for floor-based supports, in which case the passages would have remained unimpeded for as long as the concrete needed to set. Alternatively, the ledge may represent the widths of the planks. A mortar and rubble mix was piled on top, which, in the case of intramural spaces also formed the wall core.

Keep basements

Barrel-vaulted basements are a feature of several early great towers in France, including those of the early eleventh-century donjons of Loches and Beaugency, both of which were divided longitudinally by a cross wall to create two barrel-vaulted compartments. Some of the earliest vaulting to be found in an English keep is at Norwich, where, *c.* 1100, barrel-vaulting was raised across the four western angles of the basement, that is to say, between the outer walls and the central spine wall. The rationale behind this idiosyncratic expedient is uncertain; it may have been intended to strengthen the building by tying the walls together, although it would also seem to have been designed for carrying a load from above.[21] Whatever the original intention, however, the scheme was abandoned before it was completed and would not be repeated elsewhere. An early change of plan during construction resulted in the insertion of arcades and the covering of the entire basement with half barrel-vaulting.

Norwich apart, twelfth-century vaulted keep basements are largely confined to the north of England. The sequence begins with the hall keep of *c.* 1125 raised by Flambard, bishop of Durham at his castle of Norham near the Scottish border. Here, the basement was covered with transverse groin vaulting in four bays, separated by broad plain ribs in which the large dressed stones of the two outer faces sandwich a band of less regular masonry along the intrados. The ribs in the basement of the keep are similar in character to the plain buttressing arches hidden away in the galleries at Durham Cathedral (choir 1093–1099; nave 1099–1128), those of the nave having been presided over by Flambard. They would have been considered suitable for a storage area like the basement of the keep.

Groin vaulting was also used by the builder of the keep of Bamburgh Castle, a building roughly contemporary with Norham, where the west side of the basement has three bays of groin vaulting. The wider east side of the basement, however, is covered in three transverse bays of barrel-vaulting separated by two-bay arcades supported on central plain square columns. Essentially, this is the same technique that was used in the basement of Norwich *c.* 1100.[22] At first-floor level the pattern of the ground-floor vaulting is reflected in the Armoury, which occupies the south end of the keep and which probably contained the twelfth-century chapel;[23] the western bay has a groin vault, the eastern bays barrel vaulting; the bays are separated by broad ribs of Norham type springing from abaci.

Given that the earliest of these castle vaults was executed by Bishop Flambard's masons, it is worth reflecting that the impetus for this regional attachment to stone vaulting may have been the technical trajectory of the masons of Durham Priory in the development of vaulting systems. At the turn of the eleventh and twelfth centuries Durham was at the forefront of such works, raising some of the earliest rib-vaulting in Europe, and at the time that Norham was being built the high vault over the nave of Durham was being raised. It might be considered a natural corollary that the technological field in which Durham had become known for its mastery should be reflected elsewhere within the region.

One of the next in the sequence of vaulted northern keeps is the late twelfth-century great tower of Middleham.[24] As in the keep of Bamburgh the two halves of the divided basement carry vaults of different character. The east side is divided longitudinally by a six-bay arcade, which supported two long barrel-vaults. The vaulting on the west side has been variously described, but essentially it was groin vaulting of a rather unusual kind. In this instance the bays were not demarcated by transverse arches, so the groins are integral with the responds. Basically, the eastern vaulting is similar in technique to that used on the east side of the Bamburgh keep, although the orientations of the vaults in relation to the building are different. The groin vaulting on the west side of Middleham is an arrangement that could have been derived from the patterns of Norham and Bamburgh. Between these three buildings, then, there might be said to be continuity of technique.

Finally, the builder of Newcastle keep, begun *c.* 1168, also made considerable use of vaulting in the basement, and in the mural chambers of the other storeys. The mural chambers were barrel-vaulted, but two spaces in the cellar were constructed using rib-vaulting. One of these is the principal room within the main block, which is known as the 'Garrison Room'; the other is the chapel within the forebuilding. In the former, eight chamfered ribs spring from a central column; it was an arrangement that was commonly used in contemporary monastic architecture (eg Fountains Abbey) for vaulting twin bay undercrofts. The adjacent chapel was divided into three bays of cross vaulting.

Domed vaults in great towers

In France, many polygonal and cylindrical keeps were being stone-vaulted from the twelfth century onwards. An early example is the two-storey octagonal donjon of Provins built *c.* 1160, for Henry I, count of Champagne, which had domed vaults at both levels (Fig 4.18). The basement is covered by a saucer dome rising from the segmental tops of all eight walls, while over the upper floor a high pendentive dome, or sail vault, was raised. This is a more inventive feature, with greater aesthetic qualities, as befits the higher status of the room. In this unusual hybrid system the dome is carried on four pointed squinch arches springing from corbels set into the centres of the four main wall faces. The spaces behind the arches are barrel-vaulted, and the curvature of the dome begins from these corbels, and continues without a break. Pendentive vaults such as this were extremely unusual in twelfth-century Europe, and the presence of this example at Provins raises the question of its sources.

These may have included the domed churches of western France, which, since the first quarter of the twelfth century, had used pendentives over square bays to carry hemispherical vaults. At Angoulême Cathedral (Charente, 1105–1128) pendentives were associated with pointed arches, a combination that is reflected at Provins. A variation of this regional type was invented *c.* 1130 at Saint-Hilaire, Poitiers (Vienne), where squinch arches rather than pendentives were tried, in conjunction with octagonal rather than hemispherical domes. The principle was followed in the kitchen of Fontevraud Abbey (Maine-et-Loire), a mid twelfth-century building, which is of particular interest with regard to Provins. Like the donjon of Provins, the kitchen is an octagonal building and the vault is carried on four great arches forming a square bay, although in the case of the kitchen they spring from the angles of the octagon rather than the sides. Four squinch arches span the angles of this bay to create an octagon, which forms the base for a high octagonal dome. The architect of the kitchen made liberal use of the pointed arch, and the vault itself rises to a point.

A small number of French domed donjons post-date Provins. One is Châteaudun (Eure-et-Loire), which was built *c.* 1170–1190 by Henry I of Champagne's younger brother, Theobald (Thibaut) V, count of Blois.[25] It is a cylindrical building on a circular base, and contains two domed vaults of pointed section. A third brother, Stephen (Etienne), lord of Sancerre, was responsible for the donjon of Châtillon-Coligny (Loiret) of *c.* 1180–1190, a

72 Castle Builders

Fig. 4.18. Provins (Seine-et-Marne) – Domed sail vault over the first floor of the Tour de César (third quarter of the twelfth century).

sixteen-sided building on a circular base which has a plain hemispherical dome over the second floor, and two curious lower storeys each containing a central column from which springs a circular barrel-vault.[26] Far away in the south-east of the country, the twelve-sided donjon of Simiane-la-Rotonde (Alpes-de-Haute-Provence) of *c.* 1200 contains a high ribbed and domed vault,[27] though this stems from a quite different building tradition.

Domed vaults in Britain
Domed vaulting is considerably more rare in England or Wales, and seldom was a tower domed throughout, although a number of round towers do have elements of domed vaulting, usually over the basement supporting the main entrance floor. In the north of England the basement of Conisbrough (*c.* 1180), is covered by a vault of hemispherical form, a type much used in twelfth-century Angevin church architecture, from which it may have been derived, and the basement of Barnard Castle (Co. Durham), of *c.* 1190, has a low saucer vault. In south Wales the early thirteenth-century round keep of Caldicot has a vaulted basement, but the keep of Pembroke, built by William Marshal in the early years of the thirteenth century, seems to have been the first building in Britain to have had a domed upper storey, which, like the Conisbrough basement, is of hemispherical form (Fig 4.19). Between 1184 and 1186 William Marshal was in the Holy Land, so it is conceivable that the idea for the dome came from the church of the Holy Sepulchre in Jerusalem, which he would undoubtedly have visited. However, there were also Angevin precedents for hemispherical domes, and, as we have seen a hemispherical dome had already been built

in the donjon of Châtillon-Coligny. The builder, Stephen of Sancerre, had also visited the Kingdom of Jerusalem in 1170 as a prospective son-in-law to King Amalric and there is no doubt that he too would have had first-hand knowledge of the Holy Sepulchre.

Whatever the source, the Pembroke dome was something new to this side of the channel, and may have proved a challenge to local builders unfamiliar with the form and the construction methods behind it, so it is interesting to consider the manner in which they dealt with this aspect of the design. Fortuitously, there are a number of clues to the nature of the centring on which the dome was erected. Firstly, a narrow (23 cm or 9 in), but serviceable ledge extends around the interior of the building at the springing level of the dome. Secondly, a little below the ledge, are two pairs of corbels placed opposite one another, which were apparently intended to carry a pair of beams. In addition, 1.52 m (5ft) below each pair of corbels, and placed centrally between them, is another, single, corbel. Deciphering how the system of centring worked is to some extent speculative, but it seems likely the upper corbels carried a pair of beams that formed the basis of a working platform associated with the construction of the dome. The position of the lower corbel between the two upper ones suggests a post, and probably a brace, rising to support a third beam parallel with, and situated between, the first two. It also seems probable that this central beam would have been interrupted by two cross pieces jointed into the outer beams, thus forming a central aperture through which materials could have been hoisted from below. Such an arrangement would have produced a rigid structure that the builders could have used with confidence. The ledge around the base of the dome is wide

Fig. 4.19. Pembroke (Pembrokeshire) The dome over the keep (early thirteenth century).

enough to have housed a ring beam from which either a series of joists could have extended to the main beams, to extend the platform right across the keep, or upon which the centrings for the vault could have been constructed. The interior stonework of the dome does not seem to have been carried round in a continuous hemisphere, but rather in a series of short segments, which may correspond with the formwork between the centring ribs and thereby denote the configuration of the centring. The apex is a separate construction erected after the lower part of the dome had been raised.

The successful completion of this dome was emulated in a number of smaller towers in south Wales, including Tenby and Manorbier (Round Tower), both in Pembrokeshire, but the only other example of similar quality, which contains the most comprehensive vaulting system to have been built in Wales is to be found in the mid thirteenth-century cylindrical keep of Laugharne, which has three vaulted storeys.[28] The two lower are covered with saucer domes, but the dome over the upper storey (originally subdivided by a wooden floor) is of pointed section, and seems to emulate Pembroke. Because the keep of Laugharne is a smaller tower than that of Pembroke it is probable that the construction of the dome was not such a difficult undertaking. Unlike Pembroke, where there is a structural evidence regarding the method of construction, such clues are lacking at Laugharne. Here, the dome rises directly from the inner face of the wall, a characteristic that implies a different *modus operandi*. Unlike their counterparts at Pembroke the builders of the Laugharne dome seem to have raised it in continuous circular courses.

The domes of Pembroke and Laugharne rise above the battlements and were probably visible from the exterior. The same is true of the dome over the Scottish mid thirteenth-century great tower of Dirleton (East Lothian), but the dome itself is different in character because it covers a hexagonal rather than circular interior, and continues the faces of the walls which curve upwards to a point (see p. 123).

Ribbed vaulting in towers

In France, the *Tours Philippiennes*, the series of donjons raised by Philip Augustus over the thirty years between *c.* 1190 and *c.* 1220, were generally rib-vaulted at all levels (Fig 4.20). Six or eight ribs springing from responds rose to a central eye or boss. These vaults had an aesthetic purpose in that they improved the proportions of the chambers and gave them a decorative focus. However, they also represented a sound structural rationale, because they both supported stone floors above them and bound the sides of the tower together to provide it with greater strength. A prerequisite of rib-vault construction was the erection of a framework of centring on which to support the ribs, and, spanning the spaces between the rib supports at the upper level, the erection of timber formwork that acted as a mould for the webbing between the ribs. This was a job for the carpenters, but it was, of course, tailored to the design for the stone vault.

In the donjon of Coucy, which had a diameter twice the size of the *Tours Philippiennes*, there were three tiers of rib-vaulting. Here, the architect thought the better of providing the tower with stone flooring, which would have meant infilling the voids between the sides of the tower and the inward curving vault with rubble and mortar. Given that the voids were approximately 8 m (26 ft) deep and had an upper width of around 6 m (20 ft), this would have been a considerable undertaking. It would also have placed a considerable extra load

Fig. 4.20. Verneuil-sur-Avre (Haut-Normandie) Sexpartite ribbed vault over the ground storey of the great tower (first quarter of the thirteenth century).

onto a newly constructed vault, and would have necessitated a hiatus in construction to allow the mortar mixture time to set. Instead, the architect incorporated suspended timber floors directly above the vaults. This meant that the voids could remain hollow, economies could be made in time, materials and cost, and work could proceed unchecked. The floor beams extended from the twelve angles and were therefore directly above the vaulting ribs.[29] There is no doubt that this was a deliberate ploy on the part of the master builder, in order to provide bases on which to erect the centring for the ribs of the vault above.

In England, rib-vaulting is encountered less frequently in great towers than it is in France, although there are rather more examples of rib-vaulting in wall towers. The ground storey of the Bell Tower (*c.* 1190) at the Tower of London, which has an irregularly disposed semi-polygonal interior, is covered with a correspondingly asymmetrical vaulting system, having a band of barrel-vaulting across the neck of the tower, and then an inner vault over the pentagonal end of the building carried on five unmoulded ribs rising from corbels between the arrow-loop embrasures to a keystone with a carved boss. The arches of the barrel-vault, the rib-vault and those of the arrow loops embrasures are all acutely pointed. It is quite a complicated arrangement, owing to the irregularity of the cell. The barrel-vaulting of the embrasures and entrance would probably have come first, and the rib-vault second.

A number of other inventive vaults were raised over wall towers with unusually-shaped interiors built for Henry III at the Tower and at Windsor. One of these covered the basement of the D-shaped Clewer Tower (1227–1230) at Windsor. This is a considerably larger building than the Bell Tower, with a more regular plan, and, consequently, the builder was able to construct a vaulting system of greater symmetry. Here, internally, the nose of the tower was semi-octagonal and the rear rectangular. The solution was to treat the front and rear as separate compartments, divided by a transverse rib and to cover both areas with rib-vaulting. In contrast to the extravagant height of the Bell Tower loop embrasures their counterparts in the Clewer Tower were given low segmental-pointed arches.

The late twelfth-century rib-vaulted basement of the great tower of Newcastle with its ribs radiating from a central column has already been mentioned (see p. 71). A late thirteenth-century example of this type is in the basement of the north-east corner tower of Somerton Castle (Lincolnshire), a castle raised for Anthony Bek, bishop of Durham, under a licence of 1281.[30] Here too the vault is carried on a central polygonal pier and, in this case, twelve chamfered ribs spring from corbelled wall responds. Something very similar was used to cover the basement of a great tower at the south end of Morlais Castle (Glamorganshire) built by Gilbert de Clare, earl of Gloucester, probably in the 1280s;[31] both are round towers with polygonal interiors. These vaulting arrangements are reminiscent of a number of thirteenth-century polygonal chapter houses - Lincoln (*c.* 1210), Westminster (1246–1259), Salisbury (*c.* 1250–1260) and Wells (*c.* 1293–1306) - and it is likely that these models would have been in the minds of the builders.

It was only in the later Middle Ages that fully vaulted towers became common in England. One of the earliest is Caesar's Tower, at Warwick Castle, a building of unusual plan, dating from around 1350, with an external face comprising three rounded lobes, and a semi-polygonal face towards the courtyard. Despite the originality of its exterior plan, the builder facilitated the vaulting of the main chambers of the five-storey tower by making them rectangular and covering them in two bays of cross vaulting. Some forty years later, the builder of the twelve-sided Guy's Tower, at the same castle, took the same approach. Externally, the tower is twelve-sided, but, again, the chambers are rectangular, with the exception of the uppermost storey, which has a hexagonal plan. As in Caesar's Tower, the rooms were covered in quadripartite ribbed vaulting, excepting the fourth floor, which has a hexagonal vault, its ribs rising to a central crown (Fig 4.21).[32]

Barrel-vaulting in the north of England
The disparity between the north and the south of England that has already been noted in the discussion of the use of vaulting in twelfth-century keeps, was repeated in the fourteenth century, when northern builders favoured barrel-vaulted basements in contrast to the southern preference for timber floors throughout. The reason for this northern predilection for stone may have had something to do with the supply of materials, but it is probable too that the more unsettled conditions on the northern borders made the installation of fire-resistant stone vaulting a sensible precaution.

Generally, the materials used for the barrel-vaulting matched those used to face the walls. Vaults of segmental section are usual in northern castles of the fourteenth-century, but occasionally vaults of pointed section were constructed. This is the case at the Northumbrian great towers of Belsay (*c.* 1370) and Warkworth (*c.* 1390). In the case of Belsay (where the pointed vault spans the basement kitchen), the reason for this unusual profile is probably

Building In Stone 77

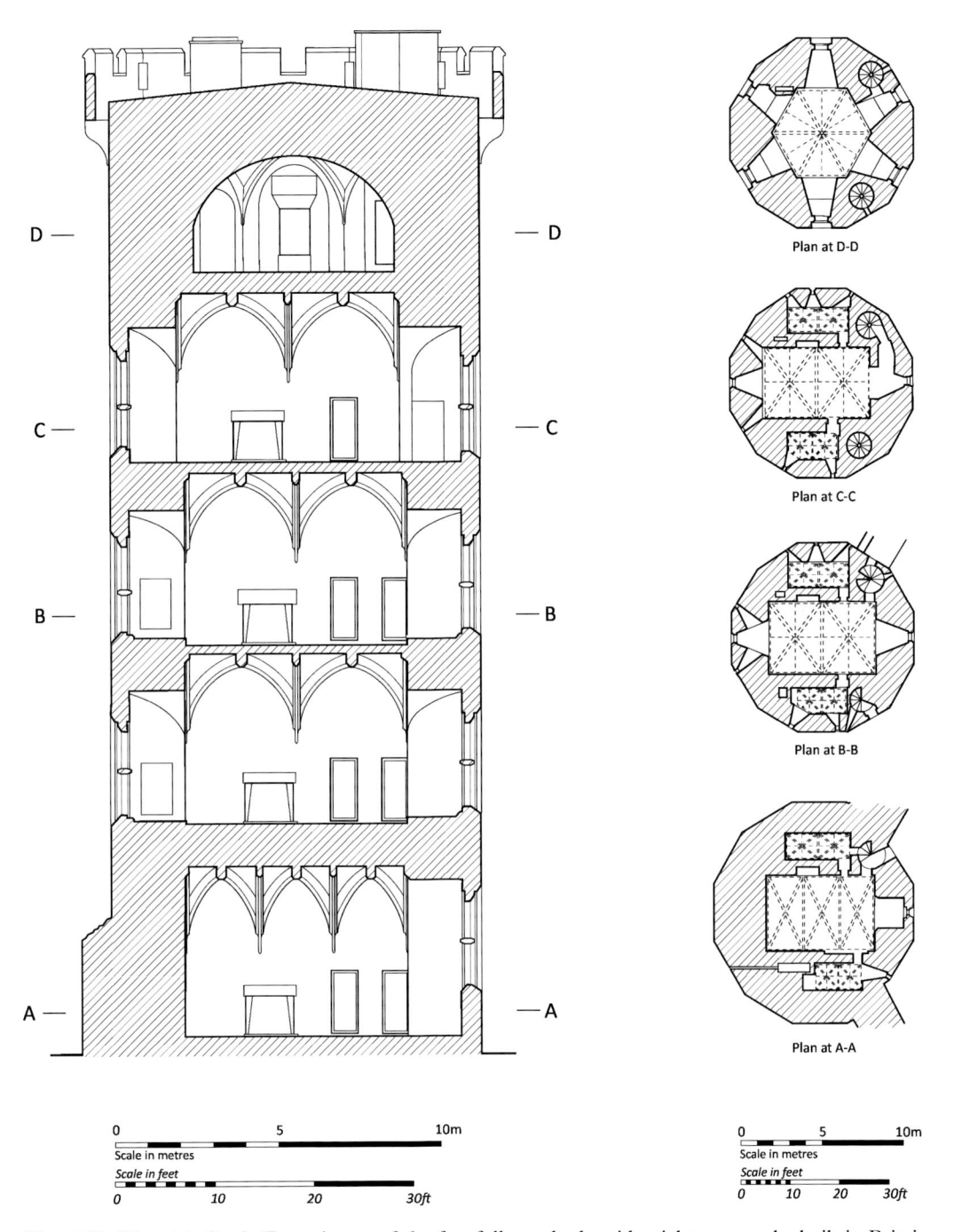

Fig. 4.21. Warwick Guy's Tower is one of the few fully vaulted residential towers to be built in Britain (last quarter of the fourteenth century); by Ric Tyler after Pugin 1895.

78 Castle Builders

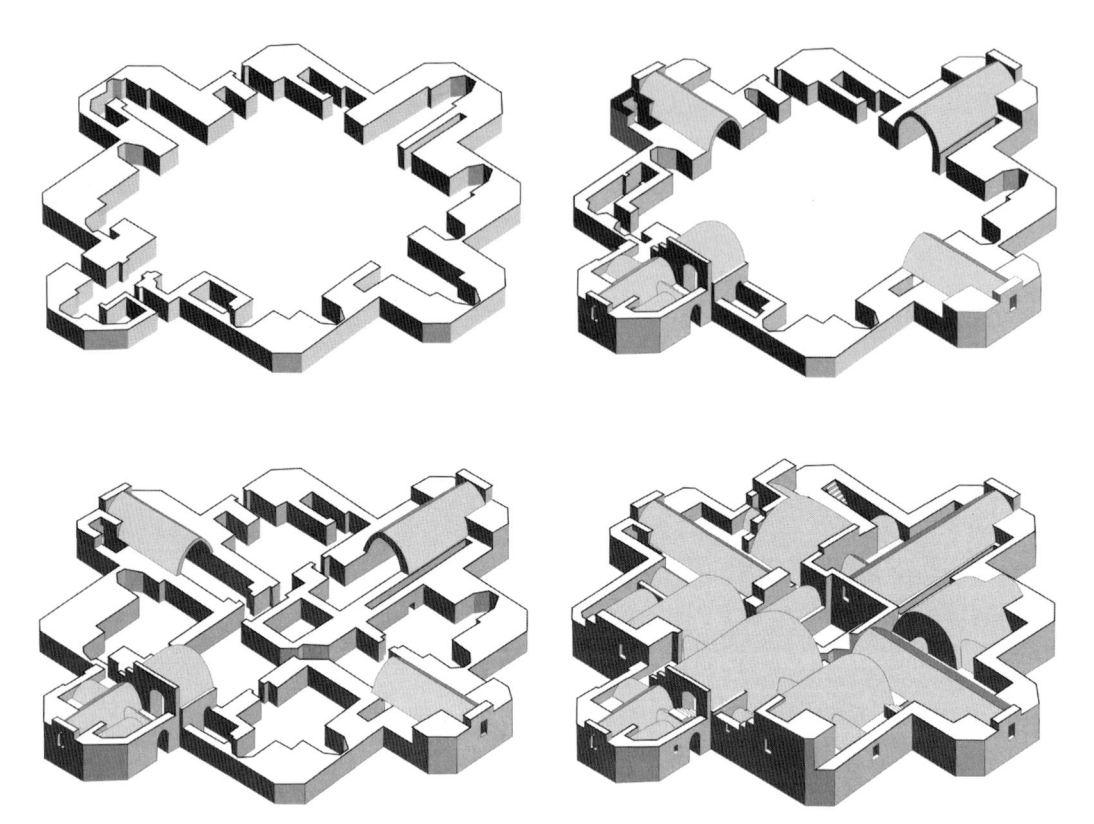

Fig. 4.22. Warkworth (Northumberland) The basement of the great tower showing the sequence of construction of walls and vaults (last quarter of the fourteenth century); by Nigel Dodds.

regional preference. William Douglas Simpson drew attention to the fact that despite being rare in England, the pointed barrel-vault was a common type in Scotland, which could perhaps be the source of the detail.[33] Simpson also deduced from a series of ragged joints in the vault that it had been built in a series of short sections, rather than in a single operation.

There was a different motive for the design of the vaults at Warkworth, which has a complex basement plan divided into a substantial number of rooms. Here, the master mason introduced a mixture of vault profiles ranging from the broad rounded segment of the entrance hall to the acutely pointed vaults of some of the peripheral rooms. The adoption of these different patterns was a practical solution to the problem of maintaining a consistent height of vault crown in rooms of various widths when the vaults sprang from the same level. The structural evidence suggests that a particular construction sequence was followed. After the outer walls of the basement had been built, the four arms of the donjon were vaulted, then the internal partitions built and vaulted (Fig 4.22).[34]

Staircases

Until the early thirteenth century, spiral staircases were universally vaulted. In the keep of Orford the sides of the well were faced in ashlar, but the vault comprises a thick mortar mix, which retains deep impressions of the planks on which it was laid. The head of the ashlar facing rises with the stair in a series of steps, which coincide with short vault sections of plank impressions that taper towards the newel (Fig 4.23). The impressions suggest overlapping planks, not unlike weatherboarding that have been configured to accommodate the twisting curve of the vault. In early newel stairs the circular stairwell, the steps, or winders, and the central newel were separate structural entities. The newel comprised a sequence of columnar stones, and the winders were composite structures, the lower ones being constructed on a solid base of rubble that was used to infill the bottom of the well. Thereafter, the winders were carried on the spiralling staircase vault, which also provided a structural link between the newel and the side of the well (Fig 4.24a). Each rotation of the vice must have formed a distinct constructional phase, the first of which rose from ground–floor level to the height of the vault crown. A hiatus in construction would have ensued during which the vault was allowed to settle and the mortar to set.

The straight mural staircase therefore represented a less demanding structural task than the vice. It was simply a matter of laying the steps on the top of the solid core of the wall and roofing the space, either with a vault or with stone slabs, stepped or angled. In the late twelfth century, however, a technical advance was achieved which was to revolutionize vice construction – masons began to cut the winder and newel section in a single piece, and this greatly simplified the building process (Fig 4.24b). On the one hand it allowed the steps to be prefabricated so that the assembly process on site was streamlined, and on the other hand, the steps were self-supporting, which obviated the need for vaulting. Consequently, vice construction times must have been significantly reduced. One of the earliest examples of this technique may be that in the keep of Carrickfergus,[35] which has been dated to the period 1178–1195.[36] On the other hand several of the newel stairs in the donjons raised by Philip Augustus between c. 1190 and c. 1220 – e.g. Villenueve-sur-Yonne (Yonne) and Verneuil-sur-Avre (Eure) - were vaulted.

Fig. 4.23. Orford (Suffolk) – Plank marks of the formwork on the stair vault (third quarter of the twelfth century).

One method of enhancing a spiral staircase was to cover the stairwell with a decorative vault. A conventional sexpartite vault was used at Castel del Monte (Puglia) in the 1230s (Fig 4.25), but a later development was to utilize a continuation of the central newel as a base from which a series of vaulting ribs might radiate in what is known as an umbrella vault; essentially this was an adaptation of the vaults with central columns discussed above. The fashion flourished in the north of England during the fourteenth century, with examples being built at Alnwick (Warder's Tower c. 1350),[37] Bothal (gatehouse c. 1350),[38] Belsay (c. 1370, Fig 4.26),[39] Haughton (c. 1370),[40] and Warkworth (keep c. 1390) all in Northumberland.[41] These

80   Castle Builders

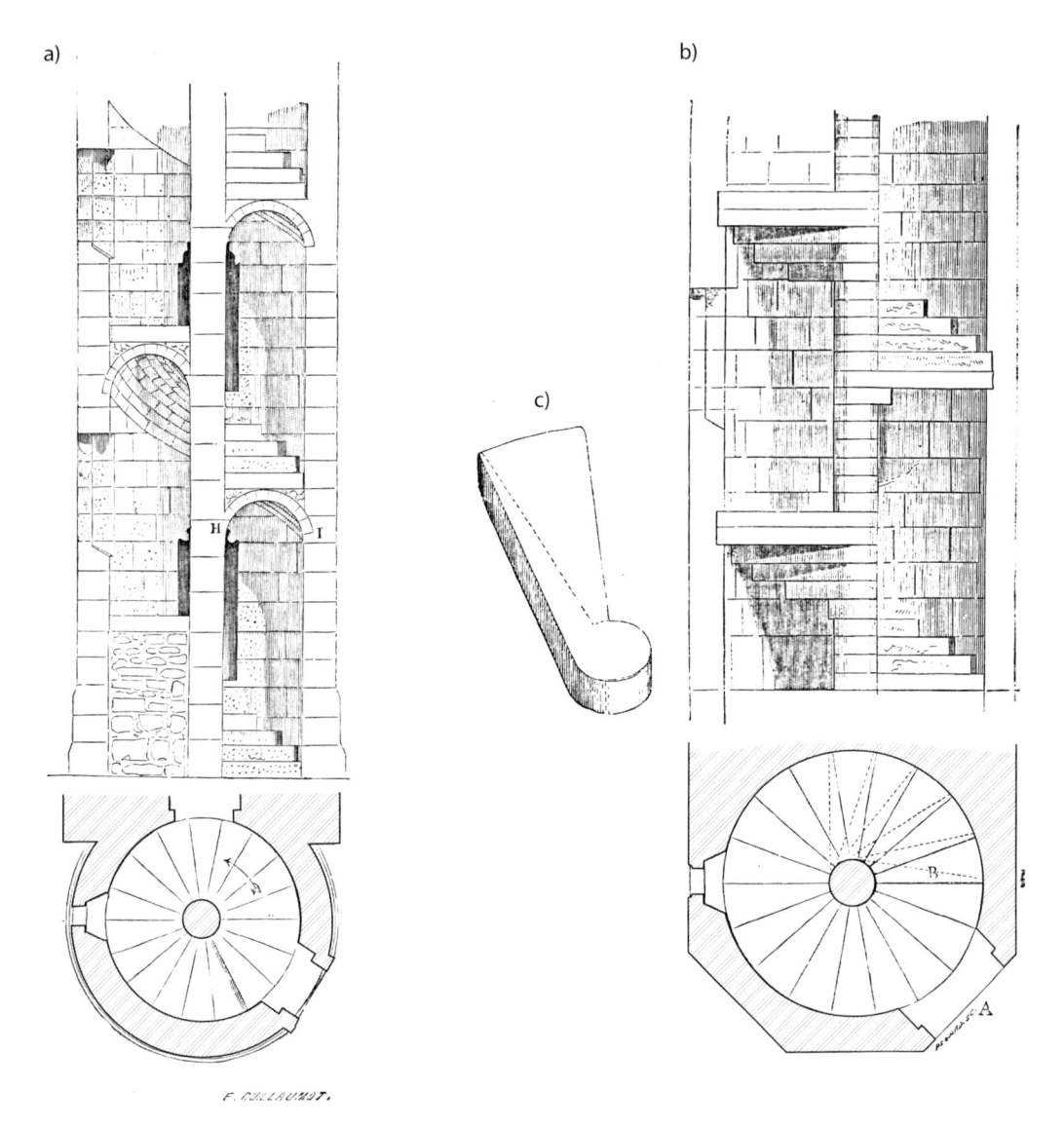

Fig. 4.24. Sectional drawings of a) a vaulted vice and b) a vice with composite winders and newel sections (c); after Viollet-le-Duc 1875.

are comparatively simple structures, but the principle was adopted to crown some of the most elaborate staircases of the medieval period.[42]

Conversion to stone and adaptation of earlier buildings

Motte redevelopments
Chapter two touched on the approaches taken to adapt a motte carrying a timber superstructure to one that would carry a stone building. Some of the most straightforward of these schemes involved no more than the replacement of a palisade with a stone perimeter

Building In Stone   81

Fig. 4.25. Castel del Monte (Puglia) Sexpartite vault over a stairwell (second quarter of the thirteenth century).

wall, the so-called shell keep, which might then contain buildings within the enclosure. Shell keeps are usually polygonal (Durham, Tamworth) or sub-circular (Arundel, Totnes, Trematon, Windsor).

Other builders, however, were more ambitious in their aims, and many sought to surmount the motte with a great tower proper. An early example is Guildford, where the early twelfth-century keep was built on the eastern edge of the motte so that its outer wall rises from halfway up the mound and the earthwork wraps itself round three sides of the building. The work probably involved cutting a section out of the motte down to bedrock. Although this would have been a substantial undertaking in itself it would have facilitated the construction process in the long run, by preparing the way for securely rooted foundations and easing the logistics of building material supply.

This was one solution to concerns about structural stability associated with the raising of a stone tower on top of an earthwork intended

Fig. 4.26. Alnwick (Northumberland) Umbrella vault over a staircase (*c.* 1370); from Hartshorne 1858

to support a timber superstructure. A different approach, which obviated any question about the suitability of the motte as a base for a stone structure, was to build an encircling wall from ground level upwards to encase the entire motte in masonry. This solution to the incorporation of the motte into the rebuilding of a castle in stone was adopted on at least two occasions during the second half of the twelfth century. The first of these conversions was probably at Robert Fitz Harding's castle of Berkeley (Gloucestershire), the second was at the bishop of Winchester's castle of Farnham (Surrey). These were obviously much more ambitious and expensive projects, and had originality in that they incorporated characteristics of both the keep and the enclosure, and thereby created powerful architectural effects.

The encased motte of Berkeley has a sub-circular plan extending to approximately 37 m (120 ft) in external diameter. Three semi-circular turrets project from the exterior face of the wall, and there may also have been a fourth on the north side where there is now a rectangular structure. In general concept this plan seems to be derived from the donjon of Houdan of c. 1130, but without its strict geometrical basis. Compared with Houdan, however, which has an external diameter of only 16 m (52.5 ft), the edifice that was constructed at Berkeley appears from the outside to have been built on a giant scale. Its height of approximately 19 m (62 ft) is respectable for an English keep of the eleventh or early twelfth century and it was evidently intended to resemble a tower. In reality, the wall encircling the motte enclosed an elevated courtyard, the revetment of the motte accounting for approximately one third of the total height.

The diameter of the enclosure is large in proportion to the height of the mound, and the motte has evidently been subjected to considerable alteration. The process of conversion began with the infilling of the ditch separating the motte from the bailey. Next, the base of the motte was revetted in stone, this revetment acting as a plinth on which to build the wall above. Because the wall is vertical and the motte was probably in the shape of an inverted cone, there would have been a widening gap between the two as the wall rose. Once the wall had reached the required level for the courtyard, this space was infilled with earth, which was probably obtained by lowering the motte. Like a keep, the converted motte of Berkeley was entered via a forebuilding which extended along one side of the building and which contained a staircase ascending to the elevated interior.

However, such instances of encasing a motte with a wall are rare, and a third option was adopted in a number of instances from the thirteenth century onwards. One such site was at Sandal where preparations for the construction work included cutting back the edge of the motte to create a rebate, or terrace, encircling the entire summit. The foundations of the keep, which was of cylindrical form, were built on this terrace, so that the outer wall of the keep clasped the higher centre of the motte. A similar approach was tried at York c. 1244, but here the quatrefoil design of the keep may not have been so suitable. By 1360 the south lobe had developed serious cracks so that the building had to be repaired; even now there is a considerable lean towards the south.[43] It is probable that the disjointed character of the multi-lobe plan, which embodied a degree of weakness, contributed to the failure of the structure.

A terracing technique was also used at Stafford Castle, when, in 1348, a great tower was raised on top of the motte there. The new keep was rectangular with projecting corner towers giving an overall length of 44 m (145 ft), slightly greater than the conjectured original diameter of *c.* 40 m at the crown. The first stage in the proceedings, then, was to provide an adequate platform by lowering the motte and extending it towards the north and east, a process that included the deliberate infilling of the motte ditch towards the inner bailey to allow for expansion.⁴⁴ The sides of the upper section of the earthwork were then cut back vertically to accommodate the four walls, and the truncated crown of the motte was incorporated within the building to serve as a raised ground-floor level, some 3.5 m above the newly made platform.

Finally, a motte that underwent two conversions is Whittington (Shropshire). In the twelfth century, a rectangular keep was built on top of the mound. Subsequently, in the 1220s, Ranulph de Blundeville, earl of Chester, encased the motte with a wall complete with a twin-towered gatehouse and round corner towers, and thereby transformed it into an inner courtyard. In this second conversion a great tower - actual or representative – played no part, and it was probably accompanied by the demolition of the twelfth-century keep.⁴⁵

Redevelopment of the enceinte

The replacement of a timber palisade with a curtain of stone was a comparatively simple operation, the foundations being cut into the crest of the bank. This is what happened during the fifteenth-century rebuilding of Tutbury, where the eleventh-century bank received a stone curtain in stages between 1400 and 1442, initially under the direction of the master mason Robert Skillington.⁴⁶ The completion of the curtain was followed by the construction of two new wall towers, which were a greater challenge because both towers were set within the eleventh-century bank.

To take the South Tower of 1442–1450 as the example, the plinth of the internal (north) elevation rises from courtyard level. However, the foot of the external (south) elevation is halfway down the bank so that the preparation for construction included the excavation of a deep section through the bank, and the creation of an undercroft accessed from the courtyard by a flight of steps. There must have been a large scale programme of earth removal before construction work could begin.

Building in Brick

Where suitable building stone was not available locally, brick might be used as a substitute. Castle building in brick proliferated in the thirteenth and fourteenth centuries along the North Sea/Baltic coastal strip from the Low Countries to the borders of Russia, being significantly boosted by the conquests there by the Teutonic Knights. In England, castle building in brick was more limited, and it is no coincidence that it has an eastern distribution. This derives firstly from the import of Flemish bricks into eastern ports, an early example being the thirteenth century, use of imported Flemish bricks at the Tower of London.⁴⁷ Secondly, centres of local manufacture were established in the eastern counties probably as a corollary of the import trade. However, even after the development of a home industry, both manufacture and building in the late medieval period were to remain heavily dependent on the skills of north European émigrés.⁴⁸

There are some fourteenth-century examples of brick defences in England: for example, the town walls of Hull (Yorkshire, 1321), the Cow Tower, Norwich (1380) and the gatehouse of Thornton Abbey (Lincolnshire, 1382). However, the brick castles generally date from the fifteenth century, because the widespread adoption of brick came towards the end of the castle building era. Also, brick castles in England are few in number, even though the medium was much used for other domestic buildings, and their distribution is restricted to the east and south-east. Because they constitute only a peripheral aspect of castle construction, the intention here is simply to dwell on a few aspects of brick castle building related to specific sites.

Brick manufacture and supply
The bricks were usually made close to the construction site. Those for Caister Castle were made of local clay, and the material for some of the earlier ones (those used in the east curtain) was sourced from an area on the north bank of the River Bure, known latterly as 'Brick Pits', situated approximately 1.25 miles to the south-east of the castle. The bricks would have been carried to the site by boat.[49] Most of the bricks for Ralph Lord Cromwell's castle at Tattershall were made by a certain Baldwin Docheman, whose name indicates a man of Flemish or German origin,[50] and they came from Cromwell's brickworks of Edlington Moor, an area that takes its name from the village of Edlington approximately 9 miles north of the castle.[51] Others were bought from John Chamberlain, lessee of Cromwell's brickworks at Boston 11 miles to the south-east, from which the River Witham probably served as the conduit. At the quadrangular castle begun by William Lord Hastings at Kirby Muxloe (1481–1483) the brick maker's name was John Ellis, and to judge by the low transport costs and the familiar references to 'the brickhouse' the place of manufacture was very close to the building site.

Construction
The use of brick simplified the construction process. Bricks were a superior material to ashlar in the sense that they eliminated the comparatively long drawn-out process of cutting the blocks to size and shape and setting them into position with lifting gear, and so the construction process was of shorter duration. Bricks were also better than rubble because their regularity meant less trimming and speedier laying. Brick construction also allowed a more exact prediction of the rate of progress, and was therefore a boon to planning.

Some insights into the working practices of the bricklayers are to be gained from the building accounts for Kirby Muxloe castle. They are first mentioned during the week beginning 7 May 1481, and over the first two weeks the team comprised a master bricklayer, John Horne, two trowel men, or layers, and three servants, who probably mixed the mortar and supplied the layers with bricks.[52] From the third week much of the brickwork was being done by contract, initially by Horne (and his team) at 18d. per thousand, and later by Robert Burrell and John Cosyn at 14d., and from 1483 by John Corbel at 18d.[53] During the first two building seasons (1482–1483) 1, 167,400 bricks were laid at piecework rates. Taking into consideration a six-day week and the number weeks worked, this amounts to an average of 21,619 per week or 3,603 per day.

If a twelve-hour day was worked,[54] then the contract work rate, including working the bricks as well as laying them, implies a work gang of three layers plus a servant each, in fact, one very much the size of the six-man day-rate team delineated in the accounts at the beginning of the 1481 season.[55] In 1482 nearly all the brickwork was done by contract, amounting to 733,000 bricks. In the third season (1483), which was curtailed owing to the execution of Lord Hastings, only 196,000 bricks were laid by contract, although the bricklayers were working on the towers at day rates until October.

The architects of brick castles
Who were the architects of these works? In the case of Kirby Muxloe we can be reasonably certain that this function was fulfilled by the mason, John Cowper, who was based at Tattershall (as builder of the church), over 100 miles to the north-east of Kirby Muxloe. It is he who is variously described in the accounts as 'master mason', 'surveyor over the stone-masons', 'surveyor of the works', or 'overseer of the masons'. When on site, he was paid a fee of 4s. per week based on a daily rate of 8d., but on nine occasions during the period 1481–1482 (the only two full years of building operations) he received a bonus of 10s. as a reward for travelling to and from Tattershall, and on each of the four such instances in 1481 he also received an additional two days pay to compensate him for the time it took to travel home.

At Caister Castle it may also have been a mason who was in charge. Although the building accounts of Caister are much less detailed, an entry regarding one Henry Wode, mason, shows that he was paid a similar weekly rate to Cowper (4s. 1d.) and that he had also submitted a claim for travelling to and from Norwich, a distance of some 35 miles.[56] The latter implies he was not permanently on site and that he, like Cowper, was also employed elsewhere. Expenses of this nature are only likely to have been allowed for particularly important personnel. This Henry Wode may perhaps be identified with Henry Mason who, along with other significant members of staff, received from Fastolf a gift of cloth. Such largesse was another mark of esteem denoting an important and esteemed servant.[57]

Documentation for Herstmonceux Castle (Sussex), built for Sir Roger Fiennes, Henry VI's treasurer, from *c.* 1441, is lacking, but the building's analogies with the contemporary royal foundation of Eton College (1441–1461), some 60 miles away, may suggest that the king's master mason, Robert Westerley, who had charge of the works at Eton from 1441,[58] was also involved in the design of Herstmonceux. The alternative suggestion that the principal figure was the brick maker, William Vesey,[59] who was also involved with the construction of Eton, is probably less likely.

It has been suggested too that Baldwin Docheman, the brick maker at Tattershall, also acted as the architect of the castle, but there is no convincing evidence to support this.[60] What we can say is that the great tower was to a considerable degree influenced by the gatehouse of Thornton Abbey, which lies approximately 50 miles to the north of Tattershall, and which was built in the 1380s, partly in brick. Although Lord Cromwell's Tower is both wider and taller, both buildings are approximately 18 m (59 ft) long, both are built on a north–south alignment, both project boldly from the curtain or precinct wall (Thornton internally, Tattershall externally), both have projecting octagonal corner turrets, and both have an eastern wall of extended thickness, which, internally, is utilized to accommodate mural chambers and passages. These analogies may suggest that an architect from the region was involved, but they might also reflect Lord Cromwell's own instructions.

One entry in the building accounts for 1434–1435 that may be pertinent with respect to identifying the master builder for Tattershall concerns wages paid to the mason John

Botiller and his two servants, which amounted to sums of 13s. and £1 0s. 2d. respectively.[61] This John Botiller could well be the John Botiller of Toddington (Bedfordshire), who, in 1435, was commissioned to take workmen and materials for works at the royal hunting lodge at Clipstone,[62] a little over 40 miles to the west of Tattershall. He was evidently a man who was in a position of authority at Clipstone, making him a suitable candidate for having charge of Tattershall; the relatively close proximity of the two properties would have allowed him to oversee the two sites simultaneously.

We can conclude, then, that brick–built castles were just as likely as their stone counterparts to have been raised under the direction of a mason. Brick was not such a dissimilar medium as to warrant the deployment of a specialist, and the process of construction (as opposed to preparation of materials) in brick or stone was to a large extent the same; the former was simply a replacement for the latter, and made no extra demands on the master mason.

Chapter 5

Great Tower Builders Part 1: *c.* 900–1190

Although it was by no means a universal component of the castle, the great tower was a frequent and conspicuous element, often forming an imposing architectural climax. The prominence of the great tower in relation to the other constituent parts of the castle has so impressed itself upon the public consciousness that it is often seen in emblematic terms, and the term is occasionally used as a synonym for a castle. This psychological impact was not incidental, for in addition to combining defensive and residential functions, there is no doubt that the great tower also had a symbolic role to fulfil in signifying lordship and its attendant implications of wealth and power. So, even though it usually formed part of a larger complex, the great tower had an architectural standing of its own, and, even though it might have acted as a focus for the wider complex, it was seldom a fully integrated constituent. Indeed, there was often a conscious attempt to isolate the great tower by encircling with its own ditch, by placing it on top of a motte, or even by siting it outside the main enceinte. It therefore lent itself to being designed in isolation as an architectural *tour de force*. The greater and more complex these buildings became, the more incumbent it was to engage a master with the proven requisite skills. These were not so much the skills of a military engineer (although defence was taken into consideration), but those of a domestic architect of a specialist kind, who had an aptitude for creating dramatic effect and for encompassing a plan that reflected the particular requirements of the client.

Great Towers in France c. 900–1050

Some of the first great towers are to be found in northern France, where the form probably came into existence during the ninth century, although the two earliest surviving examples – at Doué-la-Fontaine (Fig 5.1) and Mayenne (Mayenne) – have been dated to *c.* 900,[1] the former possibly the work of Theobald, count of Blois, and the latter perhaps raised at the instigation of Charles III, king of West Francia. There are, however, few points of resemblance. Doué, which is the simpler of the two, comprises a rectangular block, and is believed to have begun life as a single-storey hall-house, with the main entrance in the long west side and a lesser entrance in the short south side. The conversion into a tower is thought to have taken place after the building had been gutted by a fire. Following this event, the existing walls were raised to create at least one additional storey, the doorways were blocked, and a motte was subsequently raised around the former hall-house so that this latter became a basement accessible only from the interior via the upper level. The subsequent destruction of much of the upper walling means that we know a good deal more about the hall-house than the subsequent tower. Consequently, a discussion of the nature of the tower must be largely speculative, although the general design was to a great extent determined by the plan of the hall-house. It might be assumed that the activities which had

88 Castle Builders

Fig. 5.1. Doué-la-Fontaine (Maine-et-Loire) The ground-floor hall which was later raised into a great tower and encased within a motte (second half of the ninth century).

taken place in the hall-house would have been moved to the upper storey for reasons of security, and that the lower storey would have become a storage place.

The Mayenne donjon is a quite different structure. Now encased by later buildings, it occupied the elevated north-eastern apex of the castle enclosure, overlooking the River Mayenne. Possibly built under the auspices of the Carolingian king of West Francia, Charles III, one of the most striking aspects of the donjon is the reuse of materials from the Roman site of Jublains, which lies 6 miles to the south-east of the château. Roman sites provided readily accessible quarries for early medieval builders, although, given the Carolingians' known interest in appropriating the imperial past, symbolism may also have played its part in this instance. Roman sites at least would have provided materials that lent themselves to a dynastic style.[2]

The L-shaped plan comprised a three-storey, east–west-aligned rectangular main block measuring 10.7 x 7.6 m (35 x 25 ft) and rising to a height of 10.5 m (34.5 ft) at eaves level, with a four-storey square wing projecting from the west end of the south elevation and towering above the main block. A stair turret attached to the west side of the wing acted as a porch and provided the main artery of communication within the tower by giving access to the vertical sequence of rooms within the wing. It was from the wing that the two upper rooms within the main block were entered. The secure ground-storey of the main block, which was lit only by narrow loops set high above floor level, was a storage space, entered only from the floor above. This latter contained the principal reception room, or hall, the corresponding room in the wing serving as an antechamber. In contrast to the basement, the first-floor hall was brilliantly lit by a series of large round-arched windows; a group of four in the north wall form a particularly striking feature. The uppermost storey of the main block was probably a more private chamber. It is not possible to say how typical this building was, but one recognizes in it a highly specialized building type with a degree of sophistication in the internal lines of communication. At Mayenne we can see a rare early instance of a castle builder beginning to engage seriously with three-dimensional planning.

Chronologically, the next surviving donjon of note is that at Langeais, which is believed to date from *c.* 1000 (Fig 5.2); it is one of the towers usually assigned to Fulk Nerra, count of Anjou between 987 and 1040. Fulk is noted as a prolific castle builder, although the uncertain chronology of many of the donjons of the period, and the fluctuating boundaries of Angevin territory, mean some attributions must be tentative. At Langeais the two-storey rectangular main block had external dimensions of approximately 18.5 x 8.5 m (61 x 28 ft), and, as at Mayenne, there was at least one, but more likely two, square wings projecting from the long elevation of the main block.[3] One of these probably housed a staircase that provided public access to the first floor apartment, and there may have been an external timber gallery at first-floor level, extending between the two wings. The walls, which ranged in thickness from 1.48–1.68 m (5–5.5 ft) at the lower level, were faced principally using the pre-Romanesque technique of *petit appareil*. In addition, however, the east wall contained a broad band of ashlar masonry, and there were also ashlar-faced buttresses at the three surviving corners and in the centre of the east front. A striking decorative effect is achieved in the principal semi-circular arched openings through the alternation of the stone voussoirs with re-used Roman tiles, following Carolingian precedents.

Fig. 5.2. Langeais (Indre-et-Loire) The donjon from the east (*c.* 1000).

Between Mayenne and the early donjon at Langeais, there is a hiatus of up to 100 years, and although the paucity of the current evidence does not allow us to chart the progress of techniques in donjon design and construction in the tenth century, the donjon of Langeais suggests that there had been few major developments. In contrast, the early decades of the eleventh century were to witness a remarkable advance. A tower that can be assigned with greater certainty to Fulk Nerra is Loches, which has been dated through dendrochronological analysis to 1012–1035,[4] and was therefore built within Fulk's lifetime. Although we cannot be certain as to the number of years that separate the donjons of Langeais and Loches, the contrast between them is marked. The donjon of Loches rises through four storeys as opposed to two, reaching a height of *c.* 30 m (98 ft); the L-shaped plan covers a greater area, comprising a main block (*La Grosse Tour*) of 25.2 x 13.7 m (83 x 45 ft) and a wing (*La Petite Tour*) of 13.2 x 9.1 m (43 x 30 ft); the walls are much thicker at 2.79 m (9 ft); finally, the tower is faced throughout with ashlar rather than *petit appareil* (Fig 5.3).

At Loches the great tower attained maturity and established itself as an important and highly recognizable architectural form. Consequently, the architect of Loches must be considered a master builder of some significance. One clue as to his origins may be seen in the semi-circular buttresses, which form a distinctive and prominent aspect of his design. Semi-circular buttresses feature on a number of tenth-century churches in the region, including those of Autrèche, Bilazais, Cravant-les-Coteux and St Generoux, and were evidently a characteristic of late Carolingian architecture. Autrèche is approximately 23 miles to the north of Loches, Cravant-les-Coteaux is 33 miles to the west and Bilazais and St Generoux are approximately 60 miles to the west, so they form a relatively compact geographical group. The buttresses of Loches, therefore, might be seen as an aspect of a regional tradition of masoncraft, which may, in turn, be indicative of the background of the master builder.

Semi-circular buttresses were also used by the architect of the great tower of Montbazon (Indre-et-Loire), which lies approximately 18 miles to the north-west of Loches. The chronology of Montbazon is uncertain, but, on stylistic grounds, it probably belongs to the first half of the eleventh century, and may be another of Fulk Nerra's works.[5] Montbazon, however, is a less sophisticated building; it comprises a single rectangular block 19.65 x 13.75 m (64 ft x 45 ft), and its stonework is crude in comparison with the ashlar facing of Loches.

Another building of comparable date (*c.* 1015–1030) and scale (though of different proportions) is Beaugency (Loiret, Fig 5.4), which lies approximately 65 miles to the north-west of Loches. It too may be one of Fulk Nerra's works, but in this case the master builder eschewed the use of semi-circular buttresses, and created a tower of peculiar proportions, that owe little to Loches. Like Montbazon, it is shorter than the main block of Loches, at 22.4 m (73 ft), but has a width of 17.6 m (58 ft), an unprecedented measurement for a great tower, which necessitated the use of a longitudinal dividing wall in order to support a double-pile roof. The widths of Loches and Montbazon were at the limit of what could be spanned by single lengths of timber, and it is possible that it was a shortage of suitable material that occasioned this solution. Whatever the reason, the introduction of the spine wall was a breakthrough in great tower design because it allowed the building to be floored and roofed in two spans, an advance that doubled the potential width, and at the same time greatly increased the possibilities for internal planning.

Fig. 5.3. Loches (Indre-et-Loire) The donjon from the north comprising La Grosse Tour in the background with La Petite Tour in front, partly obscured by the fifteenth-century gatehouse (first quarter of the eleventh century).

Fig. 5.4. Beaugency (Loiret) Tour de César from the north east (first quarter of the eleventh century, heightened in the twelfth century).

The Pre-Conquest Great Towers in Normandy

The principle of spine walling within the great tower was developed in Normandy, where the keep of Avranches, owes its design to the concept. Avranches is situated at the foot of the Cotentin peninsula, close to the western border of the duchy. It dates from the late tenth or early eleventh century and is one of the earliest of Norman great towers.[6] The slightly irregular rectangular ground plan, which, at some 37 x 27 m (121 x 89 ft), covered a much larger area than any of the buildings discussed so far, is also distinguished from them in appearing to have had a more complex interior. The spine wall split the interior of the tower lengthways into two divisions of unequal width in order to create a double-pile plan; a transverse partition wall sub-divided the tower into four compartments. The use of semi-circular buttresses, semi-circular-arched windows with alternating stone and tile voussoirs, and *petit appareil* provide further analogies with the donjons of the Loire discussed above, and hint at cultural links between the two areas.

The lack of a firm chronology for many early towers hampers the theoretical reconstruction of their sequential development. However, a building that is related to the Avranches tower is the donjon of Ivry-la-Bataille, on the eastern border of Normandy. Ivry is one of the most interesting of the early French donjons, both for the unusual character of its design, and for the influence it exerted on one of the most famous of European great towers. Although the Ivry donjon has been reduced to its ground storey, the remains were sufficient to show that the initial plan was that of a north–south-aligned rectangle 32 x 25 m (105 x 82 ft) with an L-shaped wing attached to the north end of the east wall, incorporating an apsidal eastward projection. In a second structural phase, shortly after the donjon had been built, or perhaps even during the course of construction, the wing was extended to the south to equal the length of the main block.[7] The result was a double-pile plan, albeit of unequal proportions, with the former eastern wall of the main block now acting as the spine wall. Here at Ivry the process by which the double-pile plan evolved from the winged tower is laid bare. Unfortunately, is no longer possible to say whether a similar accretive process was responsible for the plan of the donjon at Avranches, nor is either tower sufficiently closely dated to allow us to determine which came first.

The great tower of Ivry was built c. 1000 by Aubrée, Countess of Ivry. For the first time, we have the name of the architect; he was a man called Lanfred, 'whose character as an architect transcended that of all the other French architects at the time'.[8] The plan of Ivry is certainly distinctive, and is evidently by the hand of a master builder of note (Fig 5.5a). As we have seen, wings attached to rectangular donjons had precedents, but the introduction of an apse, with its ecclesiastical or imperial associations, was new. The form, and the eastern orientation of the apse does suggest that it contained a chapel, but its asymmetrical disposition in relation to the main body of the building is quite different from that to be found in the regular hierarchical arrangements of church buildings. The arrangement emphasizes the essential secularity of the donjon, and the informality of the original plan.

One would like to know more about Lanfred, but although his pedigree is a closed book to us, Orderic Vitalis does at least provide a second (earlier) attribution, that of the great tower of Pithiviers (Loiret), approximately 70 miles to the southwest of Ivry. Unfortunately, this building is no longer extant, but it may possibly be identified with a

94 Castle Builders

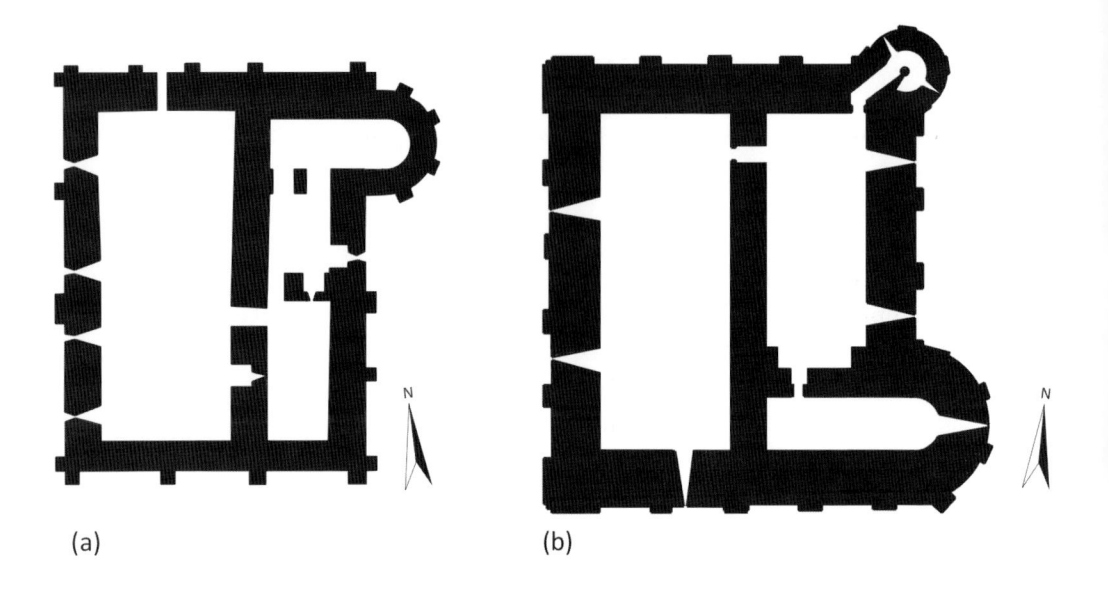

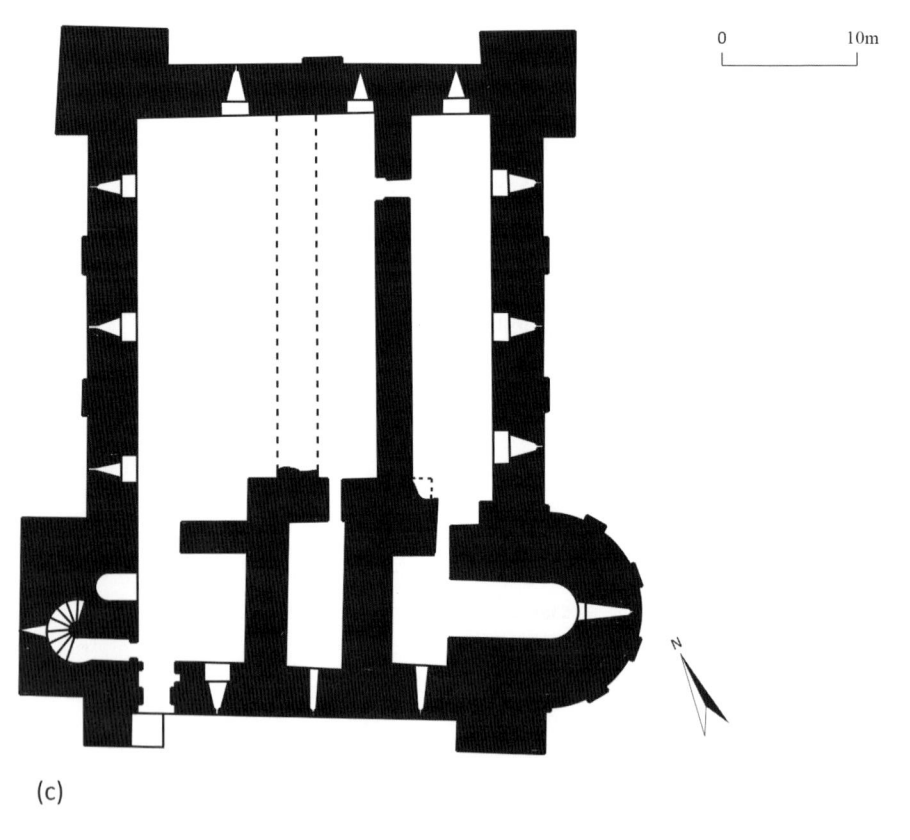

Fig. 5.5. The great towers of (a) Ivry-la-Bataille, *c.* 1000 (b) London (White Tower) *c.* 1075–1100 and (c) Colchester, begun *c.* 1075–1076; after Impey 2002 (a and b) and Crummy 1981 (c).

medieval great tower recorded in a nineteenth-century drawing of Pithiviers.[9] This too had an apsidal projection, which does suggest a common origin for the design. Whether this feature was Lanfred's own idea or whether it reflects a more widely employed style of architecture within northern France is unclear. However, the fact that it was to reappear some 70 years later in the design of the Tower of London implies that it had some special significance for the Normans.

London and Colchester

Ivry is an example of an empirical approach to architectural design, but approbation of the final result can be measured by its influence on one of the earliest and most famous Norman keeps in England: that of the Tower of London (The White Tower). The White Tower was probably begun in the late 1070s, and although work was suspended *c.* 1080, shortly after second-floor level was reached, and not resumed for at least another ten years, until the reign of William II, the building was probably complete by 1100.[10] The keep replicates Ivry's north–south-aligned rectangular block divided by a crosswall, with an apsidal projection at one end of the east side (Fig 5.5b). This a rare configuration that, together with the close correspondence of some of the dimensions, suggests that the White Tower may have been influenced by Ivry.[11]

The administration of the project is usually attributed to Gundulf, bishop of Rochester, and although his primary role is likely to have been managerial, his close association with Abbot and Archbishop Lanfranc at the abbeys of Le Bec, St Etienne, in Caen, and St Augustine, in Canterbury, bespeaks experience of large-scale building projects and a knowledge of structural practices and architectural fashion that would have stood him in good stead in consultations with the technical mastermind behind the White Tower. The name of the master-builder is unknown, but it is reasonable to suppose that he had a continental background and an understanding of the types of buildings that the Normans were introducing into England, including, perhaps, Ivry-la-Bataille.

Originally, the White Tower had three storeys, and was topped by a screen wall, containing a well-lit mural gallery, that enclosed the roofs. The screen wall rising above the roof was to become a recurrent aspect of eleventh- and twelfth-century keeps. Externally, the main distinguishing features of the White Tower are the apse at the south-east corner, a cylindrical stair turret that projects from the north-east corner, square turrets at the other two corners, the pilaster buttresses that articulate the window bays, and the blind arcading that contains the second-floor windows. There was also a forebuilding on the south side (now demolished) that contained a staircase ascending to the first-floor entrance.

The original function of the White Tower is uncertain, but as far as the development of castle design and construction is concerned it was the first example in England of large-scale secular planning in an integrated form combining both horizontal and vertical lines of communication. The only external access was at first-floor level. Internally, at all three levels, the building was divided into three main components: to the west of the spine wall there was a single large room; to the east of the spine wall, the space was divided by a transverse wall into a large rectangular space to the north and a smaller apsidal-ended space to the south. Access from outside was into the western room and thence into the north-eastern room, which acted as the hub of communication within the building. From here, access was obtained to the south-eastern room and also to a large spiral staircase at the north-east corner of the building that was the only route to both the basement and the upper floor.

The orientation and distinctive outline of the White Tower plan are replicated in the broadly contemporary keep of Colchester, which was begun *c.* 1074 or 1076 (Fig 5.5c).[12] In particular, the prime distinguishing characteristic of the apsidal projection is replicated at Colchester in an identical position, at the south end of the east elevation, and it appears evident that one tower was meant to reflect the other. However, although the demolition of the upper part of the Colchester keep has rendered a true comparison of the two buildings problematic, it is evident from the surviving fabric that they were far from being identical, and even if the original intention had been for the two towers to correspond more closely in design, the site conditions at Colchester meant that its builder would have had to make an early change of tack, because the character of the great tower was to a substantial degree influenced by its siting within the former Roman *colonia* of *Camulodunum*.

Firstly, the ruins of the Roman town provided the medieval builders with a bounty of recyclable building materials, so that the walls of the keep incorporate a heavy content of Roman tile, a material that today gives the building a quite distinct character. Secondly, and more importantly, a major difference between Colchester and the White Tower is one of scale, the former having external dimensions of 46 x 33.5 m (151 x 110 ft) as opposed to the 36 x 29.6 m (118 x 97 ft) of the latter; in fact, Colchester has the largest footprint of all great towers, eclipsing even the keep of Avranches. There is no doubt that this attribute was a consequence of the deliberate siting of the keep over the podium of a Roman temple, whereby the walls of the keep are set immediately outside the corresponding walls of the podium. It was the dimensions of the podium, then, that determined those of the medieval great tower. Otherwise, if analogies of other eleventh-century great towers are considered, it is probable that the keep would have been a more compact structure.

The manner in which the construction issue posed by the existence of the podium was approached created another problem for the master builder in that the resultant 26.5 m (87 ft) internal width of the keep seems to have been too great to allow a replication of the arrangement used for the White Tower, which was roofed in two spans. Although it would have been technically possible to cover a building of this width with a double-pile roof, it would have been on the limits of what was achievable and is only likely to have been realized by producing two cells of equal width. It is clear, however, that this did not comply with the planning brief, which required a wide western cell and a narrower eastern cell as in the White Tower plan. The solution adopted by the Colchester master was to introduce a second axial cross wall in the form of an arcade, a little to the west of the surviving one, and in doing so created a narrow aisle for the main western room. This western room, the width of which was approximately the same as its counterpart in the White Tower, was the main consideration in determining the relative widths of the axial divisions, its roof span being the limiting factor.

Apart from the differences in scale and plan occasioned by the nature of the site, there are a number of other disparities between the designs of Colchester and the White Tower which show an independence of approach. The White Tower presents a relatively simple structural plan on each floor, being divided by one axial and one transverse crosswall into three cells. Colchester is more complex, partly owing to the extra axial crosswall occasioned by its greater width. Whereas the main stair of the White Tower is contained within a cylindrical turret at the north-east corner of the building, that of Colchester is at the south-west corner, where it is housed in one of three boldly projecting corner turrets. These turrets, which provide a powerful contrast with the White Tower, were unprecedented in great tower architecture, though they were to be emulated in several twelfth-century keeps in England and France.

The discovery of a prototype for the White Tower at Ivry-la-Bataille superseded speculation that the ducal great tower of Rouen (the details of which are unknown) might have served as a model for the White Tower.[13] In confirming a continental antecedent the compulsion to comprehend the great towers of Colchester and London chiefly in terms of one another was alleviated, and opened the way to considering them instead largely as independent interpretations of a more widely distributed style. In seeking further parallels, the great tower of Avranches, which had set benchmarks with the extent of its ground plan and the number of its internal divisions, is one obvious contender, particularly with respect to Colchester, where there was also a transverse partition right across one end of the interior.

The Second Generation: Royal Keeps 1085–1140

East Anglia: The Norwich master

London and Colchester, together with their Norman predecessors, including Ivry-la-Bataille and Pithiviers, form a coherent architectural group. The keep of Norwich Castle, which followed close on the heels of the two English buildings, and which was the first major work of the next generation, is the focus of another stylistic series. Despite being the same type of building, Norwich provides a strong architectural contrast to London and Colchester, and there is no doubt that it was the work of a consummate master, and a building of seminal significance.

The keep was begun by William II, c. 1095, but only completed under Henry I c. 1115, following a break in construction,[14] perhaps occasioned by William's death in 1100. Built on a motte, a number of structural anomalies denote that the original concept was modified during the course of construction, probably during the raising of the basement, and it is possible that the combination of a new client and a new architect resulted in a general revision of the scheme.[15]

Norwich keep's stylistic independence of the White Tower group is immediately apparent in the uncompromisingly cuboid character of the main block and its comparatively narrow walls,[16] but it can also to be gauged from the centrally placed spine-wall along the east–west axis, which differs from the asymmetrical positioning of nearly all previous great tower crosswalls, and from the presence of a number of other innovatory features which imply that a highly inventive mind was responsible for the design. One of these innovations was an elaborate forebuilding (Bigod's Tower; no longer extant) approached by a grand staircase of stone, an arrangement that extended across much of the east side of the tower. This integrated combination of forebuilding and external staircase was to be emulated and developed by the builders of later twelfth-century keeps, but the concept seems to have been introduced at Norwich. Here, its aesthetic contribution to the great tower was to break up the regularity of the entrance elevation by introducing a diverting asymmetrical element that also enhanced the dramatic character of the approach.

Like the White Tower, the vertical articulation of the main elevations of the keep was based on regularly disposed pilaster buttresses. However, whereas the horizontal articulation of the White Tower was principally reliant upon the fenestration, the treatment to which the elevations of Norwich were subjected was revolutionary in castle architecture. Above the flint-facing of the basement, the keep was finished entirely in ashlar and was covered in four tiers of shafted arcading. Such extraordinarily decorative treatment was unparalleled in buildings of this type, and the only comparable instances that come readily come to mind are the later twelfth-century Sicilian palaces of La Cuba and La Zisa in Palermo. It is an approach that echoes some contemporary ecclesiastical architecture, including Norwich Cathedral, which gives some reason to suppose that the two projects, which were conceived together, were intended to reflect one another architecturally. The detail is certainly of a quality and on a scale that might be expected in a great church, and evidence in the form of masons' marks implies that the same masons worked on both projects, indicating that both may have been under the direction of the same master builder.[17]

Norwich has been linked architecturally with two other keeps.[18] The first is Falaise, in Normandy, another royal tower usually dated to *c.* 1120, and also attributed to Henry I. Falaise is of a similar cuboid character to Norwich, except for the south-east corner where the chapel is emphasized by being housed within a rectangular projection. The design of the windows lighting the main rooms of both buildings is almost identical, comprising twin unmoulded semi-circular-arched lights springing from a central shaft and impost blocks. The principal display elevation at Falaise is the north front, which faces outside the castle. This, like the main (south) front of Norwich, is divided into four bays by pilaster buttresses. Here, however, they play a more dominant role than at Norwich in articulating the façade. They are broader, thicker, set more closely together, and the corners are rebated to create a play of light and shade and so give a deeper sense of perspective. The builder of Norwich had a similar preoccupation with light and shade, but he concentrated on the blind arcading to create the effect.

There does not seem to have been an original forebuilding at Falaise, but the layout of the interior, as far as it can be reconstructed, seems to have been very similar to that of Norwich. Again, the main entrance is at the north end of the east wall at first-floor level, and the interior was divided into two (in this case unequal) halves by an east–west aligned crosswall. Here too the hall was at the east end of the north side, and the kitchen at the north-west angle. The relative position of the chapel at the south-east angle is also the same despite being accommodated in an annexe. As at Norwich the great chamber seems to have been to the south, adjacent to the chapel. The correspondence is too great to be coincidence and there is little doubt that the plan of Falaise was based on that of Norwich, and that the architect must have been conversant with its internal arrangements. Whether this was through personal experience, or secondary knowledge gained orally or by reference to plans, is uncertain, but the former seems likely.

The second great tower to be influenced by Norwich is Castle Rising, approximately 32 miles to the north-west of Norwich. Rising was built in 1138 by William d'Albini, but has a strong claim to be considered amongst the buildings of the Henrician circle of patronage in that d'Albini married Henry's widow, Adeliza. D'Albini himself was a staunch loyalist ready to identify himself with the prevailing monarch. Castle Rising is strongly derivative of Norwich. It too comprises a rectangular main block with an identical orientation to Norwich, and an elaborate forebuilding and staircase complex set against the east wall that gave access to the first floor. The upper part of the staircase building is treated with blind arcading in the manner of Norwich, but of a more advanced type appropriate to the later date.[19]

The internal plan of the Rising keep is remarkably intact, so that there is little doubt about the original intention of the designer. The keep was divided at all levels into two unequal halves by an east–west-aligned crosswall. At first-floor level the northern half was occupied by the great hall (east), which was entered from the forebuilding, and a kitchen and service room (west); the southern half housed the chapel and antechapel (east) and the great chamber (west). Both the hall and great chamber were provided with a pair of latrines in the west wall. Although the keep of Norwich was gutted in the nineteenth century so that the full details of its layout are no longer recoverable, theoretical reconstructions suggest that the scheme bore a very strong resemblance to that of Rising, and that the thinking behind the two plans is almost identical,[20] allowing the inference to be drawn that the plan of Castle Rising was based on that of Norwich, and implying also, therefore, that the architect of Rising was familiar with the internal arrangements of Norwich.

On architectural grounds alone there is sufficient reason to suggest that this group of related great towers might represent the work of a single architect, a possibility that the narrow range of patrons supports. It is, moreover, entirely feasible that the 40- to 45-year time span for the group might fall within the working lifetime of a master craftsman; there are indeed several instances of individuals from the fourteenth century (which is better documented) whose careers were as lengthy.[21] For this theory to hold good, however, the Norwich Master, as we might call him, would have carried through the most ambitious and striking of the three works (Norwich) when he was at his least experienced relative to the other two buildings. While this is not impossible, it might be suggested rather that there was a second master who had been closely associated with the first and who was involved with the latter stages of Norwich.

The south-east: Canterbury and Rochester

A second major royal keep dating from *c.* 1100 was raised at Canterbury, where it coincided with the rebuilding of the choir of the cathedral choir.[22] The design of the keep differs from that of Norwich in a number of respects, and there is little doubt that it is the work of a quite different master builder, who was, nevertheless, familiar with the earlier keep at Colchester, with which Canterbury has some analogies. Like Norwich, it has a rectangular plan, though it carries projecting square corner turrets rather than the clasping buttresses of Norwich. At least three storeys high originally, the elevations are divided into three (east and west) and two (north and south) bays by pilaster buttresses, and the interior into three main sections by two transverse (east–west) crosswalls.

Although the building has not fared well, having lost its upper storey and internal walling, surviving fragments of detailing suggest that it had considerable architectural embellishment including an elaborate moulded plinth and nook-shafted windows with chevron-moulded arches. Also decorative in intent was the unusual window embrasure design, which, instead of having the more usual splayed sides, comprised a series of unmoulded receding arched orders that must have produced an interesting perspective effect. Analogies for this latter detail are lacking, but it is just possible that it was a development of the White Tower's first-floor external arcading, which gave a similar if more limited sectional profile.

Elements that link it with Colchester are the corner turrets, the high plinth and the unusual tripartite division of the interior. At Colchester we have seen that the division into three had an empirical origin, as a response to an exceptional width imposed by the physical nature of the site. At Canterbury, however, the concept of two parallel axial walls was taken up in a more formal arrangement that had been planned from the outset. As at Colchester, the plan implies a triple-pile roof. Not that the building was unusually large and therefore difficult to span, indeed, the internal width of 21 m (70 ft) is just the sort of measurement that might have been designed to be roofed in two manageable spans with the aid of a central crosswall like that of Norwich. While the particular circumstances of the Canterbury project cannot be confirmed, and always supposing that a suitable supply of timber was available to allow a double-pile arrangement, the twin crosswall system must have been intended primarily as an alternative means of partitioning the interior to create a usable plan. In this case the plan comprised a main central room flanked by two narrower sub-divided sections.

Between 1127 and 1136, William de Corbeil, Archbishop of Canterbury, custodian of the royal castle of Rochester, raised a new keep there at the instigation of Henry I (Fig 5.6). Like Norwich, it was built with a central crosswall, but in other respects it presents a striking contrast. Firstly, it was built to a square plan, a design hitherto eschewed by great tower builders, although square towers were the norm in ecclesiastical architecture. The external dimensions of the main block are 21 m (70 ft) square, so it has a smaller ground plan than the English keeps discussed so far, and the main architectural effect relies instead on the great height of the building, which at c. 38 m (125 ft) makes it the tallest of all great towers in England. The result is a greater sense of verticality than had hitherto been seen in an English great tower, an effect that is enhanced by the pilaster buttresses, and by the square corner turrets that rise to a height of 3.7 m (12 ft) above the parapet of the main block. The general appearance of the keep is austere, and its architectural impact relies on an evocation of raw power.

The first-floor entrance is set within a lower forebuilding that stands at the east end of the north elevation. This structure, which is even plainer in its outward appearance than the main block, is approached by an external staircase that begins at the north end of the west elevation and then wraps around the north-west corner, continues through a turret at the west end of the north elevation, and along the north side. This is a different arrangement from Norwich, where the forebuilding stair ranges along a single side, but it was a scheme that was also used in the great tower of Arques-la-Bataille (Seine-Maritime) in Normandy, one of Henry I's near contemporary great towers, and the idea was to be adopted for a number of later keeps.

The crosswall divides each floor of the interior into a series of two-room apartments linked by doorways in the wall. The most interesting aspect of this division, however, is at second-floor level, which houses the principal apartment rising through two storeys. Here, the lower part of the crosswall is built as an arcade with cylindrical columns carrying scalloped capitals and semi-circular arches decorated with chevron mouldings. In a secondary operation the arches were infilled by solid walling; this may have been intended from the outset, but it

Fig. 5.6. Rochester (Kent) The great tower from the south west (second quarter of the twelfth century).

might also have been the result of a change of plan during construction or even an early alteration to the primary fabric.

This arcade is one of a number of aspects of the Rochester keep, including the projecting corner turrets, the 3.7 m (12 ft) thickness of the walls, the splayed plinth, and the substantial depth of the foundations below the top of the plinth, that have analogies at Colchester, suggesting that details of the earlier building were within the repertoire of the Rochester master.[23] There are fewer analogies with Canterbury, although significant correlations are the corner turrets and the manner in which the top of the plinth rises above ground-floor level rather than corresponding with it.

The north: The Bamburgh master

In the north of England, a different master builder was commissioned to raise a new royal keep at the ancient stronghold of Bamburgh, on the Northumberland coast, a project that was probably complete by 1135 (Fig 5.7). This may have been a mason called Osbert, to whom payments were made for work at Bamburgh in 1131.[24] Now largely devoid of twelfth-century detail, the keep, nevertheless, provides evidence of a distinct regional rendering of the great tower theme. As one of the earliest and most significant of stone keeps in the northern counties, it holds a special place in the architectural development of the region, and would be a source of inspiration for later builders.

The keep was originally three storeys in height and built to an almost square plan with plain pilaster buttresses widening at the angles to form square corner turrets. There are also

102   Castle Builders

Fig. 5.7. Bamburgh (Northumberland) The great tower from the east; perhaps the work of the mason Osbert (second quarter of the twelfth century).

a number of novel features that contribute to the great tower's individual personality. The basis for the internal floor plans, for instance, appears to have been a pair of intersecting crosswalls, a quite distinct arrangement original to the building. Also, in marked contrast to the contemporary royal keeps of southern England, the entrance is at ground-floor level and was not prefaced by a forebuilding. Instead, it is set within a shallow projection of the wall to allow for an internal vestibule from which a straight mural staircase led to the first floor.[25] The other distinguishing characteristic is a very elaborately moulded plinth, a most unusual and unexpected feature in this context.

Despite these idiosyncrasies, there are also signs that the builder had knowledge of the White Tower, certain elements of which were incorporated into the design of Bamburgh. These include, firstly, a substantial first-floor chapel that ranges along the entire length of the south wall, and which parallels the first-floor chapel in the White Tower. Secondly, the double-pile roof of the Bamburgh keep was, like those of many early great towers, concealed behind a screen wall containing a continuous gallery, an unusual feature, but one that also appears in the White Tower, which seems to have been the model. Whether these links with the White Tower denote first-hand knowledge on the part of the Bamburgh master or whether the ideas were imparted by word of mouth or document is unknown.

Bamburgh is not the only border keep to be laid at the door of this northern master; there is a good case for ascribing to him the great tower of Carlisle, which probably dates from *c.* 1120–1140 (Fig 5.8), completion of the tower probably being carried out under David I of Scotland.[26] Notwithstanding that the Carlisle keep has been even more drastically altered than Bamburgh so that a reconstruction of its original form is problematic, to say the least, it displays a number of architectural analogies that place it firmly within the same school of masoncraft, and which suggest, therefore, that the Bamburgh master played a part in its design.

Firstly, the overall character of the plan is similar; both structures being built to a nearly square plan (approximately 21 m x 18.7 m at Bamburgh and 20 m x 18 m at Carlisle). Also, both seem to have been three-storey structures, and Carlisle, like Bamburgh, was given rectangular corner turrets. The most telling analogy, however, is the entrance to the keep, which, like its counterpart at Bamburgh, was at the north end of the east face at ground-floor level, without a forebuilding, and set within a single-storey, stone-coped projection of the wall. Here too, access to the first-floor apartments was via a straight mural staircase ascending from a vestibule. This arrangement has a very limited and specific chronological and topographical distribution, and there is very little doubt that it had its origins as the hallmark of the Bamburgh master.

Fig. 5.8. Carlisle (Cumberland) The great tower from the east (second quarter of the twelfth century).

The Midlands: Kenilworth

One provincial master who emulated the royal great tower builders was Geoffrey de Clinton's mason at Kenilworth, where a great tower was raised in the 1120s (Fig 5.9). As sheriff of Warwickshire, de Clinton was the King's representative in the county, and his castle at Kenilworth, particularly the keep, was probably intended and seen as a symbol of royal authority. In such a case it might be expected that the keep would be modelled on royal buildings of this type; this is probably true of Kenilworth, but only up to a point. Kenilworth was a simplified imitation of the royal keeps; it rose to no more than two storeys, only one of which was residential, and the plain rectangular plan was based around the dimensions of the first-floor hall. It was on the exterior that the architect focused his efforts, where he deployed rectangular corner turrets of unusually bold projection. The only precedent for these was Colchester, and it may be from here that de Clinton's mason took his inspiration for this part of the design. The principal effects of the turrets were to inflate the apparent scale of the tower, and, in conjunction with the high splayed plinth, and the closely set pilaster buttresses that break up the intervening wall surfaces, they create a sense of massive

Fig. 5.9. Kenilworth (Warwickshire) The great tower from the south east (second quarter of the twelfth century).

solidity, and an interesting three-dimensional perspective. It was the outward effect that was important here rather than the internal plan.

Rectangular Keeps in the Reign of Henry II

Scarborough

The accession of Henry II ushered in a new period of castle building including a major series of great towers. The first of the new keeps was raised at Scarborough, on the Yorkshire coast, during the period 1158–1169. The name of the architect is unknown, but what we can say is that despite having some superficial similarities to the Bamburgh school in its nearly square plan, high splayed (though plain) plinth and pilaster buttressing, it nevertheless represents a quite different sphere of influence, being heavily dependent on royal and baronial works in the south and east of England. It has a much smaller footprint, is taller, and it eschews the arrangement of ground-floor entrance and straight mural staircase that is one of the most distinctive aspects of Bamburgh, in favour of a first-floor entrance approached through a forebuilding, following the example of Norwich and Castle Rising; this latter arrangement was something new for the north. The external aesthetics were addressed through the articulating buttresses, shafted angles (as at Castle Rising), and by the regularly arranged fenestration. This comprised shafted twin-light openings recessed beneath a larger arch, the type of arrangement already noted at the White Tower and at Norwich.

Following the precedent set at Norwich, the interior was divided by a central spine wall, a trait that had also been taken up by the architects of Portchester and Rochester keeps. However, at Scarborough, the builder followed the unusual expedient of making the first-floor division in the form of a great arch. This was not entirely new, a single arch like that at Scarborough, having been used to great architectural effect in the upper hall of Hedingham keep *c.* 1142. At Hedingham, where the arch cleared a span of nearly 9 m (30 ft), it helped to support the roof, but at Scarborough, where the span was nearly as wide, it also seems to have carried a solid spine wall on the next storey. This structural principle, is derived from ecclesiastical architecture, particularly the great church crossing arches that reached comparable widths to those bridged at Hedingham and Scarborough, and which were used to support the walls of a central tower.

Richard Wolveston
Soon after work had begun on the construction of the Scarborough keep, Hugh du Puiset, bishop of Durham, rebuilt the great tower of Norham (1157–1174). Du Puiset was a well-travelled and significant architectural patron, responsible, amongst other works, for the Galilee chapel in Durham Cathedral and the upper storey of the north range in Durham Castle. His master builder for Norham was Richard Wolveston of Durham, who enlarged

Fig. 5.10. Norham (Northumberland) The south-east elevation of the great tower attributed to Richard Wolveston. The greater part of the stonework in this elevation dates from the third quarter of the twelfth century, but the tower has been subjected to fifteenth century rebuilding (left) and heightening.

an existing keep, built by Bishop Flambard *c.* 1121, to create a double-pile plan measuring 25.6 x 18.3 m (60 x 84 ft) in which the eastern end of the southern component rose above the main body of the two-storey main block by at least another storey (Fig 5.10). The parallels for this unusual design have been sought in the carefully planned accommodation provided for other twelfth-century bishops.[27]

Wolveston was also connected with another great tower in the north of England that may have had some similarities to Norham. In 1171, one 'Ricardus ingeniator' was working on the keep of Bowes, for the King, a building that was still under construction in 1179 (Fig 5.11). It must surely be significant that at Bowes, Wolveston built a keep of almost exactly the same length and width as the keep at Norham; if one was based on the other then the assumption must be that Norham came first, because at Norham he was constrained by having to incorporate the earlier tower. It is clear that the two surviving storeys of the Bowes keep were each divided by a crosswall into two rooms of unequal size, evidently a hall (east) and chamber (west) at first-floor level. The ruined state of Bowes means a degree of uncertainty about the original form of the building above the first-floor, but one interpretation suggests that its chamber (western) end rose higher than the rest of the building, as in the southern component of the Norham keep.[28] It is a moot point whether this asymmetry can be associated with Richard Wolveston in particular, but nothing of the kind has been recorded in contemporary royal keeps,[29] and it may perhaps be indicative of a personal or regional preference.[30]

Fig. 5.11. Bowes (Yorkshire) The great tower of c. 1171 by Richard Wolveston from the south east; the foundations of the forebuilding in the foreground gave access to the prominent first-floor entrance to the right (north).

Some 18 miles to the south-east of Bowes is the near contemporary keep of Middleham. This is a much larger structure, with a footprint nearly twice the size as those of Norham and Bowes, but then it did serve as the principal residence of the lord of Middleham, rather than a royal outpost or an episcopal border fortress. Although diagnostic details are few, the vaulting of the basement has affinities with Bamburgh and Norham (see pp. 70–71), and there are analogies with Bowes in the stepped and chamfered plinth and the external staircase to the first-floor entrance. This latter arrangement was probably also a feature of Norham, although no structural evidence has survived the partial destruction of the keep. Potentially, Middleham is another building by Richard Wolveston.

Maurice the Mason

Contemporary with the construction of Bowes was a major building programme at Newcastle (1168–78), which included a new keep (Fig 5.12). If the Durham engineer, Richard Wolveston, was favoured by the crown at Bowes, then he might seem to have been the obvious choice for Newcastle as well, which was, after all, closer to Durham than was Bowes. Newcastle, however, is attributed to a mason (*cementarius*) called Maurice on the grounds of a payment recorded on the pipe roll for 1174–1175. The extent of Maurice's involvement in the works at Newcastle cannot be deduced from this single reference. It comes late in the construction sequence, coinciding with the resumption of building operations after a hiatus caused by the invasion of the Scots in 1174, but his remit at this stage would have included the completion of the partially constructed keep, on which the first expenditure was recorded in 1171–1172 and the last in 1175–1176.

Fig. 5.12. Newcastle (Northumberland) The south elevation of the great tower raised by the master mason, Maurice, in the 1170s, with the forebuilding to the right (east).

Subsequently, a Maurice (*ingeniator*) appears in the pipe rolls pertaining to the works at Dover Castle. The rebuilding of Dover Castle was in hand from 1180 with the keep being raised between 1181 and 1187, a period that coincides with the references to Maurice (Fig 5.13). Although the keeps of Newcastle and Dover are vastly different in scale, two features of particular interest provide an architectural link between the two buildings and suggest that they were designed by the same hand. The first of these is the long staircase approach to a second-floor entrance contained within a strongly defended forebuilding. The second is the well rising through the building, which could be drawn only at second-floor level, and its associated system of lead piping that was used to conduct water to two other parts of the

Fig. 5.13. Dover (Kent) Maurice's great tower of the 1180s from the north.

building. The significance of these two features as diagnostic traits associated with Maurice is magnified by their extreme rarity.

While second-floor keep entrances are not encountered anywhere else in England, there is a twelfth-century parallel in France in the donjon of Arques-la-Bataille, a building raised under the auspices of Henry I in the 1120s, and the interest of this donjon is compounded by the design of its forebuilding, which, like that of Dover, is wrapped around the corner of the building. Here too a well rose through the building to the second floor. Normandy was, of course, a possession of the English crown, and it is not improbable that the castle was known to Maurice, and that these aspects were developed at Dover, some sixty years later. If Arques was a source for Dover and Newcastle, so too may have been the White Tower. Interestingly, one particular feature of the White Tower that was emulated at Newcastle and Dover was the screenwall that rose above the roofline, and which contained a continuous mural gallery.

It is probably true to say that the sources of the Newcastle keep depend on the origins of its architect. Maurice's later association with Dover might suggest that he was a member of the royal school of masons based in the south-east sent to take charge of the resumption of work on Newcastle in the aftermath of the Scottish invasion. However, there are a number of reasons for supposing that a northerner might have been involved in the design of that keep. One is the vaulted basement, an unusual feature in early keeps, but one that is much more prevalent in the north of England. The three lengths of straight mural staircase that are to be found in the keep (one abandoned) also belong to a northern tradition. Both features are also found in Bamburgh, in the light of which it may not be unreasonable to suggest that the external gallery of Newcastle was also derived from Bamburgh rather the White Tower. The Newcastle chapel also follows its Bamburgh counterpart in extending across the full length of the keep and in being divided into three structural bays. We know, also, from the case of Richard Wolveston, that locally based master builders might be recruited to undertake important royal works.

In considering the origins of Maurice, it is worth noting that two villages close to Bamburgh, Ellingham (6 miles) and Eglingham (11 miles), both have churches that are dedicated to St Maurice (at Ellingham there is also a St Maurice's well). This is a very rare dedication in England, and the presence of two such instances so close together implies that this location had a particular affinity with the saint, and that he may have provided a local source of inspiration for the naming of baby boys. If Maurice the mason was a northerner, then he might have had his origins in one of these two settlements. In which case, it is quite possible that he might have gained work experience at Bamburgh, specifically on the keep, on which work was being carried out in 1163–1164, only shortly before the Newcastle keep was begun.

One other aspect of great tower building that must be taken into account in this reflection on Maurice and his origins, is that the majority of significant rectangular keeps to be built during the reign of Henry II were in the north of England. Dover was something of an anomaly in being both the first and last royal great tower of rectangular plan to be built by the Henry in the south-east. Regardless of the purpose of Dover, and to whom the design should be attributed, it is a fact that the most recent antecedents of its form were all to be found in the north of England, even though they may have been smaller in scale. It is therefore more likely that the craftsmen experienced in such projects by the time Dover came to be built would, in some measure, have had northern backgrounds.

Chapter 6

Great Tower Builders Part 2: *c.* 1100–1500

France 1100–1190

Dover brought to an end the sequence of great rectangular keeps that, in England, had begun with Colchester and the White Tower in the reign of William I, and whose antecedents stretch back to the tenth century in continental Europe. However, different forms of great tower had been built for decades before the construction of Dover, the most successful of which was based on the cylinder. Although a tradition of building cylindrical church towers had existed in northern Germany and England since the tenth or eleventh century, the origins of the cylindrical donjon are probably to be found in France in the late eleventh or early twelfth century. One of the earliest is believed to be Fréteval near Vendôme (Loir-et-Cher), which is thought to date from *c.* 1100.

Geometrically more complex plans are to be found within an interesting group of early to mid twelfth-century donjons clustered within a 50-mile radius of Paris. Houdan, which lies approximately 32 miles to the west of Paris, was probably raised, from *c.* 1120, by Amaury III de Montfort, count of Évreux (Fig 6.1). The plan of the donjon is based on a 16 m (52.5 ft) diameter circle with a 4.8 m (16 ft) diameter semi-circular turret at each of the four cardinal points, and a 9.2 m (30 ft) square interior with canted corners. The existence of the orientating turrets and the fact that the interior plan is square suggest that the builder was reluctant to make too radical a departure from the rectangularity of most early great towers, and emphasizes the point of just how revolutionary the cylindrical tower was as a domestic building and how disconcerting it might have been to those of a conservative disposition.

Elements of rectangularity and circularity were also combined in the donjon of Amblény, in Picardy (Aisne), some 50 miles to the north-west of Paris, which was probably built by Drogon II lord of Pierrefonds, perhaps *c.* 1150.[1] The plan comprises a rectangular main block with a 7.5 m (25 ft) diameter circular turret at each corner. In common with Houdan, the corners of the interior are canted. At the design stage the architect probably constructed a rectangle approximately 9 x 7.5 m (25 x 29 ft) to represent the interior and then struck the four circles for the turrets from the corners using radii equal to half the width of the figure. In practice, however, the building is not quite so regular as the geometrical theory behind its plan would have allowed, a circumstance that is probably to be explained by the failure of the builder to adhere strictly to the brief.

The architects of Houdan and Amblény were both attempting to reconcile the fashionable circle with the traditional rectangle. No such conflict of purpose can be discerned in the donjon at the royal castle of Étampes, even though it appears to be a development of Houdan in particular (Fig 6.2). Built either by Louis VI or Louis VII in the 1130s–1140s, the use of the circle in great tower planning was taken a step further by the creation of a quatrefoil design from which all rectangularity was expunged. The plan was based on a circle of approximately 24.4m (80ft) in diameter within which four smaller circles, with radii of a little under 7 m

Fig. 6.1. Houdan (Yvelines) The donjon from the east (first half of the twelfth century).

(23 ft) were inscribed to constitute the outer faces of the lobes. Étampes had no obvious progeny in France, although it was to have major influence on the thirteenth-century keep of York (see pp. 126–127).

The most recent of the buildings that make up this grouping is the Tour de César of Provins (Fig 3.9). Situated approximately 50 miles to the south-west of Paris, it was probably built by Henry I, count of Champagne, soon after 1152. Despite the architect using an octagon, rather than a circle, as the main component of the plan, there are some particularly striking points of resemblance to Houdan. The plan was based on a 17 m (57 ft) square, now represented by the plinth. As at Houdan and Amblény, there was a large rounded turret at each of the four corners but set within the angles of the main square rather than being struck from them. These have 4.8 m (16 ft) diameters, the same as those at Houdan. The octagonal interior of Provins is irregular, having shorter diagonals, and so resembles the canted square that formed the internal plan of Houdan. In fact, the dimensions of the underlying squares on which the two internal plans are based are almost the same at 8.3–9.1 m (29–30 ft). These correlations of size give reason to suppose that Houdan, whose lords, the Montforts, were Henry of Champagne's kinsmen, served as a model for the architect of Provins.

Fig. 6.2. Étampes (Essone) The Tour de Guinette from the south west (*c*. 1130).

The main storey of the Tour de César is covered by a sail vault carried on four great squinch arches that spring from central points in four of the walls (see p. 71, figs 3.9 and 4.18). This vault seems to bear no relation to the underlying building, but in geometrical terms it is a logical continuation of the manner in which the tower has been planned. The starting point for the construction of the plan is a square now represented by the plinth; superimposing a second square at an angle of 45 degrees gave the layout of the octagonal tower; the vault represents a smaller square also at an angle of 45 degrees, and so reflects the underlying rationale of the design. There were smaller vaults covering the trapezoidal spaces between the arches and the inner walls of the interior.

In the combined use of the circle and the square in formulating the plan, the shared dimensions, and the manner in which the elements of the plan are disposed, these four towers form a coherent architectural group. As they all lie within a 50-mile radius of Paris, a reasonable supposition might be that they represent a regional school of architecture centred on the city. The date range of *c*. 1120–1160 could have been spanned by the career of an individual master builder, certainly by two generations of the same family or craft school.

This group of buildings represents a search for a new aesthetic that was characterized by a receptiveness to unconventional forms and a delight in geometrical confections. The future, however, lay with less complex plans, specifically the circle, which, by the end of the twelfth century had become the standard form of great tower plan in France. The donjons built by Henry of Champagne's brothers Theobald (Thibaut) V, count of Blois and Stephen (Etienne), lord of Sancerre at Châteaudun (*c.* 1170–1190) and Châtillon-Coligny (*c.* 1180–1190) respectively, were in the first case (Châteaudun) uncompromisingly cylindrical, and in the second case (Châtillon-Coligny) sixteen-sided on a circular base. These two buildings, which appear to emulate Provins in their emphatic use of domed vaulting (see above, Chapter 4), are sufficiently close in concept, form and geographical proximity (approximately 70 miles apart) to have been the product of the same master builder.

England 1140–1190

East Anglia

William d'Albini's great tower of New Buckenham (Norfolk) is generally considered to be the earliest cylindrical keep in England with a probable construction date of 1138–1146. Diagnostic features are few, but the presence of a central crosswall marks the building out as having a structural relationship with its rectangular counterparts (for example, the keep of William d'Albini's own Castle Rising), and suggests a builder who had a greater familiarity with more conventional keeps than of circular towers on this scale. The crosswall may have been intended as a structural expedient in order to tie the building together, but it probably also had something to do with the anticipated method of flooring and roofing the building (see p. 42).

Where the inspiration for a cylindrical keep came from is uncertain; the fashion in England at the time was for rectangular keeps; indeed, as already described (see pp. 98–99), this same William d'Albini built one at Castle Rising *c.* 1138. It has been pointed out that East Anglia was a region with a tradition of building cylindrical bell towers, a practice owed to a lack of good quality building stone, and a consequent reliance on locally procured flint, a material that does not lend itself well to producing angles. It is certainly true that New Buckenham lies within an area in which cylindrical church towers are concentrated, demonstrating that this building tradition was established and current, when the keep came to be built.[2]

While the keep at New Buckenham may have represented this tradition for practical reasons, it is interesting to consider that it may also have been a deliberate evocation of the local vernacular in order to make a direct comparison of stature between d'Albini's castle and the churches of his estates, for despite being a product of regional building practices, the keep also represents a new departure. This is because one of its most striking characteristics is its great size, the external diameter of approximately 20.5 m (67 ft) being between two and five times bigger than those of the bell towers.[3] It is also larger than any cylindrical castle tower that had so far been built in France, and its diameter would not be surpassed until the thirteenth century.[4]

D'Albini's innovatory new tower did not set a trend; his cousin Hugh Bigod, earl of Norfolk, for instance, built a rectangular keep at his castle of Bungay, 15 miles to the east of New Buckenham, in the 1160s. Perhaps its uncompromising plan, however familiar to the inhabitants of East Anglia, was something that the rest of the kingdom was not quite ready for. Although Henry II's new keep at Orford, built between 1165 and 1173, was also based on a circle, it was heavily disguised, for despite having a circular interior, the exposed parts of the exterior are faceted to give it the appearance of a polygonal building (Fig 6.3).[5] Three rectangular turrets clasp the main block and rise above it, suggesting that the important thing was the central plan rather than a specific outward form. The turrets, together with the rectangular forebuilding, partially obscure the core and distract from it, though the combined massing of the various components produces a striking overall effect.

Fig. 6.3. Orford (Suffolk) The keep from the south west (third quarter of the twelfth century).

Although we do not know the name of the architect of Orford we cannot doubt that he was a man of consummate skill. Ailnoth the engineer, who held royal office from 1157–1190, has long been considered a candidate,[6] and although the attribution has no tangible evidential basis, a number of significant circumstances might be cited in support of the idea. Firstly, as keeper of Westminster Palace, Ailnoth was a trusted royal servant with a responsibility for architectural works, particularly domestic buildings. It is also the case that his skills were utilized at several other royal residences besides Westminster,[7] including Windsor Castle, where he was present on a number of occasions between 1166 and 1173.[8] Ailnoth is also known to have made at least one excursion to Suffolk, in 1174, when he took men to demolish the earl of Norfolk's castles of Framlingham and Walton in the aftermath of his rebellion. This Suffolk connection is one reason to believe that Ailnoth might also have an architectural role at Orford.[9] The association with Windsor is particularly interesting because the project there involved the construction of a courtyard house in the upper ward and the reconstruction of the defences in stone; it therefore had important elements of both domestic and defensive character. In other words, it was a development of a similar type to Orford, even if it was on a larger scale and the residential centrepiece took a different form.

The North

A near contemporary building to Orford is Conisbrough, which contains the earliest datable English cylindrical keep after New Buckenham (Fig 6.4). The castle was built by Henry II's half-brother, Hamelin, an illegitimate son of Geoffrey Plantagenet, who, in 1164, married the Warenne heiress, Isabella, adopted the Warenne family name, and took the title earl of

Fig. 6.4. Conisbrough (Yorkshire) The keep from the west (third quarter of the twelfth century).

Surrey. Hamelin died in 1202, and the tower falls into the date range *c*.1165–1190, based on the transitional foliage sculpture in the chapel. The great tower is unique in being surrounded by six wedge-shaped buttress turrets. One of the turrets houses the chapel at second-floor level, but otherwise they are solid, except at roof level. If their main function was not to provide extra accommodation capacity, they may have had an aesthetic purpose, although a plain cylinder would have been equally and probably more effective than the present building. The solid nature of the Conisbrough turrets engenders the view that the prime motive was either to create an architectural effect, or to provide structural supports for a tower of unfamiliar character. A sense of uncertainty about the structure extends to the internal doorframes, which have clearly been designed for a flat, rather than curved, wall interior, an indication, perhaps, that the original intention was to construct the interior of the keep to a polygonal or rectangular plan, and that the final form of the keep was only determined after some serious deliberation.

The geometrical basis of the plan of Conisbrough – a series of circles and the related construction of a regular hexagon for setting out the buttress turrets – contains some of the essential qualities of the Orford keep, and although in that case the clasping turrets are rectangular rather than wedge-shaped, the general principle is similar, and it would not be unreasonable on this basis alone, to suggest that a designer with the same mindset was at work, and, by extension, given the royal connection, that the same architect may have had an involvement in the design of both buildings. This group of circle-based designs with royal associations may be extended to include an eleven-sided great tower that crowned the motte of the royal castle of Tickhill Castle, in Yorkshire, 6 miles to the south-east of Conisbrough, on which work was being carried out in 1178 and 1180. Here at Tickhill, the circular plinth on which the (now demolished) tower was built emphasizes the geometrical derivation of the form. The tower itself appears to have been without a forebuilding or other projections except for a buttress at each angle.

The detailing of both Conisbrough and Orford might be described as Transitional, but although there is a degree of similarity in some areas, there is a profound variance in others, suggesting the hands of quite different craftsmen. Thus, Orford is provided with numerous square-headed windows set beneath semi-circular relieving arches; although Conisbrough is not so copiously fenestrated, it too has windows of this description. At Conisbrough, however, the profiles of the relieving arches are followed through in the barrel-vaulting of the window embrasures. This is in contrast to Orford, where the windows are set within pointed embrasures. Indeed, Orford's frequent (though not exclusive) use of the pointed arch, which is absent from Conisbrough, distinguishes Orford as

Fig. 6.5. Barnard Castle (Durham) The great tower from the north (last decade of the twelfth century).

architecturally more advanced; other such indications are the stylized nature of the shaftless trumpet capitals at the main entrance to the tower from the forebuilding, which suggest a craftsman of considerable originality, and the rather unusual nature of the joggled triangular arch over the main, first-floor, entrance to the building. Of the two, Conisbrough, wherever it falls within its stylistic date range, is the more old-fashioned in its detailing, and Orford the more forward looking. If the same architect had a hand in both buildings, a conclusion that might be drawn from these contrasting details is that not all aspects of design were the exclusive preserve of the architect.

One other cylindrical great tower begun in northern England before the end of the twelfth century is the Round Tower at Barnard Castle (Co. Durham), which dates from *c.* 1190 (Fig 6.5).[10] The proportions are modest with an external diameter of about 11 m (36 ft) and a height of about 12 m (40 ft) towards the courtyard. Like the builder of Conisbrough and the designers of several other northern English twelfth-century keeps, the architect of the Round Tower eschewed the vice in favour of the mural stair that followed the line of the walls. In addition, the Round Tower formed part of the defensive circuit, a fairly unusual arrangement, but one that is shared with the keep of Conisbrough. At Conisbrough, the main motivation seems to have been to ensure that the latrines discharged outside the courtyard; this was also an object in the disposition of the Round Tower, but the boldness of its projection in front of the curtain contrasts with the diffidence of the arrangement at Conisbrough, and the generous provision of arrow loops shows that it was clearly intended to play a part in defence.

Other polygonal great towers

In the south-east the main work of this period was Henry II's keep at Chilham (Kent) of the 1170s,[11] a building of octagonal plan with a degree of resemblance to Orford, though it was built on a smaller scale, having an external width of 13 m (42 ft). The polygonal plan recalls the faceting of Orford's main block and the projecting rectangular turret containing the main staircase echoes the staircase turret of Orford; in addition, like its counterpart at Orford, the turret had a forebuilding attached to one side. There is, therefore, enough detail to conclude that Orford influenced Chilham. Nevertheless, the geometry of Chilham's plan is quite different, for while it is possible to construct a regular octagon from a circle using a pair of compasses and a straight edge, techniques published in the medieval period suggest that it more usual to base it on a square.[12] Whatever the design technique, Chilham is an altogether simpler and less inventive building. The King's mason, Ralph, who was at Chilham in 1172, may have been the designer. We know very little about Master Ralph, but he worked on at least two other royal castles: Dover in 1170–1171 and 1181–1182, where he was probably employed on the walls, and possibly the keep, and Winchester (Hampshire) in 1174–1175.

Octagonal great towers are rare, but King John was to build one at Odiham sometime between 1207 and 1215 and another was built on top of the motte of Richard's Castle (Herefordshire), only slightly wider than Chilham at 13.4 m (44 ft). The excavators of Richard's Castle dated this building to the late twelfth century on architectural grounds, although it has not been proved whether it pre-dates or post-dates Chilham.

France: 1190–1250

Beaked towers

In a few instances, the cylindrical form was modified with a prow, or beak to create a revolutionary almond-shaped plan. One of the earliest is the donjon of *c.* 1190 at La Roche-Guyon in the French Vexin, where the castle occupies a cliff-top position above the Seine, close to the border with Normandy, then part of the Angevin domains. This type, which was clearly related to defence (see Chapter 7 below), was reproduced in a more elegant form at Richard the Lionheart's castle of Château Gaillard (1196–1198), in the Norman Vexin, some 17 miles to the north-east, which occupies a similar position above the Seine (Fig 6.6). Otherwise, the type had limited popularity in western Europe although it was better received within the domains of the Empire, where several great towers with almond-shaped plans were built during the course of the thirteenth-century.[13]

Fig. 6.6. Château Gaillard (Ain) The great tower from the south east (1196–1198).

The Tours Philippiennes

The proliferation of cylindrical donjons in France is associated with Philip II Augustus (reigned 1180–1223) who built towers of this shape at Beauvais (Oise), Bourges (Cher), Cappy (Somme), Chinon (Indre-et-Loire, Fig 6.7), Compiègne (Oise), Corbeil (Essonne), Dourdan (Essonne, Fig 6.8), Falaise (Calvados), Gisors (Eure), Laon (Aisne), Lillebonne (Seine-Maritime), Montargis (Loiret), Montdidier (Somme), Orléans (Loiret), Paris (The Louvre), Peronne (Somme), Rouen (Seine-Maritme), Verneuil-sur-Avre (Eure), Vernon (Eure) and Villeneuve-sur-Yonne (Yonne) (Fig 4.5). The form was in distinct contrast to the rectangular donjons of the Norman and Angevin kings, and one reason for its promotion by the French king may have been to make a political statement of independence, a point that is forcibly underlined by the juxtaposition of the two types at Falaise.

The earliest of the group was the Louvre, built between 1190 and 1202, and one of the last was at Dourdan, which was completed shortly before 1222. So these structures were built over a period of approximately 30 years, with the majority falling within the last twenty years of Philip's reign. The *Tours Philippiennes* have a large measure of architectural uniformity, made more apparent by the simplicity of their design, which contrasts with the often sophisticated planning of the great rectangular keeps with their wall chambers and multiple staircases. The pattern was established at the Louvre, the donjon of which served as the model for the later buildings, thereby engendering a coherent architectural group

Great Tower Builders Part 2: c. 1100–1500   119

Fig. 6.7. Chinon (Indre-et-Loire) Tour de Coudray from the south east (first quarter of the thirteenth century).

Fig. 6.8. Dourdan (Essone) The donjon from the south east (first quarter of the thirteenth century).

that symbolized royal power. Apart from the cylindrical form, common features are the good quality freestone masonry, the battered plinths and the domed rib-vaulting rising to central boss or eye at the crown. Like the donjon of the Louvre, several of the towers were encircled by their own ditches and to some extent isolated from the rest of the castle.

Nevertheless, it is evident from the surviving remains that there was no very prescriptive formula, and the towers indeed embody a good deal of individuality, which implies that individual masters had a degree of autonomy. The towers ranged in diameter from 13.7 m (45 ft) to 16.8 m (55 ft). In some (eg Chinon, Dourdan, Verneuil-sur-Avre) mural staircases followed the curving line of the wall; in others the vice was used (eg Louvre, Lillebonne, Rouen, Villeneuve-sur-Yonne). Many were built with a helicoidal scaffolding system (eg Dourdan, Verneuil-sur-Avre, Villeneuve-sur-Yonne, Rouen), while others were not (Lillebonne). The impression to be gained from a comparison of the buildings is that a general directive was issued regarding the basic requirements and that the master builders were left to interpret it as they would. The simplicity of the form gave little leeway respecting the outward appearance of the towers and ensured a broad measure of unity.

Coucy and Aigues Mortes

The climax of this style occurred in Picardy, but it was under the auspices, not of the king of France as might be expected, but of Enguerrand III, lord of Coucy, who rebuilt his castle probably during the 1220s. Eclipsing all its predecessors, the Coucy donjon had an external

Fig. 6.9. Coucy (Aisne) Reconstructed section through the donjon (second quarter of the thirteenth century); from Viollet-le-Duc 1875.

diameter of 30.5 m (100 ft) and rose to a height of 55 m (180 ft) (Fig 6.9). In order to gain some perspective, we might contrast it with the keep of Conisbrough (Fig 6.4), which has an external diameter of 15.5 m (51 ft) and which was approximately 28 m (92 ft) high, and is, in fact, smaller than one of the wall towers of the inner ward at Coucy.

Enguerrand's donjon was set within its own ditch, the outer side of which was enclosed by the curtain wall. Above the battered base of the tower were three storeys of apartments; the ground-floor entrance level was situated some 5 m (16 ft) above the bottom of the surrounding ditch. Stability lay partly in the strength of the 7.5 m (25 ft) thick walls, but also in the elaborate system of vaulting and arcading. All three storeys were rib-vaulted, the ribs springing from the twelve angles of the dodecagonal interior, and meeting in a perforated crown rather than a single keystone. The ribs were buttressed internally by wedge-shaped piers, the recesses between them being linked by arches, which diverted the vertical thrust of the walls above into the buttresses and counteracted the oblique thrust from the vault.[14]

The Coucy donjon was an extremely well-planned building, whose ultimate form had been determined before work began on site, and which underwent no discernible change of plan while being raised. We do not know the name of the master builder behind its design and construction, but the very high quality of the work and the very precise manner in which it has been thought out prior to the commencement of building operations, suggests a master of the highest ability. The donjons of Philip Augustus certainly provided models from which to draw on, and a generation of craftsmen with the relevant experience for a project of this kind. Coucy, however, was on a much grander scale, and its aesthetic qualities more ostentatious than anything in Philip's repertoire of round donjons.

Various details of the donjon are suggestive of a builder familiar with the design of superior ecclesiastical architecture. The manner in which the interior of the donjon was built up in tiers of arched recesses echoes the storied main vessels of great churches. At ground- and second-floor levels the arched recesses contained galleries, those of the upper storey being connected by a mural passage that recalls a triforium. The three high pointed domical vaults, the ribs of which rose to a perforated keystone, were, in essence, adaptations of the apsidal vaults over great church sanctuaries, while the sculptural details were also of a quality and pervasiveness that might be expected in a cathedral rather than a castle. Thus, the entrance to the donjon was framed by an order of shafts with crocket capitals, and between them a frieze of crockets alternated with trefoil foliage motifs. Above the entrance a bas-relief of a knight engaged in combat with a lion was framed by a hollow border containing onlooking figures and, beyond, a hoodmould of floral crockets. Inside, the vaulting shaft capitals were also crocketed, those of the ground floor being surmounted by further figure sculpture. Around the top of the donjon was a two-tier crocketed cornice, and surmounting the parapet coping were four crocketed pinnacles, both features that evoke ecclesiastical, rather than castle, architecture.

When Enguerrand III began his great donjon at Coucy, work was proceeding on one of the greatest of French cathedrals, at Amiens (Somme), some 60 miles to the north-west. Here, in 1220, the master mason, Robert de Luzarches, had begun the creation of a structural masterpiece with a pronounced verticality (whose height was to surpass that of any previous church), in which every part of the architectural jigsaw was accurately planned and assembled. These qualities were shared by Enguerrand's donjon at Coucy, the creation of which is to be viewed against an architectural background of intellect, precision and a desire to push against the boundary of possibility, as manifested at Amiens. That Enguerrand was aware of the Amiens project and sought to emulate the audacity of the building's scale is suggested by the fact that the height of his tower was approximately the same as that of the nave roof ridge, and its outer radius the same as that of the apsidal eastern termination of the choir. It is probable that in building his castle Enguerrand took advantage of the technological expertise with which Amiens and other great church projects were endowed, and employed a master builder from the highest ranks of the profession.

The high quality and ambitious scale of the building work at Coucy must have gained the castle a degree of celebrity at the time. Did it have much influence on later thirteenth-century castle architecture? Something of the donjon's character, albeit on a smaller scale, is certainly to be found at the Tour de Constance at Aigues Mortes (Gard). This is a great tower of two storeys over a small basement built by Louis IX *c.* 1250. At 30.5 m (100 ft) high and 22 m (72 ft) in diameter its proportions are less generous than those of Coucy, but more so than the donjons of Philip Augustus. Like the donjon of Coucy, the rooms of the Tour de Constance have high twelve-ribbed vaults rising to a perforated keystone, and the ground storey repeats the unusual feature of a mural gallery, allowing access to openings above the chamber.

Scotland in the 1240s

In 1239 Enguerrand's daughter, Marie de Coucy, married Alexander II, King of Scotland, an event that has prompted speculation regarding the influence of Coucy on Scottish castles in the years immediately following.[15] Historically, the most promising case for evidence of this seems to be that of Dirleton (East Lothian), which was rebuilt by the Queen's steward, John de Vaux, from *c.* 1240. The surviving work from the de Vaux period is concentrated at the south-west corner of the quadrilateral enclosure, where it forms an informal grouping of towers dominated by a cylindrical keep, which formed the nucleus of de Vaux's private apartments (Fig 6.10). Architecturally, the initial impressions are not very suggestive of influence from France, but closer examination gives some reason to believe that French precedents may have played a part in the design of Dirleton.

Although the highly unusual bunching of towers at the south-west angle, recalls the tower clusters of the 1220s at Dover (see

Fig. 6.10. Dirleton (East Lothian) The great tower from the east (second quarter of the thirteenth century).

p. 154), there was also a roughly contemporary instance of this arrangement at the Château de Folie at Braine (Aisne). Braine is in Picardy, only 25 km to the south-east of Coucy. The coincidence takes on a greater resonance when considering the interior of the keep, the two surviving storeys of which are irregularly polygonal in plan. On each floor the most striking feature is a high domed vault with applied ribs springing from the angles of the room. Precedents are hard to come by in Britain, but vaulting is commonly found in early thirteenth-century French donjons, including Coucy, which, given the soaring proportions of its vaults, is a particularly credible source for Dirleton. Where Dirleton differs from French practice, however, is that the ribs are purely decorative, and structural integrity lies in the self-supporting dome. If de Vaux's work at Dirleton was partly based on French antecedents, then the influence was second-hand in its nature and anecdotal rather than technical. This work is a Scottish craftsman's interpretation of a distant Gallic model with the intention of creating a similar effect, rather than the replication of a structural trait.

More convincing as a direct recipient of French influence is the great tower of Kildrummy (Aberdeenshire), known as the Snow Tower, which was probably built by Gilbert of Moray, bishop of Caithness before 1245. Like the keep of Dirleton, the Snow Tower has a diameter of approximately 15.25 m (50 ft), and although it is now reduced to basement level, formerly rose through five storeys.[16] Each of the floors was covered by a domed vault, pierced at the crown by a circular eye, in this respect following French practice as manifested at Coucy and being replicated slightly later in the Tour de Constance. A mural gallery ran all around the wall of the second storey, a feature that was also an important characteristic of Coucy and the Tour de Constance.

The third Scottish castle dating from around the 1240s that may be considered to have benefitted from French influence, especially that of Coucy, is Bothwell (Lanarkshire), which was raised by the Moray family from 1242. One of the most significant attributes of the keep is its unusually generous diameter of 65 ft, a dimension that surpassed those of all other buildings of its type in Scotland; in this respect it mirrors the donjon of Coucy, which exceeded the size of all previous French donjons. Also like its counterpart at Coucy, and unusually for a British castle, the Bothwell keep was set within its own ditch, albeit interrupted by the curtain, and entered across a drawbridge at first-floor level. It further resembled Coucy in having a polygonal interior, although it was octagonal, rather than dodecagonal. There are also signs that the first-floor entrance hall was covered with a ribbed vault, but in this case a timber structure imitating stone,[17] another instance of imitating an effect rather than reproducing a structure.

Circle-Based Keep Designs in Wales and England 1200–1300

In the early thirteenth century the initiative for great tower building was with the nobility rather than the king. The greatest concentration of cylindrical keeps in Britain is in Wales and the Marches. One of the earliest is Pembroke, built for William Marshal, who was invested as earl of Pembroke in 1199 and acquired Pembroke itself shortly afterwards. He died in 1219. The keep is about 16 m (53 ft) in diameter and rises to a height of 24 m (80 ft); it sits on a plinth with an arching profile and has two offsets marking the upper floor levels (Fig 6.11). The first-floor entrance was approached by a flight of stone steps; directly above it a window of two lancet lights with dog-tooth mouldings proclaims the keep to be a

Fig. 6.11. Pembroke (Pembrokeshire) The great tower raised for William Marshall with the remains of the inner gateway or Horseshoe Tower in the foreground (early thirteenth century).

product of the Gothic age, and introduces an element of domestic charm into its otherwise severe appearance. The keep would have had a rather different aspect when its upper parts were intact. Not only was it crowned by a timber hoarding, the sockets for which survive, but it was capped by a dome that rose above the tops of the walls and was encircled by a second line of battlements that overlooked the hoarding. Architecturally, the arrangement provided greater visual interest and balance than is evident today.

A more compact building is the keep of Longtown, which was probably built by Walter de Lacy between 1189, when he succeeded to the family estates and 1241 when he died, perhaps the most promising period for the date of construction being 1216–1223, when he was sheriff of Hereford and resident in England, having been deprived of his Irish estates. The two-storey tower surmounts a motte and, like Pembroke, had a high battered plinth extending to entrance level. The plan is based on a 13.7m (45 ft) diameter circle, from which three regularly spaced small rounded turrets project (south, north-west and north-east). In drawing up the plan the architect would have constructed an equilateral triangle within the circle in order to position the turrets, a technique previously used by the architect of the Orford Keep for the same purpose.[18] The Orford turrets had clear functions: containing the main staircase and some of the domestic accommodation. At Longtown the role of their less emphatic counterparts seems to have been to provide localized thickenings of the wall to counteract three weak points. Thus, the south turret marks the position of the spiral staircase, the north-east tower that of the fireplace and flue, and the north-west tower that of a mural latrine.

Turrets like these, though not repeated in such quantity, were a characteristic of a small number of other thirteenth-century round keeps including those built at Caldicot for either Henry de Bohun (d. 1220) or his son Humphrey (d. 1275), earls of Hereford; Skenfrith for Hubert de Burgh (soon after 1219); and further afield at Chartley (Staffordshire) for Ranulf de Blundeville, earl of Chester, c. 1220. The turrets contained a latrine at Caldicot, and a staircase at Skenfrith. These towers, with their marcher lord owners and close proximity in date form a coherent architectural group. Another Staffordshire round keep, raised by Ranulph de Blundeville's brother-in-law, William Ferrers, earl of Derby, at his neighbouring castle of Tutbury sometime between 1190 and 1247, has been lost, but given the personal connection between the owners there is a possibility that it too belonged to this regional grouping.[19]

Ranulph de Blundeville's keep at Chartley was approximately 17m (55ft) in diameter, and at the time of its construction, Chartley was one of the larger cylindrical keeps in France, England and Wales, with a diameter comparable to those of Pembroke and the Louvre. As we have seen, however, the erection of Coucy was to show the way for the more ambitious castle builders to operate on a grander scale. Bothwell is one British example, but the concept was also embraced by English builders of the mid thirteenth century, notably in Yorkshire, where the circle formed the basis for a small group of motte-sited keeps at Sandal, Pontefract and York.

Sandal Castle, near Wakefield, was rebuilt in stone during the course of the thirteenth century under William de Warenne, 5th earl of Surrey (d. 1240) and his son, John, the 6th earl (d. 1304). The keep was one of the first elements to be built.[20] Demolished in the seventeenth century, it comprised an 24.7 m (81 ft) diameter cylindrical tower with four protruding turrets of semi-circular plan. Three of these turrets correspond with the cardinal points north, east and west, while the fourth lies to the southwest of the western turret with which it flanks the entrance to the keep. These two, together with the western turret, were semicircular, but the northern turret, which was rebuilt, was semi-decagonal. The excavators of the castle believed that the original intention was to dispose the turrets regularly, but that this plan was changed in order to provide a more strongly defended, and perhaps architecturally imposing, entrance. Had the original plan been carried through, the tower would have had a resemblance to that of the early twelfth-century donjon at Houdan, although the core tower at Houdan is considerably smaller in diameter at 16 m (52.5 ft). Indeed, the diameter of the Sandal keep was unprecedentedly large in Britain, and it is uncertain whether it formed a solid tower or whether it was more akin to a shell keep with a central light well.

The second of these motte-sited keeps is at Pontefract, which lies some 9 miles to the east of Sandal. The keep dates from the first half of the thirteenth century. The chronology of the Pontefract keep is uncertain, but it was probably raised during the 1220s or 1230s, by John de Lacy, who, in 1232, became 3rd earl of Lincoln in the right of his wife, the niece and heiress of Ranulph de Blundeville. Like its counterpart at Sandal, the basis of the Pontefract keep seems to have been a cylinder – only slightly smaller in diameter at 23.5 m (77 ft) – with semi-circular turret projections. At Pontefract, however, the turrets were of an indeterminate number. Leland's observation that the tower was 'cast ynto 6. roundelles, 3. bigge and 3. smaul' is too inexact to be very helpful.[21] The surviving remains include the bases of three such projections (south, east and west) somewhat irregular in size and disposition, which give no clear indication of the original arrangement of the whole. Although several depictions of the keep prior to its destruction, in 1649, show it as a cluster of rounded turrets, it has not yet been possible to confirm the character of the original ground plan. What the remains do tell us, however, is that the designer's use of the projecting turret was less constrained than in previous examples and that he seems to have had an informal approach to their arrangement. The three surviving lobes formed part of the inner enceinte; the southern and western lobes are hard up against one another, but the eastern lobe is isolated from the others by the curving wall of the cylindrical tower and the wall of the middle bailey. The disposition of these turrets is reminiscent of the thinking behind the clusterings of towers built at Dover in the 1220s (see p. 154).

A building that has been compared with Pontefract is the keep of York Castle (Clifford's Tower),[22] begun in 1245, though not completed until c. 1270.[23] As we have seen, the design of Clifford's Tower displays a quite different type of plan and has more in common with Sandal than Pontefract, although the ultimate inspiration of its plan is to be found in France. The design of Clifford's Tower is attributed to the king's master mason, Henry de Reyns, who was sent to York in 1245 to set the project in motion. Master Henry is largely remembered as the architect of the eastern arm of Westminster Abbey, which, as rebuilt by Henry III from 1245, is a building heavily influenced by French models, notably Reims, from where Henry de Reyns appears to have derived his name.[24] However, Henry de Reyns was also a castle builder, being the principal mason at Windsor Castle in the 1240s. The plan of the keep, which is that of a regular quatrefoil, is unique in England, and there are sound reasons for supposing that it too was inspired by French precedent, specifically, by the mid

Great Tower Builders Part 2: c. 1100–1500   127

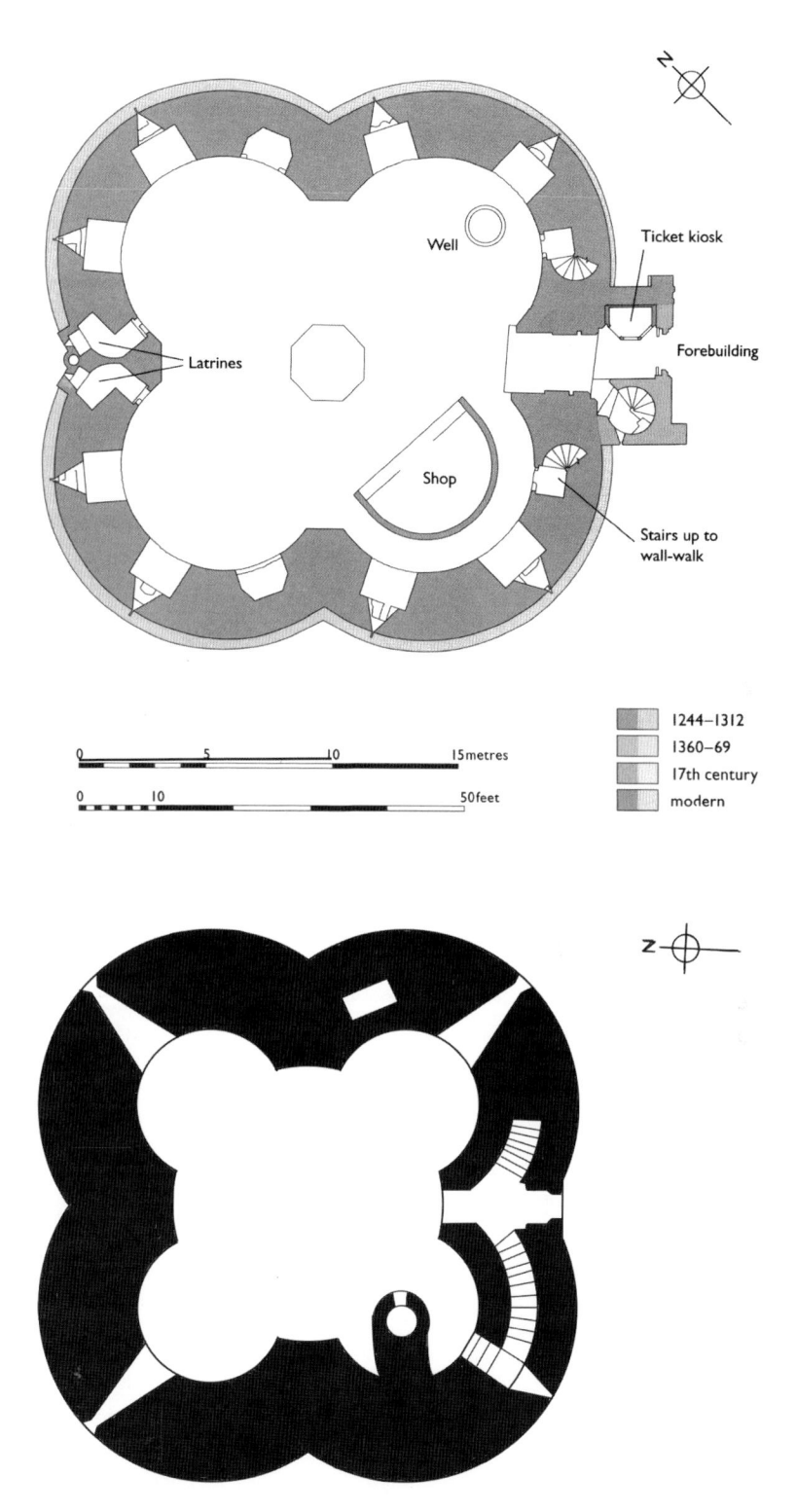

Fig. 6.12. Ground plans of the great towers of (a) York (Clifford's Tower © Historic England), and (b) Étampes (Tour de Guinette, after Viollet-le-Duc 1875), dating from 1245–c.1270 and c. 1160 respectively.

twelfth-century donjon of Étampes, known as the Tour de Guinette, despite the disparity in the dates of the two towers (Fig 6.12).

The similarity in general form alone is suggestive of a connection, but a comparison of the dimensions reinforces the probability that the plan of Clifford's Tower was derived from that of Étampes. The basis for the plans of both buildings was a 24.4 m (80 ft) diameter circle within which four smaller circles, with radii of a little under 7 m (23 ft) were inscribed to represent the outer faces of the lobes. As at Étampes the entrance of Clifford's Tower is situated at one of the points at which two lobes meet. The degree of correspondence is too great to be coincidental, and it suggests that Étampes was known to Henry de Reyns, even if only at second hand. The donjon of Étampes was old fashioned in France in the thirteenth century, but to an English mason abroad it might have seemed a highly original building worthy of recording for future reference.

Notwithstanding a relationship with Étampes, Clifford's Tower might also be seen to have analogies with Sandal. The four turrets of the latter correspond in some measure with the four lobes of Clifford's Tower, but, more significantly, the plan of Sandal also seems to be based on a 24.4 m (80 ft) diameter circle. Bearing this in mind, the brief of the king's craftsmen to consult with other masters, might very well have prompted an approach to the builder of Sandal, who was charged with a task that had much in common with that projected at York. Both projects amounted to the modernization of a motte and bailey castle through the reconstruction of its buildings in stone.

Late thirteenth-century great towers in north Wales

Another building that may be said to have had a degree of affinity with Sandal, about which more will be said anon, is the cylindrical great tower of Flint, one of the castles erected by Edward I during his subjugation of Wales. Begun in 1277, it was still under construction six years later, but at the end of the 1282 season it was given a temporary roof, and a hiatus in the building programme followed. It was only in 1286 that the temporary covering was removed and the tower received its permanent roof. It is possible that it was never completed in its intended form. The ruinous condition of the building brings with it problems of interpretation, but there is no doubt that it was a highly distinctive structure.

The keep is positioned at one corner of the castle and isolated from it by a ditch. Access was from the inner bailey across a drawbridge at mezzanine level; the entrance passage extended through the wall to a staircase leading down to the ground floor. On the left-hand (east) side of the entrance passage, a mural corridor led to a spiral staircase, which ascended to the first floor, which is where the main domestic accommodation was situated. Remains of only two storeys survive, and it is uncertain whether there was an additional floor, although the latrine shafts, of which there are four, all extend to a higher level than the first floor, suggesting that there was further domestic accommodation above or that it was intended. At ground-floor level the builders raised two concentric walls, and then vaulted the intervening space to create an intra-mural gallery from which three doorways stepped down to a circular central space. At first-floor level it is evident that the walls of the central cylinder continued upwards, and that there was a radial pattern of interconnected rooms extending around it above the ground-floor gallery. Whether the central space was a courtyard or whether it contained a single large room on each storey is uncertain. If the latter, then the ground-floor room would have been covered in a low stone dome because there are no indications of a timber floor. At basement level a central room would have received some illumination from the gallery loops, though it would, presumably have been given over to storage. At first-floor level, however, where a residential function seems likely, additional lighting would have been required, and could have been achieved by means of a clearstorey, if the wall of the central room rose above the outer wall of the tower.

The same architect was probably responsible for the cylindrical keep of Hawarden (Flintshire), some 7 miles to the south-west of Flint (Fig 6.13). This building is slightly smaller than its counterpart at Flint, having a diameter of a little over 18 m (60ft) as opposed to 21 m (69 ft), and was probably under construction by 1282. Here, too, the entrance was elevated, but in this case, by being sited on a motte; nevertheless the access pattern mirrored that of Flint, whereby the entrance passage led to the lower storey and an opening on the left-hand side of the passage communicated with a spiral staircase ascending to the upper storey. At this level a mural gallery extends around the building linking the window embrasures. It is an aspect of design that emanates from the same mindset that was behind the circular arrangement of accommodation at Flint and the mural gallery at basement level.

Precedents for the plan of the Flint keep have also been sought in British thirteenth-century shell keeps, with Restormel (Cornwall) being cited as a particularly apposite example.[25] Restormel certainly represents a similar planning principle, but because it is a much larger building with an external diameter of *c.* 38 m (125 ft), a more convincing parallel might be the great tower of Sandal, which is closer to Flint in scale and which incorporated an enigmatic concentric inner wall. As we have seen, like its counterpart at Flint, the great

Fig. 6.13. Hawarden (Flintshire) The keep from the north east (last quarter of the thirteenth century)

tower of Sandal is incompletely understood, and there is some doubt as to whether it was a solid building or whether the apartments were ranged around a central courtyard.

Notwithstanding these analogies, there are more pressing reasons to suppose that the principal sources are to be found in France. The corner position of the donjon, its isolation from the castle, and the manner in which the curtain of the inner ward follows the curving line of the keep, are indicative of French antecedents, notably the early thirteenth-century *Philippienne* castles of Lillebonne and Dourdan. A similar scheme was later adopted by Louis IX at Aigues Mortes in the juxtaposition of the Tour de Constance of *c.* 1250 and the town walls. At 21.6 m (71 ft) in external diameter, the great tower of Flint is considerably larger than most thirteenth-century round keeps, but comparable to the Tour de Constance at 21.9 m (72 ft). These similarities, coupled with the knowledge that Edward I had visited Aigues Mortes in 1270, *en route* to crusade, are good reasons for suggesting that the Tour de Constance played its part in influencing the design of Flint. Furthermore, although the circular arrangement of the accommodation that is one of the main defining aspects of Flint is not to be found in the Tour de Constance, the latter does contain a continuous mural gallery at first-floor level, thereby providing a link with Hawarden and the Flint basement gallery. This is a characteristic that has its origins in France, with a line of descent from the donjons of Châteaudun and Chatillon-Coligny via Coucy. It is a reasonable supposition that the tower was designed either by James of St Georges or by one of the foreign craftsmen that accompanied him to England and acted as his deputies.

The other main great tower built by Edward in north Wales, the Eagle Tower at Caernarfon, is something of a contrast, reviving the polygonal form that had last been used in England for King John's Odiham some 60 years previously (Fig 16.14). All the towers at Caernarfon are polygonal, but whereas most of the wall towers are based on the octagon the Eagle Tower, which also forms part of the enceinte, stands out, not only because of its greater size, but also because it has a decagonal plan, a highly unusual geometrical figure which has been used here to emphasize the tower's special status. There are other instances at Caernarfon of polygons being used in a slightly unusual way, as though the

Fig. 6.14. Caernarfon (Caernarfonshire) The Eagle Tower from the south (last quarter of the thirteenth century).

Fig. 6.15. Stokesay (Shropshire) South Tower from the south west (last decade of the thirteenth century).

designer were trying to break free of the restraints that had hitherto been imposed by more regular figures; the King's Gate and the Queen's Gate, for instance, where paired polygons are bunched together in an irregular fashion.

This tendency was taken a step further at Stokesay, where the South Tower, or keep, of *c.* 1290, raised for the wealthy wool merchant and money lender, Lawrence of Ludlow, has a unique plan based on an octagon and two smaller dodecagons integrated to form a highly innovative design (Fig 6.15). In planning this tower the master builder was pushing beyond the boundaries of a geometrically-based plan in much the same way and at much the same time as sculptors were blurring the construction lines of the monuments and buildings they embellished. The origins of this plan almost certainly lay amongst the castles of the Welsh wars, in particular, Caernarfon, begun in 1283 and the baronial castle of Denbigh (Denbighshire), which was begun in 1282, with royal support. Like Stokesay's South Tower, the Eagle Tower at Caernarfon is thrust outwards from one end of the enclosure in something of the manner of a figurehead and displays polygonal sides towards the courtyard. In these respects Stokesay appears to be modelled on Caernarfon.

The bunching together of more than one geometrical element that forms part of the concept behind the Caernarfon gateways is also evident at Denbigh, but in a much more ambitious and innovative manner (Fig 6.16). Here, the pioneering gatehouse is an amalgam of three separate polygons. In the Denbigh gatehouse we are beginning to see a more developed stage in the process that led to the design of the great tower of Stokesay a few years later. At Denbigh, the separate elements have not yet been fused to the extent that they were to be at Stokesay, but the gatehouse is a large step along the way, and very probably acted as a stage in the development of the idea behind Stokesay. In the light of these north Welsh analogues it is interesting to remember Lawrence of Ludlow's role as creditor to the King, and to consider that this might be a case of a favoured subject gaining access to the services of the royal masons.[26]

Another example of a great tower of unconventional outline is the one raised at the royal castle of Knaresborough between 1307 and 1312 by the London mason, Hugh de Tichemers. The plan of the keep is in the form of an irregular hexagon: half octagon (north) and half rectangle (south) with the polygonal prow projecting beyond the curtain wall to spearhead a triangular-shaped enclosure. A diagonally placed porch and staircase arm extends from the south-east angle of the tower, following the line of the inner curtain. The plan of the main block, then, adopts the principle of integrated geometric figures encountered at Denbigh and Stokesay, and the position of the keep thrusting forward from the apex of the curtain is reminiscent of Caernarfon

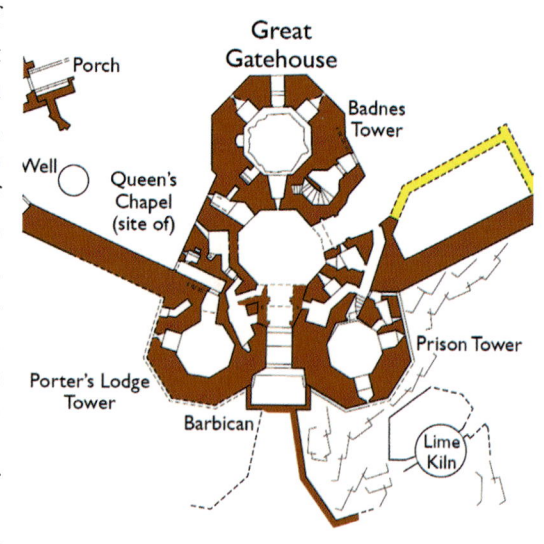

Fig. 6.16. Denbigh (Denbighshire) Ground plan of the great gatehouse. © Crown copyright (2015) Cadw.

and Stokesay. Knaresborough marks the high point of this brief period of experimentation with the fusion of geometrical forms that began in the 1280s. The final exponent of the approach was the builder of Caesar's Tower, Warwick, of *c.* 1350, which is trilobed towards the front and semi-hexagonal at the rear, and which also forms part of the enceinte.

The great tower continued to be a major component of castle design during the later fourteenth and fifteenth centuries. Regional distribution is heavily weighted towards the unstable English/Scottish border region, where the popularity of the tower as a domestic unit was driven by a need for security. It is appropriate, then, that it is to this region that one of the most original and architecturally effective great towers belongs. This is the keep of Warkworth, a building of *c.* 1390, which is probably a work of the Durham mason, John Lewyn.[27] Built on top of a pre-existing motte, it comprises a 24.4 m (80 ft) square block with a wing extending from the centre of each elevation to form a cruciform plan (Fig 6.17). Something of its skilfully planned interior is evident from Figs 4.22 and 6.18; there is no doubt that it was intended as a largely self-contained dwelling that made the most of a restricted site. A central light well suggests an evolutionary relationship to those great towers discussed above (Sandal, York and Flint) that may have had hollow centres rather than being solid, but the intricacy of the planning also points to an affiliation with contemporary quadrangular castles, a type with which Lewyn was familiar (see pp. 186–187).

Fig. 6.17. Warkworth (Northumberland) The great tower from the south; attributed to John Lewyn (last quarter of the fourteenth century).

134   Castle Builders

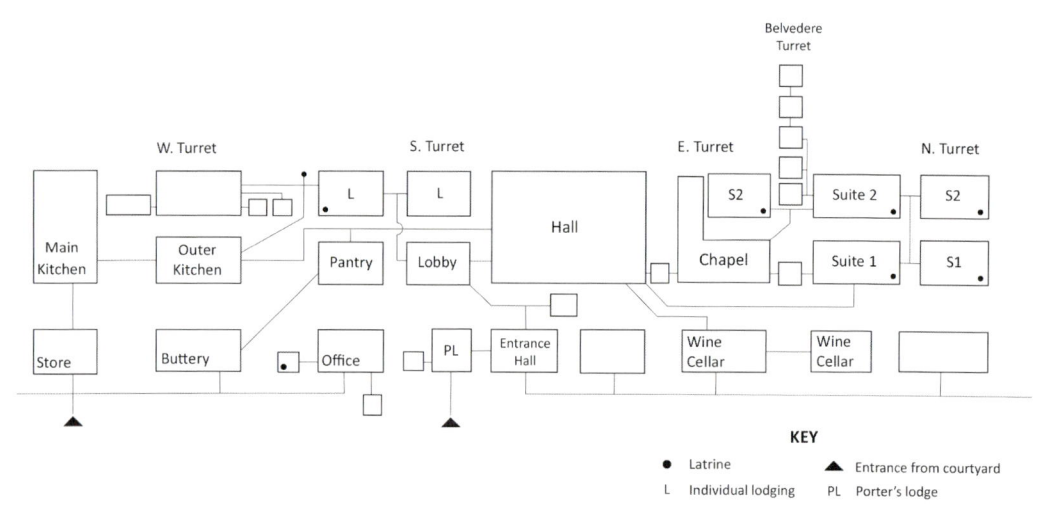

Fig. 6.18. Warkworth (Northumberland) Planning diagram for the great tower.

Warkworth represents a high point of great tower design, but there was no lack of inventiveness amongst the great tower builders of the following century. North of the border, the best of the fifteenth-century great towers is at Borthwick (Midlothian), which was raised for Sir William Borthwick under a licence of 1430 (Fig 6.19). The plan comprises a rectangular

Fig. 6.19. Borthwick (Midlothian) The great tower from the west (*c*. 1430).

main block with twin rectangular wings extending from the west front and flanking a deep recess between them to create a dramatic principal elevation, which is, in essence, an original take on the hall with end service and chamber blocks. This western elevation faces the approach to the castle and was clearly considered to be the most significant front from an architectural viewpoint. It seems as though it ought to be the entrance front, but, in fact, the first-floor entrance is tucked away in the north elevation. Some 140 years previously, a similar illusion had been created by the designer of the South Tower of Stokesay, where, from a distance, the external projections evoke a twin-towered gatehouse.[28]

The design of Borthwick may have been influenced by the Northumbrian tower of Belsay, which also has twin wings projecting from one of the long sides, albeit of a less pronounced character. Belsay dates from *c.* 1370, but is one of the more striking of the Northumbrian towers and may have had a degree of celebrity. However, if Belsay provided the germ of an idea, the builder of Borthwick transformed it into something much more emphatic and on a larger scale. In this latter respect, another possible model is Hermitage Castle (Roxburghshire), where a fortified manor house of the mid fourteenth century was converted into a tower house in an accretive development that extended into the fifteenth century. The Hermitage tower has a rectangular main block, but a key aspect of the design comprises four rectangular corner towers which project boldly so that the elevations of the main block are deeply recessed. A similar approach lay behind the west front of Borthwick.

Borthwick, like Warkworth, was a self-contained tower house; the more significant of the English great towers of the first half of the century are less independent. That of Caister Castle, the construction of which may have been overseen by the mason, Henry Wode, is an elongated cylindrical corner tower, relying for effect on the contrast between its great height and the lower courtyard buildings from which it extends. Ralph Lord Cromwell's keep at Tattershall, perhaps the work of John Botiller, was a solar tower attached to a great hall. Although it differs sharply from Caister in having a rectangular plan with projecting octagonal corner turrets, what these two contemporary buildings had in common is that they both formed part of the enceinte and carried arched machicolations. A third great tower (the High Tower), probably dating to the 1440s, was built at Cromwell's Wingfield Manor House at South Wingfield (Derbyshire). Like its Caister counterpart, it was a lodging tower (rectangular in this case) and, in common with both Caister and Tattershall, projected from the outer wall.

These three great towers on the east side of the kingdom were all primarily integrated elements of the domestic accommodation, but the contemporary keep at Raglan (Monmouthshire) embodied a greater degree of independence and security. Constructed either for Sir William ap Thomas between 1435 and 1445, or his son William Herbert, earl of Pembroke between 1460 and 1469,[29] the great tower known as the Yellow Tower of Gwent was built over a motte and was detached from the greater part of the castle by a moat, so that it had to be approached by a drawbridge. Such isolation is more in the nature of what is traditionally expected of a great tower, and argues for a defensive function. The tower was built to a hexagonal plan, and the domestic accommodation was spacious but simple in concept, comprising a horizontal succession of well-appointed rooms, one to each floor.

The Yellow Tower of Gwent is one of the most architecturally significant of great towers to be built in Wales during the medieval period and is certainly in a class of its own in the fifteenth century. In England, the most significant great tower of the fifteenth century is the Hastings Tower at Ashby-de-la-Zouch (Leicestershire), which was built for William Lord Hastings from *c.* 1472 (Fig 6.20). Despite having been partially demolished during the Civil War, its distinctive design is readily apparent in the surviving building. Hastings' tower consisted of a rectangular four-storey main block with a smaller rectangular seven-storey wing or turret attached to one end; the rooms of both elements were accessed from a single spiral staircase situated close to the ground-floor entrance. This entrance was set within a shallow projection, a feature that had been utilised by the great tower builders of Bamburgh and Carlisle in the twelfth century and Hawarden in the thirteenth century, but here at Ashby the projection was carried up as a pilaster terminating in a four-centred arched panel containing Lord Hasting's achievement of arms; its crocketed hood mould of ogee form terminates at third-floor window sill level. Additional embellishment is provided at each of the surviving angles of the main block and wing by a series of tall tourelles of polygonal section with high panelled bases that oversail the faces of the walls; these features are linked at parapet level by prominent arched machicolations carried on three tiers of corbels.

Fig. 6.20. Ashby-de-la Zouch (Leicestershire) The Hastings Tower from the north (*c.* 1472).

The name of the master builder has yet to be discovered, but there are some aspects of the plan that may stem from Tutbury (Staffordshire) some 12 miles (19 km) to the north-west. These are the juxtaposition of main block and subsidiary wing (a factor that is also found in the South Tower of Tutbury, 1442–1450) and the provision of entrance lobbies on each floor adjacent to the staircase that also appear in the North Tower (1457–*c.* 1460). Square-headed windows with returned hood moulds were used by the builders of both the Hastings Tower and the North Tower, and in both the Tutbury towers the courtyard-level entrance was set within a turret; it is a detail that might have suggested the entrance projection in the Hastings Tower. The South Tower certainly, and the North Tower probably, were masterminded by the royal mason, Robert Westerley, who disappears from the records in 1461 when his services were dispensed with by the new regime. By this time he must have been advancing in years (at least 65) and although the likelihood does not seem high, it is not beyond the bounds of possibility that he continued to work in private practice, and was still active in his eighth decade, and could, therefore, be considered the originator of the Hastings Tower.[30]

Chapter 7

Military Engineering Part 1

Defence is the attribute most popularly associated with castles, and indeed it was a theme of castle architecture throughout the Middle Ages. We have already touched on the subject of military engineering and noted a class of craftsmen (engineers) who were specialists in the infrastructure of war, including castle defences. In early castles their installations were heavily reliant on substantial earthworks with superstructures of timber. The structural natures of some of these works have been discussed in previous chapters, but since much of their substance has been subsumed, we are limited in what we can say in respect of the military thinking behind them. We are on surer ground with stone buildings, in which a greater survival of fabric and detail clarifies the intention of the builder. The widespread adoption of stone as the principal material for castle building coincides with conspicuous improvements to castle defences that took place from the later twelfth and thirteenth centuries in order to counterbalance developments in siege tactics. Although many of these improvements were empirically based, it is evident that during this period at least, attention was being paid in some measure to defensive theory, and that the military engineer was in the ascendant. There is, in addition, ample physical evidence to suggest that innovations in defensive systems continued to be made throughout the fourteenth century and beyond.

Defending the Great Tower

The significance of the great tower to castle architecture is profound, but its contribution to military engineering is less well authenticated. However, there is no doubt that many, though perhaps not all, great towers were intended to be secure and defendable buildings. The breadths of the walls supports this view, for it is in great towers, particularly those of the eleventh and twelfth centuries, that the thickest castle walls are to be found. Dimensions above the plinth of some of the greater towers are as follows:- White Tower 4.3 m (14 ft);[1] Colchester 3.7 m (12 ft);[2] Canterbury 2.79 m (9 ft 2 ins);[3] Kenilworth 4.3 m (14 ft); Guildford 4.3 m (14 ft); Scarborough 4.6 m (15 ft) (west wall), and 3.7 m (12 ft) (other walls); Dover 5.2–6.4 m (17–21 ft).

When judged against contemporary great churches these breadths appear to be out of all proportion to the demands of structural stability. Nor does the initial motive for building in such an extravagant manner appear to have been to allow for the accommodation of intra-mural chambers, for it was not until the 1150s that these became a significant element in great towers, and, furthermore, it seems to have been the thick walls that suggested the mural chambers rather than the other way round. This theory is borne out by the cylindrical keep of Pembroke, which has 4.6 m (15 ft) thick walls, but which lacks mural chambers. It is difficult to escape the conclusion that such massive walls represent a desire for security, and to maintain an ability to withstand an assault from projectiles and other aspects of siege warfare. In many cases these walls seem to have been the victims of over-engineering, but the intent inherent in their dimensions seems clear.

After the structural solidity of the keep, the most important aspect of defence is a strong entrance. Many great towers had elevated entrances, which was itself a measure that heightened security, but one that was in many cases enhanced by the elements used to control the approach. At some castles this took the form of a fortified stairway, as in the forebuildings of Castle Rising, Newcastle and Dover, which were all protected by gatehouses, a measure that increased both the exclusivity of the keep and its defensive propensities. Such arrangements might be interpreted as a means of controlling access to the lord, or of psychological control, but the defensive properties hold true.

Further aspects related to great tower security and defence are universally narrow basement windows, elevated living quarters and battlemented parapets. These measures seem to have constituted all that was deemed necessary during much of the twelfth century, just as the defence of the enceinte was relatively low key until the later twelfth century. Most of these defensive elements were passive, but the great tower also had the means to take a more active part in the defence of a castle, both by acting as a vantage point from which operations might be directed, and by serving as an elevated platform for the discharge of fusilades.

We have seen in the previous chapters that rectangular keeps, which were the dominant form from the tenth to twelfth centuries, were gradually supplanted by great towers of circular plan. An explanation that has often been given for this transition is that the latter had military advantages: it was a more stable structure than a building with angles, and therefore less vulnerable to mining, and, furthermore, the rounded wall surface had deflective qualities, so that the tower presented a less vulnerable target to missiles. These attributes may be true, but the theory cannot be proved, and it is perhaps better to evaluate on a case by case basis.

What can be said is that from the last decade of the late twelfth century onwards, in a number of cases, the military intent of the great tower seems indubitable. La Roche-Guyon and Château Gaillard are both instances in which the great tower is so integrated with the defensive scheme that their martial purpose cannot be doubted. Both these towers would have made suitable observation and command posts, each having vistas not only of the line of approach but also sight-lines along the adjacent River Seine. The idea that these towers were designed for war is reinforced by the lack of domestic comforts, and by the beaked forms of the keeps, which are streamlined towards the anticipated line of assault as though they were expected to be targets for the *petrarie*. It is a reasonable supposition that the shape was intended to have a defensive advantage, and that it was probably designed to counter a bombardment by presenting a narrower target with deflective properties. The prows also provided immensely thick walls at the expected points of impact. Another indication of the defensive role of Château Gaillard's great tower is that it was supplied with a machicolated parapet, so that the base of the tower could be defended from the alure.

In England, several great towers were endowed with quite definite defensive traits from the end of the twelfth century onwards. Those of Barnard Castle (Round Tower) and its near contemporary Pembroke (*c.* 1200) both incorporated arrow loops, while Pembroke also had provision for a hoard. Later in the thirteenth century, the great towers of York

(Clifford's Tower), Flint, Hawarden, and Caernarfon (Eagle Tower) were all endowed with arrow loops so that they could have played an active role in defence at more than one level; Flint had a timber superstructure of indeterminate nature but which could, perhaps, have acted as a hoard.

Apart from Pembroke, all these towers may be said to share another common trait, because they all, in some measure, act as part of the enceinte. The great towers of York and Hawarden are both sited on older mottes at the edge of the bailey, while their counterpart at Flint is in some ways analogous, in that it occupies a site outside the corners of the inner and outer courtyard, within its own ditch. The Eagle Tower actually forms one of the wall towers, a characteristic it shares with the late twelfth-century great tower of Château Gaillard, which was placed with great deliberation partly inside and partly outside the curtain. It was a positioning that was to recur frequently during the course of the thirteenth century, and is perhaps indicative of the greater significance of the enceinte in the field of military engineering, for it was on this aspect of the castle that developments, prompted by advances in siege warfare, were to be concentrated.

Defending the Enceinte

The early stone defences of the enceinte were, like those of contemporary great towers, comparatively uncomplicated. Primarily, they consisted of a crenellated curtain wall, with occasional interval towers of rectangular plan, and a gated entrance, sometimes, though not always, within a tower. Defence was largely conducted from the wallhead by means of an alure and, in some cases, might be enhanced by the erection of a timber hoard.

An early indication of a more scientific approach to the defence of the enceinte is the strengthening of the curtain wall through the systematic disposition of flanking towers, features that increased the defenders' control over the curtain by providing positions from which to enfilade the base of the wall. Henry II's engineers built three major schemes of this type at the royal castles of Orford (1165–1172) Dover (1168–1180) and Windsor (1172–1189). Our knowledge of the Orford curtain is based only on a seventeenth-century drawing, and survival at Windsor is only partial, but Dover gives a good idea of late twelfth-century military thinking in England at the highest level.

Maurice the Engineer and the defences of Dover

The plan of Dover Castle is an irregular wedge shape, spearheaded towards the north-west (Fig 7.1). The irregularly-shaped inner ward lies close to this north-western apex, and is surrounded by an outer curtain except to the south-east. Apart from the keep discussed above, Henry II's works encompassed the inner curtain and the north-east section of the outer curtain; the latter was evidently the first stage in a larger scheme of enclosure that was only completed under King John, but is clearly distinguished from the later work on architectural grounds. Both inner and outer curtains of this period are characterized by rectangular towers built on prominent battered plinths capped by bold stringcourses. The martial nature of the towers is underlined by their open backs, which would have been untenable if taken by an enemy and, along the outer curtain and the south-west side of the inner curtain, by multiple arrow loops through which the defenders were able to discharge forward and flanking fire (Fig 7.2). Until Dover, defence had to a great extent been conducted

140 Castle Builders

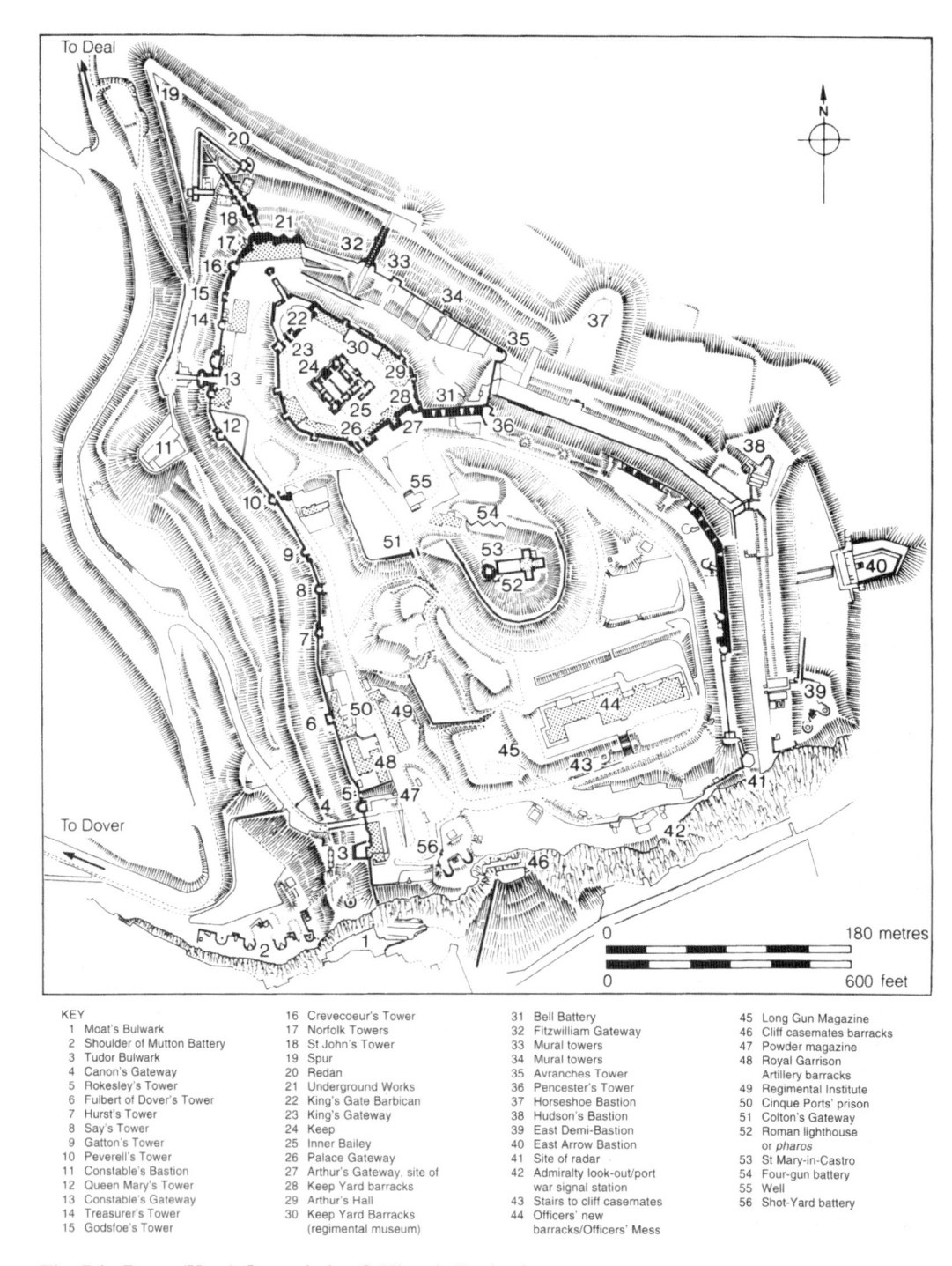

Fig. 7.1. Dover (Kent) Ground plan © Historic England.

KEY

1. Moat's Bulwark
2. Shoulder of Mutton Battery
3. Tudor Bulwark
4. Canon's Gateway
5. Rokesley's Tower
6. Fulbert of Dover's Tower
7. Hurst's Tower
8. Say's Tower
9. Gatton's Tower
10. Peverell's Tower
11. Constable's Bastion
12. Queen Mary's Tower
13. Constable's Gateway
14. Treasurer's Tower
15. Godsfoe's Tower
16. Crevecoeur's Tower
17. Norfolk Towers
18. St John's Tower
19. Spur
20. Redan
21. Underground Works
22. King's Gate Barbican
23. King's Gateway
24. Keep
25. Inner Bailey
26. Palace Gateway
27. Arthur's Gateway, site of
28. Keep Yard barracks
29. Arthur's Hall
30. Keep Yard Barracks (regimental museum)
31. Bell Battery
32. Fitzwilliam Gateway
33. Mural towers
34. Mural towers
35. Avranches Tower
36. Pencester's Tower
37. Horseshoe Bastion
38. Hudson's Bastion
39. East Demi-Bastion
40. East Arrow Bastion
41. Site of radar
42. Admiralty look-out/port war signal station
43. Stairs to cliff casemates
44. Officers' new barracks/Officers' Mess
45. Long Gun Magazine
46. Cliff casemates barracks
47. Powder magazine
48. Royal Garrison Artillery barracks
49. Regimental Institute
50. Cinque Ports' prison
51. Colton's Gateway
52. Roman lighthouse or *pharos*
53. St Mary-in-Castro
54. Four-gun battery
55. Well
56. Shot-Yard battery

from the wallhead, but the incorporation of arrow loops into the main body of the walls, in what was one of the first major deployments of this device, created a second tier of defence.

The inner ward contained the royal apartments, notably the keep, and it must be said that some aspects of its design may be more to do with controlling access to the King than equipping it for siege warfare. Nevertheless, the ward was entered via two gateways, one at each end of the enclosure, each being protected by a walled courtyard barbican. The gateways were of similar design, being recessed between twin rectangular towers, an innovative arrangement that gave the entrance greater protection than the single-towered gatehouse.

The showpiece of the stretch of the outer curtain built for Henry II is the Avranches Tower, which occupies the eastern corner. This tower is unusual in being semi-octagonal, a shape that was chosen to allow the archers a greater field of fire at an exposed angle that coincided with a break in the line of the outer ditch.[4] The three main faces of the tower were each provided with two tiers of three arrow loops, access to which was from mural galleries entered from a series of pointed embrasures and was apparently designed for the use of the crossbow.[5] Each trio of loops would have been operated by a single archer, but he would have had the flexibility of being able to fire in three different directions. A third level of fire could, of course, have been directed from the battlements. This innovatory construction was devised to address a particular weakness in the defences of Dover and is an indication that those defences were not merely for show, and that there was a military rationale behind the design.

While the Avranches Tower was the military masterpiece of Henry II's outer curtain, the ordinary rectangular wall towers were also well equipped with arrow loops having two to each of the three faces. In addition, several archery positions, each containing three loops, are built into the outer curtain itself. This sweeping provision of loops in the outer curtain and its towers contrasts markedly with the selective nature of their deployment around the inner curtain, where they are confined to the three south-western towers. It is possible that this section of the inner curtain was more strongly defended for some reason that is no longer apparent, but, equally, the discrepancy in treatment may reflect a change of plan, indicating that the south-western towers belong to a slightly later phase than the other

Fig. 7.2. Dover (Kent) One of the wall towers on the west side of the inner curtain from the south; it is equipped with twin arrow loops to all three sides (1168–1189).

towers of the inner ward, and are closer in date to the section of the outer curtain that was raised by Henry II.

Although the outer enceinte was only partially built in Henry's time, it is clear that this was only the start of a more comprehensive defensive system that was eventually completed by his son and grandson. The relationship between the inner and outer wards, whereby the former was largely surrounded by the latter, suggests that Henry intended the two lines of fortification to work in tandem. Indeed, had the outer ward been taken then the inner ward, having been deprived of communication with the outside world, would have been untenable. On the completed north-east side, the loops and parapets of the outer curtain and towers provided two levels of defence, while the parapets of the inner curtain and towers formed a third. The distance between the two curtains is approximately 15.25 m (50 ft), so the field beyond the outer curtain would have been well within the range of an archer stationed on the wall walk of the inner curtain. This is the principle behind later systems of concentric fortification, and Dover was the first castle in which such a scheme was implemented on a major scale.

Maurice the engineer has already been noted as the builder of the keep (see Chapter 5). The defences described above form part of the same scheme of work, and it is perhaps reasonable to attribute them to Maurice as well. The case has also been argued for the presence of Maurice at Bamburgh in the 1160s shortly before the keep of Newcastle was begun. Amongst the later twelfth-century works at Bamburgh are two rectangular wall towers on the north side of the inner ward, which have twin arrow loops in the front and two tiers of single loops in the sides (Fig 7.3). In considering the influences upon the works of the 1180s at Dover, together with the possibility that Maurice was a north countryman, these two towers are rather interesting. Firstly, the generous disposition of the arrow loops in the Bamburgh towers anticipates a similar level of provision in the towers along the south-west side of the inner ward of Dover, which, like the Bamburgh towers, have two loops in the front wall and two in the side walls. Secondly, the Bamburgh towers overlook the outer ward, which, at this point, forms the main route into the castle from the gateway, and which is at a much lower level than the inner ward. It is only a short step from this arrangement to the more extensively applied system of concentricity at Dover. There is, then, good reason to suppose that the defences of

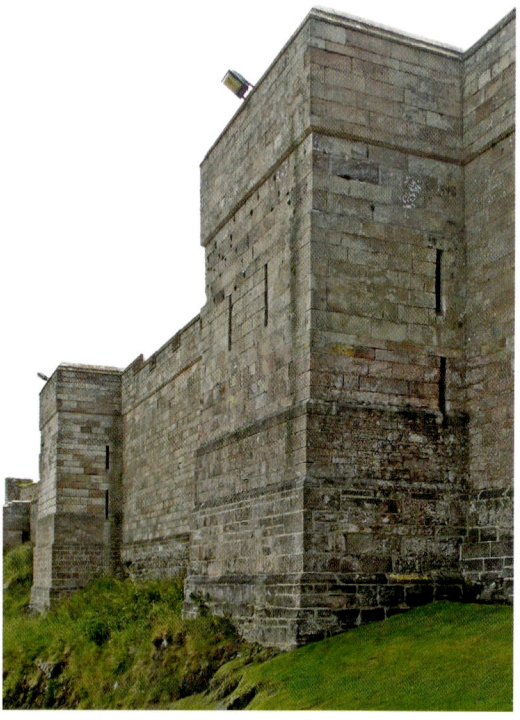

Fig. 7.3. Bamburgh (Northumberland) The wall towers of the inner ward from the north west, perhaps by the mason, Maurice (third quarter of the twelfth century).

Bamburgh may have played their part in moulding the greater scheme of Dover, and there is a strong likelihood that Maurice was the conduit by which the principle was disseminated. He must therefore be considered as one of the leading English military engineers of his age.

Reconstruction of Framlingham

Henry II's works at Dover were unfinished at the time of his death in 1189, but some of the ideas that manifest themselves at Dover were taken up and developed by the builder of the castle of Framlingham the reconstruction of which was begun for Roger Bigod, earl of Norfolk *c.* 1190. Unlike Dover, Framlingham is a keepless castle, but the principle of systematically-disposed rectangular wall towers was seized upon in the design of the inner bailey curtain. The inner bailey is only slightly smaller than the inner ward of Dover, and, curiously, is rather similar in plan, even though the outline must have been to a large extent determined by the pre-existing earthworks. At Framlingham, the opportunity was taken to increase the provision of arrow loops, but only along the southern front, so that, in common with Dover, it was still intended that the defence of much of the enclosure should be conducted from the wallhead. The reason the arrow loops were concentrated along the south is probably related to the position of the entrance to the outer bailey, which seems to have been situated towards the eastern side, so that the route of access to the gatehouse of the inner bailey would have been along the south front. As at Dover, the intention would seem to have been to make a display of strength along this route, and to furnish the possibility of hitting an enemy hard at the most likely point of their massing.

If Dover was the model for the builder of Framlingham, it was certainly not the only model, because a number of architectural characteristics and masonry details are paralleled in the keep of Orford Castle, which lies some 12 miles to the south-east of Framlingham. Firstly, the width of the Framlingham wall towers and their degree of projection from the curtain approximate closely to the measurements of the turrets that surround the Orford keep; their height, at 14.3 m (47 ft), is a little over half that of the Orford turrets, although they were, in fact, unusually tall for wall towers in the twelfth century. Both castles were built in locally-procured rubble (septaria at Orford, septaria and flint at Framlingham) and the uneven treatment of the ashlar quoins in both cases is similar, resulting in a ragged junction with the rubble. Finally, the unusual triangular inner arch of the gate passage at Framlingham, with its full panoply of joggled voussoirs, can be directly paralleled in the entrance to the keep of Orford. Exactly what these analogues mean is uncertain - to some extent they might be attributed to regional practices - but the correspondence of the tower dimensions must be a result of the direct influence of Orford. An imponderable is the nature of the now lost curtain of Orford and its towers and how they would have compared with those of Framlingham.

The architectural analogues between Orford and Framlingham, the speculation regarding Ailnoth the engineer's involvement at Orford and his known role in the dismantling of the old castle at Framlingham in the 1170s, naturally lead us to consider whether Ailnoth could have been in any way responsible for the rebuilding of Framlingham. This seems improbable, but the chronology would just about work. The reconstruction of Framlingham can only have happened from 1189 onwards, when Roger Bigod came into the properties forfeited by his father. Ailnoth's last payment from the crown was in 1190 when he received approximately one quarter of his usual annual salary. By this time he must have been an old man and by 1197 he was dead, but it is just conceivable that Framlingham was his swan song.

Early Rounded Wall Towers

One aspect of Framlingham that seems old-fashioned in the wake of Dover is the gatehouse, which is confined to a single tower rather than being based on the more up to date twin-towered design of Dover. Very shortly it would be the entire defensive circuit that seemed passé, as the rectangular tower gave way to newer designs, with a quite different aesthetic, that were, in addition, more suited to modern warfare. In fact, the process was underway even before the reconstruction of Framlingham had begun. As we have seen, the donjons of Houdan, Ambleny and Provins all incorporate round turrets, and by the 1180s some of the royal castles of Angevin France, notably Chinon, Gisors and Loches had received wall towers of semi-circular or D-shaped plan.

One of the earliest applications of rounded wall towers in England may have been at Conisbrough. Here, the curtain wall is structurally later than the late twelfth-century keep, which it abuts, but there is little reason to suppose that it is much later.[6]

Fig. 7.4. Conisbrough (Yorkshire) Semi-circular wall tower from the southeast (last quarter of the thirteenth century).

The towers themselves are solid with battered bases (Fig 7.4). By the last decade of the twelfth century, rounded wall towers had found their way to Wales. William Marshal's work at Chepstow, which seems to have been begun soon after his acquisition of the castle in 1189, included both D-shaped and circular towers.[7] These rounded wall towers at Chepstow and Conisbrough appear to have no parallels in England before the beginning of the thirteenth century and are at odds with the works of contemporary royal masons, a disparity that suggests the influence of France.

Château Gaillard

A large part of the works at Chepstow and Conisbrough may have been completed by the time Richard the Lionheart came to build an entirely new castle, Château Gaillard, at Les Andelys, in the Norman Vexin (1196–1198) (Fig 7.5). This promontory site, which sits above the Seine, comprises a sequence of three connected baileys forming a closely controlled route of access. Like Dover, the plan of the castle was wedge-shaped, spearheaded by an outer bailey orientated towards the single approach route and only feasible line of attack.

Military Engineering Part 1   145

Fig. 7.5. Château Gaillard (Aisne) The castle from the east. The outer ward is to the left, its apex marked by a round tower, the ruined outer gatehouse lying just to the right of the surviving section of curtain wall; in the background is the well preserved inner ward containing the great tower; between the two is the poorly preserved middle ward, its far side marked by a section of curtain (1196–1198).

This outer bailey, which formed an isolated enclosure surrounded by a continuous ditch, acted as an elaborate barbican, containing as it did the main gateway to the castle at the north end of its east curtain, a position that ensured the approach could be overlooked from the curtain for the full length of the enclosure. Having entered the outer bailey a second bridge had to be crossed to the middle bailey; then a third bridge had to be negotiated in order to gain access to the inner bailey. The inner bailey contained a beaked donjon, its outer side forming part of the enclosure.

Despite there being only a few years between the work of Henry II at Dover and that of Richard at Château Gaillard, the general appearance of the latter is in complete contrast to that of the former, and it is evident that it represents a profoundly different approach. The systematic disposition of cylindrical towers along the outer and middle bailey walls of Château Gaillard is one of the earliest examples of such an arrangement in Western Europe, and represents a complete departure from Henry's rectangular towers at Dover. Round towers ironed out the blind spots and allowed a less restricted field of fire from arrow loops and parapet. The outer face of the inner bailey curtain of Gaillard is even more innovatory in its closely-set broad rounded turreting, which maximized the field of fire, but also embodied deflective qualities that may have been designed to counter the effects of artillery bombardment (Fig 7.6). The streamlined character of Richard's unusual almond-shaped donjon, with the prow turned aggressively east towards the approach, was probably also owed to a preoccupation with countering bombardment. Another innovatory feature, which was incorporated into the donjon, was the system of slot machicolation, which was,

Fig. 7.6. Château Gaillard (Aisne) The inner ward from the south east.

again, one of the earliest examples in western Europe, although the system had already been used on the twelfth-century north-west tower of the inner enceinte of Krak des Chevaliers in Syria.

The sources for the design of Château Gaillard are mostly to be found in France, where Richard had spent much of his time. Comparison may be made with much older promontory sites like Chinon, an ancient castle substantially rebuilt by Henry II, which also includes a succession of three baileys, separated from each other by rock-cut ditches, although these divisions post date the arrangement at Gaillard. The round towers of the Plantagenet castles at Chinon, Loches and Gisors are also likely to have been part of the architectural background. More specifically, it is believed that the castle of La Roche-Guyon, some 17 miles to the south-west, in the French Vexin, may have exerted its influence. Most evident of a connection is the character of the donjon, which, like that of Gaillard, has an almond-shaped plan, its prow reflected in the plan of the surrounding curtain wall, both facing towards the approach. Furthermore, the design of the outer bailey of Gaillard seems to have been adapted from the layout of the outer curtain of La Roche-Guyon, including the round tower at the pointed apex of the enclosure.

Although there does not seem to be any continuity between the royal works in England and Richard's work at Château Gaillard, there is a measure of affinity between Conisbrough and Gaillard. As we have seen, the precocious use of rounded wall towers at the former provides a link with Henry II's French works and a point of connection with Gaillard, but the analogy goes further when the inner wards of the two castles are compared in more detail. These two enclosures have a similar, bow-shaped, plan in which the flanking towers

(Conisbrough) and continuous turreting (Château Gaillard) are confined to the curving section of the enceinte. The gateways are on this side; the keeps are on the opposite side, and the most striking point of comparison is that, in each case, the keep breaks the line of the curtain and so forms part of the enceinte; it is quite an unusual arrangement and therefore more worthy of attention than might otherwise be the case. The two keeps are based on a circle of approximately the same size; in both instances the first-floor entrance was approached by a stone staircase that followed the line of the keep and then made a 90 degree turn towards the doorway; in each case an inner ring of walling rose above the level of the alure and may have carried a second tier of battlements; closely set corbels extending around the interior of both towers at alure level indicate a floor, or possibly a roof.

Château Gaillard has been described as 'the final expression of all the progress made in the design and construction of fortified castles during the Norman period'.[8] If this is true, then now would appear to be a good point at which to take stock of the state to which military engineering had advanced by the end of the twelfth century, and to discuss the thinking behind the design of Château Gaillard.

The castle occupies a strategic position on the edge of Richard's domains, and was therefore well situated to act as a springboard for his intention to recover the territory that had been lost to the King of France during his captivity. It commands a superb vista of the Seine valley and its elevated site would have recommended itself to a military engineer for the tactical advantage it offered. Promontories had long been considered as advantageous locations for fortification, and would continue to be commandeered for castle building in the next century.[9] It was the topography of the site that shaped the character of the fortifications.

Firstly, the natural elevation of the location was accentuated by the excavation of ditches around the exterior and between the three baileys, thus providing barriers to siege engines. Such obstacles meant that each of the entrances could only be approached across a bridge that could quickly be immobilized by raising the inner section. One tactical aspect of the design was the positioning of the gateway to the outer bailey at the end of one of the side walls rather than facing the line of approach, where it might have been exposed to the brunt of any attack. The intention was to draw the visitor down the north-east side of the outer bailey along the entire length of the curtain whence their advance might be monitored.

This outer bailey is an interesting element of the defence, its shape and detachment from the main body of the castle appearing to anticipate the ravelin. Its isolation suggests that if it were to have been captured then the main body of the castle would still have been capable of independent resistance. This, then, may have been the strategic plan in the mind of the builder. Unfortunately, the destruction of the opposing walls of the outer and middle baileys has prevented a full appreciation of the relationship between the two elements, but a competent military engineer would have foreseen the taking of this outwork, and the requirement, therefore, to render it untenable by ensuring that its defences were dominated by those of the middle bailey. That principle was certainly adopted in the relationship between the middle and inner baileys, where there is a pronounced difference in height. The north-east curtain of the outer bailey steps down from the apex towards the ditch, indicating that the wall would have been considerably lower to the east than it was to the west. In terms of military theory this principle of relative independence of adjacent courtyards might be considered as superior to the concentric approach that Maurice had been developing at Dover, in which the inner ward would not have been capable of independent resistance for long had the outer defences been carried.

Dover is again a key point of reference when considering the entrances at Château Gaillard, since entrances were always a major point of vulnerability. At Dover, a crucial development of the 1180s had been the adoption of twin flanking towers, at the entrances to the inner ward. In contrast, the outer gateway of Château Gaillard, which was sited at the north corner of the outer ward, was, in essence, a rectangular block projecting from the line of the curtain, not unlike the slightly earlier main gatehouse of Framlingham, which, as has been suggested above, was already old-fashioned when it was begun. However, Richard's gatehouse was distinguished by a single (round) flanking tower to the east, whereas the west side of the gatehouse, which acted as a continuation of the west curtain, was protected by the adjacent ditch and was overlooked by the eastern corner tower of the middle bailey. The gateway to the inner ward also has something of the transitional about it. In a nod to the Dover gatehouses it was set between two turrets, which form part of the continuous sequence of segmental projections with which the curtain is embossed. In the gateway turrets, however, the design has been modified by the provision of flattened fronts and gate-passage returns. The result resembles a state of transmutation between one of Henry II's Dover gatehouses and one with rounded twin-towers, a type that was to become fashionable in the thirteenth century.

The general impression to be gained from the remains of the Château Gaillard is that it does not take its place very obviously within the mainstream of castle development, unlike Dover, which appears very much of its time and place. Château Gaillard is a mixture of innovation and eclecticism, with some aspects that seem idiosyncratic in the light of subsequent developments. All of this adds up to the sort of building a gifted amateur might produce, so the idea that Richard himself, given his interest in and experience of warfare, should receive a good deal of credit for the building, is an attractive one.[10] However, even if the design is to be at least partly attributed to Richard, the surviving remains leave no room for doubt that his master mason was a man of outstanding technical and aesthetic ability, and carried out the construction work with a precision and sensitivity worthy of the highest practitioners of his craft (see pp. 210–211).

Round towers are thought of as more stable structures that offered a greater degree of protection from mining, but equally, if not more important, was the broader panorama and field of fire that they offered to archers. That the provision of archery positions had become an important part of the military engineer's remit is evident in the comparatively generous though targeted provision of loops at Framlingham and Dover, with additional attention to strategically significant areas. Despite these advances, from what can be judged from the admittedly fragmentary evidence at Château Gaillard, defence was still conducted largely from the wallhead.

Corfe and related structures

Although Richard did not make much impression on the development of English castles, his successor, John, made a substantial contribution. In England, some of the earliest wall towers attributable to King John are those of the west bailey of Corfe, the defences of which were rebuilt in stone in 1201–1204. Amongst these, at the western apex of the bailey, are the fragmentary remains of a hexagonal tower known as the Butavant Tower; it was the latest addition to a small group of polygonal wall towers that had been built over the last twenty years. The earliest was probably the Avranches Tower at Dover, which is attributed to the works undertaken on the outer curtain in the 1180s. In its wake came the Bell Tower, at the Tower of London (*c.* 1190), the south-west tower of Framlingham (*c.* 1190) (Fig 7.7), and the Carrickfergus Tower at Warkworth (Northumberland, *c.* 1200). Apart from their polygonal plans these buildings are related in that each one occupies an acute angle in the curtain, and, being provided with batteries of arrow loops in their multiple faces, were designed to command a broad field of fire.

These polygonal salient towers were a short-lived phenomenon. Indeed, with the benefit of hindsight, the Butavant Tower already seems old fashioned when contrasted with the other two (north and south) towers of the West Bailey, which

Fig. 7.7. Framlingham (Suffolk) The south-east tower from the south east (last decade of the twelfth century).

are rounded. In truth, however, the Butavant Tower was already a type in the process of transition, for unlike its predecessors, its plan was unequivocally based on the circle. The process came to maturity at Kenilworth, where John rebuilt the defences of the outer ward in stone *c.* 1210–1212. The presence of the protective mere appears to have obviated the need for wall towers, but one exception is Lunn's Tower (Fig 7.8), which occupies an angle of the enceinte. Its ground storey had a circuit of five arrow loops, and so it served a similar purpose to the polygonal angle towers. Instead of being polygonal, however, it is built to a circular plan, one of the first wall towers of this form to be raised by the English crown, and one of the most unusual, because the five bays of arrow loops are articulated with pilaster buttresses, a detail that retains the sense of angularity of the polygonal corner towers. In addition, the interior of the tower is polygonal and the external buttresses coincide with the internal faces rather than with the angles, so that some of the buttresses are perforated by arrow loops. It is a very original development of the earlier theme that retains something of its origins, and is a tribute to the inventiveness of its designer.

To return to the West Bailey of Corfe, the north and south towers are semi-circular or D-shaped, like the mid wall towers of Philipe Augustus' Louvre of 1190–1202, or indeed the wall towers of Conisbrough. The difference, however, is that the Corfe towers are open

Fig. 7.8. Kenilworth (Warwickshire) Lunn's Tower from the east (first quarter of the thirteenth century)

backed rather than solid, and that they were intended to accommodate archers. Like the Butavant Tower, they each incorporated a line of four arrow loops, two facing outwards and two facing along the line of the curtain, all set within arched embrasures with square reveals. The design is similar to those of the outer bailey, where part of the enceinte was probably rebuilt in stone in 1212–c. 1215 under the supervision a mason called Stephen.[11] These later towers have the same characteristic disposition of arrow loops hard up against the curtain wall. The work of the master mason at Corfe, then, displays a familiarity with Henry II's work at Dover, but also an awareness of more recent developments in military engineering, particularly the rounded towers and more generous and systematic provision of arrow loops.

The second Dover master
John was also building at Dover in the period 1205–1216, prompted no doubt by the capture of Château Gaillard and loss of Normandy. He continued the incomplete outer curtain begun by his father, Henry II, in the 1180s. John's work on the north and west sides of the castle is characterized by state-of-the-art D-shaped wall towers with outward projecting rounded prows, a form that was extended to the main twin-towered gatehouse that he built at the north-west apex of the castle. Outwardly, the wall towers of John's engineer at Dover are somewhat similar to those at Corfe, but are solid rather than open-backed, and slightly longer in plan, their flat backs projecting inside the curtain. Towers of this type had already been used at the Angevin castles of Chinon and Gisors in the 1180s, and by Philip Augustus at the Louvre from c. 1190, and were being built at Krak-des-Chevaliers in the County of Tripoli (Syria) at about the same that they were being deployed at Dover. It was to remain a standard type throughout the thirteenth century. The D-shaped tower had the tactical advantages of the cylindrical tower but it integrated more easily into the curtain and was therefore easier to build. The form was also used for a small number of great towers in the early thirteenth century including Issoudun (Indre), Helmsley, Ewloe (Flintshire) and Castell y Bere (Merionethshire). Its appearance in England following the loss of Château Gaillard may be an indication of the presence of Angevin engineers in England. We don't have a name for the mastermind behind John's works at Dover, but Urricus the engineer (*fl.* 1184–d. c. 1216) was a man held in great favour, who in 1201 had seen service with John in Normandy who granted him a knight's fee. His craft background is obscure, although he seems to have been the Urricus who was described as an arbelaster in 1193–1194, and he was in the business of constructing siege engines at Nottingham in 1194, in Normandy in 1201 and at Carrickfergus in 1210.[12]

The third Dover master
Despite John's attention to the defences of Dover its vulnerability was tested when, in 1216, during the last days of his reign, the threat of French invasion was realized, and the castle was besieged. The weakness of the castle hinged on the position of the twin-towered main gateway at the north-west apex, which was directly in line with the main approach to the castle on the outside, and with the entrance to the barbican of the inner ward on the inside. This gatehouse bore the brunt of the French attack, and was severely damaged when its eastern flanking tower was undermined and partially brought down. In the re-organization

of Dover's defences that followed the raising of the siege, resolving the problem of the main gateway's vulnerability took top priority.

There were three main strands to the solution that Henry III's engineer devised. Firstly, it was decided to remove the entrance to a less exposed position in the west curtain, so that it was no longer in the direct line of attack. This change of position also facilitated the fulfilment of a second objective, which was to lengthen the line of approach, so that it might be monitored and guarded more adequately. By bringing the entrance route in front of the west curtain it was directly under the scrutiny of the defenders on the wall walk. A further measure of control and defence was the construction of an elongated barbican along the greater part of this section; a right-angled turn led over the castle ditch to the new gatehouse.

The third aspect of the project was to strengthen the defensive character of the gatehouse itself. Known as the Constable Tower, the new gatehouse was built $c.$ 1220–1227 and was probably the earliest in the series of castle gatehouses to be raised during the reign of Henry III (Fig 7.9). It was certainly the most remarkable; the design is highly original and requires some discussion. At the core of the new building was one of King John's D-shaped wall towers, which Henry's engineer pierced to create an entrance, a task facilitated by the backless character of the tower. In addition, he built a number of new elements around it including a two-storey rectangular residential block to the rear, a two-storey portico at the front, and three new D-shaped flanking towers immediately to the south (one) and north (two) of the gatehouse. The unprecedented character of the portico, which presents a broad flat elevation with rounded ends, is derived from the principle of two D-shaped towers placed back to back.

Fig. 7.9. Dover (Kent) The Constable Tower from the west ($c.$ 1220–1227).

Part and parcel of the new gatehouse scheme was the blocking of the north-west entrance and the strengthening of the defences in this exposed position. A new, beaked, tower was placed in front of the old entrance, and the gateway's eastern flanking tower was rebuilt in a more robust fashion, so that the former gatehouse now comprised a cluster of three towers forming a bulwark at this north-west apex, an effect that was bolstered by the construction of two additional wall towers a little to the east. The position was further strengthened by the construction of the St John Tower within the ditch to the north-west of the old gateway, and by a great earthen outwork beyond. In addition, a new postern (the Fitzwilliam Gate) was opened in the north curtain in the 1220s. This comprises two beaked towers flanking a beaked turret, itself pierced by the gate passage; the design appears to have been inspired by the form of the gatehouse blocking.

The clustering of towers in an outward show of strength was a prominent feature of the post-siege works at Dover, occurring in association with the Constable Tower, the Norfolk Towers and the Fitzwilliam Gate. All these instances can be dated to the 1220s and clearly have their origins in an empirical response to the peculiar circumstances of the remodelling whereby the old gateway was abandoned in favour of a new site. However, it is worth considering that the concept of closely-spaced towers may have been based on Richard the Lionheart's extraordinary inner bailey wall built over twenty years earlier at Château Gaillard. In England the only other examples of clustering are the great towers of Pontefract, probably of the 1230s (see p. 126) and York (1244–1272). There are, however, at least two cases of tripartite clusterings in France: the Château de la Folie at Braine (Aisne), probably of the 1220s, now no longer extant, and the Château de Montaigu-le-Blin (Allier).[13]

The use of beaked towers at Dover is unique amongst castle builders in England and reflects early thirteenth-century French practice where they had a degree of currency. Of particular pertinence, perhaps, is Loches, where the upgrading of the curtain wall, under either Richard the Lionheart or Philip Augustus, included the construction of a trio of beaked wall towers along the south front (Fig 7.10), and the early thirteenth-century castle of Coudray-Salbart (Deux-Sèvres), where the east curtain was given two large beaked angle towers.[14] It is also possible, however, that this aspect of the new works at Dover represents a harking back to Château Gaillard and the then unusual character of the donjon.

The engineer responsible for these aspects of the remodelled castle, then, appears to have been a man with knowledge of recent French practice, possibly with experience of Château Gaillard itself.[15] Another possible adaptation of an aspect of Château Gaillard at Dover is the outwork at the north-east angle, which extended the castle in the expected direction of attack, and gave the defenders the means of deploying their own *petrarie* in a more forward and defendable position. Like the outer ward at Château Gaillard, which is the topographical equivalent, the defences of the outwork split the line of approach in the manner of a ravelin and overlooked an advance along either route. In contrast to its counterpart at Gaillard, however, the outwork was not an isolated ward, the tunnels (see p. 19) allowing it to be reinforced in relative safety.

Fig. 7.10. Loches (Indre-et-Loire) A semi-circular turret of Henry II (last quarter of the twelfth century) in juxtaposition with later beaked towers (last decade of the twelfth century or first decade of the thirteenth century).

Sally ports

These Dover tunnels were a development of an existing concept in which underground access was provided from the castle enclosure to the exterior, often into the surrounding ditch. An early example descends from the south side of the inner ward of Windsor into the moat; it probably dates from the late twelfth century, in which case it was part of the defensive scheme raised under Ailnoth the engineer and the mason Godwin. A postern built in 1194 at Nottingham to give access to the motte may have been another example. A tunnel leading from the lower ward of Windsor to the ditch dates from the construction of the west curtain of the 1220s and is therefore broadly contemporary with the Dover tunnels. Two tunnels at Knaresborough, which lead to the north and south ditches respectively, may perhaps be contemporary with the excavation of the latter by King John in the early thirteenth century. Such postern gates are often interpreted as sally ports, through which parties of men-at-arms might pass in order to attack a besieging force. It is possible that some might have been used in this way, but there would appear to have been tactical limitations to those that, like the Knaresborough examples, opened out onto the bottom of a deep rock-cut ditch.

Windsor

Windsor was another royal castle that had undergone a siege in 1216, an event that had, as at Dover, highlighted the deficiencies in the defences and prompted the king (Henry III) and his counsellors to set about the strengthening them. At Windsor the two main areas that required attention were the west curtain and its three wall towers (from north to south: Cleaver's Tower, Garter's Tower and Salisbury Tower), and the south curtain of the middle bailey with its two attendant towers (Henry III's Tower and Gerard's Tower). These works, which were probably completed during the 1220s, are distinguished by large round-nosed wall towers with systematically disposed arrow loops. One architectural link with Henry's works elsewhere is the double D-shaped plan of Henry III's Tower at the west end of the middle bailey's south front. Its footprint is based on that of the portico in front of the Constable Tower at Dover, which had been completed by 1227.

The Tower of London

A third major updating of the defences of a royal castle was carried out at the Tower of London. The works of Henry's minority had concentrated on the south curtain, where, in the 1220s, he raised the Wakefield Tower and probably the Lanthorn Tower. From the late 1230s a major expansion of the bailey was undertaken towards the north and east, which entailed the construction of new lengths of curtain wall and their associated wall towers. The majority of the towers belonging to this phase are D-shaped, their closed backs flush with the rear of the curtain, but the three corner towers are different. The Salt Tower (SE) has a circular plan; the Martin Tower (NE) is akin to the D-shaped towers with a flat external face towards the west continuing the rear line of the curtain; most unusual of the three is the ovoidal Devereux Tower (NW). This special treatment of the angle towers was a continuation of the practice that had begun with the Avranches Tower at Dover in the 1180s, and which, in an earlier phase at the Tower, had manifested itself in the Bell Tower. An interesting planning development was that, in concert with this expansion of the main ward, a small inner ward was built between the White Tower to the north and the south curtain, with a twin-towered gatehouse and a curtain wall pierced by battery of arrow loops. The creation of this complex of two wards, both of quadrangular form, was a stage in the evolution of concentric fortifications that was to reach an apogee in the latter half of the thirteenth century.

The development of concentricity
The concept of concentric lines of defence is an ancient one dating back to the prehistoric period, and the example of multivallate hillforts is unlikely to have been lost on the early castle builders. Indeed a number of early castles were established within prehistoric fortifications. Moreover, there is a small number of early castles in England, with a wide geographical spread, in which the principle was adopted in one form or another. Hen Domen, Berkhamsted, Tutbury and Helmsley have all been cited as examples (See Chapter 2). At least the first three, and possibly all four, date from soon after the Conquest. It has to be said that these are relatively rare instances, but they do provide evidence that the principle was understood, and it is probable that future archaeological investigation will reveal further examples.

In England, concentric fortification systems in stone are considered to begin with Henry II. It has been argued above that a localized scheme was implemented at Bamburgh in the 1160s, and that a more thorough system was incorporated into the reconstruction of Dover Castle under Maurice the engineer, where the construction of the outer curtain

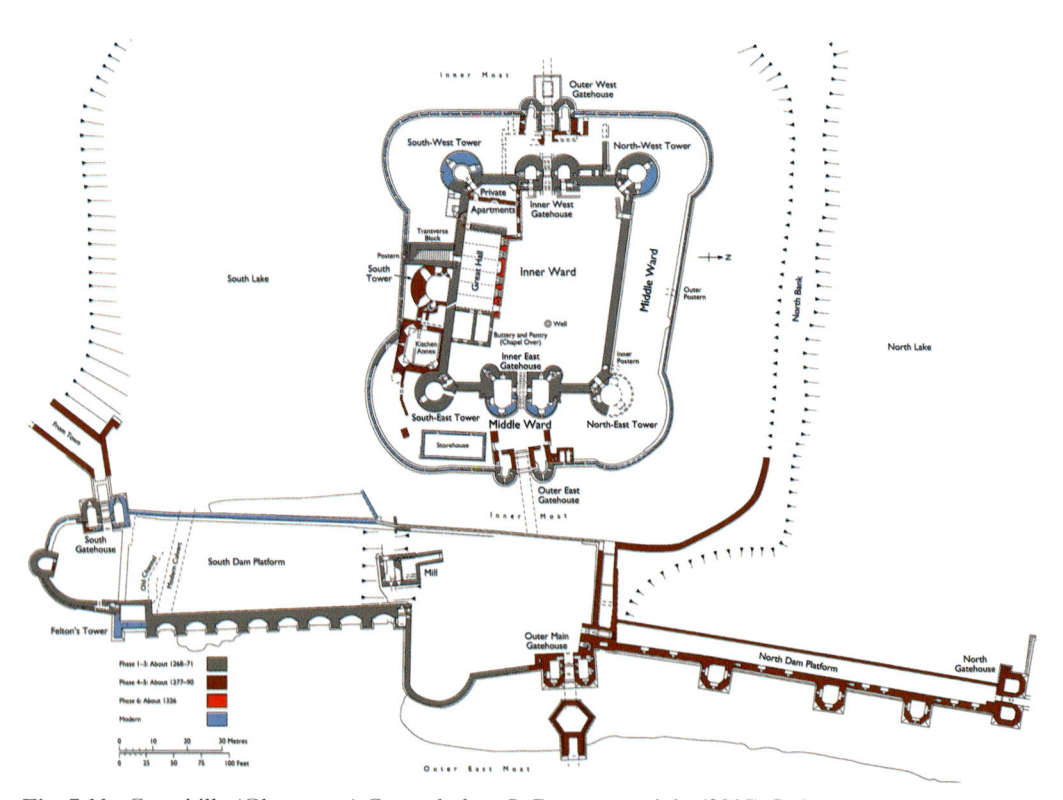

Fig. 7.11. Caerphilly (Glamorgan) Ground plan. © Crown copyright (2015) Cadw.

was probably begun in the 1180s. This principle, in which an inner enclosure dominates an outer enceinte, is also in evidence at La Roche-Guyon of *c*. 1190, and to a lesser extent at Château Gaillard. None of these three examples represents true concentricity because in none does the outer curtain fully enclose the inner curtain to create a continuous courtyard between the two, and it was not until the later thirteenth century that the principle was carried to its logical conclusion in Britain, even though the Hospitaller castle of Belvoir in the Kingdom of Jerusalem was built as a fully concentric stone castle as early as *c*. 1168.[16]

In Britain, it was not until the last years of the reign of Henry III (1216–1272), that the principle was deployed in the most systematic fashion. The instigator was Gilbert de Clare, earl of Gloucester and Hertford who raised a new castle at Caerphilly, in south Wales, between 1267 and 1271 (Fig 7.11). The identity of the technical mastermind behind Caerphilly is one of the great unknowns of medieval military architecture, because his endeavours there, which were to result in a fortification of the first rank, suggest a military engineer of great significance.

The orientation of the castle was unusual, because instead of a single progressive sequence from outer to inner ward, an arrangement that had enjoyed a good deal of popularity amongst castle builders in the past, particularly on promontory sites, the inner ward could be approached from the tip as well as the neck of the former spur, and from both sides of the artificial lake that surrounded it via the dams. Caerphilly, then, had much greater flexibility than many castles with regard to its defence and communications.

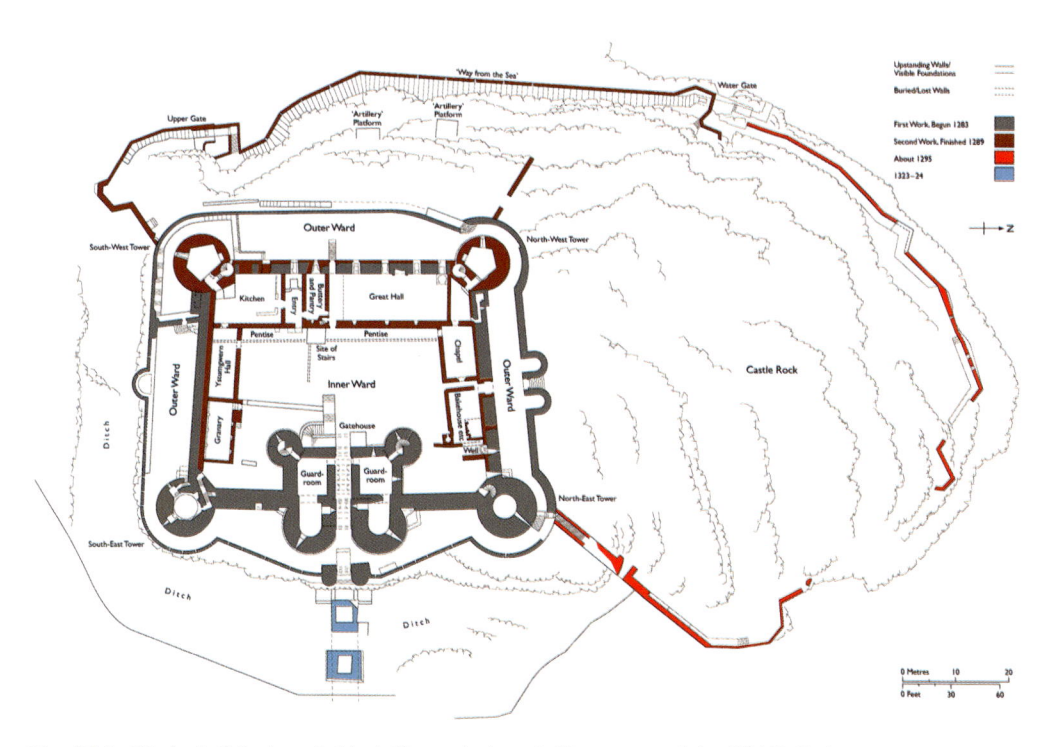

Fig. 7.12. Harlech (Merionethshire) Ground plan. © Crown copyright (2015) Cadw.

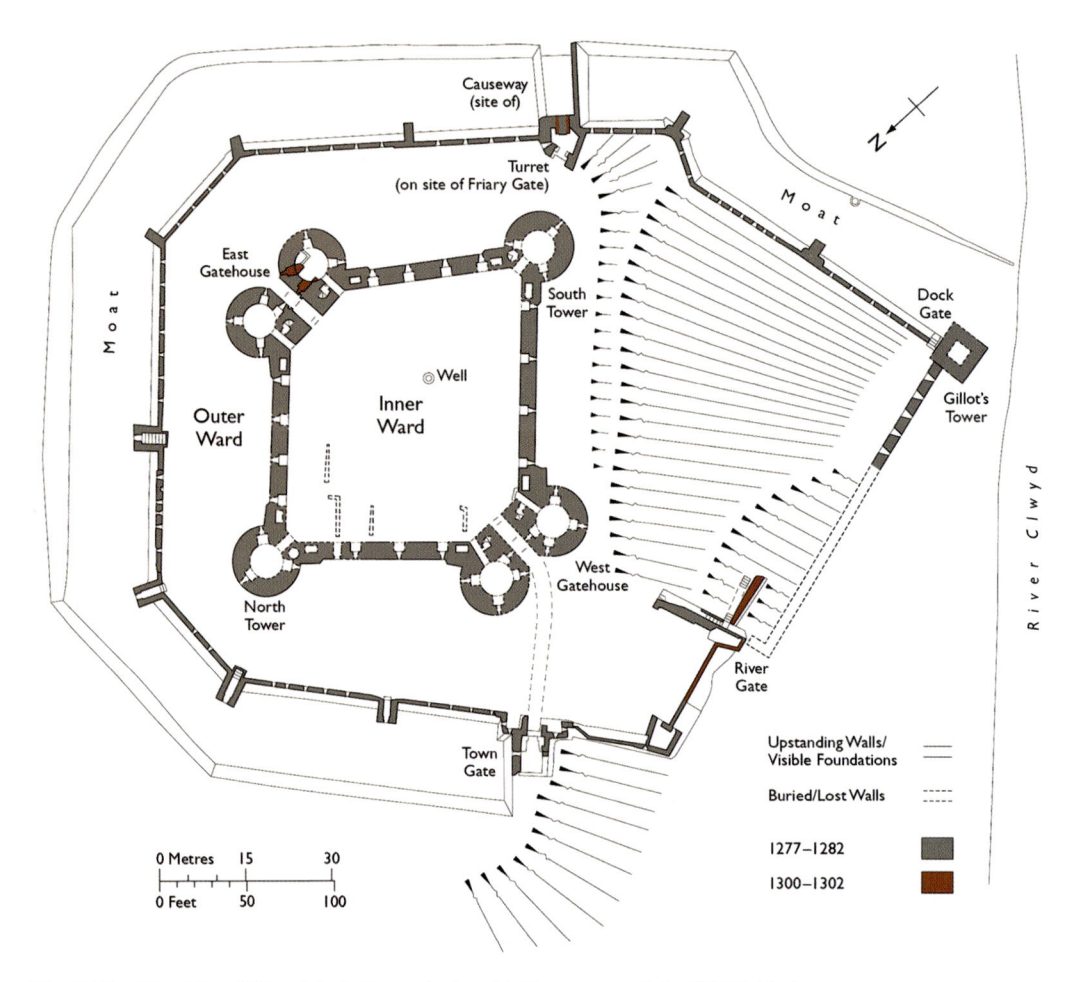

Fig. 7.13. Rhuddlan (Flintshire) Ground plan. © Crown copyright (2015) Cadw.

The inner enclosure forms a parallelogram with four round corner towers and two twin-towered gatehouses. Its antecedents are to be found in the late twelfth- to early thirteenth-century quadrilateral castles of Philip Augustus and related buildings, though lacking the great tower that so often accompanied them. Although the quadrangular form had a lengthy pedigree, what was new at Caerphilly was its context, set within an outer ward of similar plan. At Caerphilly, all three islands are contained by stone revetments, but the central one incorporates large rounded bastions, one at each of the four angles, echoing the positions of the corner towers of the inner enclosure. The ultimate origin of this particular feature may have been the Philippian castles, such as Dourdan, where the surrounding ditch with its revetted counterscarp may have suggested a complimentary outer ward.

Like Pembroke of an earlier period, Caerphilly is an instance of a provincial development making an impact on the direction taken by the royal castle builders, because the developed concept of Caerphilly was quickly followed by Edward I at the Tower of London, which he transformed into a fully concentric castle by the erection of an outer ward, between 1275 and 1285, under the direction of the master mason, Robert of Beverley. Concentricity was also to be used on a substantial scale during Edward I's conquest of north Wales: Rhuddlan (1277), Harlech (1283) and Beaumaris (1295) all have concentric lines of defence. Of these three, Harlech owes the most to the design of Caerphilly (Fig 7.12), in the broad bastions of the outer ward that shadow the corner towers, the positioning of the outer gate directly in front of the inner gate, which resulted in an arrangement akin to a barbican, and in the form of the inner gatehouse itself, all aspects that have parallels in the central island of the Caerphilly complex.

Rhuddlan had three lines of defence (Fig 7.13); firstly a stone-revetted dry moat, which encompassed three sides of the castle and which was screened by an outer palisade; then an outer ward pulled out of shape towards the south where it extended down to the River Clwyd; then the inner ward. Turrets projected from the wall of the outer ward into the moat, some of which contained flights of stairs descending to sally ports that gave access to the moat. Between these turrets the curtain contained rows of arrow loops aimed towards the wall foot. Further firepower could have been deployed from a higher level in the outer curtain and from the taller inner curtain. The outer ward could itself have been enfiladed from inner curtain, both from loops near ground level and from the parapet.

These heavily concentrated deployments of arrow loops were characteristic features of Edward's north Walian castles, though, as we have seen, had already been developed by Henry III's engineers at the Tower of London in the 1230s (see p. 151). Some of the best preserved of these 'shooting galleries' are at Beaumaris (Fig 7.14), which retains well defined rows of embrasures beneath segmental-pointed arches At Caernarfon, where concentric

Fig. 7.14. Beaumaris (Anglesey) The line of arrow loops along the west curtain with the defences of the inner ward looming up behind.

Fig. 7.15. Caernarfon (Caernarvonshire) Three tiers of arrow loops manned from the parapet and two intra-mural galleries.

fortifications were not adopted, the curtain outside the town walls contained two intra-mural galleries, one above another, which, together with the parapet, formed three tiers of closely-spaced arrow loops (Fig 7.15).

Although the late thirteenth century was the apogee of the concentric fortification, the pattern continued in use down to the late fourteenth century at Queenborough (1361), Raby (Co. Durham, 1378) and Wardour (Wiltshire, 1393).

Wallhead Defences

Hoarding
Hoarding construction has been discussed in Chapter 3, but there is more to be said with reference to their function. Hoardings were the principal means of protecting the walls from enemy attrition, and of conducting an active defence. Slots in the floor allowed missiles to be launched at the area immediately in front of the curtain, and arrow loops in the screen front made it possible to harry the enemy from a forward position in relative safety. From the later twelfth-century, the loops in the hoarding were being augmented by masonry loops in the supporting wall. At Château Gaillard, for example, a line of arrow loops set within the parapet in one of the surviving sections of the curtain around the outer ward was associated with a line of hoarding sockets, and was designed to be useable when the hoarding was in place. The hoarding itself would have provided a second tier of loops.

Slot machicolation

A stone alternative to hoarding as a means of controlling the foot of the wall from above was the slot machicolation, whereby a series of buttresses projecting from the face of the wall, was linked at wallhead level by arches carrying an oversailing parapet. Slots incorporated in the floor of the alure between the buttresses allowed the defenders to drop substantial missiles on an enemy at the foot of the walls. Slot machicolations were in use by the crusaders in Syria by the mid twelfth century when a system was built into the face of the north-east tower of the inner ward at Krak des Chevaliers. It may have been a crusader model that provided Richard the Lionheart or his engineer with the inspiration for the slot machicolations with which he equipped the donjon of Château Gaillard in the 1190s. In this instance the batter rises from the base to slightly above first-floor level, and the wedge-shaped supports for the machicolation arches begin on the batter, several feet below first-floor level. This type of system was never very popular in northern Europe and is mostly associated with the south of France, the pre-eminent example being the papal palace at Avignon from *c.* 1335. It was probably from Avignon that the idea was disseminated in the fourteenth century to the headquarters of the Teutonic Order at Malbork, Poland, where it was incorporated into the design of the Grand Master's Palace.

There are only two slot machicolation systems in England, both of which date from the late fourteenth century. One is close to the northern border, at Haughton Castle (Northumberland), and the other is on the south coast, at Southampton (Hampshire). At Haughton the machicolations were built during the heightening of a late thirteenth-century defended first-floor hall house. In constructing the machicolation arches the builders made use of the existing buttresses as supports and raised the walls of the new storey on top of the arches. A more extensive arcaded machicolation system was built in strengthening the town defences of Southampton in 1378–1388. The Southampton arcade was built in front of existing walling, mostly of houses, which was utilized as part of the defensive circuit. These two schemes, at different ends of the kingdom, were products of the peculiar circumstances with which the builders were confronted. At Haughton the existence of the buttresses provided inspiration for a novel way of increasing the house's domestic accommodation while at the same time strengthening its defences. Both are ad hoc solutions and are therefore atypical.

Corbelled machicolation

Corbelled machicolation, in which the parapet was carried on corbels rather than buttresses, was a more economical alternative, and proved more popular. That corbelled machicolations derived from timber hoardings is implied by the incorporation of stone corbelling around wall heads in concert with hoarding sockets. Such arrangements were in use from the early thirteenth century. In several towers of that date at Caldicot single corbels were set immediately beneath the sockets and must have been intended as supports for the beams and/or protection for the stonework. Single corbels are also to be found around the flanking towers of the south-west gateway of Corfe (*c.* 1235 to *c.* 1245), but here they do not supplement hoarding sockets and must have been intended to carry the hoarding framework on their own.

The loss of the upper parts of the towers hinders interpretation, but there is plenty of pictorial evidence for the donjon and wall towers of Coucy (*c.* 1225) where the builder also used corbelling as an alternative to beam slots rather than as an adjunct to them (Fig 7.16). At Coucy, the corbelling was set several feet below the level of the hoarding platform, and there were four tiers of corbels, which allowed the stonework to project substantially from the wall face in order to accommodate timber sills for the hoarding supports. A similar system seems to have been used for the later thirteenth-century town walls of Newcastle-on-Tyne where three-tier corbelling survives around the Durham Tower (*c.* 1265).[17]

These multiple-corbelled hoarding supports were only a short step from the complete replacement of hoarding with corbelled machicolations, and they show their influence on one of the earliest applications of corbelled machicolations in Britain. This is over the two gateways to Conwy Castle of *c.* 1284. Here, the parapets were carried on no fewer than six tiers of corbels, a highly extravagant form that was only occasionally to be emulated in castle building, and only once in Britain, where two or three tiers was the rule (Fig 7.17).[18] Anticipating later practice, the builders of Beaumaris constructed a three-tier set over the Gate Next the Sea at Beaumaris in the 1290s (Fig 7.18).

Fig. 7.16. Coucy (Aisne) The donjon depicting the corbelling on which the hoarding was intended to be erected, and which seems to represent a stage on the way to the adoption of corbelled machicolations (second quarter of the thirteenth century); from Viollet-le-Duc 1875.

In the north of England, one of the earliest corbelled machicolation systems that we know of was around the tower containing the gaol in Hexham, Northumberland, which was built in 1330–1332 on the orders of William Melton, archbishop of York. Whereas at Conwy and Beaumaris the system is localised by being confined to the entrances, at Hexham three tiers of corbels extend all around the wallhead, making the tower one of the first buildings in England to be entirely treated in this way. The system is continued around the angles on diagonally placed corbels. Documentary evidence suggests that in the Midlands the earliest use of corbelled machicolations may have been around the now ruined keep of Stafford Castle, built under a contract of 1348.[19] Only slightly later is Caesar's Tower, at Warwick Castle, possibly of the 1350s, which retains its machicolations. In the

Fig. 7.17. Conwy (Caernarfonshire) Machicolations over the gateway to the outer ward (last quarter of the thirteenth century).

Fig. 7.18. Beaumaris (Anglesey) Machicolations over the Gate-next-the-Sea (first quarter of the fourteenth century).

south, corbelled machicolations were raised over the new barbican to Lewes Castle built by John de Warenne, 7th earl of Surrey, in the first half of the fourteenth century.

What these early examples tell us is that by the mid fourteenth century regional differences in construction technique had emerged, the principal division being between the north and south of England. Northern (and midland) builders followed the practice of the masons at Beaumaris, in that the corbels support lintels. In the south of England (and south Wales), however, the corbels support arches, which tallies with French practice. On the whole, this dichotomy prevailed through the later Middle Ages, although the midlands was to fall within the orbit of southern practice in the fifteenth century when the builders of the great towers of Tattershall (1430s) and Ashby de la Zouch (1470s) adopted arched machicolations.

Chapter 8

Military Engineering Part 2

Defending the Entrance

Single-towered gatehouses

In early castles, the defence of the gateway could be rudimentary; the eleventh-century gateway of Richmond, for instance, simply pierced the curtain wall and may initially have been protected by nothing more than a gate. In a number of other cases the entrance comprised a single rectangular tower pierced by a gateway. The entrance would have been approached by a removable drawbridge and the tower itself gave a degree of control, but, generally, early gateways were comparatively lightly defended. At Exeter, Ludlow and Tickhill, all of which date from the eleventh century, and which represent an early type, the entrance opened out into a wider space occupying the entire ground floor of the tower, below a timber first floor.

The early twelfth-century gatehouse of Norham represents an improvement from a defensive point of view because it contained a vaulted gate passage, thereby endowing the entrance with fireproof qualities; this passage, however, was defended only by a gate at the outer end. The single-towered gatehouse remained the dominant type until the last quarter of the twelfth century, although even then it was still considered a serviceable choice by the builder of Framlingham, *c.* 1190. Here at Framlingham, though, in addition to a side-hung gate, there was also a portcullis (Fig 8.1), a device that was normally incorporated into the gate passage defences from this time onwards.

Fig. 8.1. Framlingham (Suffolk) The gate tower from the south (last decade of the twelfth century).

Early twin-towered gatehouses

A major development in gatehouse design was the adoption of an entrance flanked by a pair of towers, the two gateways to the inner ward of Dover, of the 1180s, have already been remarked upon as early instances. The Dover towers were rectangular, but, from the 1190s,

Fig. 8.2. Chepstow (Monmouthshire) The outer gatehouse from the east (last decade of the twelfth century).

gatehouses were being built with twin flanking towers of rounded form, a type that was to become a standard of the thirteenth-century castle builder's repertoire. One of the earliest is the outer gatehouse of Chepstow, built by William Marshal, who acquired the castle in 1189 (Fig 8.2).[1] The dating of the gatehouse to *c.* 1190 is based on dendrochronological analysis of samples from the original gates. There is no sign that the royal works influenced Chepstow, nor William Marshal's slightly later works at Pembroke, and he seems to have relied on the services of provincial craftsmen.

The towers of the Chepstow gatehouse, which are of unequal diameter, stand on battered bases and are pierced by arrow loops at two levels, and therefore had a greater offensive capacity than the gate towers to the inner ward of Dover, which were devoid of loops. The Chepstow towers break forward to protect a segmental-arched gateway that is recessed beneath a higher arch, and the gate passage was defended in depth by a machicolation slot in the vault extending across the entire width of the passage, an arrow loop in the south tower, a portcullis, a pair of gates secured by a draw bar and, finally, a second portcullis. Two round holes in the vault between the machicolation slot and the first portcullis have been interpreted as housings for portcullis counterweights, although it is difficult to determine the veracity of this interpretation.[2]

Twin gatehouse towers of rounded form were adopted by the royal works slightly later, at Dover, where, as part of his work on the outer curtain between 1204 and 1216, King John built a new gatehouse at the north-west angle of the castle. This was quite different in design from the gatehouse of Chepstow, having D-shaped, rather than circular, flanking towers, which were open-backed rather than closed, and therefore solely of defensive character. This gatehouse was one of the first of its kind in England. As at Chepstow, and, indeed, as in the semi-circular wall towers built by John at Dover and Corfe, the towers were provided with a trio of arrow loops in their bowed fronts.

The form of the Dover gateway was emulated at Kenilworth where, c. 1210–1212, twin D-shaped towers were added to the front of the twelfth-century outer gatehouse (Mortimer's Tower) to create a design that reflected recent thinking on defensive architecture. The existing twelfth-century gatehouse was a rectangular block with a central gate passage at the head of a salient in the curtain, and the narrowness of the new drum towers is a reflection of the restrictions imposed on the engineer by the earlier tower's retention. The new drum towers were equipped with arrow slits to the front and sides, and their addition to the older block resulted in an elongated passage with an improved sequence of defensive barriers comprising two portcullises and three sets of gates. It is interesting to consider whether this kind of development, in which an older gatehouse was re-fronted and thereby extended, was the origin of some later gatehouses with elongated entrances and multiple barriers.

Montgomery, its antecedents and successors
From 1223 a new royal castle was being built at Montgomery to replace the existing castle of Hen Domen. This is a promontory site, which had been noted by Henry III's advisors as an apt location for an 'impregnable castle'. As at Château Gaillard and some other castles, the builders created a linear sequence of linked wards through which the visitor progressed to an inner ward occupying the high point of the site (Fig 8.3). The earlier phases of this castle were carried out during Henry's minority under the auspices of Hubert de Burgh, who, no doubt, had been one of the advisors who was so taken with the possibilities of the site.

The inner ward of the castle has two distinctive gatehouses that illuminate the sources for the design and offer an intimation of the process by which the architectural development of the provinces might influence the royal works. The south gatehouse has three-quarter circle bow-fronted twin towers flanking the entrance; to the rear is a large rectangular attached accommodation block. The gate passage was protected by a pair of gates at the outer end, then a portcullis, and, at the inner end, a second pair of gates. There may also have been a machicolation slot over the passage.[3] However, there were no arrow loops within the passage, nor in either of the ground-floor rooms, which seem to have been little more than storage basements accessed from above. This arrangement is something of a contrast to the D-shaped towers of John's gatehouses, and although the accommodation block was something that had recently been developed at the Constable Tower, Dover, c. 1220, under

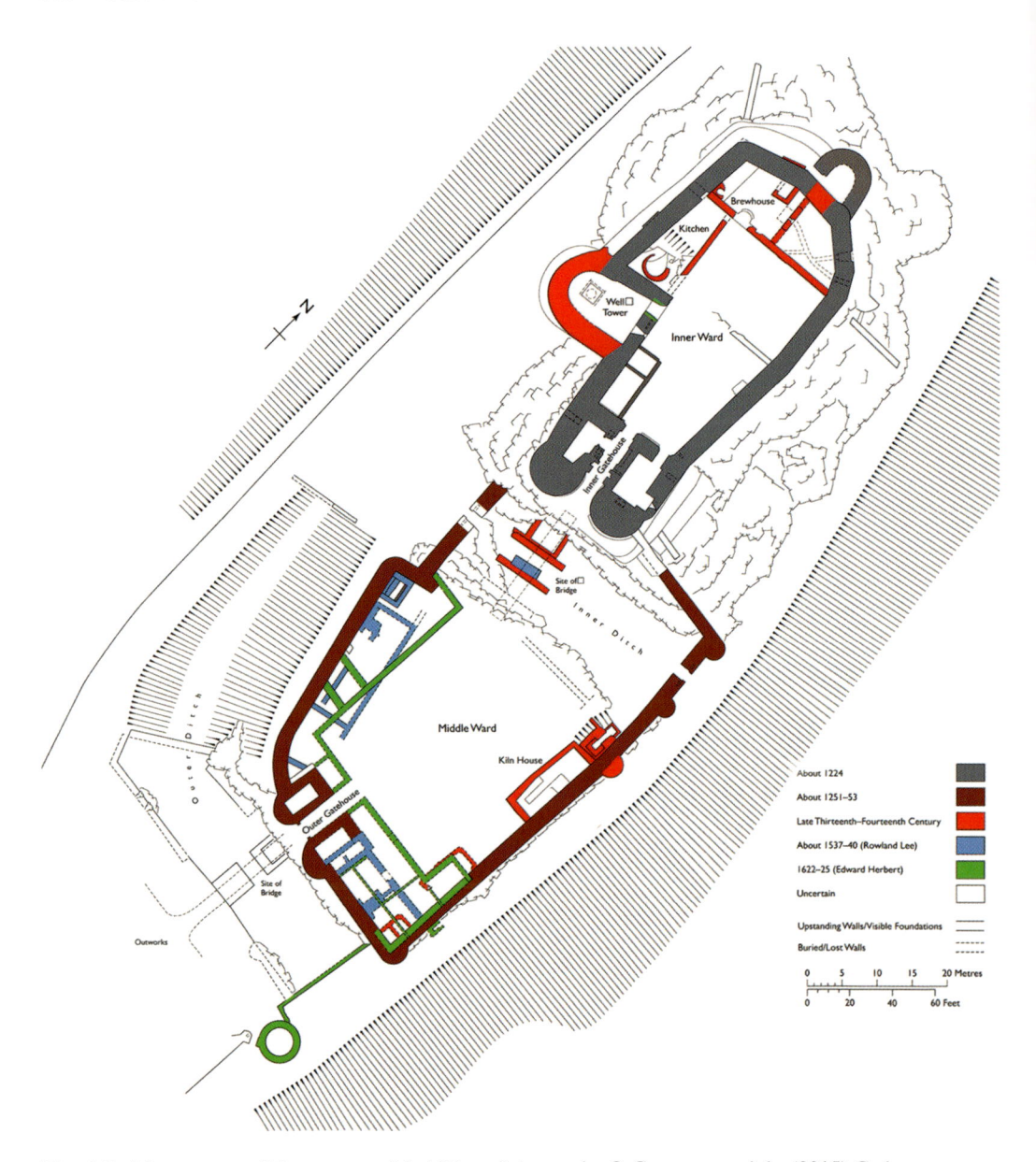

Fig. 8.3. Montgomery (Montgomeryshire) Plan of the castle. © Crown copyright (2015) Cadw.

the eye of Hubert de Burgh, the degree of circularity of the flanking towers was greater than in the royal works, and is more akin to the late twelfth-century towers of Chepstow.

In itself, the character of the gatehouse towers is perhaps not terribly significant, but in concert with the postern at the north end of the ward it takes on a greater import. The postern is entered via a D-shaped tower, with an entrance in the west side, a ninety-degree turn being necessary to enter the gateway in the curtain. Although this is a highly unusual arrangement, it has a very close parallel in the so-called Horseshoe Tower, which contained the gateway to the inner ward of Pembroke, another work attributed to William Marshal, for which Middle Eastern antecedents have been claimed.[4] These analogies at Montgomery with the works of William Marshal, could suggest the presence of a master mason with a first-hand knowledge of the Marshal castles. While the outer gatehouse of Chepstow may date from *c.* 1190, the inner ward of Pembroke belongs to the period *c.* 1200–1219. The chronology is tight enough for the Chepstow and/or Pembroke master(s) to have worked both for Marshal and at Montgomery, and it seems possible that in this instance a local master builder was engaged to erect the royal castle.

Montgomery may have influenced the form taken by two twin-towered gatehouses built by Henry at the Tower of London in the 1230s. Here, the western gateway collapsed in 1240 and no trace of it survives, although its barbican has been excavated in the moat to the north-west of the Beauchamp Tower. However, the foundations of the second gatehouse (the Coldharbour Gate), which gave access to the innermost ward, may be seen at the south-west angle of the White Tower. This building had twin cylindrical towers centred on the outer corners of a rectangular block, and so represents a different type from the gateways with D-shaped towers that were built by John, having more in common with Montgomery. The basic layout of this gatehouse was to be repeated at the Tower under Edward I in the 1270s, in the designs of the Middle Tower and Byward Tower at the main entrance.

The south-west: Corfe
At Corfe, the South-west Gatehouse of *c.* 1235 to *c.* 1245,[5] which gave access to the west bailey, has one elongated D-shaped tower and one round tower, a composition that seems to have been the result of the peculiar characteristics of the building site. The construction of the gatehouse followed on from a remodelling of Corfe in 1235, a project that included the excavation of the Great Ditch across the castle to separate the outer bailey from the west bailey and inner ward. At the same time a new wall was built 91.4 m (30 ft) to the west of the ditch to delineate the west bailey. The new gatehouse was raised in front of the wall on the strip of land, or berm, between it and the ditch, with the fronts of the towers on the lip of the ditch. Because the southern tower also formed part of the enceinte, a circular form was chosen to give it the attributes of a flanking tower, whereas the northern tower, which was wholly within the castle, had elongated sides in order to extend across the 10 m (33 ft) width of the berm. Each tower had a single arrow loop in its front at ground-floor level pointing towards the approach across the bridge, the right-hand one cruciform, the left-hand one plain. Around the wall head of each tower a line of corbels may have been to carry a timber hoard. The gate passage was defended firstly by a portcullis, then a machicolation slot divided into four sections, then a gate behind the archway secured by drawbars then, towards the rear of the gatehouse, a second portcullis.

The north
Some twenty years after the completion of the Constable's tower at Dover the double D-shaped plan of the portico was repeated at the royal castles of Scarborough, where the great gate was nearing completion in 1244–1245, and Newcastle where the Black Gate or outer gatehouse was under construction in 1247–1250 (Fig 8.4). However, this design, which is so closely identified with the royal works, was not replicated at York Castle, where rebuilding in stone was being carried out from 1244. At York, the masons raised a more conventional twin-towered gatehouse. The quadrant plan of the flanking towers and the

170   Castle Builders

Fig. 8.4. Newcastle (Northumberland) The Black Gate from the south east (1247–1250).

outer arch beneath which the gate was recessed are more reminiscent of the outer gatehouse of Nottingham Castle raised 1252–1255. Now sadly depleted, the medieval remains are incorporated into an early twentieth-century reconstruction, but the general purport of the design is apparent. Twin drum towers flanked the entrance, and there was a rectangular accommodation block to the rear.

Gatehouses of the de Clares

These royal twin-towered gatehouses were eclipsed by the monumental scale and architectural quality of the gatehouse raised by Richard de Clare or possibly his son Gilbert, at his castle of Tonbridge between *c.* 1250 and *c.* 1265 (Fig 8.5). Although it is related to the royal gatehouses raised under Henry III in its twin rounded towers, it nevertheless has a number of innovatory aspects that mark it out as a seminal building, and there is no really compelling evidence to suppose that the design was deeply influenced by royal precedents. Indeed, D-shaped flanking towers were a type that was no longer current in the royal works. The concentration of effort that has evidently been lavished on this one building had been lacking in its royal counterparts up to this point, the greater spread of buildings financed by the King seeming to have resulted in less extravagant approaches.

Although Tonbridge is not simply a defensive building, defence was nevertheless one aspect of the design that was taken very seriously indeed. The bow fronts of the flanking towers were built on bases of polygonal plan carried up as protective spurs; the bows themselves contained three tiers of arrow loops, staggered to allow an arcing range of fire around the approach to the entrance; the ditch in front of the castle had to be crossed by a drawbridge. It is the gate passage itself, however, on which the defensive aspects have been concentrated. At the outer end, there was, in sequence, a line of machicolations, a portcullis, a two-leaf gate, another row of machicolations, and beneath the latter in the sidewalls two arrow loops controlled from the two guard rooms, one each side of the gate passage. The doors to these rooms, each of which was protected by its own portcullis, come

Fig. 8.5. Tonbridge (Kent) The gatehouse from the north (mid thirteenth century).

next, occupying a centre position in each of the sidewalls, with a line of machicolations extending between them in the vault above. At the outer end of the passage there is a second sequence of defences, which seem to be designed to control egress from the courtyard. These are, from the courtyard, machicolations, portcullis, two-leaf gate and machicolations.

Each of the two guard rooms has direct access to a staircase, which communicates with the upper floors and roof, including the first-floor 'control room' from which the portcullises were operated and the inner lines of machicolations fed; the two outer lines of machicolations were operated from the parapet. Instead of the single slot machicolation that had been popular from the later twelfth century onwards, the slot was divided into a series of square apertures. The two pairs of gates both opened inwards, implying that the gatehouse was designed to control both ingress and egress. It also meant that the building was self-contained and capable of putting up an independent defence should the need arise. Hitherto, gate passage defences had acted as a single sequence of hurdles, so the Tonbridge arrangement represents an important new concept that was to have a good deal of influence.

Tonbridge was without doubt the model for Gilbert de Clare's inner east gatehouse of 1268–1271 at Caerphilly. Although the partial destruction and subsequent rebuilding of the Caerphilly gatehouse has created difficulties of interpretation, we know enough about its character to make an adequate comparison between the two buildings and confirm that the later building reproduced, to a great extent, the design of Tonbridge. The Caerphilly gatehouse was roughly the same size as Tonbridge, had similar D-shaped towers to the front with latrine projections in the re-entrant angles between them and the curtain, and similar round stair turrets to the rear. The internal plans also seem to be in broad agreement, including the ground storey with its two guard chambers either side of the gate passage entered by portcullis-defended doors and with direct access to a stair. The passage itself was defended by two pairs of doors, at least one but probably two portcullises, arrow loops towards the front, and lines of machicolations in the vault.

The concept of the self-contained gatehouse with heavily defended entrance passage, as established at Tonbridge and followed up at Caerphilly, was a short-lived phenomenon, emulated principally in some of Edward I's Welsh castles in the 1280s and 1290s, notably at Harlech and Beaumaris, both of which have closely related plans including the distinctive paired staircase turrets at the rear, and possibly even more strongly defended entrance passages. In the north gatehouse of Beaumaris, which is the best preserved, the sequence is a pair of barred gates, a portcullis, a second portcullis, a second paired of barred gates, a third portcullis, and at the inner end of the passage a third pair of barred gates. It is probable that a similar sequence existed at Harlech. In both cases the upper floor was carried on a series of diaphragm arches, which may have contained machicolations between them.

The ultimate in defended gate passages was that of the King's Gate of 1296–1323 at Caernarfon, a complex gatehouse, which is not entirely understood, owing either to it having been unfinished or partially demolished. The defences comprised, in sequence, a drawbridge pivoted on the threshold of the gateway, with a pit inside the passage, two portcullises, several lines of machicolations, a pair of gates, two more portcullises, and a second pair of gates. Between the third and fourth portcullis were the entrances to the guard rooms at the front of the gatehouse and to two rooms at the rear. The second pair of gates gave access to a vestibule, at which point a ninety-degree angle turn to the right (west) led into a continuation of the entrance passage giving access to the Lower Ward; logically, this passage would have been replicated on the east side, but, if so, there is now no trace. The western passage was protected at its eastern end by another portcullis, then a pair of gates; there was a similar arrangement of defences at its western end. In addition to these obstacles, the gate passage was monitored from both sides by a series of loops, which would have allowed the guards to fire upon anyone within it.

This formidable assembly of defences may seem excessive, but the susceptibility of the castle as a target for the Welsh had been realized when the half-finished building was captured and badly damaged during the revolt of 1294. It is, therefore, a reasonable assumption that the mason, Walter of Hereford, who took over the direction of work on the castle when it resumed in 1295, was instructed to pay particular attention to the defence of the entrance, as the potential weak spot of the defences. His response was to increase the number of conventional obstacles, and to add a touch of originality by introducing a right-angled turn, possibly providing separate entrances to the two wards. Never had the transit through a gatehouse been subjected to such a high level of control. It was the zenith of the trend towards ever more heavily defended entrances, which, by the 1280s, had accelerated into something of an obsession. The position of Caernarfon as the administrative centre of north Wales and the greater symbolic role that it embodied, made their mark upon its singular architectural character and set it apart from the other castles of the Welsh conquest. It is possible that this special status also affected the character of the gateway defences, leading Walter of Hereford to devise a distinctive scheme commensurate with the castle's extraordinary standing. No other castle gatehouse was to emulate defence on such a scale.

Barbicans

Courtyard barbicans
The earliest barbicans consisted of small courtyards in front of the gateway. They reduced the vulnerability of the gateway by screening it from the outside, and by allowing troops to gather there prior to making a sortie, so that the gateway itself was not exposed at the moment of exit. Maurice the engineer built courtyard barbicans in front of the two entrances to the inner ward of Dover in the 1180s. Each of these comprised a curtain wall containing a gateway, the latter being at the opposite end of the barbican from the twin-towered gates to the inner ward. The north barbican, which faced towards the then main gatehouse at the north-west angle of the castle, was semi-polygonal in outline, reflecting in some measure the profile of the Avranches Tower and providing the inner ward with a prow. These devices comprised another aspect of Maurice's concentric scheme of defence, the barbicans being overlooked by the gatehouse and curtain to the inner ward.

The new barbican that accompanied the resiting of the main gatehouse of Dover (Constable's Tower) in the 1220s was quite different. Firstly, although it had something of the courtyard barbican about it, it was separated from the gatehouse by the castle ditch and was elongated towards the north-west by a long walled approach that ran parallel with the curtain and was commanded by it. This approach opened out into the barbican proper, which was dominated by the gatehouse. The route from the barbican to the gatehouse was across a drawbridge so that the outwork could be isolated in a much more effective fashion than in Maurice's system.

This concept of the isolation of the barbican from the gateway was to be a recurrent theme of the thirteenth century, being developed by Gilbert de Clare's engineer at Caerphilly, in the works of the late 1260s and 1270s. Here, the approach to the main outer gatehouse was across a wide moat. Rather than spanning the moat with a single bridge, an intermediate platform housing a barbican was built within the moat. Drawbridges extended from the barbican to the outer bank of the moat and from the main outer gatehouse to the barbican. The binary division of command over the drawbridges meant that access to the castle could be closely controlled. The main outer gatehouse gave access to the south dam platform, from which an inner moat had to be crossed to the castle; effectively this platform was another barbican.

A similar principle underpinned the design for a distinct type of barbican built for John de Warenne, 6th earl of Surrey at Sandal Castle, where it stood at the foot of the motte and controlled access to the keep. Closely dated to *c.* 1265–1271 it is contemporary with Caerphilly.[6] This structure, which was ditched around so that it occupied a virtual island within the bailey, had a D-shaped plan with the arc facing outwards, away from the motte. Access was via a drawbridge across a moat into the side of the building. After a ninety-degree turn another drawbridge then had to be negotiated to reach the gateway at the foot of the motte before the ascent to the keep could be made. As the building has been reduced to its foundations, the original form of its superstructure is uncertain, although there is some evidence to suggest that it was a two-storey building with an element of domestic accommodation.[7]

Part of the interest of the Sandal barbican is its architectural relationship with two other late thirteenth-century barbicans: those of the Tower of London and Goodrich (Fig 8.6). The former (known as the Lion Tower) was part of the reconstruction of the main entrance to the Tower that was carried out between 1275 and 1285; the latter can only be assigned to the thirteenth century, and no more exactly. These are both courtyard barbicans, but, like Sandal, have D-shaped plans and side entries, and were isolated from the rest of the castle by ditches crossed by drawbridges. The relationship between London and Goodrich has long been recognized and attributed to a common source,[8] but given the closeness in date, the marked similarities in concept, and the fact that there were close personal contacts between the patrons: Warenne, his brother-in-law, William de Valence (Goodrich), and Edward I,[9] there is certainly a case to be made for adding Sandal to the equation.

One possible antecedent for the Sandal barbican is the early thirteenth-century Horseshoe Tower that stood in front of the inner curtain of Pembroke Castle, giving access to the inner ward (see pp. 168–169). This embodies two of the defining qualities of the barbicans under discussion: it was D-shaped and was also entered from one of its sides, so that a right angle had to be turned to gain entry to the gateway in the curtain; as a gatehouse, it was highly unusual. Since 1247, Pembroke had been in the hands of William de Valence, so it would not be unreasonable to suppose that he and his brother-in-law, John de Warenne, might have used it as a source for their own works at Goodrich and Sandal respectively. These three systems are unlikely to have been designed independently of one another, and as the Sandal barbican is an earlier building than the Lion Tower, so it may be that the direction of diffusion was towards rather than from the royal works.

Fig. 8.6. Goodrich (Herefordshire) The D-shaped barbican from the north west (last quarter of the thirteenth century).

Fig. 8.7. Conwy (Caernarfonshire) The castle from the west showing the low walls of the barbican in front (last quarter of the thirteenth century).

The vogue for these isolated D-shaped barbicans was not long lived, and did not supersede the simple courtyard barbican that was adopted by Maurice at Dover. Edward I himself had a pair of courtyard barbicans built at Conwy *c.* 1283 at each end of the castle to protect the main gate (west, Fig 8.7) and watergate (east), the form being dictated by the restricted topography of the site. The barbicans were provided with rounded wall turrets and the west barbican had its own twin-turreted gatehouse, but there was really little difference between them and their twelfth-century counterparts at Dover, and they adhered to one aspect of the military concept of concentricity in that the barbican was commanded by the walls and towers of the castle proper. An interesting aspect of this particular scheme is that the builders seem to have believed that the provision of a barbican obviated the need for a gatehouse. Instead, the entrances to the castle are simple gateways albeit protected by machicolations and portcullises.

Passage barbicans
In the later medieval period much more restricted passage barbicans became popular. In its conventional form, a passage barbican comprised two parallel walls that extended from the gatehouse and were linked at the outer end by a crosswall containing a gateway. A building that anticipates the passage barbican, even if it doesn't quite fulfil its purpose, is the western tower complex at Framlingham of *c.* 1190. The rectangular tower is located at the south-east corner of the lower court and is attached to the curtain by two long walls extending across the castle ditch and enclosing a passage. The passage provided access to the tower via a timber gallery and thence to the lower court. There was also external access to the passage from a doorway in the southern wall immediately east of the tower, and there must have been a staircase within the passage via which the postern in the curtain wall was reached.

The passage type of barbican was also becoming discernible in the 1220s barbican at Dover, where the long approach to the courtyard barbican anticipates later arrangements. There are hints of the Dover scheme in the thirteenth-century passage barbican at Conisbrough (now missing its gateway) which extends from the edge of the moat towards the inner ward then turns through 45 degrees to follow the line of the curtain, terminating in front of the gateway where it was necessary to turn another 90 degrees in order to enter the gateway. In shadowing the curtain the barbican was, of course, dominated by the wallhead defenders to a greater extent than at Dover. There are also elements of the passage barbican in the late thirteenth-century arrangement for the Tower of London, where bridges extend across the moat between the Lion Tower and the two twin-towered gatehouses.

It was not until the fourteenth-century, however, that the type became formalized as an architectural feature. An early example existed at Dunstanburgh, in front of the great gatehouse of 1313, which had been raised by the mason, Master Elias.[10] Master Elias has been tentatively identified with Elias de Bruton, a mason recorded as working at Conwy in 1302–1303,[11] although the architectural affinities of the Dunstanburgh gatehouse are with Harlech rather than Conwy. It is arguable, however, that the juxtaposition of great and outer gatehouses at Harlech inspired the builder of the gatehouse and barbican of Dunstanburgh. At Harlech, which is a very symmetrical castle, the outer gatehouse stands directly in front of the great gatehouse, and is only separated from it by a short distance (Fig 8.8). Architecturally, the outer gatehouse emphasizes the colossal scale of the great gatehouse,

Fig. 8.8. Harlech (Merionethshire) The outer and inner gatehouses from the east.

and thereby adds to the psychological impact; militarily, the great gatehouse dominates access to the outer ward. Very much the same arrangement pertains at Dunstanburgh but on a larger scale. Here, the foundations of the barbican suggest a building approximately 6 m (20 ft) long from the outer wall to the fronts of the bows and approximately 9 m (30 ft) wide. It comprised two parallel walls joined at the outer end by a third wall containing the entrance arch.

The mid fourteenth century saw a proliferation of passage barbicans in which an outer tower was attached to the gatehouse by the flanking walls of the barbican passage. The type was universal, although there were distinct regional and local interpretations. In the south of England, *c.* 1330, John de Warenne, 7th earl of Surrey, built a barbican before the gate to his castle of Lewes. The three-storey outer tower has round angle turrets carried on stepped corbelling in the manner of the Beaumaris water gate, and incorporated three levels of defence. The gateway itself contained two portcullises; at first-floor level there are cruciform arrow loops with oillet feet, both in the flanking turrets and in the main body of the tower, the latter squeezed to either side of the gate arch. Finally, there is a machicolated parapet over the entrance.

The theme was repeated at Warwick, *c.* 1340, for Thomas Beauchamp, earl of Warwick. The Warwick barbican also has a three-storey entrance block, in this case flanked by octagonal angle turrets, the walls of the passage being carried back to the gatehouse, initially at a lower level, though raised to the same height as the entrance block in a later phase. Originally, the barbican tower appears to have stood within the moat, being approached by a drawbridge; a second drawbridge probably linked it to the gatehouse.[12] Within the barbican tower passage was a portcullis, a line of machicolations and then a gate. In the north of England a major passage barbican was added to Alnwick Castle at about the same time as the Warwick example. It has a two-storey rectangular entrance block with square turrets flanking a recessed entrance. As at Warwick, the linking walls of the barbican crossed the castle ditch, and, in this case, is known to have incorporated a drawbridge within it.[13] Barbicans like these acted as extensions to the gate passage and, by confining traffic to a narrow space in a direct line with the gatehouse gave a much tighter degree of control over the approach than did the courtyard barbican.

The Drawbridge

Drawbridges could only span short distances and usually comprised the final element of a more permanent structure that extended across most of the ditch. In its most primitive form the drawbridge was simply removed by hand, an inefficient system that was to be supplanted by some form of mechanism using axle technology, the bearing sockets of which sometimes survive in the side walls of the gatehouse.

Lifting bridges

In the simplest form of mechanized drawbridge the inner end of the bridge was pivoted on the threshold of the gate. Chains attached to the outer end of the bridge extended to a chamber above the gate passage where they were attached to a windlass. When the windlass was turned the chains wrapped around its axle and raised the drawbridge to block the entrance. The evidence for such an arrangement usually includes apertures in the face of the wall above the gateway for the chains to pass through to the room containing the windlass. Such was the arrangement in the early thirteenth-century inner gatehouse of White Castle (Monmouthshire), where the gap between the permanent bridge and the gateway had been made structural by the creation of a stone walled pit. Despite the development of new technology, this simple form of drawbridge did not become obsolete; a lifting bridge, for instance, was installed at the outer gatehouse Kidwelly in 1390–1402.

Turning bridges

A drawback to the lifting bridge was that the process of raising it with a windlass was slow. A technological advance was the turning bridge, which was pivoted, not at one extremity, but closer to its mid-point so that it acted as a seesaw, and could be worked according to the counterbalance principle. The trick to being able to raise and lower the bridge in the most efficient manner was to weight one end so that it was slightly heavier than the other, and therefore fell naturally into a vertical or horizontal attitude so that it could only be kept in the opposite position by being secured. By releasing the locking device the bridge would swing into its natural pose. The mechanism may have been suggested by the trebuchet, which used similar counterbalance technology. An essential part of the turning bridge system was a drawbridge-pit on the castle side of the ditch in order to accommodate the inner half of the drawbridge when it was in the vertical position.

One of the earliest instances of a turning bridge in France was built into the entrance of the donjon of Coucy, a building of the second quarter of the thirteenth century, which was separated from the rest of the castle by its own ditch. In England, turning bridges were introduced during the reign of Henry III (1216–1272) but were rare before the 1240s,[14] although the mid and late thirteenth century witnessed a proliferation of their use. At White Castle, the outer gatehouse, which was probably built in 1256–1257 under the tenure of the Lord Edward (the future Edward 1), was provided with a turning bridge, in a departure from the earlier lifting mechanism of the inner gatehouse. As in the inner gatehouse there was a drawbridge pit in front of the entrance, which in this instance was deeply recessed between the two flanking towers. Unlike the inner gatehouse, however, it was pivoted on the outer wall of the pit, so that when it was in the down position its outer end spanned the gap between the permanent bridge and the gatehouse, and the inner end spanned the drawbridge pit.

A distinctive type of turning bridge had been introduced into the royal works by the 1240s, the earliest known instances being at the royal castle of Newcastle where the Black Gate of 1247–1250 incorporates two examples of an ingenious design in which the bridge was pivoted on the threshold of the gateway and worked by a system of counterbalance.[15] It seems that the drawbridge was constructed on three longitudinal beams, the ends of which extended beyond the bridge and threshold some 4 m (13 ft) into the gate passage. Instead of a drawbridge pit, these counterbalance beams were accommodated within three corresponding slots in the floor of the gatehouse, so that when the bridge was released the beams dropped through the slots and the bridge rose backwards to block the gateway.

This principle was also adopted for the drawbridge to the barbican (Lion Tower) of the Tower of London *c.* 1275, and only slightly later at Goodrich, at the entrances to both the barbican and the main gateway. Drawbridges designed on a similar principle were also used in two of the earliest of Edward I's castles in north Wales: Flint (inner gate) and Rhuddlan (Town Gate and Friary Gate), all of *c.* 1277.[16] The Lion Tower may also have been the source of inspiration for the drawbridge to the gatehouse of the inner ward of Bungay Castle, built by Roger Bigod, earl of Norfolk *c.* 1294, possibly with the assistance of royal craftsmen.[17]

Seldom can the details of drawbridge mechanisms be reconstructed entirely from the surviving remains. In his interpretation of the Bungay drawbridge, Hugh Braun deduced, from the presence of checks for the counterpoise beams, that the bridge fell naturally into the vertical position. In such cases there must have been a means of returning it to the horizontal. This would mean either raising the inner, weighted, end from within the gatehouse by means of a windlass, or, adjusting the weighting so that the outer end became heavier than the inner end. There is rarely any indication of such devices, but at Bungay, Braun recorded beam sockets on either side of the gatehouse,[18] which might perhaps indicate the housing for a temporary windlass, fixed into position when needed to lower the bridge, by raising the counterbalance beams.

It is interesting to note that this particular type of turning bridge is absent from Gilbert de Clare's castle of Caerphilly, and this is one aspect of the de Clares' castles that suggests a large degree of independence from the precedents of the royal works. At Caerphilly, Gilbert de Clare's engineer seems to have resorted to a combination of lifting and turning techniques. In the main outer gatehouse of the 1280s an inner pit within the entrance passage housed the inner end of the drawbridge when raised, a feature that indicates a turning bridge. However, above the gateway, there are also two square holes, apparently for drawbridge chains, an arrangement that suggests a lifting bridge (Fig 8.9). So there seems

180　Castle Builders

Fig. 8.9. Caerphilly (Glamorganshire) The main outer gateway with holes for the drawbridge chains above the gateway (last quarter of the thirteenth century).

to have been a hybrid system in operation here in which counterbalance technology worked in concert with a hand-turned windlass. It may represent a method of retaining a greater degree of control over the counter-balance system, in effect a type of manual overdrive.

A mixture of lifting and turning bridge technology was also installed in the later castles of Edward I in north Wales, following the war of 1283, but there is no sign of the counterpoise beam systems that were in use at Rhuddlan. At Conwy, the counterpoise pit beneath the outer gateway of 1283 suggests a turning bridge; there are also counterpoise pits at Caernarfon (Queen's Gate, 1283; King's Gate, 1295). At Beaumaris (Gate-next-the-sea 1295), there is both a counterpoise pit, and, above the gateway, holes for the chains, suggesting a dual control system like the one described at Caerphilly. The reason that the turning bridge with counterbalance beams fell out of favour in north Wales after 1283 is unknown, but may have been a result of a change of personnel. It is possible that the design of the Flint and Rhuddlan bridges had already been decided upon by the time James of St George took over the royal works in north Wales, some six months after work had begun there. In which case, Richard the engineer, who had been working for the crown since 1265, and who was in charge of the initial work at Flint and Rhuddlan from July 1277,[19] may have been responsible for the design of the drawbridges there.

Lifting bridges with counterbalanced beams
Towards the end of the thirteenth century a new type of drawbridge mechanism was introduced, also based on the counterbalance principle, but quite different in its design. Two beams were pivoted at their mid points, one each side of, and immediately above, the

gateway. The outer ends were attached to the lip of the drawbridge by chains, while the inner ends were weighted. When the drawbridge was down the beams were in a horizontal position, and when it was raised they were in a vertical position, the outer halves fitting into specially prepared grooves in the masonry above the gate and the inner, weighted, halves being accommodated inside the building on either side of the gate passage. The drawbridge itself was pulled up into a recess in the front of the entrance. This system was popular in France, but is seldom encountered in England and Wales, and then not until the mid fifteenth century; one example is at Raglan at the entrance to the keep, which was even more unusual in being a double bridge giving separate access to two adjacent entrances (Fig 8.10).[20] North of the border, however, the technology was adopted more readily and at an earlier date, one example being built at Bothwell c. 1400 at the entrance to the north-east tower. The design of the counterbalanced beam bridge obviated the necessity for a drawbridge pit because the inner end of the drawbridge was hinged on the threshold of the gate.

Fig. 8.10. Raglan (Monmouthshire) Amidst later alterations, the entrance to the keep retains the slots for the counterbalance beams that were used in operating two drawbridges. The system allowed pedestrian access while keeping the main gateway closed.

The Portcullis

Another universal mechanism that contributed to the defence of the entrance was the portcullis. Essentially a guillotine gate set within grooves on either side of the gate passage, it comprised a wooden openwork frame with closely set horizontals and verticals in a gridiron pattern, with pointed feet to the verticals. The key timbers were the horizontal (head) beam, to which the chains by which the portcullis was raised and lowered were attached, and the side posts that occupied the grooves. Many portcullises where reinforced with iron in some way, like those at Bodiam and the outer gatehouse of Carlisle (Fig 8.11), both probably dating from the late fourteenth century, and both of which have iron grids fastened to the front of the woodwork.

A crucial piece of equipment used in raising and lowering both portcullises and drawbridges was the windlass, a simple device found in various forms, comprising an axle with supports at either end; it was sited on an upper floor of the gatehouse directly above the portcullis. In the surviving portcullis windlass (date uncertain) in the fourteenth-century York gatehouse of Monk Bar, the ends of the axle, which are supported by wooden verticals, were fitted

Fig. 8.11. Carlisle (Cumberland) The iron clad portcullis (1378–1383).

with iron ratchets, and the supports with pawls, while two retractable handspikes protrude from sockets in the length of the axle.[21] To raise the portcullis the operators pulled the handspikes down to floor level so that the chains wrapped around the axle; the handspikes were then disengaged, the ratchet system preventing the portcullis from falling back, and reinserted in the axle in the vertical position; the action was then repeated as many times as was required to raise the portcullis to its full height. By releasing the pawl the portcullis could be lowered very rapidly, but a more controlled descent could also be made by means of the handspikes.

This was one system, but there were probably several others. Viollet le Duc's illustration of a portcullis in the late thirteenth-century Porte Narbonnaise at Carcassonne shows a more sophisticated mechanism in which the chain extending between the windlass and the portcullis

Fig. 8.12. Lancaster (Lancashire) Portcullis chamber in the main gatehouse (first quarter of the fifteenth century with nineteenth-century winch).

is looped over a pulley fixed at a higher level.[22] Once the portcullis had been raised it was supported in position by two retractable beams. The descent of the portcullis was controlled by a counterbalance system in which two further chains attached to the portcullis were also looped over pulleys and weights attached to the free ends. If these weights were only slightly lighter than the portcullis then releasing the latter would allow it to descend at a moderate speed, just as the judicious weighting of turning bridges produced the same effect.

Pulley systems facilitated the raising of the portcullis and were also used in a number of castles in Britain. In the late thirteenth-century south gate of Beaumaris, the chain from the windlass extended up to and over a pulley set in the rear arch of a first-floor window. The main chain would have been linked to two further chains that extended to either end of the head beam. This is the arrangement in the early fifteenth-century gatehouse of Lancaster, but the lifting mechanism itself dates from the nineteenth century (Fig 8.12). There is no unequivocal evidence for the use of counterweights in English castles, though there is no reason to suppose that that English engineers were opposed to the device and it is quite possible that some may have existed.

Usually, lifting mechanisms have left no trace, but occasionally, the accommodations made for them in the stonework remain. At Goodrich, for example, where there were two portcullises, evidence for the manner in which they worked has survived within the masonry

Fig. 8.13. Goodrich (Herefordshire) Twin windlass niches in the main gateway with holes for the portcullis chains in the floor beneath them and a slot for a second portcullis in the foreground (last quarter of the thirteenth century).

of the room above the gate passage (Fig 8.13). The outer portcullis was operated by a pair of windlasses housed in the front wall of the building where there are two rectangular recesses, each with a pair of round sockets in its sides to accommodate the housings of the axles. In the floor beneath each recess is a square hole through which the rope or chain that held the portcullis was threaded. The floor of the room is also pierced by the slot for the inner portcullis, which must have been raised and lowered by a windlass situated over or adjacent to it.

Often, the only surviving evidence for a portcullis consists of the grooves in the stonework on either side of the gate passage. Usually, they extend to the floor of the gate passage; an exception noted by Toy is in the late twelfth-century gatehouse of Warkworth Castle,[23] where the grooves stop about 2.13 m (7 ft) above the ground, coinciding with the top of a moulded string course from which the vault springs (Fig 8.14). This implies an unusual design for the portcullis itself in which the ends of a horizontal beam came to rest on top of the string courses and the portcullis grill extended both above and below it. The frame, therefore, would probably have taken the form of a capital T with a short-armed head beam. The rationale behind such a design is not immediately obvious, but one possibility is that when the portcullis was in the raised position it would have been locked in position by placing supports under the ends of the main beam. Whatever the details of the system, it is clear that the engineer responsible for this apparatus had a streak of originality, a trait that is also to be recognized in the design of the gatehouse, which is rather unusual for its time in having semi-polygonal flanking towers.

Fig. 8.14. Warkworth (Northumberland) The portcullis slot of the main gateway extends only to the top of the string course. Behind it is a machicolation slot.

Another unparalleled system was adopted in the late fourteenth century at Castle Bolton, which had six portcullises ranged around the courtyard entrances to the domestic accommodation, all of which conformed to a standard but idiosyncratic design (Fig 8.15). The entrances were recessed within tall outer arches which accommodated the portcullises when in the raised position, meaning that they were exposed to view and to the elements at all times. A small square opening in the soffit of the outer arch shows that they were each suspended from above by a single chain attached to a windlass in the second-floor rooms immediately above the entrances. The main chain would have been linked to two further chains that extended to either end of the head beam. How well this system worked in practice is debatable; it does not seem to have been repeated elsewhere.

In numerous cases the design of the surrounding stonework suggests that the portcullis was incorporated into the building during the construction of the masonry and that no consideration was given to the possibility that it might be desirable to remove it in one piece. The only way that many portcullises could be taken out of their housings would have been by dismantling them. Replacement, then, would have necessitated assembling *in situ*. This might seem a daunting task, but there is no reason why it should not have been possible. The first task would have been to get the head beam into position; after that the upper ends of the verticals could be jointed into it from below. A degree of play in the portcullis slots would have facilitated the most challenging task of assembling the horizontals. After that, securing the various elements to each other would have been would have been comparatively straightforward.

Fig. 8.15. Castle Bolton (Yorkshire) Entrance to the north range (last quarter of the fourteenth century with twenty-first century portcullis).

Conclusion

During the later twelfth and thirteenth centuries, the castle builder's emphasis had been on defence, a concern exacerbated towards the end of the period by the Welsh wars. Indeed the proliferation of gateway defences at Harlech, Caernarfon and Beaumaris, in particular, seems to indicate an obsession bordering on paranoia. Within a few years of Edward I's death, however, the priority had changed, and designers of gatehouses were able to revert to a less tense approach to security, proportionate to the expected level of risk. In the later medieval period, the drawbridge and the portcullis continued to be mainstays of the defensive repertoire, machicolations were still sometimes incorporated into the vaulting of gate passages, (e.g. Maxstoke, 1345; Bodiam, 1385), and barbicans were still built (e.g. Tynemouth, 1390). These features were workable defences, but defence was no longer the prime object of the castle builder's attention, which was increasingly drawn to domestic matters, in particular, the problem of lodging large households in the most efficient manner by optimizing space without sacrificing the quality of the accommodation.

Chapter 9

Domestic Engineering

The Art of Daedalus

On 14 September 1378 a contract was drawn up between the Yorkshire nobleman, Richard Le Scrope, Steward of the Household, and the Durham mason, John Lewyn, in which Lewyn was commissioned to build certain works at Lord Scrope's manor of Bolton in Wensleydale.[1] This contract is the earliest documentation for the construction of the late fourteenth-century quadrangular courtyard castle at what is now Castle Bolton. Castle Bolton is the outstanding English example of a late medieval type, in which large-scale domestic planning was confined within a restricted compass, rising through several storeys, to create a compact, integrated castle with a custom-designed plan of sometimes labyrinthine complexity (Fig 9.1).

At Bolton, the five-storey corner towers and three-storey linking ranges accommodated eight major domestic suites centred on several halls, together with numerous individual lodgings, and various domestic offices including two kitchens, a brewhouse and bakehouse, as well as stables.[2] The genius of the design lies in the assimilation of the various units, a task of three-dimensional degree that involved arranging very specific lines of communication in

Fig. 9.1. Castle Bolton (Yorkshire) The castle built by John Lewyn of Durham from the north east (last quarter of the fourteenth century).

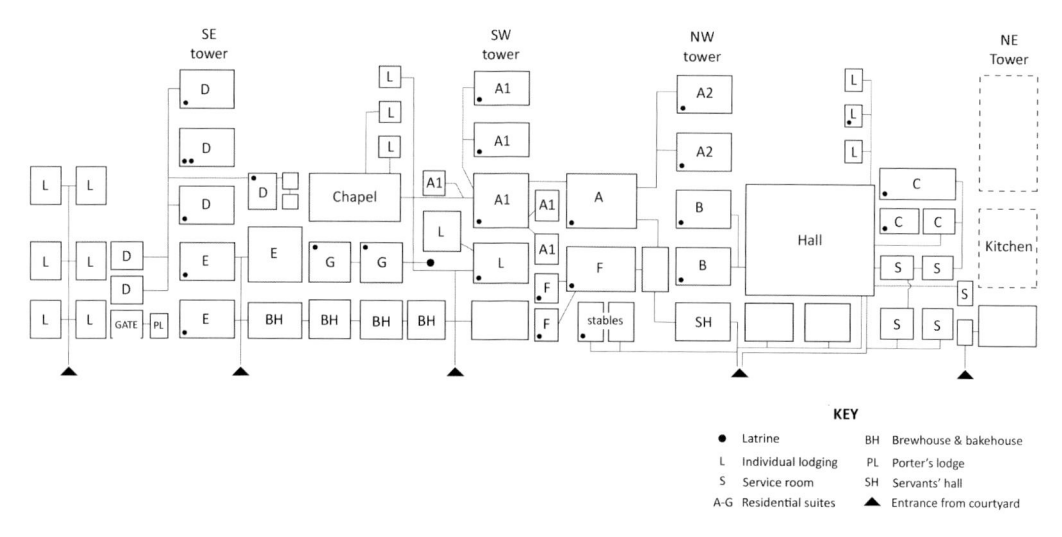

Fig. 9.2. Castle Bolton (Yorkshire) Planning diagram, after Faulkner 1963.

order to maintain a high degree of exclusivity for each residential unit (Fig 9.2). Amongst non-royal castles Bolton is the most ambitious, in scale, of this specialized type of building, and, despite the destruction of the north-east tower, one of the most easily understood, because it is otherwise comparatively little altered. We will return to Bolton and John Lewyn later, but let us first of all consider the evolution of this type of complex.

Great towers
Some of the first attempts at spatial planning within compact multi-storeyed blocks occurred in eleventh-century great towers. The breakthrough was the introduction of the crosswall into the main block, because it created greater possibilities for internal layouts, with more scope for lateral sequences of rooms, in addition to the vertical series that might be available in a multi-storey building with an undivided main block, as, for example, the donjon of Loches. The later eleventh-century great towers of London (White Tower) and Colchester were both recipients of such an approach. The White Tower, which is the most complete and therefore the best understood of the two, rises through three storeys and is divided by internal walls into three main spaces. Apparent illogicalities in the lines of communication and the possible loss of timber partitions present difficulties of interpretation. Nevertheless, it seems clear that the layout was designed to accommodate specific functions, and that the routes linking the different parts of the tower were deliberately devised to facilitate those functions even though it may no longer be possible to determine what they were.[3] The internal planning of these multi-storey blocks was refined by the second generation of royal keep builders at, for example, Norwich, Canterbury and Bamburgh, all of which had more complicated internal partitioning and carefully defined lines of communication.[4]

An interesting arrangement that anticipates late medieval planning existed within Henry I's early twelfth-century donjon of Arques-la-Bataille in Normandy, where the crosswall divided the tower into two independent halves, with no communication between them. Effectively, therefore, the donjon could have functioned as two separate entities, each comprising several spatial units or rooms. This concept of isolating groups of rooms by tailoring the lines of access, and thereby accommodating a series of independent or semi-independent sections was developed to a considerable degree in the integrated castles of the later medieval period. The great tower as a residence of palatial proportions extended down to the late twelfth century, the keep of Dover being the last in the sequence.

Courtyard houses
A second strand of compact domestic planning is represented by the early twelfth-century bishops' residences based on the claustral pattern. Roger of Caen, bishop of Salisbury, built two such complexes, at the castles of Sherborne and Old Sarum, and slightly later, Henry of Blois, bishop of Winchester, developed Wolvesey Castle along similar lines. These schemes represent a regularizing - probably under the influence of monastic planning - of the rambling collections of domestic accommodation that had hitherto been the norm in high status secular homes. Quadrangular courtyard residences were subsequently adopted in royal castles, notably the later twelfth-century apartments of Henry II built around the former Horn Court (now Waterloo Chamber) in the upper ward of Windsor Castle, which were carried out by a mason called Godwin,[5] under the eye of Ailnoth the engineer who acted as a viewer,[6] and, on a much smaller scale, those of King John in the inner ward of Corfe (the Gloriette), built in the early years of the thirteenth century.

While the details of the Windsor apartments are lost, the fragmentary remains of the Gloriette at Corfe permit a partial reconstruction of its original form. The accommodation was grouped around three sides of a rectangular courtyard, with the principal rooms at first-floor level carried on vaulted undercrofts. The more irregularly-arranged fourth (north) side was occupied by a covered staircase that ascended to a three-storey porch at the north-east angle of the courtyard. The first-floor landing within the porch may have acted as a waiting room for suppliants, a possibility indicated by the large north window, the embrasure of which contained a stone bench. Two doorways on the east side of this room gave access to what has been described as the king's presence chamber (north) and to the lower end of the King's hall (south).[7]

The courtyard, or cloister, arrangement persisted in Henry III's major rebuilding and reorganization of the royal lodgings in Windsor Castle in the 1240s. In the upper ward he reconstructed his grandfather's apartments, retaining the Horn Court at the heart of the new complex. How the various components of the accommodation (hall, chapel, chamber beside the hall, king's great chamber and adjoining wardrobe, kitchen, cellars etc) were disposed is, however, uncertain. It is probable that the technical director of these works at Windsor was Henry de Reyns, who, as we have seen (Chapter 6) was the inspiration behind the great tower of York castle (Clifford's Tower) raised from 1245 onwards, but also the eastern arm of Westminster Abbey from the same year. His successor, John of Gloucester, undertook further works on the apartments of the upper ward in the 1250s.

Thirteenth-century planning in Wales and the Marches
The example of Windsor may have been behind the plan of the royal lodgings of 1284–1286 at Conwy Castle, built by Henry's son, Edward I. Edward's principal mason in Wales, James of St Georges, who undertook the construction of the apartments, is probably to be credited

with the design. James, who had been recruited into the King's service following an early career for the counts of Savoy, had arrived in north Wales in 1278, and took charge of the royal castle building programme that had already begun at Aberystwyth, Builth, Flint and Rhuddlan. Master James is one of the first master craftsmen that we know of to have had simultaneous charge of several major castle-building projects, a responsibility that argues for a high degree of organisational ability. The extent to which he contributed to the design of Edward's castles is uncertain, but at Conwy he carried out the works of masonry for the King and Queen's chambers by contract and there is no reason to doubt that it is to him that the plan should be attributed.[8]

The lodgings were situated in the inner ward, the main domestic ranges being arranged around two sides (south and east) of a rectangular courtyard (Fig 9.3); extra accommodation was provided by the inner ward's four round corner towers, which are integral to the design. The ground storey, which was given over to storage and the preparation of food, contained a kitchen at the east end of the south range and a bread oven in the Bakehouse (south-west) Tower. As in King John's Gloriette at Corfe, the principal entrance to the first-floor apartments was from the courtyard via an external staircase. This gave access to the south end of the great chamber in the east range, whence a doorway led into the King's chamber at the east end of the south range; this apartment connected in turn with the Queen's chamber at the west end of the range. Access to the smaller chambers in the King's (south-east) and Bakehouse (south-west) towers was via spiral staircases that extended from ground-floor level to the roof, and indirectly from the King's and Queen's chambers respectively.

Fig. 9.3. Conwy (Caernarfonshire) The royal lodgings built by James of St Georges from the north east (last quarter of the thirteenth century)

A considerable part of the skill involved in planning the royal lodgings at Conwy and other such residences lay in the disposition of the communicating doorways, passages and staircases that provided access between the various parts of the complex, and gave the residence a coherent and workable plan in providing exclusive accommodation for its most important occupants, and an efficient means of serving them. As an example of this, we might cite an interesting contrivance associated with the chapel, which is housed in the north-east tower, and which takes the form of a small viewing chamber situated within the thickness of the wall at a mezzanine level. This is an extreme form of the raised private pew or gallery that was to become a recurrent feature of castle chapels in the later Middle Ages.

That the principle behind these compact courtyard residences, as favoured by the royal family, had been disseminated amongst the nobility is demonstrated by a number of marcher lordship castles. One development that shares the integrated planning principles of the royal lodgings at Conwy is the 'Gloriette' in the lower bailey of Chepstow as rebuilt for Roger Bigod, earl of Norfolk in the early 1280s by the master mason, Ralph Gogun.[9] This is a four-level domestic complex that is ranged along the north side of the lower bailey. These residential facilities represent the rational assimilation of domestic buildings that had in the castles of earlier periods been arranged less formally. The interest of the configuration is the manner in which the sloping site has been turned to advantage in order to create a bespoke design based on conventional components.

At one end of the Gloriette was an open hall, entered at courtyard level via a porch into the lower (north) end. Inside, a trio of doorways in the lower end wall led to the buttery (left), pantry (right) and kitchen (centre). The first two were at hall level, but the kitchen doorway opened to a flight of steps that descended to a service passage, also accessible from the courtyard. On the north side of the passage was a servery hatch and doorway to the kitchen, but there was also access to an office, to a room containing a double-seater latrine, and to a second staircase descending to a vaulted cellar situated under the hall. Beyond (north of) the kitchen, which was open to the roof, was the larder and beyond the larder another passage from the courtyard leading to more latrines. A first-floor chamber was built over the office and service passage, and first- and second-floor chambers over the larder.

A more comprehensive scheme on a virgin site is at Holt (Denbighshire). Sadly, Holt Castle is now substantially destroyed, but sixteenth and seventeenth-century drawings, including plans and perspectives,[10] show an integrated building of three-storey domestic ranges built to a regular pentagonal plan with four-storey towers projecting from the angles. The compressed nature of the layout suggests a very controlled internal plan, vertical communication being by way of spiral staircases in each of the towers and at several of the courtyard angles.

Another example is at Goodrich, an eleventh- or twelfth-century foundation rebuilt from the late thirteenth century by William de Valence, earl of Pembroke, as an irregular quadrangular castle with cylindrical corner towers and a series of accommodation blocks ranged around the courtyard. Architectural affinities with the works of the 1270s at the Tower of London under the master mason Robert of Beverley hint at royal influence, although several phases have been identified, which may suggest that the domestic accommodation represents an accretive development rather one that was conceived and implemented as a

Domestic Engineering 191

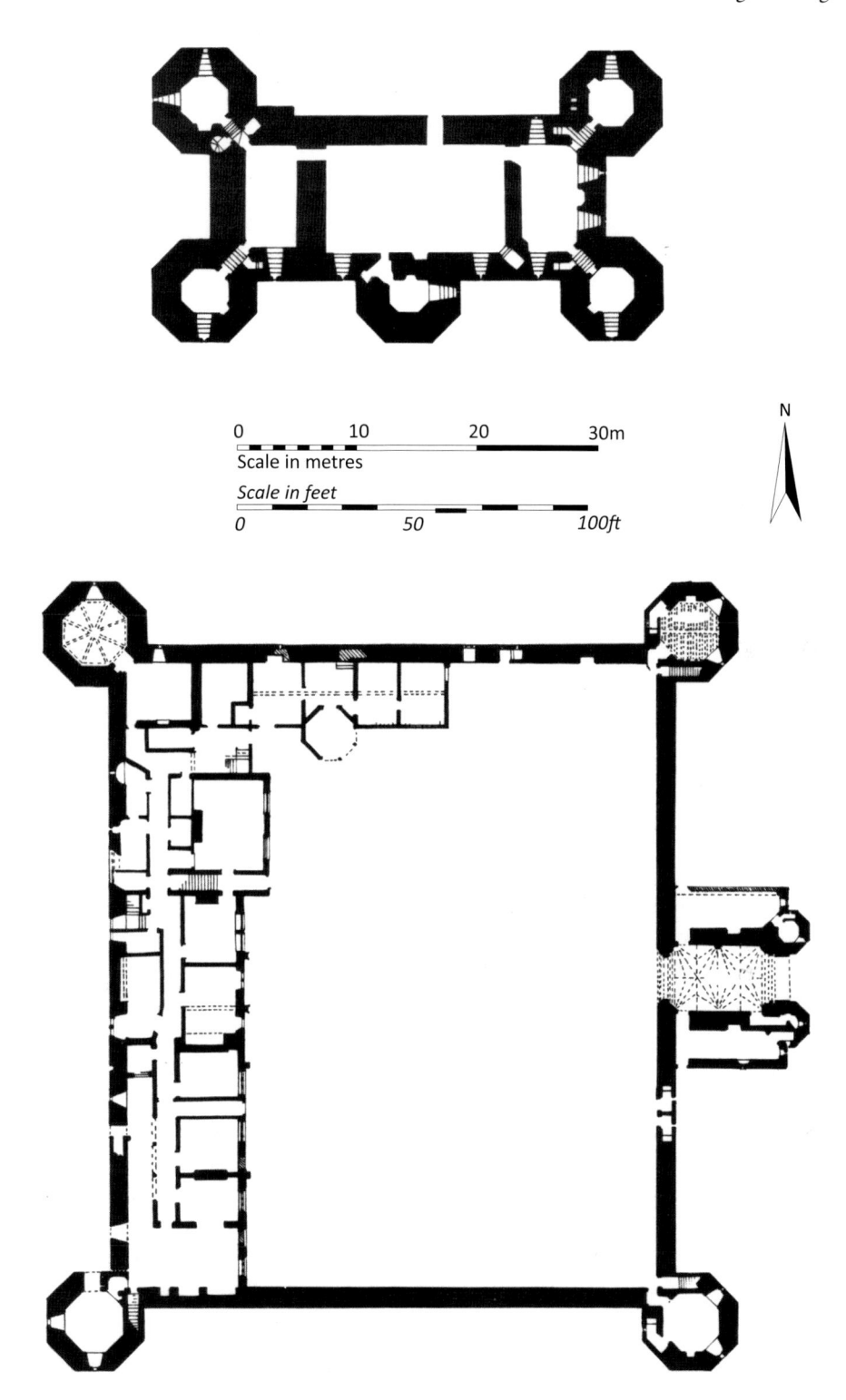

Fig. 9.4. Maxstoke (Warwickshire, after Alcock *et al.* 1978) and Stafford keep. Both buildings date from the 1340s.

single scheme.[11] In its late medieval configuration the accommodation included four halls with associated chamber blocks and other lodgings.[12]

In 1345, when William de Clinton, earl of Huntingdon, obtained a licence to crenellate for his new castle at Maxstoke,[13] the principle of the integrated courtyard castle was fully established. Built to a symmetrical plan, by 'a master architect, working with the highest possible skill',[14] Maxstoke is a quadrangular castle with octagonal corner towers, and a prominent central gatehouse. Inside, surrounding a rectangular courtyard, the curtain was lined with timber-framed ranges (Fig 9.4). The master builder may have been the Oxfordshire mason, John of Burcestre (Bicester), a craftsman known from a building contract for the keep of Stafford Castle, which was drawn up in 1348.[15]

Reconstruction of the royal lodgings at Windsor 1357–1368
The climax of such integrated residential works was Edward III's reconstruction of the royal lodgings in the upper ward of Windsor Castle between 1357 and 1368, which was the most ambitious residential scheme of medieval England. Set against the north curtain, the royal lodgings, as reconstructed for Edward III, comprised an elongated complex of two-storey ranges and taller towers covering an area of approximately 0.6 ha. The apartments were arranged around three courtyards, of which the central one was the old Horn Court that had formed the focus of the royal suite since the late twelfth century. Despite subsequent alterations the main points of the fourteenth-century plan have been partially reconstructed,[16] although the intricacies of the communication routes are no longer apparent.

Notwithstanding that the ordered planning principles behind its layout had evolved over a long period, Windsor is remarkable for the vast scale on which it was built. It is also important from the point of view that artisans from all over England were impressed to work upon it, so that it provided a conduit for the dissemination of architectural style and working practices.[17] Several building craftsmen who later achieved eminent positions seem to have worked at Windsor.[18] John Sponlee was the King's chief mason at Windsor during this period, but, from 1360, he was assisted by a mason called William Wynford.[19] Wynford, who was paid at the same rate as Sponlee, seems to have held equal status, and his subsequent history suggests that he may have made an important contribution to the design of the new works.

Northern England
Wynford's leading contemporary in the north of England was John Lewyn (*fl.* 1353–1398), who, as we have seen at the beginning of this chapter, was the mastermind behind Castle Bolton. To understand the architectural context of Bolton it is necessary to return to the second decade of the fourteenth century, the point at which the north of England had, largely independently, begun to develop its own distinctive style of castellated architecture based on the rectangular tower, a form that was once universal, but which had become deeply unfashionable in castles throughout England and France by the early thirteenth century. There is evidence of renewed interest in the form by the later thirteenth century, not only in the north, but also along the Welsh border in Shropshire where a number of rectangular great towers were built during the later thirteenth century.[20] It is the north, however, with which the rectangular tower is particularly identified in the fourteenth century.

By the 1320s rectangular wall towers had become the norm in the north, being used by the builders of three major castle schemes during the first quarter of the century. At Alnwick, where they appeared after 1309, they were interspersed with towers of different form. At Dunstanburgh (1313–1322) and Pickering (Yorkshire) (1323–1326), they were used exclusively. A series of quadrangular castles of irregular plan ensued in Northumberland at Ford (1338), Etal (1341) and Chillingham (1344); these have rectangular towers at the angles and can be seen as forerunners of the late fourteenth-century integrated castles of the north.

In addition to this general adoption of the rectangular wall tower, a number of defended hall houses with rectangular corner turrets had been built in Northumberland during the thirteenth century. These structures, though not towers, were important antecedents of later tower forms. Halls with attached solar towers were to follow, and, finally, self-contained tower houses that incorporated the hall and its associated chambers and offices.[21] One of the largest of these latter is Langley (Northumberland), built *c.* 1350–1360 for Sir Thomas Lucy. It is a four-storey rectangular block with square corner turrets extending from the ends of the long sides, and a tower porch extending from the east side. Similar in scale is Harewood (Yorkshire) of *c.* 1366, with a four-storey main block and east porch, and five-storey rectangular corner towers to the south.[22]

These complex towers follow the same compact, tightly regulated and logical approach to planning that was later espoused at Bolton, and although they were on a smaller scale, they show that the principle was understood and in use. A building of similar date or perhaps a little later is Danby Castle (Yorkshire). The exact dating of Danby is not facilitated by the contradictory heraldic evidence, but the use of the four-centred arch points to a date of no earlier than *c.* 1350, more likely later, and it is probable that the castle was built by William Lord Latimer during the 1360s and/or 1370s.[23] The significance of Danby is that it was the first integrated symmetrical courtyard castle in northern England. The castle is quadrangular with two-storey ranges and diagonally-set three-storey corner towers; although it small in scale, it may have provided a model for Lord Scrope's slightly later and more elaborate work at Bolton.[24] A second, larger model may well have been Raby (Co. Durham, see p. 196).[25]

Despite these precedents, Bolton was to be the most ambitious and coherent project of its kind in the north of England during the fourteenth and fifteenth centuries. In appointing John Lewyn to build his new castle, Scrope was obtaining the services of a highly experienced architectural practitioner. Lewyn, who was probably in his late forties or fifties when he entered into the Bolton contract, had spent around 20 years as the principal mason to the bishop and priory of Durham. The relationship came to an end in 1372, when he had serious falling out with Bishop Hatfield, an episode that resulted in him being temporarily imprisoned.[26] During his Durham period, Lewyn had superintended the construction of the monastic kitchen (1367–1374) and possibly the reconstruction of Durham Castle keep, as well as undertaking unspecified works further afield at the Durham satellite of Coldingham Priory on the east coast of Scotland (1364) and at the royal castle of Bamburgh (1368). Shortly before entering into the Bolton contract he had been engaged to undertake significant works at the royal border castles of Carlisle and Roxburgh (April and August 1378 respectively), and he was to oversee these two sites in tandem with Bolton over the next few years. He was a man at the peak of his career and as well qualified as anyone to fulfil the task that was now at hand.

To what extent Bolton may have been influenced by the royal works cannot be quantified, but it is interesting to note that the overall dimensions of its courtyard come close to replicating those of the Horn Court at Windsor, and that there is a similar correlation between the main block (courtyard and domestic ranges together) of Bolton and the immediate complex of apartments centred on the Horn Court.[27] However, in its rectilinear plan and corner towers, and its tall, compressed character, Bolton bears a degree of resemblance to some of the great twelfth-century border keeps, in particular, Bamburgh (where Lewyn had worked in the 1360s). Indeed, a trend of late medieval architecture is a blurring of the distinction between the courtyard castle and the great tower. Durham Castle keep, on which Lewyn is believed to have worked, is a case in point (Fig 9.5). Ostensibly a tower, the building had a central courtyard surrounded by four storeys of apartments over a vaulted basement, with five separate staircases giving access to the upper floors. Although the fourteenth-century interior no longer survives, the impression to be gained is of an internal plan with a high degree of complexity and there is no doubt that the formulation of its design would have provided crucial experience for the designer of Bolton.

Two slightly later northern castles, both attributed to Lewyn on stylistic grounds, are much more assured, and it is to be assumed that they are the fruit of Lewyn's experience at Bolton in working out the principles of design for this type of building. Detailed examinations of Lumley near Chester-le Street (Co. Durham) (Fig 9.6), and Wressle, near Hull (Yorkshire), both of c. 1390, in each case reveal that the architect drew on a close knowledge of Bolton

Fig. 9.5. Durham The keep from the south east (third quarter of the fourteenth century and 1839–1840).

in formulating the design. In addition to displaying a kinship with Bolton, the plans of both castles have a good deal in common with each other, and it is difficult to believe that they were designed independently. As far as the masonry details are concerned, however, there is a wide measure of disparity, suggesting that the architect may only have controlled the general planning, and that the execution of the details was delegated. Of the two castles, Wressle has a softer and more graceful character, partly engendered by the gentle colour of the limestone ashlar. The castle is sited on low-lying ground and was surrounded by a moat; there was less emphasis on height, and greater attention was paid to the aesthetic qualities of the detailing. It is indeed one step removed from its sterner contemporaries further north. To obtain a more complete impression of its former character than can be gleaned from the surviving remains, a visit to Bodiam is instructive.

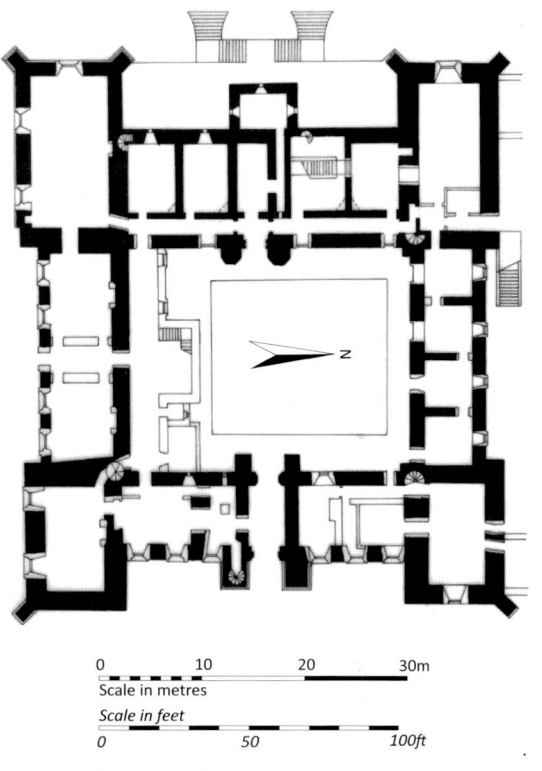

Fig. 9.6. Lumley (Co. Durham) Ground-floor plan (last decade of the fourteenth century)

Built *c.* 1385, Bodiam is the most coherent survival of the integrated quadrangular castle in the south of England, and in its general character and setting it shares a large degree of kinship with Wressle. The architect of Bodiam is not known, and although the design has been attributed to Henry Yevele,[28] the octagonal stair turrets that rise above the parapets of the towers recollect the motif that appears on William Wynford's Winchester College Middle Gate of *c.* 1387. Winchester, and Wynford's earlier work of New College, Oxford, were both tightly planned domestic complexes for communal living, the internal planning of which therefore demanded a similar approach to the integrated castle. Both the towers and ranges of Bodiam have fewer storeys than Bolton and the design process must therefore have been simpler, but the same principles apply to both. Wynford may also have been the mastermind behind the castles of Shirburn (Oxfordshire, *c.* 1373) and Wardour (Wiltshire, *c.* 1393), both of which display the same planning characteristics as Bodiam (see pp. 219–220).

While Bolton and buildings like it have a degree of kinship, they were actually planned to very specific requirements, stipulated by their owners. However, once the conditions for which the design was intended evolved, the inflexibility of its design must quickly have become apparent. It may have been this realization that caused the builder of Bolton's immediate descendants at Lumley and Wressle to dispense with the earlier castle's stone internal partitions. Other than at ground-floor level, the accommodation ranges of Lumley are largely devoid of stone walls while Wressle had even fewer such divisions. In both cases the interiors must have been divided by timber partitions, thereby giving them a greater degree of flexibility that allowed changes in the circumstances of the occupant to be accommodated more easily.

The design process
By the time Bolton came to be designed there had been a long history of integrated planning in castles, and yet the number of such ventures was small, and each one required a unique configuration. The process of designing such buildings was not a technical skill that could be easily taught or learnt except through experience, and it is arguable that only a handful of men were engaged in schemes of this nature. In the north of England, John Lewyn seems to have been the only major figure to have worked on this type of project during the latter half of the fourteenth century. Although he was the principal mason at Durham Priory during the period *c.* 1353–1372 his work appears to have been largely domestic in character, which may account for his interest in the issues of domestic living (see below, this chapter) and the technical challenges they presented. Speaking comparatively, we know a good deal about the course of Lewyn's career, and although some aspects can only be reconstructed through informed inference, he still provides a useful case study in understanding the manner in which an architect might have acquired the requisite expertise to carry out such undertakings.

Two buildings within County Durham are probably key to his professional development. One was the keep of Durham Castle, described above. The other was the manor house of the Nevilles at Raby, Staindrop, near Durham, which was converted into a quadrangular courtyard castle from the 1350s or 1360s.[29] Based largely on the similarities between the great kitchen of Raby and that of Durham Priory there is reason to believe that Lewyn may have worked at Raby.[30] There are indications that the conversion of Raby was an accretive process that was approached element by element rather than as a single coherent enterprise. Though the internal details of this complex have to a large extent been lost in the eighteenth- and nineteenth-century alterations, what is clear is that the integrated element of Raby was less extensive than at Bolton and that the intricacy of its internal plan was probably less intense. In these circumstances there was scope for a master builder to hone his skill and develop his approach to large-scale planning gradually.

The designer of Bolton, therefore, was probably already experienced in dealing with buildings of similar nature, albeit on a smaller scale. Even so, the apparent unity of the building implies a good deal of forward planning in the form of drawings, especially plans, though given the three-dimensionality of the concept, a model might have been a better way of demonstrating the nature of the internal character of the building to the client. In the case of Bolton, however, there are complications, because a close examination of its structural development suggests that to some extent it may be the product of an empirical approach and that the scale of the project grew as time went on, the internal planning becoming more intricate in successive phases of the castle.[31] It is evident, therefore, that the planning process was sometimes less straightforward than might be imagined.

Domestic Conveniences
Once the essentials of the plan had been resolved thought had to be given to the practicalities of domestic life, that is to say, heating, water supply and distribution, and sanitation, all of

Domestic Engineering 197

which had a bearing upon the design of the stonework. There is plenty of evidence to the effect that these subjects were major areas of concern and that the medieval builder did pay them a good deal of attention.

Heating
Traditionally, the great hall was heated from an open hearth, which was usually situated along the central axis of the room, close to its upper end (Fig 9.7). It was, therefore, an appropriate facility for a space that was, in origin, a communal living room, and the arrangement embodied a tradition that had its origins in the dim and distant past. The great hall was normally open to the roof, and smoke from the open hearth was usually dispersed through a louvre raised over the hearth at roof level. Typically, louvres would have been constructed of timber and would have formed an integral part of the roof structure; as such, they were usually the responsibility of the master carpenter.

Occasionally, however, it was the master mason who took on this role, as in the case of John Lewyn, who devised a different system of smoke dispersal that allowed him to dispense with the louvre. In Lewyn's scheme, flues were built into the heads of the window embrasures, which would probably have been capped by chimneys at roof level. The best-preserved examples are in Castle Bolton of *c.* 1385 (Fig 9.8) and in the keep of Warkworth Castle of *c.* 1390, but they were also used in the kitchen of Bamburgh Castle *c.* 1384, and probably in the great hall of Lumley Castle *c.* 1390.[32] Lewyn's system was doubtless intended as an improvement on the traditional louvre, and the indications are that it probably worked. At

Fig. 9.7. Stokesay (Shropshire) The octagonal open hearth in the late thirteenth-century great hall (last quarter of the thirteenth century).

Bolton, instead of a single outlet for the smoke, as represented by the louvre, there were six – one over each of the windows – a provision that must have created a more efficient scheme of smoke diffusion. John Leland, who saw the system in use in the early sixteenth century, was sufficiently interested to remark: *One thinge I muche notyd in the haulle of Bolton, how chimeneys were conveyed by tunnells made on the syds of the walls bytwixt the lights in the haull, and by this meanes, and by no lovers, is the smoke of the harthe in the hawle wonder strangly convayed.*[33] Francis Grose was similarly moved to comment on the flues in the kitchen of Bamburgh when he visited the castle in 1776: *…over each window is a stone funnel like a chimney, open at the top, intended, as it is supposed, to carry off the steam…*[34]

Lewyn's arrangement at Bolton and elsewhere suggests that smoke from the open hearth was seen as a problem; the lack of an efficient means of dispersal must, on occasion, have resulted in a constant haze. Although the open hearth remained a feature of castle halls throughout the Middle Ages, the future lay with the mural fireplace, a feature that had been in use from the tenth century, and which was to become the most common form of heating. The development of the residential tower in which there were several storeys of large rooms, encouraged the widespread adoption of the mural fireplace, because unless the floor were of stone, it was difficult to heat a room by means of an open hearth or brazier. The mural fireplace was safer and more convenient, and was made feasible by the concurrent development of the mural flue, a device that offered a more efficient method of smoke dispersal. Unlike the open hearth and the louvre, the fireplace and flue formed an integrated unit whereby the fireplace was located within a wall recess, the upward continuation of which constituted the flue.

Fig. 9.8. Castle Bolton (Yorkshire) Flue in the head of a window in the ground-floor bakehouse (last quarter of the fourteenth century).

The disadvantage of the system was that it was less efficient than the open hearth – which at least warmed the air in the room – because most of the heat was drawn up the flue. Expedients were devised in order to mitigate the problem. One of these was the hood, or canopy, which projected from the wall and so allowed the fire to be brought a little further into the room than would otherwise have been possible. The result was that the effect of the fire could be felt over a wider span than if it had been set within a deep recess. The hood was in use in France from the early eleventh century in, for example, the donjon of Loches, where each one comprised a tall conical cap over the hearth, following the line of a recess in the wall to form part of the flue. Eleventh-century examples may have existed in England, although the earliest definite evidence for the fireplace hood dates from the later twelfth century (at Conisbrough).

A common attribute of many early fireplaces, including Loches, was a curving back. It is possible that this characteristic was another attempt to counter the loss of heat up the flue by providing a means to reflect it into the room. Such a quality in a deeply recessed hoodless fireplace would have been even more desirable; and in one such example in the late eleventh-century keep of Colchester the effect would have been enhanced by the use of ceramic tiles to construct the back of the fireplace. Tiles were frequently used as bases for medieval hearths probably for their heat-resistant properties, but from an early date they were also being employed in the backs of fireplaces. Here too their heat-resistant qualities may have been a reason, but it is also probable that their use was a deliberate attempt at heat retention so that the tiles would absorb the heat of the fire and radiate it in the room. Certainly, this was an aim of the late medieval cast iron fireback, the greater conductive properties of which resulted in a much more effective device.

These early fireplaces had inclined flues that extended through the wall of the building to outlets on the exterior face. In the keep of Colchester the flue rose from the base of the fireplace to a total height of 6.44 m (21 ft), the upper part dividing into two shafts leading to vents in the outer wall situated to either side of a buttress. There are numerous examples of this outlet pattern from the eleventh and twelfth centuries. The great towers of the Tower of London, Canterbury, Rochester, Portchester, Hedingham, and Newcastle all have inclined flues with the smoke escaping from wall vents on either side of a buttress.

The challenge to the medieval fireplace builder was to obtain sufficient draught and thereby ensure the removal of the smoke, and it is debatable as to how effective some of these early fireplaces were. Certainly, the comparatively short flues with their narrow openings on the outside walls of the building must have been highly susceptible to the effect of the wind, and are likely to have had a propensity for allowing the smoke to blow back into the room. It has been implied that the siting of vents either side of a buttress was a deliberate attempt to introduce some control over downdraught, so that one of the vents could be closed when necessary (presumably by a device like a damper), in order to mitigate the effect of the prevailing breeze. While this is theoretically possible, no evidence of such a device has been discovered in a castle.

By the middle of the twelfth century, however, a breakthrough in the engineering of smoke dispersal had been achieved with the introduction of the vertical chimney flue. In France, fireplaces with short vertical flues were provided on the upper storey of the donjon of Étampes, probably of the 1140s. In England, vertical flues were being incorporated into the fabric of castles from the 1150s. One of the earliest examples is in the keep of Scarborough (1157–1159), the first of Henry II's series of great towers that culminated in Dover; it was closely followed by Orford (1165–1173) and Conisbrough (1164–1190). A concurrent development was the chimneystack, which continued the line of the flue above the building; the earliest to survive in England are the cylindrical stacks of the great hall of Framlingham Castle of *c.* 1150.

Where the open hearth continued to serve as the main source of heat in the great hall, its inadequacy as a heating system for such a large room is implied by evidence that it sometimes co-existed with wall fireplaces. The most common location for a fireplace in the hall was at the upper end where it heated the dais: a twelfth-century example can be seen in the great hall of Warkworth, where the blocked fireplace in the south wall has been partially concealed by the fifteenth-century remodelling of the building. Another example of a dais fireplace warmed the backs of those seated at the high table in the late fourteenth-century great hall of Wressle. Wressle also retained an open hearth and louvre, but in the great hall of Kenilworth, another late fourteenth-century construction, built by the mason Henry Spenser for John of Gaunt, it is probable that the open hearth was supplanted entirely by wall fireplaces including a triple fireplace at the high end and one in each sidewall.

Apart from providing warmth to the main domestic areas, the fireplace was also essential for cooking, and to that end one (or more) large fireplace formed the focus of the kitchen, though not until the thirteenth century, prior to which most cooking was probably done over an open hearth either in the open air or in a detached building. The developments in fireplace design outlined above suggest that the medieval builder did have some comprehension

Fig. 9.9. Castle Bolton (Yorkshire) Fireplace in the bakehouse containing the arched entrances to the former ovens (last quarter of the fourteenth century).

of how flues functioned, notably the principle of draught, and that this knowledge was obtained empirically. The problem of insufficient draft is something to which fireplaces with large openings are particularly prone. Yet many castle kitchen fireplaces had to be large in order to accommodate the mass catering sometimes required in a great house. Restricting the size of the flue by funnelling would have helped in retaining the heat of the smoke and maintaining draught. That the problem of insufficient draught was sometimes understood can be inferred from the presence of an aperture in the back of one of the kitchen fireplaces in the outer gatehouse of Carlisle Castle of 1378, which has been interpreted as a draught hole,[35] a device that was probably designed to be opened in order to increase the draught when necessary. The Carlisle gatehouse was, incidentally, another of John Lewyn's buildings, suggesting that he had a keen interest in domestic practicalities.

Kitchen fireplaces often incorporated an oven at the back of the hearth. Bread ovens were of standard design, with a flat base, a domed ceiling, and a small opening, though they varied considerably in size. A fire was lit inside to heat the oven before inserting the bread. The back of the fireplace was therefore a convenient position for an oven because it allowed the smoke to be dispersed up the chimney, and the embers to be deposited in the hearth. An unusual example appears at Bolton, where John Lewyn created a fireplace within one of the transverse walls of the basement for the express purpose of serving a pair of large circular ovens set against the wall and accessed from the fireplace via two archways, effectively doorways, which rise from hearth floor level, so that the ovens could be entered bodily (Fig 9.9).

Water supply and distribution
For most castles the main source of water was a well, the excavation and construction of which was a specialist occupation, often divorced from the main construction process, especially when the well was located within a courtyard rather than a building. However, it was of major consideration to the castle builder, and would have been one of the first facilities to be created, not least because a supply of water was needed for construction work.

Where the well was dug through earth, a common construction technique was to begin with a wide funnel-shaped pit tapering downwards to firmer ground, after which the well could be carried down as a narrower shaft until the water table was reached. Once the shaft had been excavated it would be lined with stone. Investigation of the well in the inner ward of Tutbury Castle in 1956, before it was partially in-filled, provided an interesting insight into construction techniques.[36] Offsets incorporated into the stone lining of the lowest section of the well, at intervals of approximately 3 m (10 ft), contained 150 mm (6 in) wide x 25 mm (1 in) deep slots, evidently intended to accommodate timbers that could have carried working platforms. They were, presumably, aids to the construction and maintenance of the stonework.

Where the well was cut through bedrock it was often unnecessary to line the shaft. The twelfth-century well within the keep of Rochester, for instance, which was approximately 18 m (59 ft) deep, was stone lined only for the first 9 m (29.5 ft). Excavating through bedrock called for quarrying or mining skills, and some rock-cut shafts were of considerable depth and undertaking. The thirteenth-century well in the inner ward of Beeston, which is said to have been cleared out to a depth of approximately 112 m (366 ft) in 1842, was entirely rock cut, although here it was lined with stone for the first 61 m (200 ft).[37]

The siting of the well was an important aspect of castle planning, and it was not accidental that it was often placed in close proximity to the kitchen and its associated services, that is to say, the part of the castle that needed copious amounts of water in order to fulfil its functions. Sometimes the well was internal, as at Bodiam, in Sussex, where it was accommodated in the basement of a tower adjacent to and only accessible from the kitchen, a system that suggests strict control of the water supply and an efficient method of distribution. At the closely contemporary Castle Bolton there was also a well chamber, the well itself being recessed within the wall of the castle. Water could be drawn either from the well chamber itself or from the service rooms on the floor above that lay between the great hall and kitchen tower (Fig 9.10). At ground-floor level there was an adjacent chute that extended through the wall to the courtyard, allowing water to be drawn from the well and directed straight into the yard possibly to a cistern or trough.

Fig. 9.10. Castle Bolton (Yorkshire) The two-level well in the north range (last quarter of the fourteenth century).

Provision for drawing the well from an upper floor was something that had been developed by the builders of great towers – structures that frequently contained their own wells – in order to furnish an efficient means of access to the basement water supply from the living accommodation above. In numerous great towers, the well could be drawn from the basement only, but this was improved on by providing access via a trap in the floor of the storey above, as occurred at Conisbrough keep. An advance on this arrangement was to extend the well shaft upwards to the next floor level, a scheme that was adopted in the donjon of Étampes. A more ambitious advance occurred at Arques-la-Bataille, where the builder of the donjon of *c.* 1123 incorporated an extended well shaft that rose to second-floor level. A similar arrangement built within the centre of the crosswall of Rochester keep *c.* 1127 ascended to the roof and had drawing positions at each level. Nevertheless, the apparent convenience of a multiplicity of access points may not have lived up to its promise in practice, a point that may have been considered by the engineer, Maurice, when he adopted the general principle of the extended well shaft in the keeps of Newcastle (1167–1177) and Dover (1180–1187), but restricted access to the second-floor. Compensation for the consequent loss of flexibility was provided by introducing a system that allowed water to be piped from the second-floor drawing position to other parts of the keep, the elevated point of access allowing the necessary inclination of the pipes.

Newcastle and Dover have two of the earliest piped water systems to have survived in English castles; it is probably not coincidental that sophisticated monastic water supply systems had been installed in the years immediately before the construction of Newcastle at, for example, Canterbury Priory, Fountains Abbey and Durham Priory.[38] It may well be that the builder, Maurice, drew his inspiration from examples like these. Few vestiges of such systems survive in castles, but they may once have been much more common, especially in the royal works. Particular attention was paid to the possibilities of piped water at Caernarfon Castle in the 1280s and 1290s. Here, the main source of water was the well that was housed within one of the northern wall towers (Well Tower). As at Newcastle and Dover, there was built-in provision for a cistern next to the well, pipes extending from the cistern through the wall to supply the adjacent kitchen.

Whereas the well was usually the main source of water, cisterns were also used for collection and storage. Hence, the later twelfth-century keeps of Orford and Conisbrough, both of which had wells in the basement, also incorporated stone water cisterns at roof level in order to gather rainwater. These arrangements may have had something to do with the domestic character of the roofs of these buildings where food preparation evidently took place. The Cistern Tower at the east end of the south curtain of Caernarfon takes its name from a stone-lined rainwater tank above the vault from which a stone outlet channel runs through the thickness of the wall to the Queen's Gate.

Latrines and foul water disposal

From an early date latrines were being situated within the external walls of castle buildings, a location that was important for ventilation and for the convenience of emptying them. These two aspects: the containment and dispersal of unpleasant smells, and the ultimate disposal of the waste were, or should have been, important considerations in the design of castle latrines. In mural latrines a vertical disposal shaft descended to ground level from where it was emptied, but the shafts themselves must have been difficult to keep clean and free from odours.

It may have been a response to such a problem that from the twelfth century some latrines were built corbelled out from external wall faces in the manner of box machicolations. Corbelled latrines were simple but effective contrivances in that they allowed the immediate deposition of excrement outside the walls of the castle, and by their nature were well ventilated, so that smells did not linger. Ideally, they were placed over watercourses or the sea for rapid disposal of the sewerage. Where this wasn't possible, they might be situated in some other strategic position that obviated the need for a latrine pit, such as overhanging a precipitous cliff, as in the case of Peveril keep (1176–1177), or above the moat.

The builder of the late twelfth-century keep of Conisbrough devised an alternative to the corbelled latrine by throwing a squinch between the main body of the tower and one of the buttress turrets at second-floor level. The latrine was housed above the squinch so that evacuations fell outside the castle onto the top of the platform. Another latrine was situated immediately below it at first-floor level, the outlet of the chute comprising a simple rectangular slot. Situated on the northeast side of the castle, these latrines would have been in the shade for the greater part of the day, quite possibly in a deliberate attempt to keep them cool.

A similar concept was adopted by the early thirteenth-century builder of Coucy, who positioned the latrines in the angles between the curtain and the wall towers on the north side of the castle; those at ground-floor level were situated within the walls of the towers themselves, but at first-floor level, where they were all *en suite* with the apartments in the towers, they were corbelled out from the face of the wall. Later in the thirteenth century such angle latrines were being enclosed in little turrets that rose from ground level, as at Windsor in the 1230s (Cleaver's Tower and Garter's Tower), in the gatehouse of Tonbridge of *c.* 1250–1265, and in the count of Savoy's castles of Yverdon and St Georges d'Esperanche, from whence they are said to have been transferred by Savoyard craftsmen to Edward I's Welsh castles of Rhuddlan (1277) Conway (1283), and Harlech (1283). This rationalizing of the design allowed a more systematic approach to the disposal of the waste.

The sanitary arrangements for castles lagged behind those of monastic complexes, the builders of which had always taken the issue seriously; the houses themselves were usually better situated geographically and socially to deal with it. The communal nature of monastic living allowed the latrines to be concentrated in a single block, rather than dispersed in a series of more or less private facilities. The reredorter, or communal latrine, was sited adjacent to or over a watercourse so that the sewage could be flushed away. Only in the castles of the military orders was such a centralized system possible, achieving its greatest architectural distinction in the castles of the Teutonic knights in the latrine towers, or *dansker*, that lay outside the main defences and which were approached from the domestic apartments by a bridge.

The *dansk* was designed for garrison living. Latrines in secular establishments were generally of a less regimented nature, and only occasionally approached Teutonic Order levels of communality. At the late thirteenth-century castle of Conwy, a single-storey turret, which contained a row of three latrines, was accessible from the outer courtyard, adjacent to the great hall, but not attached to any particular building. More ambitious and advanced in concept is the fourteenth-century ovoid-plan latrine tower built at Coity Castle (Glamorgan) on south side of the inner bailey. It projects boldly towards the moat, and contained three storeys of latrines the shafts of which dropped into a vaulted rectangular basement. At ground level there are three seats set side by side along the south wall, two of which are directly below the south window; at first-floor level there are two seats, again set side by side, against the north wall to avoid conflict with those of the lower storey; on the second floor there was a single seat, set against the south wall but to the west of those ground-floor level.

The Coity latrine tower is an early attempt to solve the problem of providing sufficient facilities for a large household within a restricted space so that the stench could be restricted to a single location and the disposal of the waste could be rationalized. A development of this approach appeared at Pierrefonds (Oise) towards the end of the fourteenth century. At Pierrefonds there were several concentrations of latrines, but the one in the D-shaped wall tower in the centre of the north front, where there were three storeys of latrines over a vaulted pit within the basement, is particularly noteworthy (Fig 9.11). The ground-storey latrines were directly over the pit, while those on the upper storeys were over stone-enclosed shafts that also dropped to the pit. As at Coity, the number of latrines diminished progressively on each successive storey.

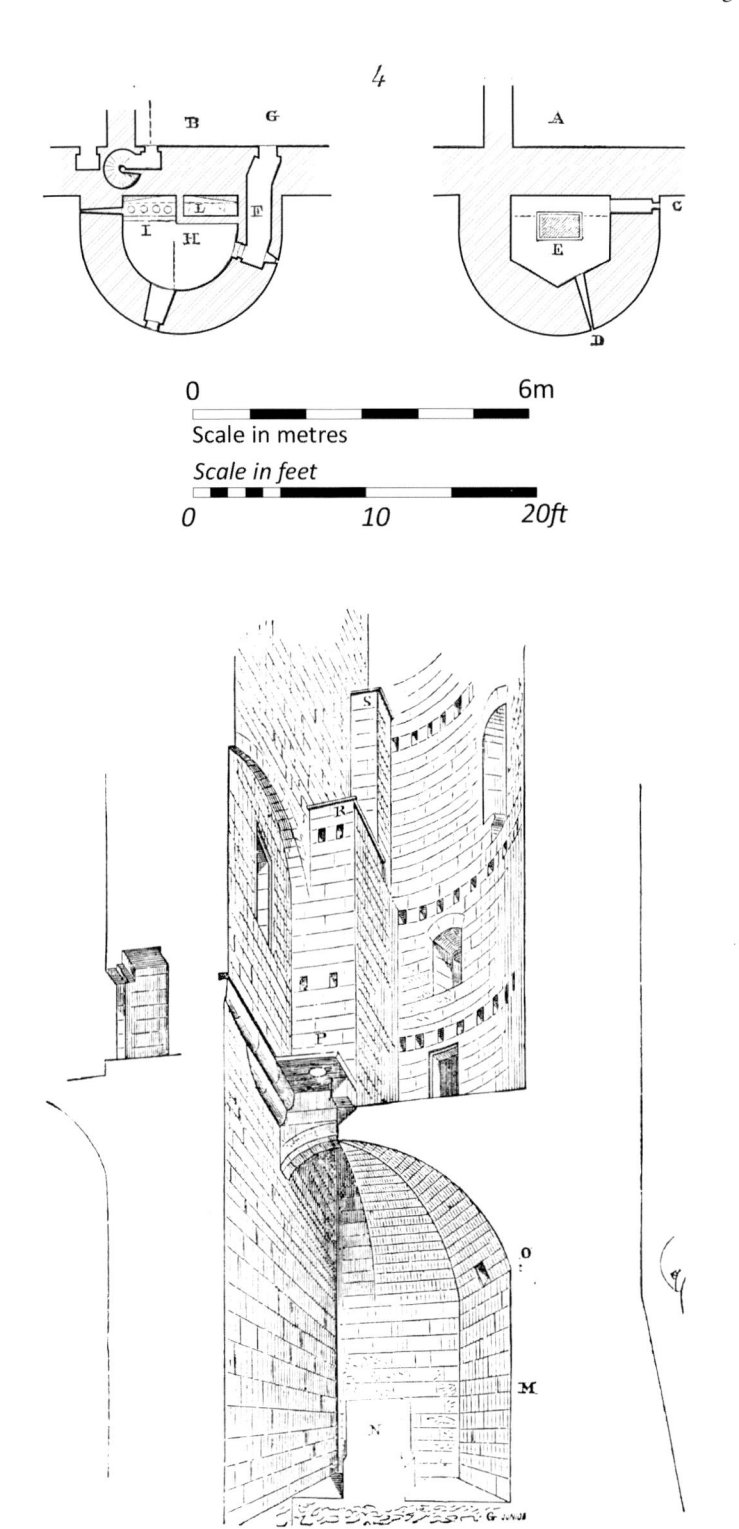

Fig. 9.11. Pierrefonds (Oise) Latrine tower (last quarter of the fourteenth century); after Viollet-le-Duc 1875.

Pierrefonds was not the only system of storied latrines in use by the end of the fourteenth century. One that displays an even more advanced solution was recorded by Viollet-le-Duc at the Château de Montagu, Marcoussis (Essone), where a narrow unfloored building set against the curtain wall housed a row of four latrines on each of three storeys.[39] These facilities, which were set within individual arched recesses, were approached along stone galleries from the adjacent lodgings. The art of the domestic engineer was to stagger the positions of the latrines at the different levels so that their respective shafts had an unimpeded drop into a communal pit. Although this example can no longer be examined, other than in Viollet le Duc's drawings, a remarkably similar arrangement of c. 1350 survives at Langley Castle in Northumberland, where one of the four corner turrets of the tower house was given over entirely to latrines disposed in a similar pattern to those at Montagu with four arched recesses on each floor (Fig 9.12). The rarity of this particular arrangement of latrines suggests a common origin.

On the whole, however, such communal arrangements were rare in the fourteenth century, when the planning of high-class domestic accommodation tended towards greater privacy and a more dispersed distribution of latrines. At John Lewyn's Bolton, where there were at least fourteen latrine outlets ranged around the exterior, these en suite facilities may have been convenient for the occupants of the various apartments, but the process of collecting and disposing of the waste cannot have been very efficient. Slightly later, c. 1390, at the quadrangular castle of Wressle, built for Sir Thomas Percy, Lewyn created an improved sanitary system by confining most of the latrines to turrets set within the angles of the towers and ranges, without compromising the arrangements for privacy.

At much the same time that Wressle was being built, Sir Thomas Percy's brother, Henry, earl of Northumberland, was building his great tower at Warkworth, where a rationalisation of the latrines is also one of the main service innovations. Here, the four shafts of the facilities serving the main apartments on the first and second floors were grouped together in a block so that they all deposited into the same ground-floor level intra-mural drainage channel, which, unusually, is situated close to the centre of the building. The contents of the channel were flushed out of the building by a supply of rainwater that was conducted into the central lightwell of the building and thence into a stone cistern in one of the basement rooms; from here it was diverted into the drainage channel. The question as to whether the discharged contents of the Warkworth latrines were then deposited in a cesspit, or whether there was a drain diverting them to the adjacent River Coquet, must for the moment remain unanswered.

Warkworth is a rare instance in which the system for flushing the latrines has survived well enough to make the principle behind it clear. Seldom are such schemes so obvious, but it is evident from other surviving remnants that they were once more widespread than they now appear. The late thirteenth-century great gatehouse of Denbigh is one example: here, the master builder built the latrines in two concentrated blocks, which discharged into communal shafts. Circular-sectioned water ducts were built into the stonework in order to convey water from cisterns on the roof to flush the shafts and expel the contents into the (dry) moat whence it must have been collected. Like the great tower of Warkworth, the Denbigh gatehouse is a building whose design suggests an architect of particular originality, who has paid close attention not only to the outward appearance – for both are designed for effect – but also to the practicalities of living in them.

INTERIOR OF GARDEROBE TOWER,   AND SECTION OF THE SAME.
LANGLEY CASTLE, NORTHUMBERLAND.

Fig. 9.12. Langley (Northumberland) Latrine turret in the tower house (third quarter of the fourteenth century); from Turner and Parker 1853.

Only occasionally, however, were castle builders able to dispense with manual collection of the waste from latrines and in so doing match the disposal facilities of the monastic houses. One example is Christchurch Castle (Hampshire), where a thirteenth-century latrine tower, which was added to the twelfth-century hall, is built out into a mill stream that connects with the River Avon. The latrine shafts dropped directly into the stream, which carried away the deposits. It has to be said that such instances are very rare, but Christchurch illustrates the point that disposal posed a problem and that where nature provided a solution it was seized upon. While the best solution to the disposal of sewage in castles was a fast flowing watercourse, for many, the wet moat acted as a substitute. If an efficient water management system allowed a flow of water to be maintained, this might not have been so unsatisfactory as might be imagined. However, an indication that the discharge of latrines into a moat was not always an unqualified success, and might have had a degree of notoriety, is the arrangement for cleaning the latrines at the late fifteenth-century moated castle of Kirby Muxloe. Here, the castle was provided with a berm between the moat and the curtain wall, of which one function was to provide access to the latrine pits, so that they could be emptied and the waste carted away rather than deposited in the moat.

Foul water was less of a problem. Generally it was dispersed via wall drains, which are commonly found in castles, often, though by no means exclusively, in association with kitchens. In the kitchen of Warkworth keep a wide floor drain for general slops was channelled towards a large spout on the exterior of the building that threw the water away from the foot of the wall. This is an unusually large example, commensurate with the

Fig. 9.13. Castle Bolton (Yorkshire) Sink/urinal draining to an external spout (last quarter of the fourteenth century).

amount of dirty water that a great kitchen might be expected to produce, but smaller spouts of similar character are often encountered, proliferating at Bolton where they serve sinks or drains built into the sills of the window embrasures (Fig 9.13). Some of these latter may have doubled as urinals (several are within latrine passages), features that were occasionally built into the fabric of a castle, including the keeps of Castle Rising (c. 1140) and Orford (1160s) and the wall towers of Coucy (c. 1220).[40]

Conclusion

By the last decades of the thirteenth century, castle builders were becoming as much concerned with developing integrated systems of domestic accommodation as they were with defensive matters. In the following century the castle builder was more of a domestic engineer than a military engineer, a change of emphasis that promoted an orderly approach to design which was not always compatible with an optimal defensive form. Indeed, in some of these late medieval castellated great houses defence, other than the installation of basic security measures, barely seems to have been an issue. After the frenetic multiplying of defensive properties in late thirteenth-century Wales, the change of tack comes as something of a relief. This emphasis on the domestic aspects was accompanied by a greater stress on architectural and decorative effect. Military architecture was about to become military chic.

Chapter 10

The Castle Builder's Aesthetic

A Beautiful Castle

In castle design, utility seldom precluded architectural effect. Castle building might have had its roots in the technical expertise required to fulfil defensive and domestic requirements, but although the castle builder was a technician, in many cases he was also an artist; indeed medieval art in general was very much the product of practical craftsmanship. A case in point is the donjon of Château Gaillard, which, in addition to being a feat of military engineering, is also a consummate work of art, its stylishly supple lines a tripartite meld of batter, body and prow a display of the stone mason's craft at its best (Fig 6.6). The inverted pyramidal supports for the slot-machicolated parapet are redolent of the same deft touch; splaying outwards and upwards from acutely pointed feet, there is nothing to match their finesse amongst the several surviving examples of this type of defensive feature; in their artistry, they contrast markedly with the slightly earlier but purely functional example at Krak des Chevaliers.

Nor was this mixture of the functional and the aesthetic confined to the keep; the curtain around the inner ward, with its shallow, closely-set, curving turrets (generally evaluated

Fig. 10.1. Château Gaillard (Eure) - The curtain around the outer ward of was decorated with alternating courses of red and white masonry (1196–1198).

only in military terms), is nevertheless a work of great attractiveness, embodying utility and art in equal measure. Making a contribution to the sensuous appeal of both structures are the alluring physical qualities of the high-quality ashlar masonry and the precision with which it has been prepared and constructed.[1] This close attention to the wall facings extends to surviving elements of the curtain around the outer ward, but goes further, because they were set with alternating courses of white and red masonry, producing an overall pattern of horizontal bands (Fig 10.1). This treatment suggests that the artistic approach to the construction of the keep and inner curtain pervaded the whole castle, and makes a *double entendre* of Richard's 'Saucy Castle', to denote not only a political provocation to the king of France but also the tantalising beauty of the building itself.

Château Gaillard is an unusually effective example of a castle with visual appeal, but a desire to make an architectural impact was a persistent objective for the castle builder, even though it seldom attained the same degree of success. This search for aesthetic effect was pursued to differing degrees, and manifested itself in different ways, but was usually present in some measure. The wall facings of Château Gaillard have been cited above as having made an important contribution to the overall impact, and there is no doubt that the finish of the walls is something that received a good deal of consideration in the wider sphere, perhaps to a greater degree than is now apparent. Where it could be afforded, ashlar provided a pleasingly regular surface, in addition to advertising one's wealth.

Patterned Masonry

Even more effective than ashlar construction was the use of masonry of different colours in order to produce patterns, as in the walls of Château Gaillard. The builder of Dover Castle keep had already experimented with this comparatively rare form of embellishment in the 1180s, by interspersing Caen stone with the Kentish rag of which the elevations are mostly composed (Fig 5.13). Only on the west front, however, is this mixture convincing as a deliberate attempt to make an ornamental impact. Broad bands of Caen stone extend across this elevation, but the scheme was not carried through the full height of the building, nor was it extended with the same degree of assurance to the other faces. There is a marked contrast between this half-hearted attempt at Dover and the confident treatment some ten years later of the outer ward curtain at Château Gaillard. Only fragments of this latter wall survive, but the overall ornamental effect must have been striking.

Continuous banding, albeit less generously applied than at Gaillard, is one of the defining characteristics of the west curtain of Windsor, built for Henry III *c.* 1225–1230.[2] This, however, is restricted to the curtain wall and does not extend to the three towers that also make up this part of the enceinte. A contrasting approach was taken in designing the enceinte of Angers Castle, of *c.* 1230–1240, where it was the towers that were banded, but not the curtain. The result was to create a more conspicuous contrast than had been achieved hitherto by juxtaposing the local black schist rubble, which comprises the main building material, and the buff limestone used for the dressings (Fig 10.2). In the wall towers, which play a very important role in defining the character of the castle, the schist is interspersed with horizontal bands of limestone. The ashlar banding around the towers of the north-east curtain is widely spaced and of single courses, while that of south-west towers is set more closely and comprises double as well as single coursing. The more extravagantly decorated

Fig. 10.2. Angers (Maine-et-Loire) The builders of the castle created a striking contrast by interspersing the local black schist rubble with bands of limestone ashlar.

south-western towers, which face outwards away from the town, are complemented by the outer gatehouse, the Porte des Champs, which terminates this part of the curtain to the east. The lower storeys of this building are entirely faced in limestone ashlar, making a contrast to the Porte de la Ville to the north-east, the decoration of which follows that of the north-east wall towers.

A similar visual hierarchy is to be found at Caernarfon Castle in north Wales, which was built for Edward I from 1283 following his conquest of Wales. Here too, horizontal banding is also a significant feature (Fig 10.3). Interestingly, the enceinte of Caernarfon has a broadly similar layout to that of Angers, the south front being terminated to the east by the Queen's Gate, which served the same function as the Porte des Champs as the principal entrance to the castle from outside the town walls. The King's Gate to the north, which faced the town, is the equivalent of the Porte de la Ville. At Caernarfon the polychrome banding was extended to the curtain wall as well as the towers, the differentiation being achieved through interspersing red sandstone with the buff sandstone that formed the main facing material. The polychrome work at Caernarfon is only to be found on that part of the enceinte that lay outside the town walls just as the more elaborate decorative effect at Angers was confined to the equivalent portion.

The Caernarfon work is believed to be a deliberate evocation of the stone and tile banding of ancient Roman buildings as a form of political propaganda. The reasons for this unusual choice of décor at Angers are unknown, but it was a frontier castle, in this case, close to the border with Brittany, and it too was built to assert and symbolize royal power in the region

Fig. 10.3. Caernarfon (Gwynedd) The castle from the south west showing decorative horizontal banding.

and to counter a threat from the duchy. Château Gaillard was built on the border of the King of England's domains with France in a provocative show of defiance and political authority, possibly as a springboard for the recovery of territory lost to the French king. Each of the builders of these three castles, then, was making a conscious attempt at conspicuous display, and it is possible that the decorative masonry was intended to make a contribution towards that end.

The most striking example of the use of differently coloured walling materials to create an ornamental effect was carried out at the Emperor Frederick II's Castel del Monte in Puglia, of the 1230s, but here it was executed in a rather different manner to the sites just described. The main facing stone was limestone ashlar, but on the exterior elevations there are splashes of colour and texture caused by the use of red breccia and white veined marble around the openings. These decorative aspects, however, are only a hint of what is to come, because the same materials were used on a lavish scale inside the building, so that the principal contrast was between the exterior and interior. Much of the breccia and marble has been stripped from the building so that only the structural elements, including columns and doorways, remain, but it seems that the walls would have been faced in breccia at ground level and in marble at first-floor level (Fig 10.4).

Castel del Monte is an extreme example - in a region with a heightened aesthetic awareness - of contrasting materials being employed to decorative effect. Although the principle was often toyed with, it was seldom applied in a systematic fashion. Generally, façades were more mundane, and the main building material was more likely to be rubble than dressed stone.

214   Castle Builders

Fig. 10.4. Castel del Monte (Puglia) - A remnant of the red breccia with which the walls of the ground-floor rooms of the castle were faced (second quarter of the thirteenth century).

Fig. 10.5. Kirby Muxloe (Leicestershire) Patterning made by bricks of contrasting colours on one of the gatehouse towers (1481–1483).

In these circumstances a castle might be given some kind of surface treatment to ameliorate its appearance and to make it stand out in the landscape. The use of rendering is sometimes attested by the survival of patches on the stonework, as in the thirteenth-century work at White Castle.[3] This site derives its name from the colour of this material, and whitewashing was one finish that was certainly in fashion during the 1240s when Henry III ordered the whitening of the three great towers of London (White Tower), Rochester and Corfe.[4]

The builders of later brick castles emulated this use of polychrome stonework to create ornamental effects by using differently hued bricks in order to achieve more versatile results. The construction of Kirby Muxloe in the 1480s corresponded with a fashion for decorative brickwork in which patterns were woven into the elevations with darker bricks (Fig 10.5). Some of this work at Kirby consisted of regular geometric designs, but there were also more specific images, including references to the builder, Lord Hastings. Two main instances of this type of decorative work are recorded in the accounts. The first was in April 1482, when the elevations of the intermediate towers were reworked with 'pictura'; the second such instance was in March 1483, and concerns the gatehouse.[5] Although the towers are no longer extant, the gatehouse survives and retains its decorative brickwork. To the right of the entrance on the canted face of the south turret is a very clear depiction of Lord Hastings' arms as emblazoned on his shield; above it, at first-floor level, is a representation of a ship. In addition, there are abstract geometrical patterns. When first made, these pictorial representations must have looked stunning, the newly baked bricks contrasting much more vividly than they do today. At Kirby, the men who undertook this work were considered to be more highly skilled and were paid at the higher daily rate of 7d., as opposed to the usual bricklayer's daily rate of 6d.

Geometrical Castles

The exterior finish was one way in which a building might draw attention to itself, but such a finish would not make up for a deficiency in design. From the twelfth century, castle builders were making increasing use of geometry to create distinctive plans for aesthetic purposes. In the twelfth century, the focus was principally on the keep, a prestige building detached from the main defensive works, which therefore lent itself to this kind of treatment; something of this has been discussed in Chapter 5. By the thirteenth century, however, it was entire castles that might be given plans derived from geometrical constructions.

This seems to have been the case in thirteenth-century Sicily and southern Italy, where the great castle builder of the age, Frederick II, King of Sicily and Emperor of the Romans, built a string of symmetrical castles in which the domestic accommodation was integrated with the defences. For the best known of these, we return to Castel del Monte, a compact castle built from new to an octagonal plan, with two storeys of apartments surrounding the central octagonal courtyard and octagonal turrets projecting from each of the angles (Fig 10.6).

Fig. 10.6. Castel del Monte (Puglia) The castle from the east (second quarter of the thirteenth century).

Outside Italy the influence of Castel del Monte is to be felt at Bellver, which was built for the Mallorcan king, Jaime II, near Palma, Mallorca, in the early fourteenth century, and which, like Castel del Monte, is a centrally planned hilltop castle. Like the builder of Castel del Monte, the architect, Pedro Salvá, who was working on Bellver in 1309, adhered to a strictly geometrical design, but in this instance the plan was circular rather than octagonal, a figure that avoided some of the anomalies in the vaulting that are a feature of Castel del Monte. At three of the cardinal points there is a D-shaped tower, and at the fourth (north), detached from the main body of the castle and linked only by a bridge, a cylindrical *torre de homenaje*. The curtain is lined with domestic apartments, and an integral two-storey loggia surrounds the central courtyard.

In England, the first castle to achieve a similar degree of regularity was at Holt, built between 1283 and 1304 by John de Warenne, 6th earl of Surrey (Fig 10.7).[6] This was in the form of a regular pentagon rather than a circle, but the circle would, nevertheless, have formed the basis of the geometry behind the plan, a derivation that is emphasized by the projecting cylindrical corner towers. It is unfortunate that there is no contemporary documentation for the construction of Holt Castle because this is one building for which one would like to know the name of the architect, not least because it represents a new aesthetic for English castles, even though it was one that would be emulated only occasionally. The date range suggested for Holt, and the circumstances under which it was built, as the centre of a new marcher lordship granted to Warenne by Edward I, might suggest an architectural connection with the King's works in Wales. However, the Warennes had a history of erecting striking architectural pieces at their castles, including Hamelin's great tower of Conisbrough and the great tower built by John de Warenne's father, William, at Sandal. John himself was behind the unusual D-shaped barbican tower at Sandal of *c.* 1270. It is an appealing thought to consider Holt as part of this family tradition and John de Warenne as the principal inspiration behind it.

The only English castle that emulates the circular form of Bellver is Queenborough on the Isle of Sheppey, which was built for Edward III between 1361 and 1375. Queenborough was a concentric castle, comprising a circular curtain surrounding a circular main block, or rotunda, containing the domestic apartments from which six round towers projected. In drawing up the rotunda the designer struck a circle, then drew a regular hexagon within it. The four lower angles of the hexagon were used as centres from which to strike the circles of four of the towers. At the fifth angle was the gateway, which was flanked by the other two towers. There were six entrances from the inner courtyard to the interior of the main block. Each gave access to one of the six towers and to one of the ground floor rooms. All six towers contained a hexagonal room, each one acting as a vestibule to a staircase leading to the upper floor(s). At first-floor level, the King's hall, chambers and oratory, as well as a kitchen were located.

The antecedents of Queenborough are uncertain. Bellver may have been an influence, but there were possible forebears nearer to home, including the royal castle of Restormel, which originated as a ringwork of *c.* 1100 in the form of a slightly irregular circle. The timber superstructure of the castle was replaced in stone, probably during the later thirteenth century, to create a tightly planned castle with two storeys of apartments lining the curtain. The outer diameter of 38 m (125 ft) and the courtyard diameter of *c.* 20 m (6 ft)

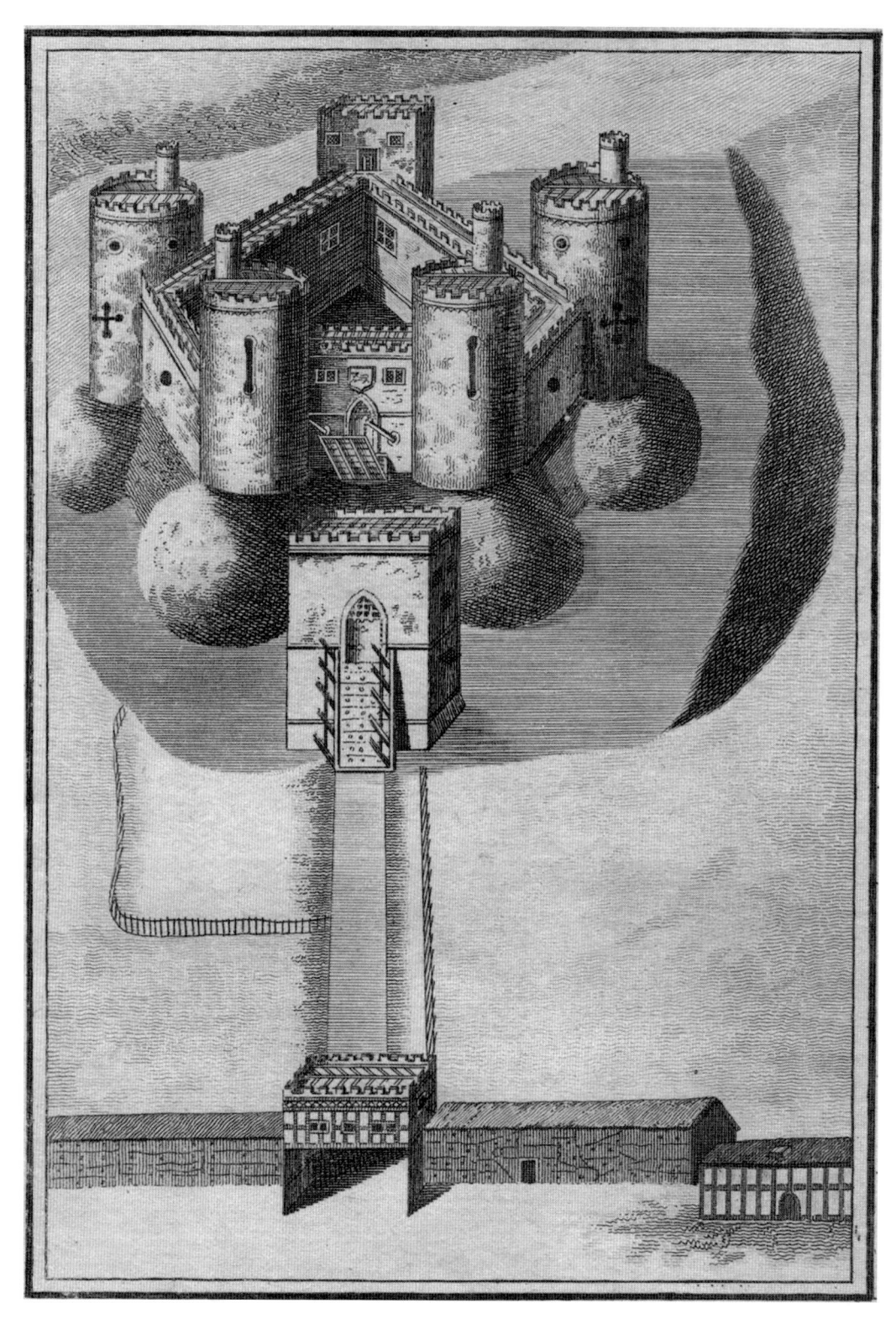

Fig. 10.7. Holt (Flintshire) View of the pentagonal castle prior to its demolition (between 1283 and 1311).

are extraordinarily close to those of the Queenborough rotunda, and the two buildings must have formed similar types of dwelling. A model that was closer in date to Queenborough might have been the 'Round Table', a short-lived circular building with a central courtyard built for Edward III in the upper ward of Windsor in the 1340s;[7] it was probably demolished in the late 1350s to make way for the reconstruction of the royal lodgings under the master masons John Sponlee and William Wynford.

The construction of Queenborough was carried out under the direction of John Box, a mason highly experienced in royal domestic and military architecture, having previously been in charge of works at Westminster Palace, the Tower of London and Calais, and it may be that he was responsible for the design. However, there are also grounds for suggesting that William Wynford, who was working at Windsor by 1360, made a contribution. One architectural feature shown in Hollar's view of Queenborough that might denote the influence of Wynford is the polygonal stair turret that extends above the battlements of each of the towers. These turrets recall features that were associated with Wynford's later work at Winchester College (Middle Gate, 1387). It is interesting to note that between April 1361 and October 1362, ie during the first two seasons of work at Queenborough, Wynford was absent from his post at Windsor for a total of 159 days.[8] It is perhaps noteworthy too that the clerk of works at Windsor from 1359 was William of Wykeham, who also had charge of Queenborough from 1361. Wykeham acted as patron to Wynford in subsequent years, notably at New College Oxford, Winchester College and Winchester Cathedral.

The formal plan was less favoured in the north of England than it was in the south. John Lewyn's Bolton, which seemingly had the potential to rival its more southerly predecessors, failed to achieve such a degree of regularity, possibly owing to a disjointed development.[9] Nevertheless, the experience paved the way for Lewyn's more symmetrical quadrangular designs of Lumley and Wressle, two buildings, both of which date from *c.* 1390, that have much in common, including the approximately 46m (150ft) square size of the main block. Lumley's regularity of plan was derived from the popular medieval proportion of one to the square root of two, or the relation of the side of a square to its diagonal;[10] Wressle was laid out to an equivalent degree of accuracy. These two castles achieved a level of regularity on a par with the south.

The Formal Front

The symmetrical plan inevitably produced the formal front, thirteenth-century examples of which include Dourdan (1222), Harlech (1283) and Beaumaris (1295), in each of which a twin-towered gatehouse is linked by lengths of curtain wall to two corner towers. The powerful impact of the Harlech front is given depth and contrast by the low outer curtain, above which it looms menacingly (Fig 8.8). There are only slight gradations in height between the gatehouse, curtain and corner tower, but the gatehouse maintains an absolute dominance over the whole composition. This tripartite arrangement of gatehouse, curtain and corner towers, used at Harlech to instil a sense of awe, formed the basis of the symmetrical castle front. The simplicity of this grouping, however, was not without flexibility. Harlech was a military outpost, its walls intended to counter an assault, and its formality constituted a symbol of an uncompromising new order. Although the castle has ceased to be a facet of political power and subjugation, the face it presents to the modern world is still somewhat grim.

What a contrast it makes with the equally formal entrance front of Maxstoke (Warwickshire) a castle that dates from the 1340s (Fig 10.8). Despite being equipped with the necessities of defence, Maxstoke was, primarily, a nobleman's country house, and its appearance reflects that role. While still comprising the basic components of central gatehouse, curtain and corner towers, these have been used to achieve an effect of martial gentility rather than belligerence. The central gatehouse dominates the elevation to a greater extent than at Harlech, a result achieved by its more pronounced projection, the contrast it makes with the low accompanying curtain and corner towers, and the diminished width of the flanking turrets that emphasize the height. A distinguishing aspect of the design is the use of the octagonal tower, a fairly uncommon choice, but a feature that was to enjoy a degree of popularity in the years following the completion of Maxstoke.[11]

As an exercise in formal architecture, this well proportioned and elegant frontage has few equals amongst English castles. It is in fact the product of a precise and rational mindset that pervades the whole design of the castle and which bears comparison with the near contemporary keep of Stafford Castle (1348), another building in which a symmetrical plan and frontage were manifestations of the underlying rationale and in which octagonal corner towers formed a major element of the design.[12] The master builder of Stafford keep was a man called John of Burcestre, who took his name from the Oxfordshire town of Bicester, which is some 75 miles from Stafford. Given the similarities in approach to the design of the two buildings, coupled with their chronological proximity, it is reasonable to suggest that John of Burcestre may also have worked at Maxstoke, which is only some 50 miles distant from Bicester.

The symmetrical entrance front was to be a recurrent theme of castle design during the fourteenth and fifteenth centuries. It was certainly an important aspect of the now much

Fig. 10.8. Maxstoke (Warwickshire) The entrance (east) front from the south east (c. 1345).

altered Oxfordshire castle of Shirburn, which, incidentally, lies some 18 miles to the south-east of Bicester. Shirburn, which was erected for Warin, Lord Lisle under a licence to crenellate of 1377, is a moated quadrangular castle with round corner towers and a central rectangular gate tower flush with the front of the adjoining ranges. The proportions of the castle were altered in the eighteenth century, but originally, the three-storey gatehouse and corner towers rose above the two-storey ranges.[13] The name of the architect is not known, but William Wynford was working at Abingdon Abbey, 12 miles to the west of Shirburn, in 1375–1376,[14] and the quadrangular form and understated square gate tower fall within the same architectural tradition as his later work at Winchester College and New College, Oxford.

Another castle that has been tentatively linked with Wynford is Bodiam (Sussex), for which Sir Edward Dallingridge was granted a licence in 1385 (Fig 10.9). Bodiam has a very similar plan to Shirburn, but a somewhat larger footprint. Here again, the stress is on the (symmetrical) entrance front, only, at Bodiam, the much more emphatic gatehouse dominates the elevation. Bodiam's gatehouse is a T-shaped building, with a short stem; the head of the T breaks forward from the curtain, and additional projecting square turrets flank the entrance. This structure is a comparatively thin block, and functions principally as a façade designed to create an outward effect. The impact is heightened by the breadth of the tower and the shorter lengths of curtain to either side that link it to the round corner towers.

Wynford's name has also been put forward as the possible architect of Old Wardour castle, near Tisbury (Wiltshire). Built for John Lord Lovel under a licence of 1393, it is a

Fig. 10.9. Bodiam (Sussex) The entrance (north) front from the north west (fourth quarter of the fourteenth century).

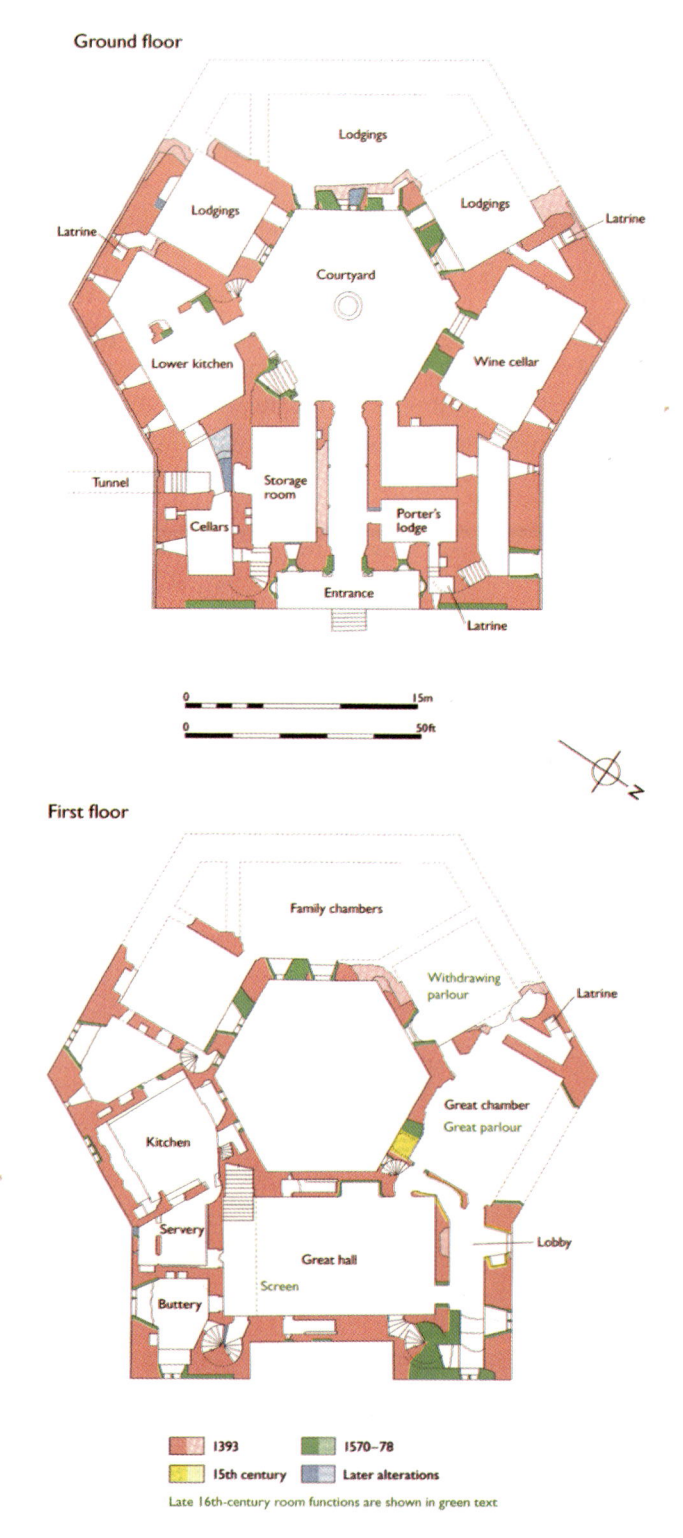

Fig. 10.10. Old Wardour (Wiltshire) Ground and first-floor plans of the inner ward; perhaps by William Wynford (last decade of the fourteenth century) © Historic England.

symmetrical building of highly original design in which the concentric plans of the inner and outer wards were based on a regular hexagon. The main survival is the partly ruined inner ward, a building that incorporates some of the characteristics of a keep, though a closer analogy might be one of the shell keeps that were remodelled with new lodgings in the fourteenth century at, for instance, Alnwick, Durham and Windsor, in which a central courtyard was retained (Fig 10.10).

There is an obvious comparison to be made with Queenborough, built some thirty years earlier, a site already mentioned as a possible recipient of William Wynford's influence. The main point of correlation is the geometrical configuration of the plans, both of which were based on a series of concentric circles. The central rotunda at Queenborough was also very similar in concept to the inner ward of Wardour, forming a compact courtyard residence. The former had an external diameter of approximately 40 m (130 ft), while its counterpart at Wardour was only slightly smaller at 37 m (120 ft). These are buildings of a similar broad scale to the stand-alone quadrangular castles of Shirburn and Bodiam,[15] but at Wardour, where angle towers were eschewed, the inner ward has something of the proportions of a tower.

The entrance front, on the north-east side of the enclosure, takes the form of a rectangular block thrusting forward from the hexagon with two flanking 'towers' framing a broad recessed centre containing the (remodelled) entrance. The overall effect is dramatic, an impression that is enhanced by the two lofty windows of the first-floor great hall above the entrance, and by the uniformity of height between the 'towers' and the recess (Fig 10.11). An element that has now largely disappeared, but which would have heightened the impact,

Fig. 10.11. Old Wardour (Wiltshire) Entrance front; perhaps by William Wynford (last decade of the fourteenth century with sixteenth-century alterations).

is the corbelled machicolation that carried the parapet over the recess and contributed to a sense of depth and three-dimensionality.

There are some affinities with the gatehouse of Bodiam, not least the rectangularity of the block, the recessed entrance and the machicolated parapet, but, in comparison, Wardour is on a giant scale. Like that of Bodiam, this entrance is something of a deceit: the 'towers' are not true towers, but rather extensions of the block, and the full length of the hall does not appear in the elevation, the two ends extending behind the fronts of the 'towers'. The composition uses conventional aspects of castle design in an original way to create a plan that is not quite as it seems from the exterior.

A not dissimilar approach is evident in the treatment of the exterior elevation of the great hall complex of Kenilworth, one of the more intriguing instances in the story of formal fronts in castles. Here, in the 1370s, John of Gaunt's master builder designed this frontage as a regular façade that is far from reflecting the reality of the interior (Fig 10.12). The hall is recessed between two square flanking towers adorned with octagonal corner turrets. Triangular-sectioned projections or buttresses articulate the bay divisions of both the hall and towers, though not towards the bailey, where buttresses of a more conventional stamp were used. These triangular buttresses are features that are seldom encountered in medieval architecture, and may have been intended to complement the octagonal turrets. This is a rare example of a formalist creating the semblance of order in an older, irregular, structure.

Little is known about the chief mason, Henry Spenser, who worked at Kenilworth between 1373 and 1380, and who was, presumably, responsible for this façade However, it has been ascertained that, like Wynford, he had worked at Windsor Castle in the 1360s,

Fig. 10.12. Kenilworth (Warwickshire) The west front of the great hall as remodelled in the 1370s by Henry Spenser for John of Gaunt, duke of Lancaster.

during the remodelling of the royal apartments in the upper ward by John of Gaunt's father, Edward III.[16] One of the principal distinguishing aspects of the royal lodgings was the south front, which was raised in 1363–1365 by the masons John Martyn and John Welot under the direction of John Sponlee and William Wynford.[17] The slightly irregular collection of buildings and courtyards that made up the complex was unified by the imposition of this highly disciplined façade. The front was divided into two main sections of unequal length framed by the polygonal Rose Tower to the extreme left (west), and by gateways flanked by twin polygonal turrets to the left of centre and to the extreme right (east). At first-floor level, the longer, eastern, portion contained the hall and chapel, while the western portion contained the King's great chamber. This upper storey was fenestrated with high arched windows in an uninterrupted display of unprecedented length. It is arguable that the hall range at Kenilworth was designed as a smaller-scale version of its counterpart at Windsor, framed between two towers, just as the hall of Windsor was framed between two gateways.

Informality

Formality was one way of creating an effect, but, as we have seen at Château Gaillard, it was not the only approach, nor was it always feasible when existing buildings and earthworks imposed restrictions. One such example is the north-east side of Warwick, a motte and bailey castle founded in the 1060s, has one of the most imposing entrance fronts in England covering a distance of nearly 90 m (300 ft). Entirely a creation of the fourteenth century, it was nevertheless constructed over a period of 30–50 years.[18] Instead of attempting unity the builder(s) chose to punctuate the curtain with three components of contrasting character comprising a roughly central gatehouse with a barbican and two angle towers. Guy's Tower at the north end of the front has a regular dodecagonal plan, while the plan of Caesar's Tower to the south is unique in having a tri-lobed front and a polygonal back. The gatehouse is a rectangular block with angle turrets, round at the front and polygonal to the rear, with a substantial barbican, the entrance to which is flanked by polygonal turrets. Each of these components is a major piece of architecture in its own right and all three are perhaps best considered independently, and yet, the composition seems to work, the juxtaposition of polygonal and round turrets at the entrance helping to reconcile the different characters of the two corner towers. The exaggerated sense of verticality that is engendered by the monumental scale of the towers and their positions on top of the high earthen bank, is countered by the long thrust of the barbican that roots the scheme to the ground, focuses the eye and draws one in to appreciate the spectacle.

The tower was the basis of a number of informal compositions in the north of England during the later fourteenth century. The development of the tower in the north owed much to the widespread fortification of previously undefended manorial sites and the fluidity of architectural forms that it engendered. First-floor halls with angle turrets were being built by the mid thirteenth century, accompanied by the conversion of older undefended manor houses into something approaching a tower; these structures contributed to the development of the tower house. A related development at Raby Castle (Durham) occurred with respect to the great hall, initially a single-storey structure that had a second storey raised on top of it, a solar tower built at the upper end and a cluster of towers at the lower end. This clustering of towers, which was developed to particular effect by the Durham master, John

Lewyn, was to become a significant component in northern English architecture during the later fourteenth century. Despite the destruction of the solar tower at Raby, it is still the towers that are the dominating factor in the castle's skyline.

The same comment on the arrangement of the towers may be made of Brancepeth (Co. Durham), another Neville castle, in which tower clustering was taken a step further. Here, at the south-west angle of the castle, is a cluster of three large rectangular residential towers with projecting angle and mid wall turrets. The Bulmer Tower to the north is on an east–west alignment, the others, which form an entity known collectively as the Neville Tower but are attached to each other only at one corner, are both aligned north–south, the northernmost component abutting the south wall of the Bulmer Tower. The composition, which forms part of the enceinte, is an interesting massing of three-dimensional aspect.

This facet of Brancepeth probably influenced the form of one of the highlights of northern castle architecture, namely the great tower of Warkworth Castle, built *c.* 1390 on top of the ancient motte. It is a square building with a wing projecting from the centre of each face (Fig 6.17). The massing of the main block and the wings represents the same approach to design that was behind the south-west tower cluster at Brancepeth, and produces a very similar though more refined three-dimensional effect. At Brancepeth the angles of the towers were highlighted by diagonally-projecting turrets, whereas at Warkworth the emphasis is achieved through canting, the result being a less cluttered composition which relied on the essential merit of the main concept. It is probable that this approach was followed at Warkworth in order to harmonize with existing twelfth- and thirteenth-century semi-polygonal towers, and thereby reflect the existing character of the castle.

Fig. 10.13. Raglan (Monmouthshire) The gatehouse front (mid fifteenth century).

A less compact tower-clustering arrangement was created at Raglan (Monmouthshire) in the following century, where the late fifteenth-century architect created a stirring piece of architectural choreography in his design of the main entrance front (Fig 10.13). Taking into account the form of the existing (mid fifteenth-century) hexagonal great tower that stood forward of the castle and dominated the main approach, he built a twin-towered gatehouse and an adjacent corner tower all reflecting the shape of the great tower. The result is a loosely disposed group of differently sized towers unified by their hexagonal forms and extravagantly machicolated parapets. The composition was evidently intended to create a striking architectural effect.

Gatehouses

The gatehouse at Raglan is one of the later manifestations in which the main entrance was exploited as an architectural centrepiece. In fact, gatehouses had been used as visual foci throughout the medieval period. An eleventh-century example is Tickhill, a rectangular building projecting from the curtain wall, on the front of which is a primitive sculptural frieze, which was evidently intended to lift the gatehouse above mere functionality and give the observer pause for thought. Single-towered gatehouses provided the architect with limited opportunities, but the adoption of twin-towered gatehouses delivered a boost to the architectural possibilities of the entrance.

The designer of William Marshal's twin-towered gateway of c. 1190 at Chepstow (Fig 8.2), the first in Britain to incorporate round towers, set the agenda for future castle builders by endowing the gateway with the status of a major design feature. The plan is a simple one, but it is visually effective, and although defence may have been the underlying motive in devising its form, that does not detract from its aesthetic appeal. The bows of the towers sweep outwards and inwards drawing attention to the recessed centre bay containing the gateway; the composition has depth and the opportunity for the play of light and shade, and the gentle rising curve of the plinth gives a sense of depth and balance.

Around 1200, the master builder employed by Robert, son of Roger, lord of Warkworth, to reconstruct his castle in stone, raised a relatively low two-storey gatehouse with twin polygonal-fronted towers (Fig 10.14). The form is in tune with the contemporary Carrickfergus tower that occupies one angle of the entrance front, and which itself may have been influenced by Maurice's work at Dover (see pp. 148–149), though nowhere else do polygonal towers seem to have been used for a gatehouse. An interesting feature of the Warkworth gatehouse is the application of polygonal buttresses to the angles of the flanking towers, in a diminutive echo of their form. Their faceted caps which recede into the arrises shortly below the original parapet, and the skilful manner in which their bases are mitred into the battered plinth, continuing the lines of the arrow loop splays, are exquisite details that have been conceived by a master craftsman gifted with definite panache.

Warkworth, for all the skill lavished on it, was not to be emulated; it was the general concept of the Chepstow front that was to become popular with most of the thirteenth-century builders of royal castle gatehouses, and indeed with much of the nobility. The one diversion from this general trend was the portal devised in the 1220s for the new gatehouse at Dover (Constable Tower), which resembles two D-shaped towers set back-to-back to produce a plain flat front with rounded ends (Fig 7.9). The design is startlingly original and

Fig. 10.14. Warkworth (Northumberland) The gatehouse of *c*. 1200 from the south east; the uppermost storey is an addition of *c*. 1400.

must have made a striking impact when it was first built. In effect, the builder was harking back to the idea of single-tower gatehouse, while paying his respects to the twin-towered type by incorporating the rounded ends. However, despite its originality, in architectural terms, it is difficult to see this stark façade as an improvement on the type with twin rounded towers. Certainly, when some twenty years later the architect of the Black Gate in Newcastle made use of the same type of frontage, he made a distinct improvement by breaking up the surface with a central projection containing the entrance. This was a deliberate reversal of the twin-towered gatehouse with recessed central entrance, although the projection contained a deep portal under a high arch. The brash and uncompromising frontage of the Constable Tower was exchanged at Newcastle for one with far greater interest and decorative intent, a point that is underlined by the incorporation of a pair of image niches, one each side of the entrance.

Despite this interesting development of the Dover concept, the Black Gate failed to inspire any further emulation of the theme; most other gatehouses from this period, through to the fourteenth century, adhered to the rounded twin-tower model. A stunningly effective interpretation of the type was built for the de Clares at Tonbridge *c.* 1250–1265 (Fig 8.5). Here, the bases of the twin towers are gripped by high faceted spurs to create a powerful scalloping effect at the intersection between the two elements, to give the appearance of stylized waves lapping at the walls. The central entrance bay, which is only shallowly recessed between the towers at the upper level, has been given a sense of diminishing perspective by a high outer arch of five orders, which frames the entrance, captures the attention and directs the eye down towards the deeply recessed gate. Immediately below the outer arch, the curving fronts of the flanking towers, which are curtailed by the central bay at the higher level, sweep round under the arch to meet the gate passage and form the sides of an outer portal. It is an extremely interesting composition and Tonbridge must be considered one of the high points of gatehouse design, both as a military building (see pp. 171–172), a residence, and as an effective piece of architecture. It engendered a number of thirteenth-century imitations, which have been dubbed 'Tonbridge-style gatehouses',[19] though none was as successful.

The dominance of the round-towered gatehouse was broken by the architect of Caernarfon (begun in 1283), a castle whose design must have been ratified under the aegis of James of St Georges. Both the main gatehouses (the King's Gate and the Queen's

Fig. 10.15. Caernarfon (Caernarfonshire) The Queen's Gate from the south east (last quarter of the thirteenth century).

Gate) have twin polygonal towers, but there is quite a contrast in appearance and effect. Of the two frontages, the most original is the smaller Queen's Gate, which serves as the outer entrance (Fig 10.15). This has a deeply recessed entrance with splayed sides, its cavernous character contrived by the joining together of the two towers at the uppermost floor level, the central portion being carried on a many-ordered arch, which bridges the central recess. This, again, references the single-towered gatehouse, but may also make an oblique allusion to Dover.

The Queen's Gate makes an imposing spectacle, partly by virtue of the uninterrupted exposure of its full height. Its sternly martial character is determined by its exposed position on the outer side of the curtain. The King's Gate, which is within the walls of the borough, is less grim and more regal, the large windows on the upper storey drawing attention to its residential function (Fig 10.16). There is a link to Tonbridge in the staged recessing of the central entrance bay, with its high outer arch of multiple orders. Above this, forming the centrepiece of the façade is a canopied niche containing a statue of the King. The polygonal towers and decorative sculpture of the King's Gate were to serve as sources of inspiration for a number of castle gatehouses over the next century and beyond.

Fig. 10.16. Caernarfon (Caernarfonshire) The King's Gate from the north (last quarter of the thirteenth century).

Sculpture

From the thirteenth century displays of sculpture were being used on castles as marks of ownership but also as decorative foci, a favourite position being over the main gateway, where it was certain to be seen. One early example was carved in relief on the tympanum of the entrance to Enguerrand III's donjon of Coucy of *c.* 1220, taking the form of a knight in combat with a lion, apparently commemorating an encounter of one of the lords of Coucy.[20] Lions are beasts with imperial associations, which may account for their appearance at the main gateway to the emperor Frederick II's Castel del Monte of the 1230s where a pair sits above the capitals of the flanking colonettes (Fig 10.17). The other main piece of sculpture at Castle del Monte is in the courtyard next to the main entrance into the apartments where there are the remains of an engaged equestrian statue, possibly emulating the works of classical antiquity. A sculpture of a 'lion passant guardant' existed over the gateway to the late thirteenth-century Holt Castle, and a panel bearing a giant relief of the Percy device of a lion rampant was exhibited on the north front of the late fourteenth-century great tower of Warkworth (Fig 10.18). The Warkworth lion forms the centrepiece of a collection of now poorly preserved sculpture around the upper walls of the great tower, but which seem to have comprised both angels and knights holding escutcheons in front of them. The shields are now blind but would originally have been painted with the arms of the Percies and their allies.

The heraldic shield was probably the most commonly depicted type of sculpture on castle exteriors, and clearly distinguished the builder. There is no doubt that such shields would have been painted with the appropriate tinctures that formed an essential part of the heraldic identification system in concert with the base design. Very often there is more than one shield, representing not only the lord of the castle but also family members and allies. Although the shield was usually considered sufficient, a small number of

Fig. 10.17. Castel del Monte (Puglia) Sculpture of a lion at the entrance to the castle (second quarter of the thirteenth century).

Fig. 10.18. Warkworth (Northumberland) The Percy lion on the north front of the great tower (last decade of the fourteenth century).

fuller achievements of arms survive from the late fourteenth century, of which there are well-preserved examples at the castles of Bodiam (Sussex), Lumley (Co. Durham) and Hylton (Co. Durham). The largest collection is at Lumley, built for Ralph 1st Baron Lumley, where six achievements of arms complete with shields, helms and crests, were placed over the outer gatehouse. In addition to Lord Lumley's arms are those of King Richard II, Henry Percy, 1st earl of Northumberland, Ralph 6th Baron Neville (brother-in-law), Sir Thomas Gray of Heton, and William 5th Baron Hylton (Fig 10.19). The shields are set at an angle following the convention of heraldic artists in depicting achievements in the rolls or arms, and it is from such rolls that the sculptors no doubt took their designs.

Figure sculpture in the round was probably being made to adorn English royal castles by the mid thirteenth century, as is suggested by the two image niches surviving on the Black Gate of 1247 at Newcastle-upon-Tyne. Niche figures were to become a recurrent theme over late medieval gateways, primarily town and bridge gates. The decoration of castle parapets with figure sculpture was underway by the late thirteenth century, some of the earliest examples known being those that decorate the merlons of Marten's Tower, Chepstow Castle, of *c.* 1287–1293.[21] The Chepstow examples are mostly demi-figures that merge into the merlon copings; they have been interpreted as personifications of aristocratic attributes.[22] Two sculptures from the late thirteenth-century town walls of Newcastle, which were salvaged during redevelopment work in the nineteenth century, are, like those of Chepstow, demi-figures that merge into the merlon copings, one apparently a musician playing a pipe or a shawm.[23] Slightly later are the sculptures of eagles that were raised on the battlements of the Eagle Tower at Caernarfon Castle in 1316–1317.[24] The eagles were closely followed by the installation of a statue of King Edward II in 1319–1320, not on the battlements, but within a niche over the King's Gate (Fig 10.20),[25] a motif that was repeated over the main gateway to Denbigh Castle, a building strongly influenced by Caernarfon.

It was in the north of England, however, during the fourteenth-century, that the fashion for heraldic and merlon-mounted figure sculpture seems to have been most popular. A project that was to have a major influence on later fourteenth-century works in the north of England in this respect was the new gatehouse to the inner ward of Alnwick Castle, which

Fig. 10.19. Lumley (Co. Durham) Heraldic sculpture over the outer gateway, from top to bottom and left to right: The royal arms of Richard II 1377–1399; Henry Percy First Earl of Northumberland 1377–1408; Ralph Sixth Baron Neville 1388–1425; Sir Thomas Grey d. 1400; Ralph First Baron Lumley 1384–1400; William Fifth Baron Hylton 1376–1435.

Fig. 10.20. Caernarfon (Caernarfonshire) Canopied niche on the front of the King's Gate containing a statue of the King (First quarter of the fourteenth century).

was raised by Henry, 3rd Baron Percy between 1340 and 1345. The gatehouse is rectangular with twin semi-octagonal towers projecting boldly from the outer angles. It is embellished with thirteen heraldic shields.[26] In the centre, over the gateway, are the royal arms, while the others are disposed on the flanking towers in a single line beneath the battlements, as though hanging from the parapet string. In addition, eight figures in a variety of attitudes, and representing different activities, surmounted the merlons of the towers. Unlike the Chepstow and Newcastle figures, which blend into the merlons, the Alnwick statues stand on top of the copings, their lower limbs fully delineated.

Alnwick was probably the model for the gatehouse of Bothal Castle (Northumberland), approximately 20 miles to the south, to which it bears a close resemblance. The builder was Sir Robert Bertram who obtained a licence to crenellate in 1343. Another extravagant display of heraldry, comprising no less than fourteen shields, including that of the Percies, was emblazoned across the front elevation. The battlements were surmounted by at least three figures, two of which survive; one seems to be a musician, the other a wild man frozen in the act of hurling a boulder.[27] Like its Alnwick counterpart the Bothal gatehouse had semi-octagonal twin towers at the outer angles, which, with Alnwick, share the distinctive trait of projecting not only forward from but also to the sides of the main rectangular block. The similarities between the two buildings suggest that the same master builder was involved in both. The sculpture, then, may be the products of the same workshop.

Ralph, fourth Baron Neville, and his architect may have drawn on these sources in the design of the eastern gateway to his courtyard castle of Raby (Co. Durham), probably of the 1360s. Here, it was the barbican that accommodated most of the heraldry. The Bucks' view shows that above the entrance arch, and carried right across the front elevation, was placed a bas relief of the Neville bull. In addition, there were several heraldic shields and figures of armed men on the battlements of the gatehouse. The barbican was demolished in the eighteenth century but much of the carved work survives *ex situ* including three figure sculptures, which now ornament the battlements of the outer gatehouse; two are men at arms with swords and shields, while the third is another boulder thrower.

The climax came at the turn of the fourteenth and fifteenth centuries, when William Fifth Baron Hylton, a minor member of the Durham nobility, rebuilt his castle at Hylton (Co. Durham) near Sunderland.[28] This was a small courtyard castle with a hall range sited opposite the gateway. The architectural centrepiece of this complex, and now the only surviving above-ground element, was the gatehouse, which was built in the form of a self-contained great tower (Fig 10.21). In designing the gatehouse, Hylton's architect borrowed freely from the slightly earlier castle of Lumley, some 7 miles to the south-west of Hylton, on which Lord Hylton's arms are depicted. The front of the gatehouse was reserved for

Fig. 10.21. Hylton (Co. Durham) The great gatehouse embellished with heraldic devices on and between the turrets flanking the entrance, and with figure sculpture on the battlements. These aspects of the building take their cue from the great mid fourteenth-century Northumbrian gatehouses of Alnwick and Bothal (c. 1400).

one of the most lavish displays to appear on any medieval castle. There were eighteen shields and two large banners, extending above the gateway and across its two flanking turrets. The banners were those of Hylton himself and the royal banner of Henry IV; the shields all represent members of the north-eastern nobility.[29] In addition, set into the rear of the gatehouse, is the white hart of Richard II, and Lord Hylton's achievement of arms complete with shield, helm and crest. The richness of the heraldic display is equalled by further sculptural work, notably the copious amount of figure carving, which occurs both inside, on the roof timber corbels in the hall, and outside, surmounting the parapet. On the battlements between the two turrets flanking the gateway the eye would have been drawn to the *chef d'œuvre* of a pair of dragons, of which the right-hand one (and perhaps the left hand one also) was in combat with a knight. Like the combat scene at Coucy some 180 years before it probably depicts a legend of ancestral prowess.[30]

Other Wallhead Embellishments

The mounting of sculpture on the battlements was the crowning element of a more general interest in embellishing the wallhead. Machicolations, which had their origins as practical aspect of defence, were also appreciated for their decorative qualities, by adding depth and interest to a castle's profile and sometimes counterbalancing a battered base. An ornamental aspect is already apparent in the slot machicolations of Château Gaillard in the 1190s, where the streamlined elegance of the parapet supports contrasts markedly with the functional version at Krak des Chevaliers. In the fourteenth-century, slot machicolations of more sober aspect were employed with considerable impact in articulating the elevations of papal palace at Avignon and the of grand master's palace at the castle of Malbork. Nevertheless, it was as ornamental crestings that machicolations were to prosper in the corbelled versions that gradually replaced hoarding during the course of the thirteenth century. By the later fourteenth century corbelled machicolations were probably valued as much for their visual attractiveness as for their defensive function. The fourteenth-century castle builders of the south of England took their cue from France, in that the corbels support arches rather than flat lintels. Indeed, it was in France the aesthetic possibilities of such systems were exploited to the full. Northern English builders preferred the flat lintel, a trait that extended even to the extravagant display on Henry IV's gatehouse of *c.* 1400 at Lancaster (Fig 10.22).

Fig. 10.22. Lancaster (Lancashire) The great gatehouse from the south (first quarter of the fifteenth century).

Another wallhead embellishment that began as a defensive feature was the bartizan, or over-sailing angle turret, a detail that, in Britain, seems to have had its origins in Edward I's Welsh castles. At Harlech (*c.* 1285) construction of the two semi-circular flanking turrets of the outer gatehouse began not at ground level but on the battered plinth of the outer curtain from which the bases were corbelled outwards and upwards in a continuous plane to form inverted demi-cones. Corbelling of a different kind was used by the masons of the Gate-next-the-Sea at Beaumaris (*c.* 1295, Fig 10.23); in plan, the base of the western turret of the gatehouse is an irregular polygon with a pointed prow; the upper part of the tower is D-shaped, the transition from one form to the other having been achieved by stepped and chamfered corbel coursing.

Stepped corbelling was used by the builder of the barbican at Lewes *c.* 1330 but it also appears in a series of bartizans in the north of England, including the fourteenth-century gateways of the city of York: Micklegate Bar (1350–1375), Monk Bar, and Walmgate Bar (the barbican) as well as the Northumbrian towers of Chipchase and Belsay (*c.* 1370). The inclined corbelling technique of Harlech also proved popular in the north-east at, for example, Langley (*c.* 1350), Edlingham (*c.* 1360), Halton (*c.* 1370), Tynemouth (*c.* 1390) and Hylton (*c.* 1400). While these fourteenth-century examples oversail the sides of the parent building they maintain the line of the angle, providing a sense of rootedness. In the fifteenth century there was a tendency to oversail the angle as well, which produced a more exaggerated but less tidy effect.

Fig. 10.23. Beaumaris (Anglesey) Corbelling of the bartizan at the Gate-Next the Sea (last decade of the thirteenth century).

Conclusion

While castles always embodied elements of defence, it is also true that they often incorporated a sense of the aesthetic, and that the latter was as much a deliberate part of the design as the former. There was nothing self-effacing about a castle; a constant theme of the castle builder's approach was to make the building stand out in the landscape in proclamation of the power, wealth and social status of its lord. The strength of the fortifications was one way of driving that message home, but there is little doubt that from early in the castle-building story high-quality architecture (most notably the great tower), including decorative embellishment, was also highly valued for its contribution to a castle's character and its owner's prestige.

Sometimes, perhaps, functional necessity might have inhibited the aesthetic impulse, but, as our initial example of Château Gaillard demonstrates, in the hands of a gifted architect, this didn't have to be the case: here, beauty and functionality converged without the one compromising the other. At Château Gaillard, the emphasis was on defence; increasingly, in the later thirteenth and fourteenth centuries, a major focus of the castle builder was the integration of the domestic accommodation with the defences. This was a trend that provided exciting opportunities for the architect, but, again, not every master builder was able, for one reason or another, to turn that to maximum advantage. The temperament and will of the patron, no less than the ability and inclination of the builder, was no doubt a highly significant factor in determining the degree of ornamental detail and the visual impact of the design.

Afterword

In this survey of the castle builder's art we have encountered a number of outstanding individuals whose names have been preserved alongside the monuments for which they were responsible. Sometimes there is enough information to recreate a career, or at least part of one, and to identify personal design traits. These details add a human dimension to the study of the buildings and enrich our understanding of the castle-building phenomenon, and the manner in which it evolved. For every name, however, an undefined quantity remains undiscovered, representing generations of castle builders who have long been forgotten and whose identities are unknown to us. Yet every so often the distinguished character of a castle building provokes us to ponder over the anonymous master builder, in what is a natural reaction to being confronted by a work imbued with the personality of its maker. To take this a step further, although the builders of such seminal buildings as the great tower of Pembroke, the Tonbridge gatehouse and Caerphilly Castle cannot be named, their respective works allow us to confirm their former existence and serve as a basis for reconstructing something of their careers. Works such as these are at the top end of the spectrum, but the principle that something of a craftsman's persona is to be found in his creations can also be applied to lesser works. Consequently, there is scope for filling in some of the gaps that punctuate the list of castle builders even though their names may never be known. The key to furthering our knowledge of the human story is the detailed recording of the elements and combinations of elements that make up the works of a particular period or region. Amongst them are to be found the hallmarks that may be attributed to individual master builders, but also the regional building practices that were adhered to by many as a matter of proven tradition within a particular locality. There is a degree of overlap, partly because some of these traditions might have had their origins in a personal style, but also because a gifted provincial builder who rose to prominence might have been trained in such practices, and used them as the basis of his stylistic approach. As more becomes known so will we construct a wider picture of building craft practices and their geographical and chronological distributions, which will assist in clarifying the lines of development and bringing the personalities behind them into sharper focus.

Glossary

Alure: the circulatory path around the top of a wall behind the parapet, used as a fighting platform. Also known as a wall walk.
Arcade plate: in an aisled building, a horizontal timber that extends along the top of the arcade(s) and on which the feet of the rafters rest.
Arch-braced collar: a collar (*qv*) supported from each end by arching braces extending from the soffits (*qv*) of the rafters to the soffit of the collar.
Arris: a sharp edge where two surfaces meet at an angle.
Axial beam: a horizontal timber extending along the length of a building, usually supporting a floor.
Barefaced lap dovetail: a variant of dovetail joint in which only one side of the dovetailed timber is shaped (barefaced), and, once joined, stands proud of (lapped), rather than flush with, the other timber.
Barrel-vault: a continuous arched vault extending between two parallel walls.
Base cruck: one of a pair of timbers forming the main components of a type of timber cross-frame. Base crucks rise from a point well down the side walls of a building to the soffit of the collar (*qv*).
Bas-relief: a relief sculpture of only low projection from the surrounding surface.
Centring: a timber framework used to support arches and vaulting during construction, and kept in position until the stonework is self-supporting.
Chase: recess within a wall surface to accommodate a timber.
Collar: a horizontal timber located between the tie beam and apex of the roof, and set between a pair of principal rafters to which it gives lateral support.
Colonia: the most important category of ancient Roman city.
Crocket: a stylized curling leaf moulding popular amongst Gothic architects.
Crown plate: horizontal axial roof timber extending the full length of the building, carried by crown posts (*qv*) to support the collars (*qv*).
Crown post: vertical roof timber extending from a tie beam to a crown plate (*qv*) or collar purlin, which in turn supports the collars.
Cruck: one of a pair of timbers forming the main components of a type of timber cross-frame. Crucks rise from a point well down the side walls of a building as far as, or close to, the apex of the roof; they carry the purlins (*qv*) and ridge piece (*qv*).
Damper: a movable plate installed in a chimney flue and adjusted to regulate draught.
Double-pile roof: two parallel roof spans covering the same building.
Earth-fast post: a major vertical timber set into the ground by being placed in a pit, which is then infilled with firmly packed material.
Formwork: temporary timber support for vault webbing designed to the intended shape of the vault.
Fossatores: ditch diggers.
Groin vault: vault formed by the intersection of two barrel vaults at right angles to one another; the point of juncture produces an arris (*qv*) known as a groin.
Halved joint: similar to the halved lap joint (*qv* **Lap joint**) except that both timbers are channelled to form a tighter joint.
Indenture: a legally binding agreement between two parties written in duplicate, the two copies being separated by cutting a jagged (indented) line between them.
Joggle: the break or rebate in the line of a joint between two stones, made to prevent slipping or sliding.
Keystone: voussoir (*qv*) at the apex of an arch.
King post: vertical roof timber extending from the tie beam to the ridge piece.
King strut: vertical roof timber extending from the collar to the junction of the principal rafters.
Lap joint: in its simplest form a lap joint is formed by two crossing timbers in which the surface of one is fixed to that of the other by a peg; a sturdier variant is the halved lap joint in which the surface of one

of the timbers is channelled at the point of crossing in order to accommodate the other and so form a proper joint.

Machicolation: projecting stone gallery at the head of a wall, with slots in the base through which projectiles could be dropped. Also, an aperture in the vaulted roof of a passage (usually a gate passage), capable of fulfilling the same function.

Mitre: joint between two stones or pieces of wood meeting at an angle (as, for example, in an arch); in which the two joining faces are bevelled along the line produced by a bisection of the angle.

Passing brace: long timber extending across and jointed to more than one vertical and/or horizontal timber; typically part of the cross-frame of an aisled building and intended to contribute to lateral stability.

Pendentive dome: a structure in which the transition between a square substructure and a dome of circular section is effected by the means of pendentives. Pendentives are concave triangular spandrels rising from the angles of the substructure and splaying inwards to act as a circular base for the dome.

Petrarie: stone-throwing engines.

Podium: raised base or plinth for a columned building.

Posthole: archaeological feature representing the former presence of an earth-fast post (*qv*).

Purlin: longitudinal member in a roof structure giving intermediate support to the rafters.

Queen strut: vertical roof member extending from the tie beam to the collar.

Raking strut: angled roof member extending from the tie beam or collar to the principal rafter.

Ravelin: pointed fortification designed to split an attacking force.

Revetment: a wall or palisade that buttresses and retains a body of earth like a bank or a motte.

Ridge piece: horizontal timber extending along the apex (ridge) of a roof to which the ends of the rafters are attached.

Sail vault: type of dome related to pendentive (*qv*) construction; circular in plan, the sides are shaved off to accommodate a square substructure.

Saucer dome: low dome with the profile of an inverted saucer.

Sill-beam: horizontal timber forming the base of a timber-framed structure.

Slip tenon: loose tenon morticed into two adjoining timbers.

Squinch arch: arch built diagonally across the right angle formed by two adjoining walls to support an upper structure.

Soffit: underside of a horizontal timber or stone.

Spine beam: axial beam (*qv*) extending down the centre of a building.

Tip lines: archaeological layers in an earth construction, such as a bank, indicating the direction in which the soil has been tipped by the workmen.

Tourelle: a type of small turret adorning the upper part of a larger building; akin to a **Bartizan**, but larger, starting at a lower level and accessible from the interior of the main structure.

Transitional: the period of transition between the Romanesque and Gothic styles of architecture, dating from *c.* 1150 to *c.* 1220.

Triforium: an arcaded wall passage or blind arcade above the main arcade and below the clearstorey of a great church.

Trumpet capital: a late Romanesque form of capital decorated with stylized elongated scalloping the components of which resemble trumpets.

Vintenarius: a commander or foreman of a group of around twenty soldiers or workmen.

Voussoir: wedge-shaped stone used in the construction of an arch.

Wall plate: horizontal timber extending along the top of an outside wall on which the feet of the rafters rest.

Webbing: the in-filled compartments of a rib vault.

Referenced Works

Abbreviations
CPR Calendar of Patent Rolls
DMBC Dudley Metropolitan Council
NYCRO North Yorkshire County Record Office
RCAHMS Royal Commission on the Ancient and Historical Monuments of Scotland
RCHME Royal Commission on Historical Monuments (England)

Bibliography
Addyman, P. V. and Priestly, J. (1977) Baile Hill, York. *Archaeological Journal* **134**: 115–156.
Alcock, N. W., Faulkner, P. A. and Jones, S. R. (1978) Maxstoke Castle, Warwickshire. *Archaeological Journal* **135**: 195–233.
Alcock, N. and Miles, D. (2013) The earliest dated base-cruck house: 21 High Street, Alcester. *Vernacular Architecture* **44**: 74–51.
Allen, D. and Stoodley, N. (2010) Odiham Castle, Hampshire: Excavations 1981–1985. *Hampshire Studies* **65**: 23–101.
Arnold, A. J., Howard, R. E. and Litton, C. D. (2004) *Tree-ring Analysis of Timbers from Carlisle Castle, Carlisle, Cumbria*. Centre for Archaeology Report 25/2004.
Arnold, A. J., Howard, R. and Litton, C. (2010) List 223: dendrochronological dates from Nottingham Tree-ring dating Laboratory. *Vernacular Architecture* **41**, 92–102.
Ashbee, J. A. (2008) 'The function of the White Tower under the Normans'. In Impey (2008a), 125–139.
Austin, D. (2007) *Acts of Perception: A Study of Barnard Castle in Teesdale*, 2 vols, Architectural and Archaeological Society of Durham and Northumberland Research Report 6. Durham: A. A. S. D. N. and English Heritage.
Avent, R. (1995) *Laugharne Castle*. Cardiff: Cadw.
Avent, R. (2006) 'William Marshal's castle at Chepstow and its place in military architecture'. In Turner and Johnson, 81–90.
Avent, R. and Miles, D. (2006) 'The main gatehouse'. In Turner and Johnson, 51–62.
Avent, R. and Turner, R. (2006) 'The middle bailey'. In Turner and Johnson, 63–70.
Barker, P. A. and Barton, K. J. (1978) Excavations at Hastings Castle, 1968, *Archaeological Journal* **134**: 80–100.
Barker, P. and Higham, R. (1982) *Hen Domen, Montgomery: A Timber Castle on the English-Welsh Border, Volume 1*. London: Royal Archaeological Institute.
Barnes, H. D. and Simpson, W. D. (1951) The Building Accounts of Caister Castle (AD 1432–1435). *Norfolk and Norwich Archaeological Society* **30** (3): 178–188.
Barton, K. J. and Holden, E. W. (1977) Excavations at Bramber Castle, Sussex, 1966–67. *Archaeological Journal* **134**: 11–79.
Bates, C. J. (1891) *Border Holds of Northumberland*. London and Newcastle-upon-Tyne.
Bennett, P., Frere, S. S. and Stow, S. (1982) *Excavations at Canterbury Castle*. Maidstone: Kent Archaeological Society.
Beresford, G. (1987) *Goltho: The Development of an Early Medieval Manor c 850–1150*. London: English Heritage.
Bett, H. (1950) *English Legends*. London: Batsford.
Boüard, M. de (1973–1974) De l'aula au donjon: les fouilles de la motte de la Chapelle à Doué la Fontaine (x^e–xie siècle). *Archéologie Médiévale* 3–4.

Braun, H. (1935) Bungay Castle: report on the excavations. *Suffolk Institute of Archaeology and Natural History* **22** (2): 201–223.
Braun, H. (1936) *The English Castle*. London: Batsford.
Brindle, S. (2002) 'Fire, restoration, archaeology and history'. In Keen and Scarff, 110–124.
Brindle, S. and Sadraei, A. (2015) *Conisbrough Castle*. London: English Heritage.
Brown, P. (2003) *Whittington Castle Guidebook*. Whittington Castle Preservation Trust.
Brown, R. A. (1964) *Orford Castle*. London: HMSO.
Brown, R. A. (1976) *English Castles*, 2nd edn, London: Batsford.
Brown, R. A. Colvin, H. M. and Taylor, A. J. (1963) *The History of the King's Works. Volumes 1 and 2: The Middle Ages*. London: HMSO.
Butler, L. A. S. and Knight, J. (2004) *Dolforwyn Castle, Montgomery Castle*. Cardiff: Cadw.
Chibnall, M. (1969–1980) *The Ecclesiastical History of Orderic Vitalis*, 6 vols. Oxford Medieval Texts.
Clark, G. T. 1884 *Mediaeval Military Architecture in England*, 2 vols. London: Wyman and Sons.
Coad, J. (1995) *Dover Castle*. London: Batsford.
Coldstream, N. (2003) Architects, advisors and design at Edward I's castles in Wales. *Architectural History* **46**: 19–36.
Constable, C. (2003) *Aspects of the Archaeology of the Castle in the North of England c. 1066–1216*. University of Durham PhD thesis.
Cooper, T. P. (1911) *The History of the Castle of York*. London: Elliot Stock.
Coppack, G. (1990) *Abbeys and Priories*. London: Batsford.
Cruden, S. (1981) *The Scottish Castle*, 3rd edn. Edinburgh: Spurbooks.
Crummy, P. (1981) *Aspects of Anglo-Saxon and Norman Colchester*, CBA Research Report 39. London: Colchester Archaeological Trust and Council for British Archaeology.
Cunliffe, B. (1977) *Excavations at Portchester Castle. Volume 3: Medieval, the Outer Bailey and its Defences*. London: Society of Antiquaries.
Cunliffe, B. and Munby, J. (1985) *Excavations at Portchester Castle. Volume 4: Medieval, the Inner Bailey*. London: Society of Antiquaries.
Curnow, P. E. (1977) 'The Wakefield Tower, Tower of London'. In M.R. Apted, R. Gilyard-Beer and A. D. Saunders, *Ancient Monuments and their Interpretation*. London and Chichester: Phillimore.
Curnow, P. E. (1979) Some developments in military architecture c. 1200: Le Coudray-Salbart. *Proceedings of the Battle Conference* 2.
Darlington, J. (ed.) (2001) *Stafford Castle: Survey, Excavation and Research 1978–1998. Volume 1 – The Surveys*. Stafford Borough Council.
Davison, B. (1972) Castle Neroche: an abandoned Norman fortress in south Somerset. *Somerset Archaeology and Natural History* **116**, 16–58.
Devaut, J. (1886) Essai sur les premiers seigneurs de Pithiviers, *Annales de la Société Historique et Archéologique du Gâtinais* **4**: 94–129, 290–320.
Dixon, P. W. (1990) The donjon of Knaresborough: the castle as theatre. *Château Gaillard* **14**: 121–139.
Dixon, P. W. (1993) 'Mota, Aula et Turris: the manor houses of the Anglo-Scottish Border'. In G. Meirion-Jones and M. Jones, *Manorial Domestic Buildings in England and Northern France*. London: Society of Antiquaries, 22–48.
Dixon, P. W. (2008) 'The influence of the White Tower on the great towers of the twelfth century'. In Impey (2008a), 243–275.
Dixon, P. W. and Marshall, P. (1993) The great tower in the twelfth century: the case of Norham Castle. *Archaeological Journal* **150**: 410–432.
Dixon, P. W. and Marshall, P. (2002) 'Norwich Castle and its analogues'. In Meirion-Jones *et al.*, 235–243.
Drury, P. J. (1982) Aspects of the origins and development of Colchester Castle. *Archaeological Journal* **139**: 302–419.
Drury, P. J. (2002) 'Norwich Castle keep'. In Meirion-Jones *et al.*, 211–234.
Drury, P. J. (2009) *Rochester Castle Conservation Plan*. Part 1. The Paul Drury Partnership.
DMBC (n. d.) *Dudley Castle Archaeological Project*, 2 vols.
Dunning, G. C. (1950) Pottery from the Abinger motte. In Hope-Taylor, 33–41.
Early, R. (2003) 'Methodology and systems of analysis: the château at Mayenne'. In X. M. Ayán Villa, R. Blanco Rotea and P. Mañana Borrazás, *Archaeotecture: Archaeology of Architecture*, BAR International Series 1175. Oxford: Archaeopress, 61–81.

Ellis, P. (1993) *Beeston Castle, Cheshire: Excavations by Laurence Keen and Peter Hough, 1968–85*. London: Historic Buildings and Monuments Commission for England.

Elsworth, D. W. and Mace, T. (eds) (2015) *Aldingham Motte, Cumbria and its Environs in the Medieval Period*, Cumbria Archaeological Research Reports No. 5. Cumberland and Westmorland Antiquarian and Archaeological Society.

Emery, A. (1996–2006) *Greater Medieval Houses of England and Wales*, 3 vols: Volume 1: Northern England (1996), Volume 2: East Anglia, Central England and Wales (2000), Voume 3: Southern England (2006). Cambridge University Press.

Faulkner, P. A. (1963) Castle planning in the fourteenth century. *Archaeological Journal* **120**: 215–235.

Fisher, E. A. (1969), *Anglo-Saxon Towers: an architectural and historical study*. Newton Abbot: David and Charles.

Frere, S. S. and Stow, S. (1982) 'Excavations at the castle keep'. In Bennett *et al.*, 60–88.

Geddes, J. (1991) 'Iron'. In J. Blair and N. Ramsay (eds), *English Medieval Industries*. Hambledon and London: Hambledon Press, 167–188.

Gebelin, F. (1964) *The Châteaux of France*. London: Ernest Benn.

Goodall, J. (2004) The great tower of Carlisle Castle. In S. Brown (ed) *Carlisle and Cumbria: Roman and Medieval Art and Architecture*. British Archaeological Association Conference Transactions 27: 39–59.

Goodall, J. (2010) 'The baronial castles of the Welsh conquest'. In Williams and Kenyon, 155–165.

Goodall, J. (2011) *The English Castle*. London: Yale.

Goodall, J. (2012) The early development of Alnwick Castle *c*. 1100–1400, *Newcastle and Northumberland: Roman and Medieval Architecture and Art*. British Archaeological Association Transactions **36**, 232–247.

Grose, F. (1783–1797) *The Antiquities of England and Wales*, new edn, 8 volumes. London: Hooper and Wigstead.

Grundy, J., McCombie, G., Ryder, P., Welfare, H. and Pevsner, N. (1992) *Northumberland*, The Buildings of England, 2nd edn. Harmondsworth: Penguin.

Guy, N. (2011) The rise of the anticlockwise newel stair. *Castle Studies Group Journal* **25**: 113–174.

Harbottle, B. (1967) An excavation at Warkworth Castle, Northumberland, 1966. *Archaeologia Aeliana*, 4th ser., **45**: 105–121.

Harbottle, B. and Ellison, M (1981) An excavation in the castle ditch, Newcastle upon Tyne, 1974–6. *Archaeologia Aeliana*, 5th ser., **9**: 75–250.

Harris, R. (2008) 'The structural history of the White Tower, 1066–1200'. In Impey (2008a), 29–93.

Hartshorne, C. H. (1858) *Feudal and Military Antiquities of Northumberland*. London: Bell and Daldy.

Harvey, J. H. (1944) *Henry Yevele: The Life of an English Architect*. London: Batsford.

Harvey, J. H. (1948) The western entrance of the Tower. *Transactions of the London and Middlesex Archaeological Society* **9**: 20–35.

Harvey, J. H. (1950) *The Gothic World 1100–1600: A Survey of Architecture and Art*. London: Batsford.

Harvey, J. H. (1972) *The Mediaeval Architect*. London: Wayland.

Harvey, J. H. (1984) *English Mediaeval Architects*, 2nd edn. Gloucester: Alan Sutton.

Hawkyard, A. (2005) 'Sir John Fastolf's 'Gret Mansion by me late edified': Caister Castle, Norfolk'. In L. Clark, *Of Mice and Men: Image Belief and Regulation in Late Medieval England*. Woodbridge: Boydell and Brewer, 39–68.

Heslop, T. A. (1991) Orford Castle nostalgia and sophisticated living. *Architectural History* **34**: 36–58.

Heslop, T. A. (1994) *Norwich Castle Keep: Romanesque Architecture and Social Context*. Centre of East Anglian Studies.

Hewett, C. (1980) *English Historic Carpentry*. London and Chichester: Phillimore.

Higham, R. and Barker, P. (1992) *Timber Castles*. London: Batsford.

Higham, R. and Barker, P. (2000) *Hen Domen, Montgomery: A Timber Castle on the English-Welsh Border: A Final Report*. University of Exeter Press.

Hislop, M. (1991) Master John of Burcestre and the castles of Stafford and Maxstoke. *Transactions of the South Staffordshire Archaeological and Historical Society* **33**: 14–20.

Hislop, M. (1992) The castle of Ralph fourth Baron Neville at Raby. *Archaeologia Aeliana*, 5th ser., **20**: 91–97.

Hislop, M. (1996a) Lumley Castle, its antecedents and its architect. *Archaeologia Aeliana*, 5th ser., **24**: 83–98.

Hislop, M. (1996b) Bolton Castle and the practice of architecture in the Middle Ages. *Journal of the British Archaeological Association* **149**: 10–22.
Hislop, M. (2000) *Medieval Masons*. Princes Risborough: Shire.
Hislop, M. (2007) *John Lewyn of Durham: A Medieval Mason in Practice*, BAR British Series 438. Oxford: Hedges.
Hislop, M. and Kelleher, S. (2011) Beaudesert Hall: a house of the bishops of Coventry and Lichfield. *Transactions of the Staffordshire Archaeological and Historical Society* **45**: 41–61.
Hislop, M., Kincey, M. and Williams, G. (2011) *Tutbury: 'A Castle Firmly Built': Archaeological and Historical Investigations at Tutbury Castle, Staffordshire*, BAR British Series 546. Oxford: Archaeopress.
Hodgson, J. F. (1885) Raby. *Transactions of the Architectural and Archeological Society of Durham and Northumberland* **3**: 113–127.
Hodgson, J. F. (1895) Raby. *Transactions of the Architectural and Archeological Society of Durham and Northumberland* **4**: 49–122.
Holmes, S. (1896) The walls of Newcastle-upon-Tyne. *Archaeologia Aeliana*, 2nd ser., **18**: 1–25.
Hope-Taylor, B. (1950) The excavation of a motte at Abinger in Surrey. *Archaeological Journal* **107**: 15–43.
Impey, E. (2002a) The *donjon* at Avranches. *Archaeological Journal* **159**: 249–257.
Impey, E. (2002b) 'The *Turris Famosa* at Ivry-la-Bataille, Normandy'. In Meirion-Jones *et al.*, 189–210.
Impey, E. (ed.) (2008a) *The White Tower*. New Haven and London: Yale.
Impey, E. (2008b) 'The ancestry of the White Tower'. In Impey (2008a), 227–243.
Impey, E. and Lorans, E. (1998) Langeais, Indre-et-Loire. An archaeological and historical study of the early *donjon* and its environs. *Journal of the British Archaeological Association* **151**: 43–106.
Jardine-Rose, P. (2012) Newnham Castle excavations, Kent: interim report. *Castle Studies Group Journal* **26**: 196–200.
Keen, L. and Scarff, E. (eds) (2002) *Windsor: Medieval Archaeology, Art and Architecture of the Thames Valley*. British Archaeological Association Conference Transactions 25.
Kennedy, H. (1994) *Crusader Castles*. Cambridge University Press.
Kent, J., Renn, D. and Streeten, A. (2013) *Excavations at South Mimms Castle, Hertfordshire 1960–91*. London and Middlesex Archaeological Society Special Paper 16.
Kenyon, J. R. (2003) *Raglan Castle*. Cardiff: Cadw.
Kenyon, J. R. and O'Connor, K. (eds) (2003) *The Medieval Castle in Ireland and Wales*. Dublin: Four Courts Press.
Kincey, M. (2011) 'The Earthworks'. In Hislop *et al.*, 118–131.
Knight, J. K. (2000) *The Three Castles*, rev. edn. Cardiff: Cadw.
Knoop, D. and Jones, G. P. (1933) The rise of the mason contractor. *RIBA Journal*, 3rd ser., **43**: 1061–1071.
Knoop, D. and Jones, G. P. (1937a) The impressment of masons for Windsor Castle, 1360–1363. *Economic History* **3**: 350–361.
Knoop, D. and Jones, G. P. (1937b) The impressment of masons in the Middle Ages, *Economic History Review*, Series 1, **8**: 57–67.
Knoop, D. and Jones, G. P. (1949) *The Mediæval Mason*. Manchester University Press.
Larking, L. B. (1859) Cowling Castle. *Archaeologia Cantiana* **2**: 95–102.
McLees, A. D. (1973) Henry Yevele: disposer of the king's works of masonry. *Journal of the British Archaeological Association*, 3rd ser., **36**: 52–71.
McCarthy, M. R., Summerson, H. R. T. and Annis, R. G. (1990) *Carlisle Castle: A Survey and Documentary History*. London: Historic Buildings and Monument Commission for England.
Mackenzie, J. D. (1896) *The Castles of England*, 2 vols. New York: Macmillan.
McNeill, T. E. (1981) *Carrickfergus Castle*, Northern Ireland Archaeological Monographs 1. Belfast: HMSO.
McNeill, T. E. (2003) 'Squaring circles: flooring round towers in Wales and Ireland'. In Kenyon and O'Connor, 96–106.
Markland (1893) Carisbrooke Castle. *Proceedings of the Hampshire Field Club Archaeological Society* **2**: 257–70.
Mayes, P. and Butler, L. (1983) *Sandal Castle Excavations 1964–1973*. Wakefield: Wakefield Historical publications.

Meeson, R. A. (1980) Tenth Tamworth excavation report 1977: the Norman bailey defences of the castle. *Transactions of the South Staffordshire Historical and Archaeological Society* **20**: 15–28.

Meirion-Jones, G., Impey, E. and Jones, M. (2002) *The Seigneurial Residence in Western Europe AD c 800–1600*, BAR International Series 1088. Oxford: Archaeopress.

Mesqui, J. (1998) La tour maîtresse du donjon de Loches. *Bulletin Monumental* **156**: 65–125.

Mesqui, J. (2013) *Châteaux et Enceintes de la France Médiévale: De la Défense à la Résidence*, 2nd edn. Paris: Picard.

Mesqui, J. and Faucherre, N. (1988) Le Château de Châtillon-Coligny. *Bulletin Monumental*, **146** (2): 73–108.

Middleton, A. (1910) *An Account of Belsay Castle*. Newcastle-upon-Tyne.

Miles, D. and Bridge, M. (2010) Tree-ring dates from the Oxford Dendrochronology Laboratory List 224: general list. *Vernacular Architecture* **41**:102–105.

Miles, D. and Worthington, M. (1998) List 94: Welsh dendrochronology – Phase Two. *Vernacular Architecture* **29**: 126–129.

Miles, D. and Worthington, M. J. (1999) Tree-ring dates from Oxford Dendrochronology Laboratory. *Vernacular Architecture* **30**: 98–113.

Miles, D., Worthington, M. J. and Bridge, M. (2008) Tree-ring dates from the Oxford Dendrochronology Laboratory List 201: general list. Vernacular Architecture **39**: 132–135.

Molyneux, N., Baines, N. and Tyers, I. (2003)The detached bell tower, St Leonard's parish church, Yarpole, Herefordshire. *Vernacular Architecture* **34**: 68–72.

Moran, M. (2003) *Vernacular Buildings of Shropshire*. Logaston Press.

Morley, B. (1976) Hylton Castle. *Archaeological Journal* **133**: 118–134.

Morris, R. K. (2006) *Kenilworth Castle*. London: English Heritage.

Munby, J. (1993) *Stokesay Castle*. London: English Heritage.

Munby, J. Barber, R. and Brown, R. (2007) *Edward III's Round Table at Windsor*. Woodbridge: The Boydell Press.

Oswald, A. (1962–1963) Excavation of a thirteenth-century wooden building at Weoley Castle, Birmingham, 1960–61. *Medieval Archaeology* **6–7**: 109–134.

Oswald, A. and Ashbee, J. (2007) *Dunstanburgh Castle*. London: English Heritage.

Oswald, A., Ashbee, J., Porteous, K. and Huntley, J. (2006) *Dunstanburgh Castle, Northumberland: Archaeological, Architectural and Historical Investigations*. English Heritage Research Department Report Series No. 26/2006.

Page, W. (ed.) (1908) *The Victoria History of the County of Hertford, Volume 2*. London.

Page, W. (ed.) (1914) *The Victoria History of the County of York, Volume 1*. London.

Palmer, A. N. (1907) The town of Holt in County Denbigh: its castle, church, franchise, and demesne. *Archaeologia Cambrensis*, 6th series, 7: 311–334, 389–434.

Parkyn, A. and McNeill, T. (2012) Regional power and the profits of war: the east range of Warwick Castle. *Archaeological Journal* **169**: 480–518.

Payne, G. (1905) The reparation of Rochester Castle. *Archaeologia Cantiana* **27**: 177–192.

Peers, C. (1957) *Kirby Muxloe Castle*, 2nd edn. London: HMSO.

Pugin, A. W. (1895) *Examples of Gothic Architecture*, 3 vols. Edinburgh: John Grant.

Renn, D. F. (1969) The Avranches traverse at Dover Castle. *Archaeologia Cantiana* **84**, 79–92.

Renn, D. F. (1973) *Norman Castles in Britain*, 2nd edn. London: John Baker.

Renn, D. F. (1982) 'Canterbury Castle in the early Middle Ages'. In Bennett *et al.*, 70–74.

Renn, D. F. (2003) 'Two views from the roof: design and defence at Conwy and Stokesay'. In Kenyon and O'Connor, 163–175.

Renn, D. F. (2012) Ailnoth the engineer and Orford Castle. *Castle Studies Group Journal* **26**:201–202.

Rolland, D. (1980) Le donjon d'Ambleny et son histoire. *Bulletin de la Fédération des Sociétés d'Histoire et d'Archaéologie de l'Aisne*, 105–128.

RCAHMS (1920) *Seventh Report with Inventory of Monuments and Constructions in the County of Dumfries*. Edinburgh: HMSO.

RCHME (1970) *An Inventory of the Historical Monuments in Dorset, Volume 2*. London: HMSO.

RCHME (1972) *An Inventory of the Historical Monuments in the City of York. Volume 2: The Defences*. London: HMSO.

RCHMW (1991) *An Inventory of the Ancient Monuments in Glamorgan. Volume 3, Part 1a: The Early Castles*. London: HMSO.
Ryder, P. (1979) Ravensworth Castle, North Yorkshire. *Yorkshire Archaeological Journal* **51**: 89–100.
St John Hope, W. H. (1913) *Windsor Castle: An Architectural History*, 2 vols. London: Country Life.
Salzman, L. F. (1952) *Building in England Down to 1540*. Oxford University Press.
Scott-Robertson, W. A. (1877) Couling Castle. *Archaeologia Cantiana* **11**: 128–144.
Shelby, L. (1972) The geometrical knowledge of medieval master masons. *Speculum* **47**: 395–421.
Shoesmith, R. (ed.) (2014) *Goodrich Castle: Its History and its Buildings*. Logaston Press.
Shoesmith, R. and Johnson, A. (eds) (2000) *Ludlow Castle: Its History and its Buildings*. Logaston Press.
Simpson, W. D. (1923) *The Castle of Kildrummy: Its Place in Scottish History and Architecture*. Aberdeen: D. Wylie.
Simpson, W. D. (1940) Belsay Castle and the Scottish tower-houses. *Archaeologia Aeliana*, 4th ser., **17**: 75–84.
Simpson, W. D. (1942) Herstmonceux Castle. *Archaeological Journal* **99**: 110–122.
Simpson, W. D. (1949) Further notes on Dunstanburgh Castle. *Archaeologia Aeliana*, 4th ser., **27**: 1–28.
Simpson, W. D. (ed.) (1960) *The Building Accounts of Tattershall Castle 1434–1472*. Lincoln Record Society 55.
Simpson, W. G. and Litton, C. D. (1996), Dendrochronology in cathedrals. In T. Tatton-Brown and J. Munby, *The Archaeology of Cathedrals*. Oxford University Committee for Archaeology Monograph 42.
Soden, I. (ed.) (2007) *Stafford Castle: Survey, Excavation, and Research 1978–1998. Volume 2 – The Excavations*. Stafford Borough Council.
Stevenson, D. (1982) 'The *Colchester Chronicle* and the early history of Colchester Castle: a preliminary analysis'. In Drury, 409–413.
Summerson, H. (1993) *Dunstanburgh Castle*. London: English Heritage.
Tabraham, C. (2010) 'Scottorum Malleus: Edward I and Scotland'. In Williams and Kenyon, 181–192.
Taylor, A. J. (1949) *Rhuddlan Castle, Flintshire*. London: HMSO.
Taylor, A. J. (1957) The building of Flint: a postscript. *Flintshire Historical Society Journal* **17**, 34–41.
Taylor, A. J. (1961) 'Castle building in Wales in the later thirteenth century'. In E. M. Jope (ed.) *Studies in Building History*. London: Odhams, 104–133.
Taylor, H. and Taylor, J. (1965) *Anglo-Saxon Architecture, Volumes 1 and 2*. Cambridge University Press.
Thompson, A. H. (ed.) (1913–1920) The building accounts of Kirby Muxloe Castle, 1480–1484. *Transactions of the Leicestershire Archaeological Society* **11**: 193–345.
Thompson, M. W. (1960) Recent excavations in the keep of Farnham Castle, Surrey. *Medieval Archaeology* **4**: 81–94.
Thompson, M. W. (1977a) *Kenilworth Castle*. London: English Heritage.
Thompson, M. W. (1977b) 'Three stages in the construction of the hall at Kenilworth Castle, Warwickshire'. In M. R. Apted, R. Gilyard-Beer and A. D. Saunders, *Ancient Monuments and their Interpretation*. Chichester: Phillimore, 211–218.
Thompson, M. W. (2000) 'The great hall and great chamber block'. In Shoesmith and Johnson, 167–174.
Toulmin Smith, L. (1906–1910) *The Itinerary of John Leland in or About the Years 1535–1543*, 5 vols. London: G. Bell and Sons.
Toy, S. (1963) *The Castles of Great Britain*, 3rd edn. London: Heinemann.
Turner, R. (2010) 'The life and career of Richard the engineer'. In Williams and Kenyon, 46–58.
Turner, R. and Johnson, A. (eds) (2006) *Chepstow Castle: Its History and Buildings*. Logaston Press.
Turner, R. Jones-Jenkins, C. and Priestly, S. (2006) 'The Norman great tower'. In Turner and Johnson, 23–42.
Turner, R., Priestley, S., Coldstream, N. and Sale, B. (2006a) 'The New or Marten's Tower'. In Turner and Johnson, 151–166.
Turner, R., Priestley, S., Coldstream, N. and Sale, B. (2006b) 'The 'Gloriette' in the lower bailey'. In Turner and Johnson, 135–150.
Turner, R., Priestly, S. and Jones-Jenkins, C. (2006) 'The Marshalls' use of the Great Tower'. In Turner and Johnson, 91–100.
Turner, T. H. and Parker, J. H. (1851–1859) *Some Account of Domestic Architecture in England*, 3 vols: Volume 1: From the Conquest to the end of the Thirteenth Century (1851); Volume 2: From Edward I to Richard II (1853); Volume 3: From Richard II to Henry VIII (1859). London: J. H. Parker.

Tyers, I. and Groves, C. (1999) List 104: tree-ring dates from the University of Sheffield Dendrochronological Laboratory. *Vernacular Architecture* **30**: 113–128

Tyers, I., Groves, C., Hillam, J. and Boswijk, G. (1997) List 80: tree-ring dates from Sheffield University. *Vernacular Architecture* **28**: 138–158.

Viollet-le-Duc, E. (1875) *Dictionnaire Raisonné de l'Architecture Française*, 10 vols. Paris: Morel.

Weaver, J. (1998) *Middleham Castle*. London: English Heritage.

West, J. (1981) 'Acton Burnell Castle, Shropshire'. In A. Detsicas (ed.) *Collectanea Historica: Essays in Memory of Stuart Rigold*. Kent Archaeological Society, 86–92.

Wheeler, W. H. (1897) *A History of the Fens of South Lincolnshire*. Boston and London.

Wilcox, R. P. (1981) *Timber and Iron Reinforcement in Early Buildings*. London: The Society of Antiquaries.

Williams, D. M. and Kenyon, J. R. (eds) (2010) *The Impact of the Edwardian Castles in Wales*. Oxford: Oxbow.

Williams, G. (2010) 'History of the castle'. In Hislop *et al.*, 88–117.

Wilson, C. (2002) The royal lodgings of Edward III at Windsor Castle: form, function, representation. In Keen and Scarff, 15–94.

Wilson, P. R. (1989) Excavations at Helmsley Castle. *Yorkshire Archaeological Journal* **61**: 29–33.

Wood, R. (2010) The Norman chapel in Durham Castle. *Northern History* **47** (1): 9–48.

Internet sources

Holmes, G. (2004–2014) William Latimer. In *Oxford Dictionary of National Biography*, Oxford University Press. [http://www.oxforddnb.com/view/article/16103, accessed 7 May 2015]

Summerson, H. (2004–2015) Lawrence of Ludlow. In *Oxford Dictionary of National Biography*, Oxford University Press. [http://www.oxforddnb.com/view/article/892, accessed 24 February 2014]

Walker, R. F. (2004–2014) Henry Audley. In *Oxford Dictionary of National Biography*, Oxford University Press. [http://www.oxforddnb.com/view/article/892, accessed 10 Feb 2014]

Waugh, S. L. (2004–2015) John de Warenne. In *Oxford Dictionary of National Biography*, Oxford University Press. [http://www.oxforddnb.com/view/article/892, accessed 26 February 2014]

Notes

Chapter 1
1. Harvey 1984, 2–3.
2. Harvey 1984, 91.
3. Turner 2010.
4. Salzman (1952), 370.
5. Printed in Salzman 1952, 459–460.
6. His surname may, however, indicate an origin in Tichmarsh, Northamptonshire.
7. Brown *et al.* 1963, 689. See also Dixon 1990 for an explanation of Edward's special concern with the enterprise.
8. Brown *et al.* 1963, 115.
9. Thompson 1913–1920, 200.
10. See Hislop 2007 for Lewyn's career.
11. *CPR 1377–1381*, 596.
12. Harvey 1944, 37–40; Scott-Robertson (1877), 130–132; Larking (1859).
13. Knoop and Jones 1933.
14. Brown *et al.* 1963, 344.
15. Knoop and Jones 1937b.
16. Taylor 1961.
17. Knoop and Jones 1937a.
18. Walter of Hereford's toponymic is thought to derive from Harford in Gloucestershire. See Harvey 1984, 136.
19. Mclees (1973, 63), however, suggests that the name 'Yevele' is derived from the Somerset town of Yeovil.
20. Harvey 1984, 345.
21. Coldstream (2003, 26–28) has speculated that the Tonbridge and Caerphilly works may have been the work of the royal mason, Robert of Beverley. Given that Robert Beverley subsequently undertook comparable works at the Tower of London, this is not an implausible suggestion, but there is no conclusive evidence in the form of royal precedents, and it seems just as probable, if not more so, that the works of the De Clares influenced the royal works rather than *vice versa*.
22. Goodall 2011, 198.
23. For a brief explanation of these systems see Hislop 2000, 16–20.
24. This technique is based on the principle that the sides of a right-angled triangle will be in the proportion of 3:4:5, so that setting out a triangle to those proportions will automatically produce a right angle.
25. Hislop 1996b.
26. For example, the rebuilding of Kenilworth and the great tower of Warkworth in the late fourteenth-century.

Chapter 2
1. RCHME 1972, 88.
2. Addyman and Priestly 1977, 124.
3. See Addyman and Priestly 1977, 123, Fig 3. The conjectural profile of the ditch differs from the one given in Fig 4 but is more likely to be correct.
4. Mayes and Butler 1983, 31, Fig 23.
5. Kincey 2011, 122.
6. Soden 2007, 11.

7. Steps were found cut into the motte during excavations at Baile Hill, York: Addyman and Priestly 1977, 124.
8. Barton and Holden 1977, 69–70.
9. Davison 1972, 56–57.
10. Barton and Holden 1977, 22–24.
11. Barton and Holden 1977, 69.
12. Barker and Barton 1978, 85, 88.
13. Cooper 1911, 18.
14. Addyman and Priestly 1977.
15. Markland 1893.
16. Soden 2007, 9–11
17. DMBC n. d. 2: 77.
18. Cooper 1912, 201.
19. Higham and Barker 1992, 198, 232–233.
20. Elsworth and Mace 2015, 18–27.
21. Kent *et al.* 2013, 22.
22. Kent *et al.* 2013, 32.
23. Beresford 1987, 101. On the one hand the excavator states that 'about half of the original height of the motte was destroyed in the mid twelfth century', and on the other that 'there was no evidence to indicate the original height of the motte'.
24. Kent *et al.* 2013, 30, Fig 26.
25. Kent *et al.* 2013, 32.
26. Beresford 1987, 101–102.
27. Elsworth and Mace 2015, 27–28.
28. Elsworth and Mace 2015, 27–28.
29. Thompson 1960, 87.
30. Beresford 1987, 89–90, Fig 93.
31. These measurements are extrapolated from Bennett *et al.* 1982, Fig 15.
32. Kent *et al.* 2013, 23–25, Fig 11.
33. Jardine-Rose 2012, 197–198, figs 2 and 5–6.
34. Mayes and Butler 1983, 31, Fig 10.
35. Higham and Barker 2000, 35–38.
36. Bennett *et al.* 2013, 13, figs 8–9.
37. Mayes and Butler 1983, 32; Fig 39, sections 39 and 40.
38. Soden 2007, 23.
39. Allen and Stoodley 2010, 39.
40. Cunliffe, 1977, 25–26.
41. Cunliffe 1977, figs 132–133.
42. Brown *et al.* (1963), 372.
43. Higham and Barker 2000, 5, Fig 4.
44. The visible earthworks today comprise bank, ditch and counterscarp bank, but excavation in the inner ward has revealed an inner ditch. It has been postulated that this must have been contained on the inner side by a raised scarp or bank defining a smaller inner ward. See Hislop *et al.* 2011, 186–188.
45. Davison 1972, 24.
46. Brown *et al.* (1963), 619.
47. Brown *et al.* (1963), 619.
48. Brown *et al.* (1963), 740.
49. Geddes (1991),169.
50. Walker 2004–2014.
51. Brown *et al.* 1963, 756.
52. Ellis 1993, 104.
53. Page 1908, 168–170.
54. Wilson 1989.
55. RCHME 1972, 60 and Fig opposite.

56. Brown *et al.* 1963, 708.
57. Another castle moat that was supplied by a tidal river was at Ogmore (Glamorganshire), around the courtyard castle raised by William de Londres *c.* 1100 on the east bank of the River Ewenni. Here again, for this to have been effective, there would have to have been sluice gates at the two points at which the moat joined the river in order to maintain the water levels. See RCHMW 1991, 274–288.
58. Brown *et al.* 1963, 716.
59. Taylor 1949, 7–8; the map at the back of the booklet shows part of the old course of the river.
60. Brown *et al.* 1963, 411.
61. RCAHMS 1920, 445 (2); see also Tabraham 2010, 186–188, for the chronology of Lochmaben.
62. Brown *et al.* 1963, 414.
63. Oswald *et al.* 2006, 65–75; Oswald and Ashbee 2007, 22–23.
64. The measurements coincide with dimensions given in the building accounts for 1313–1314, which also describe a depth of 18ft (5.5m), although the current depth has been estimated at 3m (10ft): Oswald *et al.* 2006, 66; Oswald and Ashbee 2007, 22.
65. Ryder 1979.
66. *CPR* 1343–1345, 106.
67. Mackenzie 1896, 283.
68. Barnes and Simpson 1951, 181.
69. Barnes and Simpson 1951, 183 and 185.
70. Simpson 1960.
71. Lincolnshire was particularly badly hit by flooding in 1439 after a period of heavy rain. See Wheeler 1897, 28
72. Thompson 1913–1920.
73. Peers 1957, 21.

Chapter 3
1. Higham and Barker 1992, 140–142.
2. Meeson 1980.
3. Hope-Taylor 1950, 27.
4. Barker and Higham 1982, 29–30.
5. Higham and Barker 2000, 65.
6. Dunning 1950, 33 for the date.
7. Hope-Taylor 1950, 27–29.
8. At Dol, Dinan, Rennes and Bayeux.
9. Kent *et al.* 2013.
10. The excavation report (Kent *et al.* 2013) does not discuss this possibility.
11. E.g. Higham and Barker (1992), 244–246; Beresford (1987), 103–106.
12. Molyneux *et al.* 2003, from which the following description is derived.
13. Tyers and Groves 1999, 120.
14. Tyers *et al.* 1997, 144, 153–154.
15. Miles and Bridge 2010, 103.
16. Kent *et al.* 2013, 36.
17. Higham and Barker 2000, 73.
18. Higham and Barker 2000, 75, Fig 4.14.
19. A nave span of 13.7m (45ft) was achieved at Speyer Cathedral in south-west Germany (Rhineland-Palatinate) by *c.* 1060. Speyer, however, was exceptional; Romanesque roof spans were seldom much more than *c.* 11m. (36ft); indeed, eleventh-century nave spans of Norman great churches were usually shorter. The largest great towers of the eleventh century, the White Tower at the Tower of London and the keep of Colchester Castle, had internal spans of 10.7m and 11.2m respectively. The slightly later great tower of Norwich had a maximum span of 11.5m.
20. Mayes and Butler 1983, 32, 73–75; figs 6, 41–43.
21. Beresford 1987, 106–109.
22. Higham and Barker 2000, 49.
23. Oswald 1962–1963.

24. Wilcox 1981, 12–21, 28–35.
25. Wilcox (1981, 13) has identified one of the practitioners concerned as Waldin the engineer, who built the curtain wall of Lincoln Castle on a timber framework, which was itself set on an earthen bank.
26. Turner *et al.* 2006, 29–32.
27. Turner *et al.* 2006, 32.
28. Measurements extrapolated from the drawings of the keep in Bennett *et al.* 1982, figs 37–51.
29. Harris 2008, 75–85.
30. Simpson and Litton 1996, 189, Fig 15.4.
31. If the keep was begun *c.*1127, when the castle was granted to the archbishop of Canterbury, William of Corbeil, then, based on the assumption that medieval towers progressed by 10–12ft in height per year, the roofs of the 34m (113ft) high keep would probably have been raised some nine to ten years later. See Harvey 1950, 17, and Renn 1973, 25–26, for the building rates of medieval towers.
32. Miles and Worthington 1999, 99; Miles *et al.* 2008, 133. Drury (2009, 31–32) suggests that scissor bracing might have been used, though whether scissor bracing existed at this date is uncertain; one of the earliest known examples of scissor bracing in England is that over the nave roof of Peterborough Cathedral of 1169–1189.
33. Cunliffe and Munby 1985, 80–81, plate XXI, Fig 84.
34. One possibility is that they were designed to facilitate a water collection scheme, the garrets being intended to house storage tanks.
35. Allen and Stoodley 2010, 93: Work was being carried out on Odiham between 1207 and 1215, but excavations at the site have established that the keep was not the first building on its site, although it seems to have been in existence by 1216.
36. Allen and Stoodley 2010, 32, 33.
37. Viollet le Duc, 1875, 4: 268–270; Fig 145.
38. Clark 1884, 2: 222.
39. Curnow 1977, 167–168
40. McNeill 2003 for some thirteenth-century flooring arrangement sused in Ireland and Wales.
41. The form of the roof is discussed in Brown 1964, 16, 20; see also the section drawing of the keep.
42. Arnold *et al.* 2010, 96. For a drawing of this structure see Hewett (1980), 83 (Fig 70). The turret was part of Archbishop Ernulf's reconstruction of the east end from 1093. Although the roof was considered to have been destroyed by the fire of 1174, the dendrochronological dating suggests that it might have survived.
43. RCHME 1972, plate 2. There is some question as to the structural character of this roof. For many years it was believed to have been supported on a central column, denoted by the presence of a stone base. Recent investigations have cast doubt on this, and it may be that the tower had a central courtyard or light well with timber buildings ranged around the walls in the manner of a shell keep. See *Castle Studies Group Bulletin* (2015) 19: 13–14.
44. Moran 2003, 45.
45. Thompson 2000, 169.
46. Moran 2003, 116–117.
47. Alcock *et al.* 1978, 208, Fig 5.
48. Alcock and Miles 2013.
49. Harvey 1984, 337.
50. Emery 2000, 403–404. An arched-braced collar roof is also shown in the conjectural reconstruction of the great hall of Kenilworth in Morris 2006, 19. This drawing, however, gives an inaccurate representation of the existing structural evidence.
51. It is also possible that there was already a single-span roof of the same dimensions over the predecessor of Gaunt's great hall of Kenilworth that may have affected the design of the later one: see Thompson 1977b.
52. West 1981, 86–87.
53. Harvey 1984, 7. John of Alverton's surname denotes present day Northallerton in Yorkshire, which was a manor of the bishops of Durham, and the site of a palace (Page 1914, 418–433).
54. Hodgson 1880–1885, 159. The Barons' Hall is not closely dated but the detailing of the window tracery suggests the influence of the chapter house windows of 1350–1353 by John Sponlee.

55. Harvey 1984, 350.
56. Arnold *et al.* 2004.
57. Timber vaults were certainly in use in England by the 1160s, a notable example being that of the Temple church, London of *c.* 1160. See Heslop (1991), 52–53 for an alternative suggestion of how the Orford room might have been ceiled.
58. E.g. Lichfield and York cathedrals.
59. Brown *et al.* 1963, 2: 868.
60. Cruden 1981, 80.
61. See for example the Modena Cathedral capital depicted in Higham and Barker 1992, 160, Fig 5.9.
62. Taylor 1957, 39

Chapter 4
1. Drury (1982), 315.
2. Payne (1905), 184.
3. The keep rises to a height of 34m (113ft) to the top of the parapet.
4. Harbottle 1967, 108–110.
5. The exceptional height of the Colchester plinth is owed to the keep having been built around the podium of a Roman temple, which raised the height of the ground storey.
6. An exception is the early twelfth-century keep of Portchester.
7. For Ralph Gogun see Turner *et al.* 2006, especially 135, but also 136, 137, 148, 151, 167, 175; Harvey 1984, 239.
8. Impey 2002a.
9. Viollet-le-Duc 1875, 5: 104–106.
10. In the mid to late fourteenth century a number of northern English castles, including Alnwick (barbican, *c.* 1350), Raby (west gateway, c. 1350–1370) and Lumley (gateway, *c.* 1390) incorporated semi-circular arches.
11. See Renn 1969, 86–89, for a consideration of the date.
12. Joggled arches are used, for example in the Great Mosque of Cordoba between 785 and 987.
13. An eleventh-century example of a joggled lintel is over the east doorway to the keep of Chepstow. For a discussion of the date of this building see Turner *et al.* 2006, 35–42.
14. A monumental form of this type of construction was used in the fifteenth-century rebuilding of the Alsatian castle of Haut-Kœnigsbourg (Bas-Rhin) to carry the floor of the late fifteenth-century great hall. See Viollet-le-Duc (1875), 4: 231–236, Fig 235.
15. Another late fifteenth-century example of the technique has been recorded over a former fireplace at Beaudesert Hall (Staffordshire). See Hislop and Kelleher (2011), 48.
16. Brown *et al.* 1963, 848.
17. See McNeill 1981, 41–41, for the dating of the keep.
18. Emery 1996, 303, who also notes that the practice of socketing the bars of the window grills into the lintels was also discontinued.
19. Wood 2010.
20. Drury 1982, 311.
21. The plan of the first floor as built is no longer certain, and two different reconstructions have been suggested for the area above the vaulting. See Heslop 1994 and Dixon and Marshall 2002.
22. Drury 2002, 213.
23. Goodall 2004, 50.
24. The dating of the Middleham keep to 1170–1180 is based on the similarity of a waterleaf capital in the oratory, and the stepped plinth, which are similar to details in the keep of Newcastle upon Tyne of 1168–1178: Weaver 1998, 22.
25. Mesqui and Faucherre 1988, 91, Fig 18.
26. Mesqui and Faucherre 1988, 84–90, Fig 9.
27. Mesqui 2013, 137, Fig 153.
28. Avent 1995, 34–36.
29. Viollet-le-Duc 1875, 4: 268.
30. *CPR 1272–1281*, 440.

31. Clark 1884, 312–322.
32. For a recent description and analysis of the east range of Warwick Castle, which includes Caesar's Tower and Guy's Tower see Parkyn and McNeill 2012, especially 489–496.
33. Simpson 1940, 83–84.
34. Hislop 2007, 44–45.
35. Guy 2011, 164.
36. McNeill 1981, 42.
37. Hartshorne 1858, plate VI, opposite p. 72.
38. Bates 1891, 293.
39. Middleton 1910, 24.
40. Bates 1891, 293.
41. *NCH* 5: 88.
42. For example, see Guy 2011, 169, Fig 89 for a late fifteenth-century staircase at Château Blois.
43. RCHME 1972, 61.
44. Soden 2007, 33–34.
45. Brown 2003, 28.
46. Williams 2010, 103–104.
47. Salzman 1952, 140.
48. E.g. See Thompson 1913–1920, 205–206, 208; Salzman 1952, 142–143.
49. Barnes and Simpson (1951), 186–187.
50. Simpson 1960, xxv–xxvi.
51. The site identified by Simpson as that of the Edlington Moor brickworks lies some 4 miles south-east of Edlington near Stixwould (Simpson 1960, 46n). The authority on which this identification was based is not disclosed, but the site was in use as a brickworks in the late nineteenth century.
52. Thompson 1913–1920, 234–236.
53. Thompson 1913–1920, 237.
54. See Knoop and Jones 1949, 116–118 for hours of work.
55. The calculation made here is based on a laying rate of 120 bricks per hour observed by Gilbreth during motion studies. The figures accord well with the widely accepted rate of 1,000 bricks per 10-hour day described by Lloyd (1925, 26).
56. Barnes and Simpson 1951, 186.
57. Hawkyard 2005, 44, n.37.
58. Brown *et al.* 1963, 280; Harvey 1984, 331.
59. Simpson 1942, 119–120.
60. Simpson 1960 xxviii–xxix.
61. Simpson 1960, 45. John Botiller seems to have been one of the freemasons, because the rough masons, or layers, were listed separately. His servants, therefore, are more likely to have been more akin to apprentices than labourers: see Knoop and Jones 1933, 69–72, on masons' servants.
62. Brown *et al.* 1963, 921.

Chapter 5
1. For Doué see Boüard 1973–1974; for Mayenne see Early 2003, 65.
2. Early 2003, 64, 67.
3. Impey and Lorans 1998.
4. Mesqui 1998, 101.
5. Impey 2008b, 232.
6. For a description and estimation of the date see Impey 2002a, 255–256.
7. Impey 2002b, 190.
8. Chibnall 1983, 4: 290.
9. Devaut 1886, opposite 304.
10. Harris 2008, 29.
11. Impey 2008b, 240.
12. Drury 1982, 399; Stevenson 1982, 413.
13. Brown 1976, 66.

14. Heslop 1994, 7–8. A comparison of the masons' marks in the keep with those of the cathedral may allow a narrowing of the date range to *c*. 1098–1110: Drury 2002, 219–220.
15. Heslop 1994, 51–55; Drury 2002, 212–213.
16. The walls of Norwich keep are approximately 1.8m (6ft) thick.
17. Heslop 1994, 7.
18. Brown *et al.* 1963, 39.
19. The principal model for this decorative stonework at Rising may be Castle Acre Priory, which is situated only 11 miles to the south-east of Rising. Common features include buttresses with rebated angles containing nook shafts, a combination of plain and interlaced shafted arches, and grotesque head sculptures. It is possible too that the decorative axed stonework within the blind arcading of Rising is in imitation of more refined texturing at the priory.
20. Dixon 2008, 256.
21. John Lewyn (*fl.* 1353–1398), William Wynford (*fl.*1360–d. 1405) and Henry Yevele (*fl.* 1353–d. 1400).
22. See Renn 1982, 70–73 for a discussion of the date of the keep. The replacement of Lanfranc's choir was carried out by Prior Ernulf between 1096 and 1114.
23. At Colchester the base of the foundations lie some 4.2m (13ft 9ins) below the top of the plinth, which rises to the entrance-floor level, whereas the foundations of Colchester were at least 4.3m (14 ft) below ground-floor level and at least 6m (20ft) below the top of the plinth. Here, however, the plinth rises above floor level.
24. Bates 1891, 234.
25. John Goodall (2011) has dubbed this kind of arrangement a 'swallowed forebuilding'.
26. Goodall 2004, 56.
27. Dixon and Marshall 1993.
28. Constable 2003.
29. Although something similar was created during the first half of the thirteenth century in the remodelling of the keep of Chepstow Castle in south Wales. See Turner *et al.* 2006, 91–100, especially Fig 80.
30. Some 100 years later the two-storey hall range of Haughton Castle (Northumberland) was built with an attached three-storey solar tower in an arrangement that recalls the vertical asymmetry of the keeps with which Wolveston is associated.

Chapter 6
1. Rolland 1980, 107.
2. There are at least fifteen round church towers within 10 miles of New Buckenham, at least five of which are Anglo-Saxon (Aslacton, Forncet, Gissing and Quidenham: see Taylor and Taylor 1965, 31, 241–242, 250, 502, 605–607) and at least seven Norman (Eccles, Fritton, Long Stratton, Needham, Roydon, Rushall and Shimpley: see the National Heritage List).
3. The walls are 3.4m (11ft) thick It has been noted that the round church towers of East Anglia range in internal diameter from 8 ft (2.4m) to 20ft (6m) and in wall thickness from 2½ft (0.76m) to 6ft (1.8m): Fisher 1969, 76.
4. Houdan, for instance, has a diameter of 15m (49ft).
5. For an explanation of the underlying geometry see Heslop 1991.
6. Braun 1936, 45; Harvey 1984, 2.
7. His presence has been recorded at the Tower of London, Rayleigh Castle (Essex), Windsor Castle (Berkshire) and Woodstock Palace near Oxford. See Harvey 1984, 2–3.
8. St John Hope 1913, 19. The resident mason at Windsor in Ailnoth's time was one Godwin.
9. Renn 2012, 202.
10. Austin 2007, 163–172, 263–265.
11. Brown *et al.* 1963, 613.
12. Shelby 1972, 413.
13. These include Falkenstein (Saxony-Anhalt) in central Germany; Araburg in Lower Austria; Zvikov, Strakonice and Svojanov in Bohemia; and Bítov in Moravia. The Premyslid kings of Bohemia were responsible for Zvikov, Svojanov and Bítov, and the lords of Strakonice were wardens of Zvikov, so there are personal links that might explain the architectural analogues of this Bohemian group. Hrad Bítov, in being situated on a promontory next to the River Zeletavka, is in a similar position to

Château Gaillard and La Roche-Guyon, and is the castle that follows these two sites most closely in the siting of its beaked bergfried. This is set immediately inside the curtain of the inner courtyard, at the furthest distance from the main gateway, pointing inwards towards the approach. At other sites, although the beaked prows were always deployed towards the expected line of attack, the towers occupy forward positions; at Zvikov, Strakonice, dominating the main gateway with the prow pointing towards the approach. At Svojanov it is at the apex of a roughly triangular courtyard pointing towards the main approach and protected by a *Schildmauer* (in this like Bitov).

14. Viollet-le-Duc 1875, 4: 265–269, figs 145, 146 and 146 *bis*.
15. Simpson 1923, 151–170; Cruden 1981, 18.
16. Simpson (1923), 106–107.
17. Cruden 1981, 80.
18. Heslop 1991, 45–47, Fig 4.
19. The castle had been destroyed following William's father's participation in the revolt against Henry II of 1173–1174. William came into his inheritance in 1190 and married Ranulph's sister, Agnes, in 1192. The great tower was probably raised in the See Williams 2011, 91–92.
20. Mayes and Butler 1983, 3.
21. Toulmin Smith, 1: 39.
22. Toy 1963, 123–126. The illustration of the keep shown on p. 124 of Toy's book is an inaccurate reconstruction of the plan.
23. Brown *et al*. 1963, 890.
24. Harvey 1984, 251–252.
25. Goodall 2010, 162.
26. Renn (2003) has made comparisons between the South Tower of Stokesay and the royal works. The licence to crenellate for Stokesay dates from 1291 (*CPR 1281–1292*, 450); in the same year Edward I arranged to repay a loan of 1,000 marks: Summerson 2004–2015.
27. Hislop 2007, 40–45.
28. Munby 1993, 35.
29. Kenyon 2003, 6–7.
30. One of the most striking features of the Hastings Tower are the corner turrets, which seem to have affinities with the full height turrets of a drawing made for a tower at King's College (though never built). John Harvey has suggested that the King's College drawing might be attributed to Robert Westerley; if so, this would be a major contributory piece of evidence to support his involvement in the design of Ashby-de-la-Zouch castle. See Harvey 1984, 330–331; the drawing is reproduced in Harvey 1972, Fig 49 (BL Cotton MS. Augustus I. I, 3).

Chapter 7
1. Extrapolated from the plans.
2. Extrapolated from plan in Drury 1982, 318, Fig 9.
3. Frere and Stow 1982, 63.
4. The outer ditch is considered to be a prehistoric construction representing a univallate hillfort, and that the gap on this side was the entrance. See Brown *et al*. 1932, 630; Coad 1995, 12–14, 16–17.
5. Renn 1969, 84–86.
6. In the English Heritage guidebook the keep is dated to the 1170s or 1180s and the curtain to *c.* 1200: Brindle and Sadraei 2015, 6 and 14. Goodall (2011, 150–151) assigns the keep to the early 1180s and the curtain to 'around 1200'. Both cite parallels for the wall towers at the royal castles of Knaresborough and Scarborough.
7. The chronology of Chepstow under William Marshal is based on the tree-ring dating of the main gatehouse doors, which suggest a felling date range of 1159–1189: Miles and Worthington 1998, 127; Avent and Miles 2006; Avent and Turner 2006.
8. Gebelin 1964, 50.
9. At, for example, Monmouth in 1230.
10. Brown 1976, 92.
11. Brown *et al*. 1963, 619. This Stephen has been identified with the principal mason of the same name who was paid for work carried out on the hall of Winchester Castle in 1222 (Harvey 1984, 283).

12. Harvey 1984, 305.
13. Mesqui 2013, 299.
14. Curnow 1979.
15. We know that at least one building craftsman from the vicinity of Gaillard, Master Nicholas de Andeli, carpenter, was in the royal service in England, soon after the loss of Normandy at the head of a small band of foreign workers: Brown *et al.* (1963), 61–62.
16. Kennedy 1994, 58–61.
17. Murage was granted in 1265 and was at least partially in existence by 1280: Grundy *et al.* 1992, 439.
18. Six tiers of corbels were also used over the gateway to the Percies' castle of Warkworth on the heightened gatehouse of *c.* 1400. This feature is perhaps a legacy of Sir Henry (Hotspur) Percy's custody of Conwy Castle in 1400–1402.
19. Darlington 2001,157.

Chapter 8
1. Avent and Miles 2006, 51–54.
2. Avent and Miles 2006, 57.
3. Butler and Knight 2004, 42.
4. Avent 2006, 89–90, Fig 72. A very plausible suggestion, given that William Marshal spent several years in the Holy Land. Another parallel is the de Bohun Gate at Caldicot Castle, which probably also stems from Pembroke.
5. Brown *et al.* 1963, 620.
6. Mayes and Butler 1982, 27.
7. A sixteenth-century drawing (reproduced in Mayes and Butler 1983, Fig 2) shows it as a two-storey tower with cruciform arrow loops to the lower storey, a window with shouldered head to the upper storey and two chimneys. This cannot be considered entirely reliable evidence of the thirteenth-century character of the building.
8. Harvey 1948, 22; 1984, 24.
9. Waugh 2004–2015.
10. See Oswald *et al.* 2006, 39–41 for a discussion about the chronology of the barbican.
11. Simpson 1949, 3; Summerson 1993, 11.
12. Parkyn and McNeill 2012, 496–500.
13. Goodall 2012, 240.
14. There seems to have been one at Winchester Castle by 1235. See *CCR 1234–1237*, 37.
15. Harbottle and Ellison 1981, 80–85, figs 3–4.
16. The Flint and Rhuddlan drawbridges had two rather than three counterbalance beams.
17. Braun 1935, 221–223.
18. Braun 1935, 221, Fig X.
19. Turner 2010, 46.
20. Kenyon 2003, 50.
21. RCHME (1972), 131, plates 38 and 40.
22. Viollet-le-Duc 1875, 7: 343, Fig 23.
23. Toy 1963, 146–147.

Chapter 9
1. NYCRO ZBO MIC 2424/640.
2. Faulkner 1963, 225–230.
3. See Ashbee 2008 for the eleventh-century internal plan of the White Tower, and Dixon 2008, 245–247 for that of Colchester keep, and for planning diagrams of both.
4. Dixon 2008.
5. Harvey 1984, 121.
6. Brown *et al.* 1963, 865.
7. RCHME 1970, 57–78.
8. The associated carpentry work was done by Richard the engineer and Henry of Oxford.
9. Turner *et al.* 2006b, 135.

10. Reproduced in Palmer 1907, 393–398, figs 2–4.
11. Shoesmith 2014, especially chapters 14, 16 and 17.
12. Faulkner 1963, 221–225.
13. *CPR 1343–1345*, 444.
14. Alcock *et al.* 1978, 195.
15. Hislop 1991, 17–19.
16. Wilson 2002.
17. Knoop and Jones 1937a.
18. Brindle 2002, 118–119.
19. Harvey 1984, 352.
20. At Alberbury, Clun and Hopton Castle.
21. See Dixon 1993 for an exposition of the sequential development of border manor houses.
22. Emery 1996, 339–344.
23. Latimer was in France throughout much of the 1360s, returning a wealthy man in 1368 when he was summoned to Parliament: Holmes 2004–2015.
24. Latimer, and Scrope, the builder of Bolton, were certainly known to each other. Both had fought at Crécy, both held political office in the early 1370s and both served under John of Gaunt in France in 1373.
25. John Fifth Baron Neville, one of the builders of Raby, was known to both Latimer and Scrope. Like Scrope he was a supporter of John of Gaunt, under whom both men had served at the Battle of Nájera in 1367. In the early 1370s he was closely associated with Latimer in Parliament and in 1381 married Latimer's daughter. His arms appear on Danby Castle.
26. Hislop 2007, 11.
27. The dimensions are: Bolton 28m (91ft) x 16.5m (54ft) and 52m (170ft) x 36.5m (120ft); Windsor 29m (96ft) x 15.5m (51ft) and 53m (175ft) x 39m (127ft).
28. Harvey 1944, 41.
29. The chronology of Raby is uncertain, but four principal medieval phases are evident: 1) The great hall of the manor house, which dates from *c.* 1300 2) The incorporation of the existing ground-floor hall into a new two-storey hall range with associated service and solar towers. 3) The creation of a quadrangular courtyard enclosed by three residential ranges on the west side of the hall range. 4) Additions to the west front by John, Fifth Baron Neville between 1381 and 1388. Details that probably stem from Windsor are: Phase 2 - The four-centred arches of the fireplaces in the great kitchen and formerly in the first-floor hall, and the first-floor hall windows, which seem to be simplified versions of John Sponlee's chapter house windows of 1350–1353. See Hislop 2007, 9–10.
30. Hislop 2007, 8–9.
31. Hislop 1996b.
32. One indication of this is that, in common with Warkworth, a fireplace was inserted into one of the window embrasures in the sixteenth century.
33. Toulmin Smith 1906–1910, 5: 139. By 'tunnels in the syds of the walls bytwixt the lights in the haul' Leland meant the wall passages that link the window embrasures.
34. Grose IV, pp. 56–58.
35. McCarthy *et al.* 1990, 43.
36. Hislop *et al.* 2011, 5–6.
37. Ellis 1993, 104.
38. Coppack (1990), 86–87.
39. Viollet-le-Duc 1875, 6: 166, Fig 3.
40. Viollet-le-Duc 1875, 6: 164–165, Fig 1.

Chapter 10
1. The lower courses of the keep, for example, are of equal height.
2. Brown *et al.* (1963), 866.
3. Knight (2000), 39.
4. Ashbee (2008), 144–145.
5. Thompson 1913–1920, 266, 305.
6. Brown *et al.* 1963, 334.

7. Brown *et al.* 1963, 870–872; Munby *et al.* 2007.
8. Harvey 1984, 352.
9. Hislop 1996b.
10. Hislop 1996a.
11. Cf. Alnwick inner gatehouse, *c.* 1340; Bothal gatehouse, *c.* 1343; Stafford keep, 1348. Guy's Tower at Warwick Castle of *c.* 1350 is twelve-sided.
12. Hislop 1992.
13. Emery 2006, 154.
14. Harvey 1984, 353.
15. The external dimensions of the medieval main block of Shirburn were approximately 34m (112ft) x 22m (72ft), while those for Bodiam are approximately 46m (151ft) x 42m (138ft).
16. Brindle 2002, 118–119.
17. Brown *et al.* 1963, 877.
18. Emery 2000, 440–442.
19. Goodall 2011, 194, 213, 227.
20. Restored in the nineteenth-century and now destroyed along with the donjon, the exact form of this sculpture is uncertain, but it was recorded in drawings, and in its restored form by photograph.
21. Turner *et al.* (2006a), 151.
22. Turner *et al.* (2006), 161–162.
23. Holmes (1896), 24.
24. Brown *et al.* (1963), 385, n.
25. Brown *et al.* (1963), 388.
26. From left to right these are: 1. Tyson, 2. A cross: de Vescy. The de Vescys were lords of Alnwick Castle from 1096 until 1307 when Sir William de Vescy of Kildare sold it to Henry Percy. 3. Clifford,. Roger 3rd Baron de Clifford (d. 1344) or Robert, 4th Baron de Clifford (d. 1350) 4. Richard Fitzalan, 3rd earl of Arundel 5. Bohun, 6. Three lions passant with a label of five points: probably Henry of Grosmont before he became earl of Lancaster in 1345 7. The royal arms of England quartered with France, as adopted by Edward II in 1340. 8. John, 7th and last Warenne earl of Surrey who died in 1347. 9. A lion rampant: Percy. Henry 2nd Baron Percy (d. 1352) 10. Umfreville, Gilbert de Umfraville, 9th earl of Angus. (d. 1381) 11. A lion rampant: Percy, Henry de Percy, 3rd Baron Percy from 1352. A saltire: Neville. Ralph 4th Baron Neville (d. 1367) 13. A fess between two chevrons: Fitzwalter. John 3rd Baron Fitzwalter (d. 1361).
27. The date of the licence to crenellate: *CPR 1343–1345*, 30. The shields are 1. Black Prince 2. Edward III 3. Wake of Lydel 4. Aton 5. Greystock 6. Percy 7. Bertram 8. Darcy 9. Conyers 10. Felton 11. Delaval 12. Scargill 13. Horsley 14. Ogle.
28. Morley 1976.
29. Morley 1976, Appendix 1 for identifications of the heraldry.
30. Morley (1976) has drawn attention to the worm legends of several northern families in interpreting this sculpture. See, for example, Bett 1950, 93–97.

Index

Aberystwyth Castle, Cardiganshire 189
Abinger Castle, Surrey 31, 32, 34
Abingdon Abbey, Berkshire 220
Acton Burnell Castle, Shropshire 48
Adam the Fleming 23–24
Adeliza of Louvain, queen of England 98
Aigues Mortes, Gard, Tour de Constance 122, 130
aisled construction 30, 33, 45
Ailnoth the engineer 1–2, 114, 143–144, 155, 188
Albini, William d', earl of Arundel 98, 113
Alcester, Warwickshire 47
Aldingham Castle, Lancashire 12
Alexander II, king of Scotland 122
Alnwick Castle, Northumberland
  de Vescy lords of 259 (n. 26)
  passage barbican 178
  inner gatehouse 231–232
  wall towers 193
  semi-circular arches 253 (n.10)
  sculpture 231–232
  shell keep 222
  umbrella vault 79, *4.26*
Alton Castle, Staffordshire 18, 56
Alverton, John de, carpenter 49
Amalric, king of Jerusalem 73
Amblény Castle, Aisne 110–112, 144
Amiens Cathedral, Somme 121–122
Angers Castle, Maine-et-Loire 41, 68, 211–213, *3.6, 10.2*
Angoulême Cathedral, Charente 71
Angus, Gilbert de Umfraville, 9th earl of 259 (n. 26)
Arques-la-Bataille Castle, Seine-Maritime, great tower 100, 108, 187–188, 202
arrow loops 75, 77, 117, 138–143, 149–151, 155–156, 159–160, 166, 167, 169, 171–172, 177, 226
Arundel Castle, Sussex 81
Arundel, Richard Fitzalan, 3rd earl of 259 (n. 26)
Aubrée, countess of Ivry 93
Audley, Henry de 18
Aumary III de Montfort, count of Évreux 110
Ashby de la Zouche Castle 135–136, *6.20*
Autrèche, Indre-et-Loire 90
Avignon, papal palace 161

Avranches Castle, Manche, great tower 59, 93, 96, 97
Avranches, Hugh d', see Chester, Hugh d'Avranches, 1st earl of

Bamburgh Castle, Northumberland
  and Carlisle 103
  and John Lewyn 193, 194, 197–198
  and Maurice 109, 142–143
  and Middleham 107
  and Newcastle 109
  and Osbert the mason 101
  and Scarborough 104
  and the White Tower 102
  great tower 55, 70, 101–103, *5.7*
  plinth 55
  vaulting 70
  wall towers 142–143, *7.3*
bank construction 15–17, 28
barbicans 173–178
Barnard Castle, Co. Durham, Round Tower 72, 138, *6.5*
bartizans 235
Beaudesert Hall, Staffordshire 253 (n. 15)
Beaufort-en-Vallée Castle, Maine-et-Loire 58
Beaugency Castle, Loiret, great tower 35, 70, 90, *5.4*
Beaumaris Castle, Anglesey
  arrow loops 159, *7.14*
  bartizan 235, *10.23*
  coastal location 23
  concentric fortifications 158–159
  corbelled machicolations 52, 162, *7.18*
  drawbridge 180
  gatehouse defences 172
  portcullis mechanism 183
  symmetrical elevation 218
Beauvais Castle, Oise 118
Beeston Castle, Cheshire 18, 19, 63, 201, *2.2*
Bek, Anthony, bishop of Durham 77
Belsay Castle, Northumberland 77–78, 79, 135, 235
Bellver Castle, Palma, Mallorca 216
Belvoir Castle, Israel 157
Berkhamsted Castle, Hertfordshire 17, 20, 156
Berkeley Castle, Gloucestershire 14, 82
Bertram, Sir Robert 232
Beverley, Robert of, mason 6, 62, 65, 158, 190 249 (n. 21)

Bigod, Hugh, see Norfolk, Hugh Bigod, 1st earl of
Bigod, Roger, see Norfolk, Roger Bigod, 2nd earl of
Bigod, Roger, see Norfolk, Roger Bigod, 5th earl of
Bilazais, Deux-Sèvres 90
Blois, Henry de, bishop of Winchester 188
Blundeville, Ranulph de, see Chester 6th earl of
Bodiam Castle, Sussex
  gatehouse 220, *10.9*
  machicolations 185
  and Old Wardour Castle 223
  portcullis 181
  sculpture 231
  well 202
  wet landscape 24
  and Wressle Castle 195
  and William Wynford 195, 220
  and Henry Yevele 195
Bohun, Henry de, see Hereford, Henry de Bohun, 1st earl of
Bohun, Humphrey de, see Hereford, Humphrey de Bohun, 2nd earl of
Bolingbroke Castle, Lincolnshire 25
Borthwick Castle, Midlothian 134–135, *6.19*
Bothal Castle, Northumberland 79, 232
Bothwell Castle, Lanarkshire 40, 50, 123, 181
Botiller, John, mason 85–86
Boudon, Hugh of, mason 4
Bourges Castle, Cher 118
Bourne Castle, Lincolnshire 20
Bowes Castle, North Riding of Yorkshire, great tower 6, 55, 106–107, *5.11*
Box, John, mason 5, 218
Bramber Castle, Sussex 10–11
Brancepeth, Co. Durham 225
brick construction 83–86, 214–215
Bridgnorth Castle, Shropshire 38–39, *3.4*
Bronllys Castle, Breconshire 56
Brookland, Kent, church bell tower 32
Builth Castle, Brecknock 189
Bungay Castle, Suffolk 58, 113–114, 179
Burcestre, John of, mason 192, 219
Burgh, Hubert de, earl of Kent 125, 167–168

Burnell, Robert, bishop of Bath and Wells 48
Burrell, Robert, brick mason 84

Caernarfon Castle, Caernarvonshire
 and Angers 212
 arrow loops 139, 159–160, *7.15*
 Carnarvon arch 67
 coastal location 23
 decorative stone banding 212, *10.3*
 drawbridge 180
 Eagle Tower 130–132, 139, *6.14*
 timber flooring 36, 41
 and James of St Georges 228
 joggling 65, *4.14*
 King's Gate 172–173, 180, 228–229, *10.16*
 water supply 203
 polygonal towers 130–131, *10.3*
 Queen's Gate 180, 228–229, *10.15*
 revetment of town defences 17
 roof structure 44
 sculpture 231, *10.20*
 and Stokesay 132
Caerphilly Castle, Glamorganshire
 barbican 174
 drawbridges 179–180
 and Tonbridge 172
 and the royal works 6–7, 158–159
 inner east gatehouse 172
 main outer gatehouse 179–180, *8.9*
 plan 157–158, *7.11*
 spurs 57, *4.2*
 water defences 21, *2.4*
Caister Castle, Norfolk 25, 84, 85, 135
Caldicot Castle, Monmouthshire 58, 72, 125, 161
Camulodunum 96
Canterbury, Michael of, mason 6
Canterbury Castle, Kent
 and Colchester 100
 and Rochester 101
 chimney flues 199
 ditch 15, 20
 flooring 36
 great tower 99–100, 137
 plinth 55
Canterbury Priory 2, 43, 203
Cappy Castle, Somme 118
Carew Castle, Pembrokeshire 57
Carisbrooke Castle, Isle of Wight 12
Carlisle Castle, Cumberland
 great tower 59,103, *5.8*
 and John Lewyn 5, 193, 201
 outer gatehouse, 201
 portcullis 181, *8.11*
 roof structure 49, *3.13*
Carreg Cennan Castle, Carmarthenshire 57
Carrickfergus Castle, Co. Antrim 67, 79, 151
Castel del Monte, Puglia
 decorative stonework 213, *10.4*

 plan 215, *10.6*
 sculpture 229, *10.17*
 vaulting 79, *4.25*
Castell y Bere, Merionethshire 151
Castle Bolton, North Riding of Yorkshire
 domestic planning 3, 186–187, 218, *9.1, 9.2*
 flues 197–198, *9.8*
 foul water disposal 209, *9.13*
 joggling *4.13*
 and John Lewyn 5, 186, 192, 193–194, 196
 latrines 206
 lintel failure 67
 and Lumley Castle 194–195
 ovens 201, *9.9*
 portcullis 184–185, *8.15*
 roof structure 49
 and Windsor Castle 194
 well 202, *9.10*
 and Wressle Castle 194–195
Castle Neroche, Somerset 11, 17
Castle Rising, Norfolk 56, 98–99, 104, 113, 138, 209
Chamberlain, John, brickmaker 84
Charles (the Simple) III, king of Western Francia and Lotharingia 87–88
Chartley Castle, Staffordshire 125
Château de Folie, Braine, Aisne 123
Château de Montagu, Marcoussis, Essone 206
Châteaudun, Eure-et-Loire, great tower 71, 113, 130
Château Gaillard, Eure
 aesthetic character 210–211, 236
 and concentricity 157
 and Conisbrough 146–147
 decorative stonework, 211, 213, *10.1*
 description 144–148, *7.5, 7.6*
 great tower 39, 118, 138, 139, 210, *6.6*
 hoarding 160
 inner bailey curtain 145, 154
 machicolations 145–146, 161, 234
 plinth 56
 and Richard the Lionheart 4, 118, 144–148, 154, 161, 211
Châtillon-Coligny Castle, Loiret, great tower 71–72, 113
Chepstow Castle, Monmouthshire
 floor construction 35–36
 gloriette 190
 joggling 253 (n. 13)
 Marten's Tower 57
 outer gatehouse 6, 166–167, 169, 226, *8.2*
 sculpture 231
 spurs 57
 and the royal works 6, 166
 wall towers 144
Chester, Hugh d' Avranches, 1st earl of 17

Chester, Ranulph de Blundeville, 6th earl of 18, 83, 125, 126
Chilham Castle, Kent, great tower 117
Chillingham Castle, Northumberland 193
chimney flues 197–201
Chinon Castle, Indre-et-Loire 18, 19, 118, 119, 144, 146, 151, *6.7*
Chipchase Castle, Northumberland 235
Christchurch Castle, Hampshire 208
Clare, Gilbert de, see Gloucester, Gilbert de Clare, 7th earl of
Clare, Richard de, see Gloucester, Richard de clare 6th earl of
Clifford, Robert, 4th Baron 259 (n. 26)
Clifford, Roger, 3rd Baron 259 (n. 26)
Clinton, Geoffrey de, sheriff of Warwickshire 20, 103
Clinton, William de, see Huntingdon, William de Clinton, 1st earl of
Clipstone Manor, Nottinghamshire 86
Cobham, John Lord 5
Colchester, William, mason 6
Coch Castle, Glamorganshire 57
Coity Castle, Glamorganshire 204
Colchester Castle, Essex
 and Canterbury 100
 great tower 96–97, *5.5*
 fireplace and flue 199
 foundations 54
 herringbone masonry 58
 and Kenilworth 103
 plinth 55
 and Rochester 101
 roof span 37
 sub-crypt 69
 vault 69
 wall thickness 137
 and the White Tower, 96–97
Coldingham Priory, Berwickshire 193
Compiègne, Oise 118
concentric fortifications 6, 142, 156–160, 173, 176, 216, 220–222
Conisbrough Castle, West Riding of Yorkshire
 barbican 176
 and Barnard Castle 117
 and Château Gaillard 146–147
 fireplaces and flues 199, 200
 floor construction 39
 masonry 59–60
 great tower 114–117, 121, 216, *6.4*
 joggling 65, *4.11*
 latrines 203
 and Orford 116–117
 plinth 55–56
 vault 72
 wall stitching 61, *4.8*
 wall towers 144, 149, *7.4*
 water supply 202, 203
 window 65, *4.17*
Conwy Castle, Caernarvonshire
 barbicans 176, *8.7*

drawbridge 180
and Elias de Bruton 176
estuarine location 23
and James of St Georges 5, 188–189
latrines 204
machicolations 52, 162, *7.17*
royal lodgings 188–190, *9.3*
scaffolding 60
and Warkworth 255 (n. 18)
Cooling Castle, Kent 5
Corbeil, Essonne 118
Corbeil, William de, archbishop of Canterbury 100
Corbel, John, brick mason 84
Corfe Castle, Dorset
  ditch 17
  gatehouse 169
  Gloriette 62, 188
  great tower 37–39, 214
  herringbone masonry 58
  hoarding 161
  roof construction 37–39
  segmental arch 63
  wall towers 148–151
Cosyn, John, brick mason 84
Coucy-le-Château, Aisne
  and Aigues Mortes 122
  and Amiens Cathedral 121–122
  drawbridge 178
  floor construction 39
  great tower 119–122, 125, 130, *6.9*
  hoarding 51–52, 162, *7.16*
  latrines 204, 209
  relieving arch 68
  scaffolding 60
  and Scottish castles 40, 122–123
  sculpture 229, 234
  vaulting 74–75
Cowper, John, mason 4–5, 85
Cravant-les-Coteaux, Indre-et-Loire 90
Cromwell, Ralph, Lord 25, 84, 85, 135
Crump, Thomas, mason 5

Dallingridge, Sir Edward 24, 220
Danby Castle, North Riding of Yorkshire 193
David I, king of Scotland 103
Denbigh Castle, Denbighshire 132
  gatehouse 132, *6.16*
  latrines 206
  sculpture 231
Derby, William Ferrers, 5th earl of 125
Dinefwr Castle, Carmarthenshire 56
Dirleton, East Lothian 74, 122–123, *6.10*
Docheman, Baldwin, brick maker 84, 85
domestic planning 186–197
donjons: see great towers
Doué la Fontaine Castle, Maine-et-Loire 58, 60, 87–88, *4.3, 5.1*
Dourdan, Essonne
  and Caerphilly Castle 158
  and Flint Castle 130

formal front 218
great tower 118, *6.8*
scaffolding 119
staircase 119
Dover Castle, Kent
  barbicans 152, 173–174
  Avranches Tower 141, 149, 155
  and Bamburgh Castle 142–143
  and Château Gaillard 144, 147–148, 154
  concentricity 142, 147–148, 156–157
  Constable Tower 152, 169, 226–228, *7.9*
  and Corfe Castle 149–151
  decorative stone banding 211, *5.13*
  Fitzwilliam Gate 154
  forebuilding 138
  and Framlingham Castle 143
  general description 139–143, 151–154, *7.1*
  great tower 62,107–109, 137, 188, *5.13*
  and Henry II 139–143
  and Henry III 151–154
  inner gateways 141, 165–166
  and King John 151
  and Ralph, mason 117
  and Maurice, mason and engineer 1–2, 107–109, 142–143, 147–148
  Norfolk Towers 154
  north-west gateway 151, 154, 167
  and Richard of Cornwall 4
  Saint John Tower 154
  spurs 56
  tower clusters 122–123, 126, 154
  tunnels 19, 154
  and Urricus 151
  wall stitching 61, *4.7*
  wall towers 139–141, 151, *7.2*
  water supply 202–203
  and Windsor 155
drawbridges 178–181
Drogon II lord of Pierrefonds 110
Dudley Castle, Staffordshire 12
Dumfries, Dumfriesshire 23
Dunstanburgh Castle, Northumberland
  barbican 176
  and Elias de Bruton 176
  and Harlech 176–177
  plinth 55
  wall towers 193
  water features 24
Durham Castle
  chapel 69
  and John Lewyn 193, 194, 196
  great hall roof 49
  great tower 81, 193, 194, 222, *9.5*
  north range 105
  and Richard Wolveston 6, 105
Durham Priory
  and John Lewyn 193
  vaults 70
  water supply 203
Dyker, Matthew, master dyker 25

earth-fast post construction 29–31, 32, 33–34
Edlingham Castle, Northumberland 65, 235, *4.12*
Edward I, king of England 2, 5, 6, 22–23, 52, 60, 128, 130, 158–159, 169, 172, 174, 176, 179, 180, 185, 188, 204, 212, 216, 235
Edward II, king of England 4, 232
Edward III, king of England 6, 192, 216, 218, 223–224
Eglingham, Northumberland 109
Elias of Oxford, engineer 1, 2, 6
Ellingham, Northumberland 109
Ellis, John, brick maker 84
Ely Cathedral, Cambridgeshire 37
Enguerrand III, lord of Coucy 60, 119, 121, 122, 229
Etal Castle, Northumberland 193
Étampes Castle, Tour de Guinette 110–112, *6.2*
  affinities with York 112, 126–128, *6.12*
  chimney flue 199
  plan 110–112, *6.12*
  roof 44
  well 202
Eton College, Buckinghamshire 4, 85
Ewloe, Flintshire 151
Exeter Castle, Devon 54, 58, 165

Falaise Castle, Calvados 98, 118
Farnham Castle, Surrey 14, 82
Fastolf, Sir John 25, 85
Ferrers, William, see Derby, Williams Ferrers, 5th earl of
Fiennes, Sir Roger 85
Fitzalan, Richard, see Arundel, Richard Fitzalan, 3rd earl of
Fitz Harding, Robert 82
Fitzwalter, John 3rd Baron 259 (n. 26)
Flambard, bishop of Durham 70, 106
Flint Castle, Flintshire 23, 52, 128–130, 139, 180, 189
flooring 34–36, 39–41, 49–50, 51, 74–75
Fontevraud Abbey, Maine-et-Loire 71
forebuildings 62, 71, 82, 95, 97, 98, 99, 100, 102 and n. 25, 103, 104, 107, 108, 114, 116, 117, 138
Ford Castle, Northumberland 193
formal fronts 218–224
fossarius 20
Fossour, John le, master dyker 23
foul water disposal 208
foundations 2, 18, 27, 28, 31, 33, 34, 54–55, 81, 82, 83, 101 and n. 23
Fountains Abbey, West Riding of Yorkshire 71, 203
Framlingham Castle, Suffolk
  and Ailnoth the engineer 1, 114, 143–144
  chimney stacks 200

gatehouse 148, 165, *8.1*
general description 143
joggling 63
and Orford 61, 63, 143
south-west tower 149, *7.7*
wall stitching 61, *4.6*
western tower 176
Frederick II, king of Sicily and emperor of the Romans 213, 215, 229
Frétéval Castle, Loir-et-Cher 110
Fulk (Nerra), count of Anjou 89, 90

gatehouses 165–173, 226–229
geometry and geometrical planning 3, 7–9, 110–113, 114, 116, 128, 130–132, 215–218
Gaunt, John of, see Lancaster, John of Gaunt, duke of
Gilbert of Moray, bishop of Caithness 123
Gisors, Eure 118, 144, 146, 151
Gloucester, Gilbert de Clare, 7th earl of, and 6th earl of Hertford 21, 57, 77, 157, 171–172, 174, 179
Gloucester, Richard de Clare 6th earl of, and 5th earl of Hertford 57, 171
Gloucester, John of, mason 6, 188
Godwin, mason 155, 188
Gogun, Ralph, mason 57, 190
Goltho Castle, Lincolnshire 13, 15, 20, 33
Goodrich Castle, Herefordshire
architectural analogues 57, 174, 179
arches and voussoirs 63
barbican 174, *8.6*
domestic planning 190–192
drawbridge 179
portcullis 183–184, *8.13*
roof 48
spurs 57
Gray, Sir Thomas, of Heton 231
great towers
circle-based plans 110–112, 113–117, 118–130
composite plans 132–133
polygonal plans 112–113, 117, 130, 135
rectangular plans 87–109, 133–135, 136
timber 3–32
Grosmont, Henry de, see Lancaster, Henry de Grosmont, 3rd earl of
Guildford Castle, Surrey 81, 137
Gundulf, bishop of Rochester 95

Halton Castle, Northumberland 235
Hamell, William, mason 4
Harewood Castle, West Riding of Yorkshire 193
Harlech Castle, Merionethshire
bartizans 235
coastal location 23
concentricity 159

corbelling 235
gatehouse 172, 176–177, 185, *8.8*
latrines 204
plan *7.12*
scaffolding 60
symmetrical elevation 218
Hastings Castle, Sussex 11
Hastings, William, Lord 26, 84, 136
Hatfield, Thomas, bishop of Durham 49, 193
Haughton Castle, Northumberland 79, 161
Haut-Kœnigsbourg, Bas-Rhin 253 (n. 14)
Hawarden, Flintshire, great tower, 129, 130, 136, 139, *6.13*
heating 197–201
Hedingham Castle, Essex, great tower
diaphragm arch 105
flue and smoke vent 199
plinth 56
Heighley Castle, Staffordshire 18
Helmsley Castle, North Riding of Yorkshire
concentric fortifications 156
great tower 151
moat 20
Hen Domen Castle, Montgomeryshire
bailey bank 15, 17
concentric fortifications 17, 156
timber-framed buildings 31, 33, 34
Henry I, count of Champagne 43, 71, 112
Henry I, king of England 97, 100, 108
Henry II, king of England 104, 109
Henry III, king of England 4, 18, 22, 61, 75, 126, 152, 155, 157, 159, 167, 171, 179, 188, 211, 214
Herbert, Thomas ap 135
Herbert, William, earl of Pembroke, see Pembroke, William Herbert, earl of
Hereford, Henry de Bohun, 1st earl of 125
Hereford, Humphrey de Bohun, 2nd earl of 125
Hereford, Walter of, mason 6, 65, 173
Hermitage Castle, Roxburghshire 135
Herstmonceux Castle, Sussex 85
Hertford Castle 2
Hexham Gaol, Northumberland 162
hoardings 51–53, 161–162
Holt Castle, Denbighshire 190, 216, 229, *10.7*
Honnecourt, Villard de 3
Horne, John, brick mason 27, 84
Houdan Castle, Yvelines, great tower
architectural analogues 82, 110–113, 126
geometry of the plan 8–9, 42, 110, *1.1*, *6.1*
Hull, East Riding of Yorkshire 83
Huntingdon, William de Clinton, 1st earl of 192

Hylton Castle, Co. Durham, gatehouse 231, 233–234, 235, *10.21*
Hylton, William 5th Baron 231, 233
Hyndeley, Thomas, mason 6

Ivry-la-Bataille Castle, Eure, great tower 58, 59, 60, 93–95, 97, *5.5*

Jaime II, king of Mallorca 216
Jerusalem, Church of the Holy Sepulchre 72–73
joggling 63–66, 68, 117, 143
John, King of England 18, 19, 21, 56, 62, 117, 139, 148, 149, 151, 155, 167, 169
Jublains, Mayenne 88

keeps: see great towers
Kempley, Gloucestershire, Church of St Mary 37
Kenilworth Castle, Warwickshire
great hall 47–48, 200, *3.12*, *10.12*
great tower 103–104, 137, *5.9*
Lunn's Tower 149, *7.8*
masonry 59
outer gatehouse (Mortimer's Tower) 167
roof 47–48, *3.12*
and Henry Spenser 223–224
symmetrical front 223
water defences 20–21, *2.3*
and Windsor 223–224
Kidwelly Castle, Carmarthenshire 57, 178
Kildrummy, Aberdeenshire 123
Kingdom of Jerusalem 73, 157
Kirby Muxloe Castle, Leicestershire
bricklaying 84–85
decorative brickwork 214–215, *10.5*
latrines 208
moat 26–28, *2.5*
and John Cowper 4–5, 85
and Robert Steynforth 5
Knaresborough Castle, West Riding of Yorkshire 4, 6, 18, 132–133, 155
Krak des Chevaliers Castle, Syria 57, 146, 151, 161, 210, 234

Lacy, Walter de, sheriff of Hereford 125
La Cuba, Palermo, Sicily 98
Lancaster Castle 49–50, 183, 234, *3.14*, *8.12*, *10.22*
Lancaster, John of Gaunt, duke of 2
Lancaster, Henry de Grosmont, 3rd earl of 259 (n. 26)
Lancaster, Thomas, 2nd earl of 24
Lanfranc, abbot of Le Bec and St Etienne, Caen; archbishop of Canterbury 95
Lanfred, master builder 93–95
Langeais Castle, Indre-et-Loire, great tower 59, 60, 67, 89, *4.4*, *4.16*, *5.2*

Langley Castle, Northumberland 193, 206, 235, *9.12*
Laon Castle, Aisne 118
La Roche-Guyon Castle, Val d'Oise 19, 118, 138, 146, 157
Latimer, William 4th Lord 193
latrines 99, 117, 125, 128, 172, 190, 203–209, *9.11*, *9.12*
Laugharne Castle, Carmarthenshire 74
Laval Castle, Mayenne 51, *3.15*
Lawrence of Ludlow, merchant 132
La Zisa, Palermo, Sicily 98
Leeds Castle, Kent 22
Leicester, Simon de Montfort, 8th earl of 21
Lewes Castle, Sussex 62, 164, 177, 235
Lewyn, John, mason 5, 6, 7, 133, 186–187, 192, 193–195, 196, 197–198, 201, 206, 218, 224–225
Lichfield Cathedral, Staffordshire 50
Lillebonne Castle, Seine-Maritime 67, 118, 119, 130
Lincoln Cathedral chapter house 77
Lincoln, John de Lacy, 3rd earl of 126
Linlithgow Castle, Linlithgowshire 24
Lisle, Warin, Lord 220
lintel 65–68, 164, 234
Llawhaden Castle, Pembrokeshire 57
Loches Castle, Indre-et-Loire
  and tenth-century churches 90
  fireplace 199
  great tower 90, 187, *5.3*
  masonry 59
  scaffolding 60
  vaulting 70
  wall towers 144, 146, 154, *7.10*
  windows 67
London, Tower of
  Beauchamp Tower 62
  Bell Tower 62–63, 75, 76, 149
  chapel of St John 69
  Coldharbour Gate 169
  imported bricks 83
  inner ward, Henry III's expansion of 155
  and John Box 218
  Lion Tower 174, 179
  moat 22–23
  outer ward, construction of 158
  and Robert of Beverley 61–62, 65, 158, 190
  roof 36–37
  St Thomas's tower 65
  Wakefield Tower 40, *3.5*
  western gateway 169
  White Tower 36–37, 55, 69, 95–97, 187, 199, 214, *5.5*
London, Temple church 253 (n. 57)
Longtown Castle, Herefordshire, great tower 56, 125
Louis VI, king of France 110
Louis VII, king of France 110
Louis IX, king of France 122, 130

Lovel, John, Lord 220
Lucy, Sir Thomas 193
Ludlow Castle, Shropshire 45–46, 50, 54, 165, *3.11*
Lumley Castle, Co. Durham 194–195, 195–196, 197, 218, 231, 233 *9.6*, *10.19*
Lumley, Ralph, 1st Baron 231
Luzarches, Robert de, mason 121

machicolations 52, 135, 136, 161–164, 166–167, 169, 171–172, 176, 178, 185, 234
Malbork Castle, Poland, Grand Master's Palace 161, 234
Mamble, Herefordshire 32
Manorbier Castle, Pembrokeshire 74
Mapilton, Thomas, mason 6
Marie de Coucy, queen of Scotland 122
Marshal, William, see Pembroke, William Marshal, 4th earl of
masonry
  ashlar 59, 61, 66, 78, 89, 90, 98, 143, 195, 211–212, 213
  decorative banding 211–213
  herringbone 58 (*opus spicatum*)
  petit appareil 59, 89, 90, 93
  rubble 12, 13, 17, 55, 58, 59, 60, 61, 69, 74, 79, 143, 211, 213
Maurice, mason and engineer 1–2, 6, 61, 107–109, 139–143, 148, 156, 173–174, 202–203, 226
Maxstoke Castle, Warwickshire 46–47, 185, 192, 219, *9.4*, *10.8*
Mayenne, Mayenne, great tower 87, 88–89, 90
Melton, William, archbishop of York 162
Mettingham Castle, Suffolk 25
Middleham Castle, North Riding of Yorkshire, great tower 55, 70–71, 107
miners 17–19
moats 15, 20–28, 135, 159, 169, 174, 176, 177, 195, 203, 206, 208, 220
Montaigu-le-Blin Castle, Allier 154
Montargis Castle, Loiret 118
Montbazon Castle, Indre-et-Loire 90
Montdidier, Somme 118
Montfort, Simon de, earl of Leicester, see Leicester, Simon de Monfort, 8th earl of
Montgomery Castle, Montgomeryshire 167–169, *8.3*
Montgomery, Robert of, see Shrewsbury, Robert of Montgomery, 1st earl of
Moray family 123
More Castle, Shropshire 12
Morlais Castle, Glamorganshire 77
Mortain, Robert count of 17, 20
mottes 4, 10–14, 19, 20, 28, 31, 32, 33, 44, 80–83, 87, 97, 116, 117, 125, 126, 128, 129, 133, 135, 139, 155, 174, 224, 225

mural galleries 95, 102, 109, 121, 122, 123, 128, 129, 130, 141, 160

Neville, John, 5th Baron 258 (n. 25, and n. 29)
Neville, Ralph, 4th Baron 233, 259 (n. 26)
Neville, Ralph, 6th Baron 231
New Buckenham Castle, Norfolk, great tower 42, 113
Newcastle-upon-Tyne Castle
  Black Gate 169, 228, 231, *8.4*
  drawbridge 179
  flue and smoke vent 199
  fore building 62, 138
  great tower 55, 71, 107–109, 199, *5.12*
  and Maurice 1–2, 6, 107–109, 142
  plinth 55
  sculpture 231
  vaulting 71
  water supply 202–203
Newcastle-upon-Tyne town walls 162, 231
Newnham Castle, Kent 15
Newport Castle, Monmouthshire 58
Norfolk, Hugh Bigod, 1st earl of 113
Norfolk, Roger Bigod, 2nd earl of 143
Norfolk, Roger Bigod, 5th earl of 57, 179, 190
Norham Castle, Northumberland
  great tower 59, 70–71, 105–106, *5.10*
  gatehouse 165
  masonry 59
  vaulting 70
  and Richard Wolveston 6, 105–107
Northampton, Simon of, carpenter 4, 5, 6, 44
Northumberland, Henry Percy, 1st earl of 206, 231
Norwich Castle, Norfolk, great tower 59, 70, 97–99, 100, 104–105, 187
Norwich Cathedral 98
Norwich, Cow Tower 83
Norwich, John de 25
Nottingham Castle 18, 19, 151, 155, 170

Odiham Castle, Hampshire 16, 39, 43–44, 117, 130
Ogmore Castle, Glamorganshire 251 (n. 56)
Old Sarum Castle, Wiltshire 188
Old Wardour Castle 160, 195, 220–223, *10.10*, *10.11*
open hearths 197–199, 200
Orford Castle, Suffolk
  architectural analogues 42–43, 61, 116, 117, 125, 143
  and Ailnoth 114
  fireplace flues 200
  great tower 114, *3.8*, *6.3*
  joggling 63, *4.10*

plinth 56
pointed arches 62
roof construction *3.8*, 42–43
staircase construction 78–79, *4.23*
timber ceiling 50
urinal 209
wall stitching 61
wall towers 139
water supply 203
Orléans Castle, Loiret 118
Osbert, mason 101
ovens 189, 201
Oxford Castle 4
Oxford, Elias of, engineer 1, 2, 6
Oxford, Henry of, carpenter 258 (n. 8)
Oxford, New College 195, 218, 220

Paris (Louvre) 56, 118, 119, 125, 149, 151
Pembridge, Herefordshire 32
Pembroke Castle, Pembrokeshire
architectural analogues 125, 168–169
dome 72–74, *4.19*
floor construction 40
great tower 123–125, 137, 138–139, 237, *6.11*
Horseshoe Tower 168, 174, *6.11*
plinth 56
and the royal works 6, 166
Pembroke, William Herbert, earl of 135
Pembroke, William Marshal, 4th earl of 6, 72, 123, 144, 166, 168–169, 226
Pembroke, William de Valence, earl of 190
Percy, Henry, 2nd Baron 259 (n. 26)
Percy, Henry, 3rd Baron 177, 259 (n. 26)
Percy, Henry, 1st earl of Northumberland, see Northumberland, Henry Percy 1st earl of
Percy, Sir Thomas 206
Peronne Castle, Somme 118
petrarie 138, 154
Peveril Castle, Derbyshire 58, 203
Philip II Augustus, king of France 60, 74, 79, 118, 121, 122, 149, 151, 154, 158
Pickering Castle, North Riding of Yorkshire 193
Pierrefonds 110, 204–206, *205*
Pithiviers Castle, Loiret 93–95, 97
Plantagenet, Hamelin, earl of Surrey 114, 216
plinths 55–58
Poitiers, Vienne, church of St Hilaire 71
Pontefract Castle, West Riding of Yorkshire 4, 55, 125, 126, 154
Popeshal, Ralph de, master dyker 19
Powell/Ap Howell, John, master dyker 27
Portchester Castle, Hampshire 16–17, 37–39, 105, 199

portcullis 2, 3, 165, 167, 169, 171, 172–173, 176, 177, 178, 181–185
Powis Castle, Montgomeryshire 57
Provins Castle, Seine-et-Marne, Tour de César 43, 71, 112–113, 144, *3.9*, *4.18*
Prudhoe Castle, Northumberland 55
Puiset, Hugh du, bishop of Durham 6, 105

quarrymen 17–19
Queenborough Castle, Kent 5, 160, 216–218, 222

Raby Castle, Co. Durham 49, 160, 193, 196, 224–225, 233
Raglan, Glamorganshire 135, 181, 226, *8.10*, *10.13*
Ralph, mason 117
Ravensworth Castle, North Riding of Yorkshire 24
rendering 214
revetment 12, 13, 14, 15, 17, 25, 27, 28, 30, 31, 82, 158
Reyns, Henry de, mason 4, 5, 44, 126–128, 188
Red Castle, Shropshire 18
Restormel Castle, Cornwall 129, 216
Rhuddlan Castle, Flintshire 23, 41, 159, 179, 180, 189, 204, *3.7*, *7.13*
Richard I, the Lionheart, king of England 4, 118, 144–148, 154, 161, 211
Richard II, king of England 231, 234
Richard, duke of Cornwall 4
Richard the engineer 2, 180, 258 (n. 8)
Richmond Castle, North Riding of Yorkshire 35–36, 54, 59, 69, 165, *3.2*
Rochester Castle, Kent
early stone castle 54
flues and air vents 199
great tower 37, 54, 55, 56, 69, 100–101, 105, 199, 201, 202, 214, *5.6*
herringbone masonry 58
plinth 55, 56
roof 37
well 201, 202
roof construction 33, 34–35, 36–39, 42–50, 90, 96, 100
Rouen Castle, Seine-Maritime 97, 118, 119
royal works 5–7
Roxburgh Castle, Roxburghshire 5, 193
Ryhull, Henry of, carpenter 52

St Calais, William of, bishop of Durham 69
St Generoux, Deux-Sèvres 90
St Georges d'Esperanche Castle, Switzerland 204
St Georges, James of, mason 5, 130, 180, 188–189, 228

Salisbury Cathedral, Wiltshire, chapter house 43–44, 77
Salisbury, Roger, bishop of 188
sally ports 155
Salvá, Pedro, master builder 216
Sandal Castle, West Riding of Yorkshire
aisled hall 33
bailey earthworks 15–16
barbican 174, 216
great tower 82, 125–128, 129, 133, 216
motte 10
scaffolding 2, 60, 119
Scarborough Castle, East Riding of Yorkshire 6, 59, 104–105, 137, 169, 200
Scrope, Richard Lord 3, 186, 193
sculpture 229–234
Sens, William of, mason 2
Sharndale, William, mason 5
shell keep 14, 62, 80–81, 126, 129, 222
Sherborne Castle, Dorset 188
Shirburn Castle, Oxfordshire 195, 220, 222
Shrewsbury, Robert of Montgomery, 1st earl of 17
Simiane-la-Rotonde Castle, Alpes-de-Haute-Provence 72
Skenfrith Castle, Monmouthshire, great tower 56, 62, 125, *4.1*
Skillington, Robert, mason 83
smoke vents 199
Somerton, Lincolnshire 77
Southampton town wall 161
South Mimms Castle, Hertfordshire 13, 14, 15, 31–32, 34
South Wingfield, Derbyshire, see Wingfield Manor House
Spenser, Henry, mason 200, 223–224
Sponlee, John, mason 6, 192, 218, 224
spurred towers 56–58, 171, 228
Staindrop, Co. Durham 49, 196
staircases 69, 78–80
Stafford Castle 10, 12, 16, 82–83, 162, 192, 219, *2.1*
Stephen (Etienne), lord of Sancerre 71, 73, 113
Steynforth, Robert, mason 5
Stokesay Castle, Shropshire
arch failure 63, *4.9*
flooring 36, *3.3*
great tower 132, 135, *6.15*
north tower timber upper storey 52–53, *3.16*
open hearth *9.7*
roof 44, 45, 47, 48, 50, *3.10*
Surrey, Isabella de Warenne, 4th countess of 114
Surrey, John de Warenne 6th earl of 125, 174, 216
Surrey, John de Warenne, 7th earl of 164, 177

Surrey, William de Warenne, 5th earl of 125, 216
Swillyngton, John, mason 4
symmetrical façades 218–224
symmetrical plans 215–218

Tamworth Castle, Staffordshire 29–30, 31, 34, 81
Tattershall Castle, Lincolnshire 25, 84, 85–86, 135, 164
Tattershall church 4, 85
Tenby Castle, Pembrokeshire 74
Theobald (Thibaut) I, count of Blois 87
Theobald (Thibaut) V, count of Blois 113
Thetford Castle, Norfolk 10
Thornton Abbey, Lincolnshire 83, 85
Threave Castle, Kirkcudbrightshire 52
Tichemers, Hugh de, mason 4, 6, 132
Tickhill Castle, West Riding of Yorkshire 116, 165, 226
timber ceilings 50
timber framing 15, 29–32, 33–53
Tonbridge Castle, Kent, gatehouse 6, 57, 171–172, 204, 228, 229, 237, *8.5*
Totnes Castle, Devon 81
Tours Philippiennes 60, 74, 118–119, 130
tower clusters 122, 126, 154, 224–226
Trematon Castle, Cornwall 81
Tretower Castle, Breconshire 56
tunnels 19, 154–155
Tutbury Castle, Staffordshire
  and Ashby-de-la-Zouche 136
  bank and ditch system 17, 156
  curtain wall 83
  great tower 125
  joggling 65–66, *4.15*
  motte 10
  timber vaulting 50–51
  well, 201
  and Robert Westerley 4, 6
Tynemouth Priory and Castle 185, 235
tympana 62, 68, 229

Umfraville, Gilbert de, see Angus, Gilbert de Umfraville, 9th earl of
urinals 209
Urricus, engineer 1, 151

vaulting
  barrel 69, 70, 76–78, 79, 116
  chapels 68–69
  domes 71–74, 112, 113, 123
  great tower basements 70–71
  groin 69, 70–71
  rib 74–76, 79, 119, 121, 123
  sail, see domes
  Stairs and wall passages 69
  timber 50–51

umbrella 79–80
Vaux, John de, steward of Marie de Coucy, queen of Scotland 122
Verdon, Bertram de 18
Verneuil-sur-Avre Castle, Eure 79, 118, 119, *4.20*
Vernon Castle, Eure 118
Vesey, William, brick maker 85
Villeneuve-sur-Yonne Castle, Yonne 118, 119, *4.5*
Vitalis, Orderic 93
voussoirs 62–65, 89, 93, 143

Waldin the engineer 252 (n. 25)
wall stitching 60–62
Walter of Flanders, master dyker 23
Walton Castle, Suffolk 1, 114
Warenne, Hamelin de, see Plantagenet, Hamelin, earl of Surrey
Warenne, Isabella de, 4th countess of Surrey, see Surrey, Isabella de Warenne, 4th countess of
Warenne, John de, 6th earl of Surrey, see Surrey, John de Warenne, 6th earl of
Warenne, John de, 7th earl of Surrey, see Surrey, John de Warenne, 7th earl of
Warenne, William de, 5th earl of Surrey, see Surrey, William de Warenne, 5th earl of
Warwick Castle
  barbican 177–178
  Caesar's Tower 77, 133, 162
  east front 224
  Guy's Tower 76, *4.21*
Warkworth Castle, Northumberland
  Carrickfergus Tower 149
  dais fireplace 200
  drain 208
  foundations 54–55
  gatehouse 226, *10.14*
  great tower 133–134, 225, *4.22, 6.17, 6.18*
  latrines 206
  machicolations 255 (n. 18)
  portcullis 184, *8.14*
  sculpture 229–230, *10.18*
  vaulting 78, 79, *4.22*
  window flues 197
water ducts 206
water features 20–28
water supply 201–203
Wells Cathedral, Somerset, chapter house 43–44, 77
Weoley Castle, Birmingham 33–34
Westerley, Robert, mason 4, 6, 66, 85, 136
Westminster Abbey 4, 44, 77, 126, 188

Westminster Palace 1, 114, 218
White Castle, Monmouthshire
  drawbridges 178, 179
  rendering 214
  wall stitching 61
William I, king of England 11, 110
William (Rufus) II, King of England 95, 97
William of Boston, master dyker 23
Winchester College, Hampshire 195, 218, 220
Windsor Castle, Berkshire
  and Ailnoth 114
  decorative banding 211
  defences 139, 155
  great hall roof 47–48
  and Henry de Reyns 126
  and Henry Spenser 223–224
  latrines 204
  round table 218
  royal lodgings 6, 188, 192, 194
  shell keep 81, 222
  timber vaulting 50
  tunnels 155
  vaulting 75–77
  and William Wynford 218
Wingfield Manor House, Derbyshire 135
Wintringham, William, carpenter 2, 6, 47
Wode, Henry, mason 85, 135
Wolveston, Richard, engineer 6, 105–107, 109
Wolvesey Castle, Hampshire 188
Woodstock Place, Oxfordshire 256 (n. 7)
Wrek, Thomas, mason 5
Wressle Castle, East Riding of Yorkshire 194–196, 200, 206, 218
Wright, William, carpenter 49
Wykeham, William of 218
Wynford, William, mason 6, 192, 195, 218, 220, 222, 223–224

Yarpole, Herefordshire 32, 34
Yevele, Henry, mason 5, 6, 195
York, Baile Hill 10, 12
York Castle
  Clifford's Tower 44, 82, 112, 125, 126–128, 133, 138–139, 154, *6.12*
  gatehouse 169
  and Henry de Reyns 4, 5–6, 44, 126, 188
  King's Pool 20
  and Simon of Northampton 44
  motte 11–12
  roof 44
York city walls 181–182, 235
Yverdon Castle, Switzerland 204